SRINI,
May 20, 1982

Multinational Management

Multinational Management

David P. Rutenberg

Queen's University, Canada

Little, Brown and Company   Boston   Toronto

Library of Congress Cataloging in Publication Data

Rutenberg, David.
  Multinational management.

  Bibliography: p.
  Includes index.
  1. International business enterprises — Management.
I. Title
HD62.4.R87   658'.049   81-23641
ISBN 0-316-76365-9   AACR2

ISBN 0-316-763659

9 8 7 6 5 4 3 2 1

MV

Published simultaneously in Canada
by Little, Brown & Company (Canada) Limited

Printed in the United States of America

Jacket and interior design by Jennie Bush/Designworks

Contents

Introduction   xi

Acknowledgments   xv

O N E: Organizational Structures and Tensions   1

Introductory Note to the Case 1
First National City Bank   2
Multinational Corporate Banking 2
Historical Growth 3
International Organization 3
The Multinational Corporate Client 5
Internal Problems 6
Matrix Resolution 7
Questions 8

Introduction 10
Experience Curves in a Product-Structured Corporation 12
Risk-Spreading in a Geographically Organized Corporation 18
Geocentric Balance in a Matrix Organization 23
Bibliography to Chapter 1 33

PART ONE

Multinational Financial Management   35

T W O: Exchange Management in a Multinational Corporation   37

Introductory Note to the Case 37
Dozier Industries   38

History of the Company   38
Foreign Exchange Risk and Hedging   41

Introduction   46
Polycentric View of Exchange Management   49
An Ethnocentric View of Exchange Management   56
The Geocentric View of Exchange Management   59
Conclusion   64
Questions from Other Viewpoints   66
Bibliography to Chapter 2   68

THREE: Maneuvering Liquid Assets   70

Introductory Note to the Case   70
Paisley S.A.   71
The Organization   73
Financial Policies   74
Outline of the Memo   75

Ethnocentric — Introduction   81
Geocentric Model — A Generalized Network   82
Adjusted Transfer Prices $A(p_{ij}^t)$ 86
Fees and Royalties $A(f_{ij}^t)$ 90
Intersubsidiary Loans $A(l_i^t; {}_j^{t+1})$ 92
Dividends $A(d_{ij}^t)$ 95
Local Loans   98
The Optimal Capital Structure of a Subsidiary   99
Systems within Systems   100
Implementing the Model in a Polycentric Corporation   102
Conclusion   103
Questions from Other Viewpoints   104
Bibliography to Chapter 3   106

FOUR: Multinational Expansion to a New Nation   108

Introductory Note to the Case   108
Michelin Tires Manufacturing Co. of Canada Ltd.   109
The Michelin Organization   109
The Canadian Operation   111
The Agreements   112
Industry Reactions   115
The Canadian Tire Industry   115
Industry-Government Relations   116
Industry-Government Negotiations   117
The U.S. Industry and Its Responses   119
Remedy Sought   120

Introduction 122
Polycentric Process 122
Ethnocentric Process 125
Geocentric Process 131
Closing Decisions 136
Conclusions 137
Questions from Other Viewpoints 139
Bibliography to Chapter 4 141

Summary of Multinational Financial Management   143

PART TWO

Multinational Manufacturing   145

F I V E: Logistics   147

Introductory Note to the Case 147
Ascendant Electric of England Ltd.   148
Cost Review of Supplying Los Angeles Customer by Sea 148
Thinking about Airfreight 150
Negotiating Strategy 152

Introduction 153
First Phase: Product-Centered View of Logistics (Ethnocentric) 153
Second Phase: Subsidiary-Centered View of Logistics
   (Polycentric) 163
Third Phase: Geocentric View of Logistics 164
Conclusions 170
Questions from Other Viewpoints 170
Bibliography to Chapter 5 172

S I X: Production Smoothing   174

Introductory Note to the Case 174
Ford Motor Co. Ltd.   174
A Matter of Economy 176
The Early Stages 176
Five Years, Five Chairmen 178
"General Animosity" 179
Questions 180

Introduction 182
Ethnocentric Production-Focused Production Smoothing 182
Polycentric Nation-Focused Production Smoothing 184
Geocentric Production Smoothing 187

Conclusions   202
Questions from Other Viewpoints   202
Bibliography to Chapter 6   204

SEVEN: Multinational Plant Location   206

Introductory Note to the Case   206
Bell Schönheitsprodukte GmbH   207
The Company and Its Products   207
Competition and Prices   208
Alternative Courses of Action   210
Questions   219

Introduction   220
How Governments Perceive Factories   220
Plant Location Decisions in a Geographically Decentralized
   Corporation   223
Ethnocentric Plant Location to Minimize Cost   228
Geocentric Perspective on Plant Location   231
Questions from Other Viewpoints   236
Bibliography to Chapter 7   237

Summary of Multinational Manufacturing   239

PART THREE

Multinational Marketing   241

EIGHT: New Product Launch   243

Introductory Note to the Case   243
Philip Morris International   244
The Canadian Market   244
The Competition   248
Questions   254

Introduction   255
Ethnocentric Similitude   255
Polycentric Production Smoothing   259
Geocentric Launch   263
Ethnocentric Appendix   267
Geocentric Appendix   270
Questions from Other Viewpoints   273
Bibliography to Chapter 8   275

NINE: Pricing   277

   Introductory Note to the Case 277
   Tyler Abrasives Inc.   278
   Background of Genag 279
   Tyler's International Operations 280
   The Second Meeting with Genag 282
   The Selling Process 285
   Sales Overseas 286
   Further Developments with Genag 286
   Summary 290
   Questions 291

   Introduction 293
   Umbrella Pricing 294
   Constraints on Price Policy 296
   Data Required for Multinational Pricing 298
   Three Pricing Schemes 299
   Polycentric Pricing Scheme 300
   Geocentric Pricing Scheme 302
   Ethnocentric Pricing Scheme 303
   The Three Pricing Schemes Discussed 305
   Appendix 1. A Mathematical Formulation of the Pricing Model 306
   Appendix 2. Mathematical Formulation of Geocentric Pricing
    Scheme 309
   Appendix 3. Mathematical Formulation of Ethnocentric Pricing
    Scheme 310
   Questions from Other Viewpoints 312
   Bibliography to Chapter 9 314

TEN: Product Design   315

   Introductory Note to the Case 315
   Black and Decker (Canada) Inc.   317
   The Birth of the Workwheel 317
   Standards Requirements 318
   Regulations 318
   Technical Considerations 321
   The Product Development Cycle 322
   The Concept Study 324
   Intercompany Business 327

   Introduction 331
   Polycentric View of Product Design 331
   Ethnocentric View of Product Design 333
   Geocentric View of Product Design 334
   Conclusions 339
   Appendix. Two Market Research Techniques 339

Questions from Other Viewpoints   341
Bibliography to Chapter 10   343

Summary of Multinational Marketing   344

PART FOUR

Multinational Executive Development   347

ELEVEN: International Executive Development   349

Introductory Note to the Case   349
The Road to Hell . . .   350
Questions   356

Introduction   358
Future Management Needs   358
Program Development   363
Bibliography to Chapter 11   372

Summary of the Book   374

Index   379

Introduction

This book is designed to help the reader understand the rationale of multinational corporations. Each of the nine central chapters focuses on the question of how a centrally directed multinational corporation (called a geocentric) can earn more profit than an identical corporation which lacks central direction (called a polycentric). Although some central direction is usually good, too much can be bad: Other multinationals (called ethnocentric) straitjacket their subsidiaries into acting in ways appropriate only in the headquarters' nation.

Throughout the book, the words polycentric, geocentric, and ethnocentric are used to describe attitudes that are fundamental influences on organizational structure. A *polycentric* corporation tolerates many centers of decision making. This occurs when a geographically organized corporation is run in a decentralized manner, with independent national subsidiaries. The *geocentric* corporation is one in which the executives consider the global consequences of each decision; this necessitates good information and excellent staff work, which can occur in an effective matrix structure. Ethnocentrism is a belief in the inherent superiority of one's own people. In an *ethnocentric* corporation all corporate executives are of the same nationality, and the home nation dominates their thinking to the extent that other countries seem foreign and secondary. A product manager in the home nation who is assigned international responsibility without adequate preparation will usually think ethnocentrically.

The words polycentric, geocentric, and ethnocentric were first applied to multinational corporations in the early 1960s by Howard Perlmutter, now at the University of Pennsylvania. His background in social psychology caused him to think about the power relationship between headquarters executives and subsidiary managers, and to perceive these three consistent patterns of interaction cutting across hundreds of different multinationals. Several patterns of interaction may be found within one corporation. For example, the finance function may be run in an ethnocentric manner, with headquarters keeping tight control, while simultaneously, the marketing function may be run in a decentralized polycentric manner. The three typical organizational patterns are described in Chapter 1.

In this book, you will be working to understand the operating decisions of an executive at the headquarters of a large multinational corporation, with competent functional managers in each subsidiary. Your challenge is to identify decisions that are worth centralizing. There is no point in headquarters making decisions the subsidiary is able to make on its own; unnecessary duplication is both wasteful and frustrating. Each chapter of this book deals with a decision that might justify duplicated effort. The first chapter deals with the organizational problems of making a global enterprise cohesive. Plow straight through Chapter 1. Don't linger on details, but make a note to yourself to reread Chapter 1 when you finish the book.

The body of the text deals with decisions to be made in finance, production, and marketing. Each chapter begins with a case. Working in a corporation you will be faced with caselike problems, but you will have no case book to support you. As a student, run the risk of feeling befuddled: Read the case and rough out a solution *before* continuing with the chapter. In corporate terms, the information in the chapter corresponds to detailed staff work that usually *follows* an executive's rough decision. Such staff work shows how approximations could be refined and develops the broader consequences of that rough decision. View each case as an opportunity for you to practice making a rough decision, *then* read the chapter to see how your decision could be extended and refined.

The Scope of This Book

The scope of this book is restricted to just one aspect of multinational corporations, although the "Questions from Other Viewpoints" at the end of each chapter broaden its scope. The book concentrates on:

1. *The Corporation, Not the Society.* The focus of this book is the corporation. Most governments are concerned about multinational corporations and have legislated to control their operations. For more thoughts on this extremely important issue, read Behrman (1970), Blake and Walters (1976), and Bergsten, Horst and Moran (1978) [see Bibliography to Chapter 1].
2. *Headquarters, Not Subsidiaries.* This book views worldwide corporations, as personified by their headquarters. Someday researchers will explore the delicate balance of life in a subsidiary, especially the aspiration of each subsidiary manager to maximize autonomy, but we are concerned only with headquarters.

3. *Rationalism, Not Emotionalism.* We will consider the question of *why* one must communicate and interact with people of other nationalities, but not the process or the emotions engendered. Many of the ways in which we perceive and communicate with others are nonverbal. Even experienced anthropologists suffer culture shock as they grope to function in an unfamiliar culture. Although we do not cover the psychodynamics of interaction, we shall look at the goals towards which managers strive.

4. *Normative, Not Descriptive Aspects.* Multinational corporations have been described by journalists, historians, and case writers. They have also been described more quantitatively in the massive statistical collection of Vaupel and Curham (1969, 1973), part of the decade-long Multinational Enterprise Project at the Harvard Business School. In this book we endeavor to clarify the goals toward which some multinational corporations *aspire* and develop computer-based models to achieve these aspirations.

5. *Manufacturing, Not Trading or Mining.* Most mines are expensive, and once developed, they are easy targets for nationalization. It is especially fascinating to study multinational mining because symbolically, depletable resources are a nation's birthright, and so to understand the risks of multinational mining requires a psychological interpretation of the meaning of nationhood. We shall not do so.

   Although there are some great Japanese and British trading companies whose ability to process information has been compared to government intelligence agencies, a serious academic study of trading companies will have to wait for a more completely developed *theory* of information as a management resource.

6. *Tactical Planning, Not Policy.* Corporate policy questions the nature of the corporation, its degree of vertical integration, its prowess in research or manufacturing or marketing, whether or not to become multinational, and all the other questions of identity. In this book we take the corporate policy as given, and work to *implement* a stable and consistent corporate policy. If the policy will be stable long enough, the tier of short-run decisions can improve the tier of medium-term decisions, which in turn will improve the long-term decisions.

   Corporate policy can be quite modestly described as an articulation of that which the corporation does well, with an eye to disentangling inconsistencies. This is appropriate when no *significant* discontinuities are foreseen. In this definition of corporate policy, this text provides a framework for improving the policy of a multinational manufacturing corporation.

   If the fundamental corporate policy is in serious question, top executive attention should focus on the long-term decisions of forming alliances with stakeholders, deciding on suitable products, and choosing where to make and where to sell. The emotional agony associated with these policy decisions is such that it is better not to clutter executives with short- and medium-term operating decisions, no matter how rationally they can be formulated. The policy questions of reformulating corporate objectives and fundamental strategies have to be made in a consciousness that is deeper than rationality. This book can help you structure management decisions; executive decisions should be both entrepreneurial and visionary.

A very different book would result from taking alternative approaches to any of these issues. Even the first four issues allow $2^4 = 16$ possible permutations of issues, each of which is a distinct way of looking at a multinational problem. You will have an opportunity to grapple with the other ways of looking at each problem at the end of the nine central chapters.

The purpose of this book is to explain the rationale behind the operations of multinational corporations. Reality has been greatly simplified; real shades of gray have been forced into a neat dichotomy of black and white. This simplification is similar to the highway map that ignores minor trails, vegetation, and geology. A real multinational corporation, staffed by real managers and real workers, is immensely more complex. This road map will help you navigate through the living detail of a real multinational corporation.

Acknowledgments

My wife, Sandra, and sons, Michael and Andrew, have enriched my life while I wrote this book. I began working on it while at Carnegie-Mellon University, and am grateful to Richard Cyert, now President but then my first dean, for encouraging me to teach finance, production, marketing, human behavior, and policy. At the time, it seemed a rather daring combination; now, it seems a necessary preparation for multinational management.

The research for this book was funded by the internal funds of Carnegie-Mellon and Queen's Universities. A grant from the Center for International Studies at Queen's supported a research assistant.

Three student-research assistants have labored to improve the book as a whole. Daniel Hogue helped to integrate the early concepts, then primarily mathematical. Elizabeth de Merchant pieced together the first draft, and persuaded me that words are more readable than is mathematics. Barbara Lee provided continuity, discipline, and polish. The reviewers James C. Baker of Kent State University and Dennis E. Logue of Dartmouth University's Amos Tuck School were very helpful. The copy editor of Winthrop Publishers has also been surprisingly helpful, and the continued support from the staff of Little, Brown and Company has been essential.

Chapter 1 was inspired by the ideas of Howard Perlmutter, University of Pennsylvania. C. West Churchman and Richard Holton of the University of California (Berkeley) helped me to develop their relevance to management science and international business. Endel Kolde of the University of Washington had legitimized for me the thoughtful analysis of multinational structures. That structure has been enriched by the comments of many international managers and academic colleagues. My task has been to keep the chapter short and crisp.

In Chapter 2, my debt is to Alan Shapiro, University of Southern California; we have written two articles on foreign exchange management in which we labored to conceptualize the problems. Donald Lessard of

MIT has been a valuable critic, and first gave voice to the distinction between financial risk and the ability of the multinational to adjust its physical assets.

Chapter 3 originated in my doctoral dissertation at Berkeley. When I published some of the raw ideas, Representative Vanek of Ohio denounced maneuvering liquid assets as "a cruel insult to the taxpayer who does his share" (*Congressional Record*, Vol. 116, No. 117, July 13, 1970, pp. H6640–4). I felt obliged to analyze the concepts more thoroughly.

I was fortunate to be a consultant to the corporate planning group of Westinghouse Electric Corporation when Patrick Lynch, Ed Uber, and Lou Greulich were struggling to conceptualize a corporate stance to help the Westinghouse Nuclear Division negotiate its role with the government of France. The government of France had other ideas, so the participants learned a great deal. Ion Amariuta, now at Coopers-Lybrand, taught me about joint ventures, and John Matthews and Joan Lang of IREX guided me in Eastern Europe. Executives in many other multidivisional corporations contributed ideas that are woven into Chapter 4.

Chapter 5 probably originated when I worked on oil refinery planning at Standard Oil of California, and included tankers in linear programs. I am grateful to transportation managers at Gulf Oil, National Steel, and U.S. Steel. Michael Potter of Massey-Ferguson and Donald Bridewesser, now an independent consultant, sharpened my thinking.

Chapter 6 owes most to Ulf Peter Welam of Boston University's Brussels campus, with whom I worked to develop many algorithms for production smoothing. For this book, I wanted a very simple algorithm, and developed it with Kenneth Fraser, now with the Canadian Department of National Defence.

I evolved my understanding of plant location working with Ram Rao, now at Purdue University. After we had completed one joint paper, we proudly explained its ideas to Lee O'Nan of Alcoa, who explained the problem of uncertainty due to rivalry, which led us to model preemptive rivalry. Chapter 7 shows that heritage.

The theme of Chapter 8 is the coexistence of inadequate information and rivalry when a new product is launched. I am extremely grateful to W. W. Cooper, now of the University of Texas, from whom I learned to model partial information, and to Roger Wets (Kentucky), Stanley Garstka (Yale), and Morris de Groot (Carnegie-Mellon) with and from whom I learned stochastic programming with recourse and the nature of optimal adaptivity.

Chapter 9 originated at IBM World Trade when I worked for Emil Schell. The chapter took form with the help of mathematical ideas from Erwin Diewert of the University of British Columbia, tractor price data from Norman McDonald of Corporation House Ltd., and experience curve concepts from my students who joined the Boston Consulting Group.

Tim Shaftel, University of Arizona, and I wrote two papers which provided the skeleton for Chapter 10. As Manfred Padberg, now McKinsey Germany, worked to apply the ideas of product design, the case study on Black and Decker Canada Inc. took form. We are very grateful to Jack Beckering for the many hours he spent educating us.

For Chapter 11, my intellectual debt is again to W. W. Cooper, University of Texas at Austin. The U.S. Navy was forecasting that retirements would lead to an acute shortage of civilian aircraft mechanics, just as their aircraft were becoming more complex. Bill Cooper and his colleagues responded to this ONR challenge by modeling simple jobs as stepping stones to more complex jobs. Simultaneously, I worked with executives who were bemoaning their inability to expand abroad for lack of qualified managers, so I saw the obvious analogy. My work with Richard Fleming of Pittsburgh has enriched the human qualities of this chapter. Material about executive development is so extensive yet nebulous as to deserve an entire volume. Joan Huang, then a Queen's student, helped me prune it to fit this book.

I sometimes think of this book as a stained glass window. The visions of the whole have been shared with me by experienced international executives. The stone structure and lead latticework is the rigorous theory which I have drawn from my academic colleagues at Berkeley, Carnegie-Mellon, and Queen's. Individual pieces of colored glass have come from the vivid examples of managers and students.

The richness of these streams of people has encouraged me to become a good listener, and I am grateful to each in addition to those specifically acknowledged. Conversely, I am responsible for any errors and misinterpretations that remain in my thinking and in this book.

Multinational Management

CHAPTER ONE

Organizational Structures and Tensions

Introductory Note to the Case

First National City Bank

Case studies about the organizational structure of a domestic business usually focus on the merits of decentralization and centralization. In a multinational multiproduct corporation such an evaluation cannot begin until the different ways in which the corporation could be centralized have been identified. This evaluation is colored by the technological problems of the corporation, and so most available case studies provide a block of details about the technology, and whether the corporation's skill lies chiefly in manufacturing the product (centralization by product division) or in helping the society adopt it (centralization by nation). Usually a bank falls into the second group, and at the start of the case discussed here the First National City Bank is organized by nation, with each national office headed by a senior officer (called a senof) who appears to view his nation as his fiefdom, a vivid display of polycentric thinking.

However, some of the bank's customers are multinational corporations which, it is claimed, would like consistency of treatment on a global basis, as seen later in the chapters on finance. Consider the usefulness to a multinational manufacturer of banking with many national banks versus banking with one global bank: Should an American multinational manufacturer bank with a Japanese, Canadian, or British global bank?

The questions at the end of the case bring the discussion from conceptualization to action plans.

Citibank, as First National City Bank has been called since 1976, went ahead with twinning its organization. This reorganization assured easier communication within the bank, although it did diffuse responsibility. But technical change was underway. During the 1970s Citibank embraced minicomputers and distributed data bases.

A loan officer is responsible for his or her client list, and this computing and text recall ability provides the loan officer with very flexible analytical capability. Citibank minicomputers are interconnected as a network, so that a senior loan officer dealing with a multinational client can access information on all the bank's global dealings with that client as well as the names of the Citibank employees responsible for each deal. Since information now could be centralized when and where needed, Citibank could undo its formal organization, thus sharpening individual responsibility. This reorganization was completed in 1980. Other reorganizations will surely occur as needs arise.

First National City Bank

Multinational Corporate Banking

In June 1973 senior management at First National City Bank was close to reaching a decision about its international corporate banking business. At that time, Citibank was the second largest bank in the world. International activities accounted for 59 percent of its total revenue and 60 percent of its net income. The bank's senior officers abroad seemed to give borrowing preference to local rather than international corporate clients in their belief that the returns were greater and that local clients did a greater volume of business in their country than did the foreign corporations. New data, however, had shown that the multinational corporate market was indeed profitable and that the bank was not taking full advantage of it. Multinational corporations were serviced by the bank geographically, through account managers located in the bank's offices in the home country of the client company. This meant that the domestic business of U.S.-based multinationals was handled by the Corporate Banking

This case was prepared by Professor Stanley M. Davis of Boston University School of Management, and is reproduced by permission. Copyright 1975 by the President and Fellows of Harvard College.

Group (CBG) while the international business of these same firms was serviced by the International Banking Group (IBG). The International Banking Group also managed the accounts of all European, Japanese, and other multinational corporate clients. Senior management of Citibank was not satisfied with the arrangement.

Historical Growth

Citibank opened its first international branch in London in 1902, then opened in five Asian countries that same year. It moved to Buenos Aires in 1914, and opened six more Latin American branches the following year. By 1939 it had 100 overseas offices. The branch network contracted sharply during World War II but accelerated rapidly after the mid-1950s. Between 1956 and 1965 the number of overseas branches increased from 69 to 125. By 1973 Citibank was operating in 95 countries. Overseas it had 242 branches, 320 affiliate offices, and 69 banking subsidiary and representative offices. The Bank of America, its closest rival, was a poor second with 103 branches in 44 countries.

International Organization

In 1973, the bulk of Citibank's international activities was organized geographically, under the IBG (see Exhibit 1.1). The group was led since its creation by G.A. Costanzo, executive vice president. Five divisions, each headed by a senior vice president, reported directly to him: (1) Asia and Pacific, (2) Canada and Caribbean, (3) South America, (4) Europe, and (5) South Asia, Middle East, and Africa. In each country where the bank operated there was a senior officer (commonly referred to as the senof) in charge of all Citibank activities. Each senof reported to one of the division heads. Traditionally, the senofs were the main line of Citibank's international organization and were very strong guardians of their domains. In some foreign countries, where the bank had a major share of business, a senof may have controlled as many as 5000 employees.

Within a country, the various business segments are organized basically along the same pattern as in the United States. A corporate Banking Department in each country handled the banking needs of both local and multinational industrial corporations in that nation. Depending on the particular country, the corporate banking unit might be broken down further by industry and then by account manager.

INTERNATIONAL BANKING GROUP

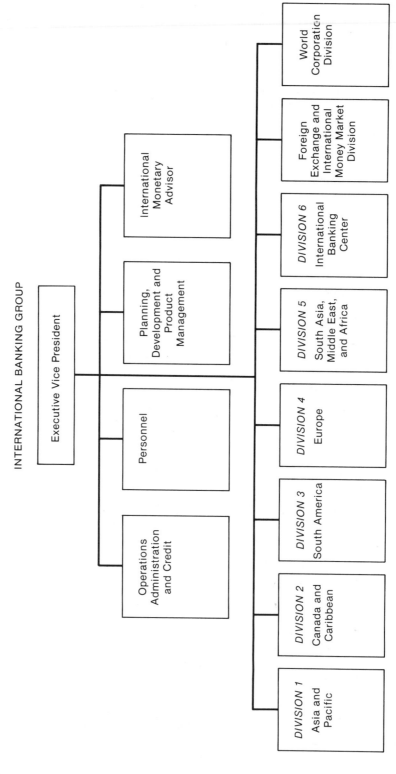

EXHIBIT 1.1

International Banking Group. Note that in Divisions 1 to 5, each country senof reports directly to a division head. (Source: company records.)

The Multinational Corporate Client

During the period between 1968 and 1973 a great deal of literature appeared about the multinational corporation. In both popular and scholarly works, in business and in government circles, the multinational corporation came into its own as a genus distinct from the national corporate business sector. About 25 percent of all U.S. corporate profits (after taxes) comes from investments abroad. The top 300 industrial firms and the seven largest banks earn about 40 percent of their profits outside the United States. Many of the largest U.S. corporations such as Mobil, IBM, and ITT earn more than 50 percent of their profits abroad. According to the International Monetary Fund, multinationals accounted for an estimated $450 billion a year in goods and services, or over 10 percent of the gross world product. This represented more than a doubling of output in a decade, and a 50 percent increase in the share of the noncommunist world's gross product between 1950 and 1970. The increasing trends toward globalization and concentration clearly made the multinational corporation a distinct business market. While domestic assets from corporate customers showed a relatively flat growth curve, Citibank's overseas loans to multinationals were growing substantially.

Citibank's multinational corporate business, in the earlier part of the century, was centered on routine banking transactions along the world's trading routes. As multinational enterprise grew, however, so did the need for indigenously oriented banking services in other countries on the same scale as was offered in the United States. The early and extensive branch network of Citibank put it in the forefront of this development in multinational corporate banking. Although the domestic growth of Citibank and of global corporations tapered off in the mid-1960s, both nevertheless grew rapidly in their international operations. The international portion of any one corporate banking relationship therefore became increasingly significant. Growth and profitability in the CBG brought it into increasing contact with the IBG, which, in turn, produced frequent internal problems.

The most common problem between the CBG and the IBG resulted from the preference shown by the bank's branch in a foreign country to lend money to a local borrower rather than to the foreign subsidiary of a global company operating in that country. The general belief was that the "spreads" — the difference between cost of funds and percentage interest to be charged — were greater when lending to local borrowers, partly because there were greater risks involved. The general consensus was that Citibank's foreign branch managers preferred local corporate clients to global ones. Besides providing larger profits from the spreads, local borrowers often required other financial services that the bank was able to supply. By contrast, the multinational subsidiary was more likely to turn to its headquarters staff for the same service. The local orientation was also helpful in demonstrating to the host country that Citibank was a good corporate citizen.

Although Citibank was well received by its multinational corporate clients, this nonpreferential treatment in some of the bank's overseas offices was occasionally troublesome. For example, if the foreign subsidiary of a multinational client was having difficulty securing a loan from the bank's branch in that country, the firm's financial officer at U.S. headquarters would be likely to contact the Citibank account manager in New York to resolve the matter. The client's position would be, "After all, we are a major customer worldwide. Just because this Uruguayan matter is not a major contract we still expect you to service us there with the same interest and attention you would lavish on our larger European deals."

Internal Problems

Even when local versus global client preference was not an issue, problems of internal communication existed between the two groups in Citibank. If a U.S. company wanted to build a plant in Argentina, for example, the firm's financial officer might go to the bank's account manager in the CBG for assurance of the necessary loan. To help his client, the account manager would then make contact with the IBG. "Among other grim realities," recounted one CBG manager, "we didn't know who the bank officer in Argentina was. We were a big bank there with hundreds of people, and so you'd write to 'The Manager.' God knows whether he ever got it." To avoid this, the CBG would present its case to the IBG in New York and they would filter the request down to the appropriate party in the field.

This process did not become cumbersome until the 1960s. The personal network of relationships within the bank had smoothed the flow; but with increases in the volume of business and the number of people involved, the screening process in New York broke down. In the mid-1960s *de facto* direct communication began between CBG account managers in New York and the counterpart local account managers in the IBG branches.

Despite these problems, however, Citibank still continued to satisfy its global customers. The major dissatisfaction was internal, between the CBG and the IBG. Neither CBG nor IBG took maximum advantage of opportunities that presented themselves, though there was no serious breakdown in bank performance with corporate clients.

Matrix Resolution

On August 6, 1973, William I. Spencer, President of First National City Bank, sent a memorandum to all officers and supervisors. The memo began:

> In 1968, we undertook a revolutionary reorganization to better position ourselves opposite our major markets. Our earnings results since that time speak for the success of the change.
>
> Last Friday, senior management finalized plans to build on this success by systematically evolving further organizational changes over the next five months.
>
> In brief, our blueprint has three major elements. First, our experience in recent years has identified an important global market: the delivery of financial services to the major corporations that operate worldwide. The potential of this market is so great that we are creating opposite it a new major organization unit, the World Corporation Group.
>
> Secondly, in the domestic arena, the Commercial Banking Group has successfully demonstrated how to build a viable business approach to the medium-size corporate customer. To capitalize on this approach we intend to extend it throughout the country. To accomplish this we will realign what are now our Commercial Banking Group regional centers into the organizational structures of the other Groups.
>
> Thirdly, the building of Citicorp Center is one of the larger risks to be managed over the next few years. This will require additional senior management expertise and talent, especially in the area of client and tenant relations.

Another memorandum followed immediately, stating assumptions being made "in order to develop a list of tasks which must be completed in order to implement these changes." It read, in part:

> 1. *The Commercial Banking Group.* The functions in the Com-

mercial Banking Group will be transferred into the organizational structures of other Banking Groups as follows:

. . .

E. Selected multinational accounts to World Corporation Group.

2. *World Corporation Group.* This group will be newly formed by transferring selected multinational accounts from the Corporate Banking Group, the Commercial Banking Group and the International Banking Group in New York. This group will also have responsibility for services provided to these multinational accounts by our overseas offices with the earnings from these services being reported in parallel in the International Banking Group and the World Corporation Group.

3. *International Banking Group.* Selected multinational accounts will be transferred to the new World Corporation Group and the unit responsible for services to higher net worth individuals will be transferred to the Investment Banking Group.

4. *The Corporate Banking Group.* The following changes will be made in the CBG: [A National Banking Group was created from the CBG to service large domestic corporate clients.]

. . .

E. Responsibility for services to all selected multinational accounts will be transferred to the World Corporation Group.

Questions

Executive Vice President Thomas C. Theobald assumed responsibility for the new World Corporation Group. January 1, 1974 was set as the date to officially transfer all accounts and begin operating the WCG. During the coming months many decisions would have to be made, including the following:

1. How would the business objectives and strategy of the new group be articulated?
2. Which corporate customers would be transferred to the WCG, what criteria would be used to make the selections, and how many multinationals are headquartered in each nation?
3. How should interactions between WCG and IBG be structured and managed, with particular regard to (a) financial, (b) human, and (c) physical resource allocations in all countries?
4. How many people would be needed, where would they come from, and where would they be assigned?
5. What were the management information system requirements?

6. When and how should clients be informed of the changes?
7. When a client corporation is transferred to WCG, the political power of its headquarters treasurer in his dealings with his national subsidiaries is enhanced. What banking consequences should WCG anticipate if the organizational archetype of the client is: a) Ethnocentric? b) Polycentric? c) Geocentric?
8. After operating the WCG and IBG in tandem for several years, what is the next reorganization you predict for Citibank?

Introduction

Many manufacturing corporations became international by a process of creeping incrementalism rather than strategic choice. Unsolicited export orders required the commissioning of agents abroad, establishment of warehouses, and development of a sales force. Established markets in less developed countries became hostages as local governments exerted pressure on corporations to build plants. Subsidiaries grew, gradually finding themselves subject to further pressure to increase local manufactures and to train nationals for some managerial positions. Simultaneously, the corporation probably licensed technology and entered into joint ventures. Very rarely were these moves part of a comprehensive strategy. A patchwork of *ad hoc* relationships became established.

In the 1960s corporations of all nationalities expanded beyond their national boundaries. They jostled aggressively to become multinational, expanding and acquiring blindly, as it now appears in hindsight. What propelled them? There are many theories: younger executives had seen the world during World War II; there were few travel restrictions; international telephone and the newly introduced jet airliners made business communication easy; research and development for products such as computers and pharmaceuticals (to name only two) became so expensive that no one market (not even the United States) was large enough to justify the next generation of products; the normal life cycle of a product could be extended by operations abroad; and internationally executives perceived low risk of financial and political instability. Governments, particularly of the Third World nations, wanted to industrialize and worked to encourage investment from abroad. In addition, the tendency of European competitors to form cartels to exclude outsiders appeared to be abating, and prudent foreign corporations moved to become established in Europe while they could. At the same time, the wave of European mergers and production rationalizations (Vernon, 1974) led some to predict that international mergers would not cease until there remained just 300 giant global corporations. To remain static seemed untenable: Acquire or be acquired! Whatever ignited the process, once some corporations moved for multinationality, competitors followed in fear of being left behind.

Consolidation follows expansion. Through the 1970s executives struggled to bring coherence to the organizational structure of their corporations. For most multinational executives, this was a sobering decade in which the meaning of a finite globe with finite resources would be understood. The exuberance of the 1960s led many citizens to believe in a conspiracy theory: The difference between profitable and unprofitable multinational companies is that the former have used their massive bargaining power to extract concessions from temporarily weak host governments. During the 1970s multinational executives lived with the backlash from that view. Although the public was awed by the vast resources of multinationals, the executives knew that only governments can claim sovereignty. Attempts to change government policy by bribery usually fail.

The problems of the 1970s revolved around the question of how a headquarters is organized to relate to its operations abroad. Such relationships are affected primarily by the nature of the operations. There are technical licensing agreements with autonomous partners, intimate cross-licensing in which know-how is exchanged for equity (and the hope for more), many kinds of joint ventures, and even management service contracts. In many cases wholly owned subsidiaries are acquired but not fully assimilated, and even those that the corporation itself has developed vary in structure, for most grow rapidly and unevenly.

During the 1970s most corporate organizational structures were evolving. The formal structures may have remained unchanged, but informal practices evolved in three ways. The first organizational evolution was that power relationships matured among headquarters, regional centers, and national subsidiaries, especially in corporations containing merger fragments. Because the most effective power may not be overt, the subsidiary-headquarters interface may take many possible positions. Suppose, for example, there has been a trend to centralization. The identical decision may initially have been made locally, then made locally with a memo to headquarters, made locally with merely the formality of a review at headquarters, prepared locally for presentation at headquarters, made at headquarters then sold to the subsidiary, or perhaps finally made at headquarters with a memo to the subsidiary. During this evolution (or an equivalent trend to decentralization), the formal organization chart may have remained unchanged.

The second organizational evolution is that managers become more familiar with how decisions should be made in their own corporation. This is more than a question of familiarity with an office manual, for it involves an executive's ability to categorize a decision in whichever of the ways just mentioned is appropriate and to do so with confidence and without anxiety. As an analogy consider a child playing in a yard; a parent is nearby. If the yard is fenced, the child can have autonomy inside that boundary; the parent need not monitor the child continuously. Conversely, if the yard has no fence, the parent must oversee constantly to assure that the child is safe. This second evolution refers to establishing, agreeing upon, and testing mental fences.

The third organizational evolution is that managers around the world now feel more legitimate in their roles. The subtle difference between a federation and a confederation is that members of a confederation agree on a goal. A multinational corporation is a confederation with the economic goal of long-run profit. Managers pursue many other goals, but it is easy to predict that the capital shortages forecasted for the 1980s will result in worldwide profit being the dominant confederation goal, to which other goals may be sacrificed.

Relationships evolve as people more clearly understand their purposes. As a multinational corporation evolves, it is vital that headquarters executives clarify (in their own minds) why they want to be multinational. The challenge to multinational executives in the 1980s is to articulate the value that multinational corporations contribute to sovereign governments.

Every corporation elaborates a myth about its birth and early international experience. This myth gives courage to the fainthearted and gives consistency to the integration of newly hired executives. The myths can usually be distilled to two economic reasons that sustain most international diversification. The first reason is economies of scale as explained by experience curves; the second is risk-spreading. Experience curves, carried to the extreme, lead to an ethnocentric attitude. Risk-spreading, carried to its extreme, leads to a polycentric attitude. We examine each separately before uniting them to get the best of each in a geocentric corporation.

Experience Curves in a Product-Structured Corporation

Each time an activity is repeated it becomes easier, though at a decreasing rate. Unit cost usually drops 15 to 25 percent with each doubling of cumulative experience. In industrial practice (Boston Consulting Group, 1970) an experience curve is a graph of unit cost (deflated for inflation) plotted against cumulative production (the total quantity since the very first unit was manufactured). The data plotted on log-log paper fit a sloping straight line. In a competitive oligopoly, market share is an important asset because each competitor moves down the experience curve at a rate proportional to its market share in a product line. It therefore behooves corporate executives to exercise self-restraint and allow their corporation to expand only into market niches in which they can become preeminent on a worldwide basis. Many corporations have fragmented their attention on too many product lines: Although their total size may appear vast, they have failed to become the world's lowest-cost producer in any particular product market.

Consider a single factory that produces items for export to several national markets. The factory has its experience curve (based on cumulative production), and each national marketing force has its experience curve (based on cumulative sales in its nation). Each marketing force could struggle alone to reduce its unit cost of distribution or, with communication and coordination, each could learn from its sister subsidiaries. In other words, the corporation can improve its productivity in both manufacturing and marketing by pooling the corporation's international experience.

This phenomenon suggests a crucial question for a multinational corporation with several plants manufacturing the same item. Is each plant progressing along its separate experience curve, or is the corporation as a whole working down one experience curve several times as fast? Is each subsidiary confronting and solving the same problem on its own, or is the corporation organized to share experience? To share cumulative experience is to have product specialists and task forces in manufacturing and marketing who jet around the world. Mid-career training assignments are in sister subsidiaries. The cost accounting system is designed to highlight those subsidiaries that are not borrowing experience rapidly enough. Markets are reallocated in order to reward plants that can reduce costs fastest. The focus is on the product: Productivity of the current designs must be improved, and the next generation of products must be developed to keep ahead of competitors.

The competitive advantage of market share is greatest for relatively young products. For example, iron castings have been manufactured for thousands of years; there is already substantial cumulative production. This year's production by one corporation will not add significantly to cumulative production, and the expected drop in unit cost will be even smaller. On the other hand, the cumulative production of jet engines or integrated circuits is low, so that a year's production adds measurably to experience. For these products there is a clear economic rationale for viewing the world as one market and computing market shares on global demand.

Organizational structures are commonly described as centralized or decentralized. Multinational multiproduct corporations can be decentralized in several ways. To view the world as one market for a product,

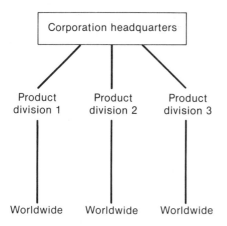

EXHIBIT 1.2
Organization by product can lead to ethnocentrism.

it is usual to organize the entire corporation into world product groups. Within one product group, activities around the world are highly centralized; thus there can be only weak coordination between product groups either at headquarters or in any of the subsidiary nations, so the corporation appears decentralized in any nation.

In a multinational corporation global product standardization fully exploits a separate experience curve of each product; however, standardization can be carried to excess. The multinational could be too brittle to counter nimble national competitors. If managed inflexibly, the cost-cutting virtue of standardization could become a vice.

Product centeredness, when carried to excess, takes on emotional overtones. Product standards of nations with the greatest cumulative production tend to become the product standards for the world. In the first half of the century, dye chemicals were associated with Germany, and anyone who wanted to keep up in the field found it helpful to read German. In the second half of this century, computers have U.S. connotations. The emotional overtone inherent in this situation is that domestic executives may become ethnocentric: They may come to believe in the *inherent* superiority of their own nation.

> Ethnocentrism denotes the well-known tendency to make rigid ingroup-outgroup distinctions. Ethnocentrics make their own groups the normative center of all their thinking. Unable to love their own kind without expressing antipathy toward others, they draw sharp lines of exclusion. Insofar as they idolize and remain submissive to and uncritical of their ingroup, they are likely to blame outsiders for their own ills and regard them as both inferior and hostile. (Olson, 1963, p. 3)

Ethnocentrism is dangerous because it leads to the self-assurance of an old-style missionary. "We (people of country A) are superior, and have greater resources, facilities and competence than you (people of country B). We will build facilities in your country if you accept our inherent superiority, and our methods and procedures for doing the job" (Perlmutter, 1967). If the corporation has been successful domestically, it will feel especially sure that its standard methods and procedures for problem solving represent a unique contribution that, as an alien corporation, it can make to the economy of the host country. The headquarters therefore requires that these standards and procedures be used by subsidiaries.

A product specialist who flies about the world may not take the trouble to understand the environmental details of each separate national subsidiary, hence he cannot tailor his communications. Leavitt (1972, Chapter 13) would describe the headquarter's behavior toward its subsidiaries as being direct rather than manipulatively indirect. In a multiproduct corporation, each product division has worldwide line responsibility.

For expositional purposes, let us consider a caricature. Each subsidiary product manager tends to identify with his worldwide product. Loyal to his product, he may view himself as only temporarily stationed in some particular subsidiary. Furthermore, his advancement is likely to be in the form of lateral moves, within the same product division, to larger subsidiaries. As a member of a group of product specialists, he will be affected by consistent norms of behavior, whether he is in headquarters or in the subsidiaries.

An individual whose recommendations transcend group norms is eased out of the group. If a subsidiary production manager recommends a nonstandard design, tailoring products to a certain nation, he may find himself stuck at that plant for the rest of his working life. Perhaps this group identification is the basis for Martyn's (1964, p. 139) reflection on his Unilever experience:

> It is a strict rule among the long-established international firms to manufacture the same products or to deliver the same services on which their home success was founded in as many countries as possible. If one of these products will not sell in a country for peculiar national reasons (soap with a carbolic smell was associated with brothels in France), the international concern prefers to withdraw rather than modify the product. Accepting variations would leave the company without consistent standards, which could disturb its accounting and its marketing, as well as its production arrangements.

Corporations organized along product and functional lines (to assure that the local subsidiaries will be run well) have a problem of coordinating several divisions in each nation. Until 1980 Westinghouse Electric was organized by global product divisions. "Not long ago, a company salesman called on a Saudi Arabian businessman. After the preliminaries, the Saudi reached into his desk drawer and drew out the business cards of twenty-four other Westinghouse salesmen. Spreading them out on his desk the Saudi exasperatedly inquired 'who speaks for Westinghouse?'" (Menzies, 1980). Operationally, each division reports to its global product division manager. Legally, each reports to the national subsidiary. The role of the president of that national subsidiary is to make public appearances to remove the negative impression his host nation has of foreign corporations in general. For this purpose, a cosmetic solution is to hire a distinguished and well-connected national as the local president. He may not understand the language of each product and professional group, and he is likely to develop a suspicion that their decisions are not in the best interests of his subsidiary. He can do little about it, however, because though he has formal authority he lacks professional authority (Etzioni, 1964, Chapter 8). His reaction frequently evolves to xenophobia — distrustful fear of foreigners and their machinations.

The U.S. group presidents of RCA have worldwide authority over the manufacture and sale of products within their group. Dundas (1979) relays the very serious frustration experienced by Canadian regional managers:

> A further source of concern to senior managers in RCA Canada stemmed from a combination of the organization structure and the changing nature of competition in the subsidiary's major businesses. Several senior managers stated that the subsidiary was not making maximum use of its resources and that this situation would get worse rather than better as increasing competition brings about change in the existing operation. In the opinion of these managers there were profitable opportunities in Canada which were being missed. The structural side of the problem had two aspects. One was that the major product groups were preoccupied with their existing activities and were unprepared to consider new proposals by the subsidiary. The second aspect lay in the perspective of the divisional vice presidents, which seemed to be bounded by the conventions of their respective major product groups.

Subsidiary product managers are unequivocally subordinate, organizationally to the local president and technically to the alien experts. Individuals act out their own patterns of subordinacy in a variety of ways (Zaleznick and Kets de Vries 1975, Chapter 7). The unequivocal subordinacy of the local product managers results in the active ones becoming either impulsive or masochistic, depending on whether they are dominant or submissive. Similarly, the passive ones become either compulsive or withdrawn. These extreme characterizations are muted in humane managers, but behavioral dynamics within subsidiaries retain the potential for instability, which provokes headquarters to send even more help and become even more imperious.

A national company can survive, if competing with multinationals, only if it adapts to national tastes. It must sense and develop market niches peculiar to its own nation. If the national company can license technology from abroad, so much the better, but only if company engineers have the creative flexibility to select and adapt the technology to manufacturing in the national niche. The national company's unique advantages are its flexibility and its ability to reposition products as its niche moves. Both could be compromised by the wrong kind of licensing arrangement.

Ethnocentric Planning Guidelines

The focus on the product, if carried to an ethnocentric excess, will result in definite planning guidelines. Let us preview each chapter from an ethnocentric viewpoint.

Chapter 2. Exchange Management in a Multinational Corporation. The corporation uses only the spot exchange rates for cost and profitability analysis, and because its shareholders are American, its bookkeeping will be in U.S. dollars. Because foreign currencies are viewed as risky, the treasurer will set up an accounting system to monitor the corporation's net assets or liabilities in each currency and will act to reduce exposure to fluctuating exchange rates, in accordance with the advice of the Financial Accounting Standards Board.

Chapter 3. Maneuvering Liquid Assets. Headquarters staff evaluates all expansion plans and cash flow forecasts. To move cash to illiquid subsidiaries, the staff will orchestrate intersubsidiary dividends and sometimes will waive the usual fee for royalties and headquarters costs. Headquarters could adjust transfer prices using the excuse that costs fluctuate and new products are always being introduced but rarely does for fear of distorting cost comparisons.

Chapter 4. Multidivisional Expansion to a New Nation. Because the corporation is in business to make a profit, its divisions must compete with one another for funds. A global product manager who has a unique relationship with a government may not want to jeopardize his relationship just to help bring in another division. Hence coordination attempts by headquarters will be resisted.

Chapter 5. Logistics. Each division will manage its own inventory flows and charter its own space on vessels and aircraft. Headquarters may facilitate the paperwork.

Chapter 6. Production Smoothing. Each division produces wherever in the world is cheapest at the time. Sometimes one division will be hiring workers in a nation while another division would like to lay off in the same nation. Most production-smoothing problems center on closing out old products and launching new ones.

Chapter 7. Multinational Plant Location. Return on investment calculations are made *after* taxes on repatriated profits to the United States. Since the company wants the lowest costs in the world and is not afraid of automation, it will operate a few very large export factories.

Chapter 8. New Product Launch. Because the United States is the home market, and fortunately the most advanced market in the world, new products are first launched here. After the product has succeeded and been improved in the U.S. market, the division manager will allow its introduction in other nations.

Chapter 9. Pricing. The same price is charged worldwide for each item (except where there are price controls). This policy provides the consistent data that marketing professionals need to gauge performance in various markets. Different prices for the same items would encourage customers to buy from the cheapest market, which would seriously impair the sales incentive system. Import duty plus freight from the home plant is sometimes added to the price.

Chapter 10. Product Design. The U.S. design will be sold in all nations, except where law may necessitate minor modifications. Product standardization will be justified by the high cost of research and development and thus the fixed cost of introducing another product. Few new products will be introduced.

Chapter 11. International Executive Development. Planning guidelines for managerial rotation will be explicit for Americans, who will be moved among subsidiaries and then back to headquarters. The acute shortage of local managerial talent will necessitate that nationals stay within their subsidiaries, where their contribution is greatest.

Risk-Spreading in a Geographically Organized Corporation

The second economic reason for being multinational is to spread risk. Risk can be reduced by geographic decentralization. Let us consider how risk can be reduced by geographically decentralized marketing, production, and finance.

A marketing executive, concerned with units sold, is reassured by the fact that national business cycles are not synchronized. When sales are slack in some nations, there are exciting growth prospects in others. Mathematically, total worldwide sales can be predicted to a lower standard deviation than sales in a single average nation.

A manufacturing executive also finds reassurance in this predictability of the total demand, for total plant capacity must be adequate to satisfy total market demand. Moreover, having plants in many different nations means that the corporation can maintain production even if it loses some plants to striking trade unions or to accidents. Whatever the scenario, having many self-contained plants adds a comfortable measure of robustness to the whole system.

A finance executive may compare the corporation to a mutual fund in which each national subsidiary is an asset: The multinational constitutes a geographically diversified portfolio of net income streams. It is important then to differentiate between perceived risk and actual risk. A French executive may perceive higher risk in an investment in the United States while, simultaneously, an American perceives higher risk in France. Furthermore, a French and an American executive visiting Casablanca may perceive quite different risks to the future of Morocco. Therefore, a team of various nationalities can develop a more objective decision than a team of executives of any one nationality. The multinational group process is time-consuming and difficult, but the quality of the ultimate decision may justify the effort by virtue of the fact that a group decision often comes closer to identifying actual risk, not merely perceptions of risk.

Historically, most corporations began international activities with an export department, which organized its activities geographically. There was a tendency, perhaps unconscious, to let "our man in Rio" conduct business in what he said was "the Brazilian way." In the resulting geographical organization, each national manager (a senof at Citibank) ran his own fiefdom. The tendency of the organization is toward greater geographical decentralization. A national manager generally avoids asking headquarters to help, for to do so would invite control; conversely, national managers usually run tight ships to avoid any excuse for interference. Thus a corporation that appears decentralized at the top may be tightly centralized within each national subsidiary.

Autonomous national subsidiaries can make deals with sister subsidiaries. If one subsidiary proposes unacceptable contract terms to another subsidiary, the latter is under no compulsion to continue negotiation. To use a legal phrase, only arms-length contracts will be signed. The advantages of dealing within a multinational corporation are that communication is easier and corporate headquarters can administer justice if a subsidiary defaults on a deal with a sister subsidiary.

In microeconomics, price theory, and elementary welfare economics, we learn that the invisible hand of price works to ensure that resources are allocated optimally. In advanced price theory and advanced welfare economics, we learn that sometimes it is impossible to write contracts with adequate contingent clauses, and so a judge who has enforcement power is needed (Williamson, 1975). For example, negotiated transfer pricing works well only if the buyer has alternative sources and the seller alternative outlets. If one buyer can purchase from only one seller, economists describe the situation as a bilateral monopoly. If either seller or

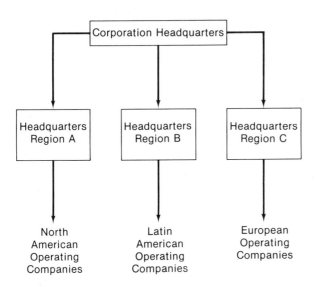

EXHIBIT 1.3
Organization by nation can lead to polycentrism.

buyer takes the advantage during negotiations, the price may be bid so high or so low that lower total profits are achieved than if an enforcer insisted on joint profit maximizing (Fouraker and Siegel, 1960).

Multinational manufacturing corporations emphasize the uniqueness of their products, a uniqueness sustained by both patents and image building in a market. Because the buying subsidiary may have no alternative sources and the selling subsidiary insufficient alternative outlets, each would like to avoid bilateral monopoly by the presence of a headquarters executive. To write a contract in such circumstances is difficult; it is easier to have a headquarters integrator and enforcer.

If geographical decentralization is to avoid a polycentric extreme, the corporation needs a headquarters with a staff of honest auditors, diligently snuffing out personal cheating. It also needs a judiciary. Commercial transactions always give rise to misunderstandings, and arms-length deals between autonomous subsidiaries likewise occasionally go into dispute. The headquarters executive hears evidence and renders verdicts in the tradition of fairness and leadership. An enterprising leader, the headquarters executive must inspire trust and have great interpersonal skills. These qualities are discussed in Chapter 11.

The purpose of the headquarters of a geographically organized business is to relay messages, anticipate misunderstandings, and mediate conflicts. This calls for a deep and sympathetic understanding of each subsidiary, joint venture, or licensee. The appropriate measure of whether headquarters achieves this is whether it can accurately anticipate how the subsidiary will accept its guidance.

Exxon consists of 13 affiliated companies, most organized on geographical lines such as Esso Middle East, Esso Europe, Exxon USA, and Imperial. Each functions independently, in its *operations*. But both capital expansions and personnel moves require the direction of headquarters, which is organized into 17 staff departments, including corporate planning, law, and public relations. Jerome Rosow (1974, p. 156) of Exxon has articulated the delicate fabric of decentralization in a geographically decentralized organization.

> Decentralization permits variety, easier adaptability, and less uniformity in management style. Therefore, the multinational requires high tolerance for differences, a great risk-taking ability, and subtle methods for maintaining variations within a range of central tendencies. Decentralized initiatives can allow room for centralized synthesis. The art of management requires distribution of power without loss of control over results.
>
> Effective decentralized management is a delicate balancing act. It is an organizational and authority structure which is spun like a delicate web. Its survival and its strength depend upon trust at the top and self-sufficiency at the periphery. Of course some decentralized organizations are more a matter of form than of substance. They are inhibited by man's natural reluctance to share, much less fully delegate, power. Decentralization depends upon adequate delegations without inadequate control.

Geographical decentralization is most viable if the corporation manufactures mature products, if the market in the headquarters nation is less than half the total sales, and if rivalry is stable. Clee and Sachtjen (1964) described one such corporation.

[In the early 1960's Massey-Ferguson,] Ltd., a huge international farm equipment manufacturer whose operations had been organized along regional lines, adopted an organizational structure built around a series of largely self-contained marketing and manufacturing *operations* units . . . [These are] centered on important individual markets (the United Kingdom, France, Germany, the United States, and Canada). Supplementing these units is an *export marketing* unit to cover sales in parts of the world where [Massey-Ferguson] has no manufacturing operations.

Longer-range corporate strategy — determination of the basic world-wide product line, decisions on major facilities, and changes in the logistic product flow from production sources to markets — is set at corporate headquarters. But these decisions are heavily influenced by *operations unit* judgments and recommendations. Each unit is responsible for determining the product lines best suited to its local markets.

If carried to excess, a virtue can become a vice. In 1980 Massey-Ferguson almost became bankrupt, and had to be recentralized. Geographical decentralization can slip into polycentrism if the regional officers at headquarters relate too closely to the subsidiaries they control. The regional officer occupying the Mexican desk should have had some experience with Mexican problems if he is to understand and effectively manipulate the Mexican subsidiary. Nevertheless, constant immersion in a wide stream of communication from Mexico causes the regional officer to identify closely with the Mexican subsidiary. He then risks becoming merely its chief proponent and headquarters becomes a debating society rather than a unifying center.

Polycentric Planning Guidelines

If a corporation has slipped into the extreme of polycentrism, the pattern of interaction within the headquarters and the relationships with subsidiaries result in unambiguous planning guidelines within which a problem should be formulated and optimized. In a polycentric corporation one might find strong sentiment for the following guidelines.

Chapter 2. Exchange Management in a Multinational Corporation. Now that the major exchange rates are floating, nobody can expect to gain by speculating. The administrative rule is no hedging; the sophisticated rationale is to diversify risk over many currencies.

Chapter 3. Maneuvering Liquid Assets. Headquarters reserves the right to specify the dividend payout of each subsidiary. The formula for allocating headquarters overhead will rarely be altered. Intersubsidiary loans may be facilitated by headquarters, but at a fair market interest. Transfer prices will not be mandated, except for an equity rule that all purchasing subsidiaries be charged the same f.o.b. price for the same item by a particular manufacturing subsidiary.

Chapter 4. Multidivisional Expansion to a New Nation. The corporation will rarely expand to a new nation except at the request of a licensee in trouble or a floundering joint venture. Hence the product line that is introduced will be the one that is requested, rather than the one best suited to the corporation's competitive position on a worldwide basis.

Chapter 5. Logistics. Details of shipping between subsidiaries are to be arranged by those concerned.

Chapter 6. Production Smoothing. If factories in some nations are excessively busy while others are not, regional officers in headquarters may suggest transferring export orders to less busy subsidiaries. Unfortunately, the lack of standard designs will limit this possibility.

Chapter 7. Multinational Plant Location. Marketing subsidiaries will inform headquarters of every instance of government and customer pressure for them to manufacture locally and will speak of factory and market as one organic unit. Headquarters staff analysts, who might argue for a rationalization of production, tend to find that data are unobtainable.

Chapter 8. New Product Launch. Each national subsidiary will introduce new products when it wants to. There may be a casual sharing of information such as "product XB155 is selling well," but there will be no comprehensive market research to clarify the underlying relevance of this information to other subsidiaries.

Chapter 9. Pricing. No pricing scheme will be imposed on subsidiaries. Hence national sales managers will constantly bicker about price; those in high-priced nations will use incidents of product leakage to accuse managers in low-priced nations of poaching customers.

Chapter 10. Product Design. Products will be designed to suit each national subsidiary even though this means forgoing the mutual benefit of experience curves. By tailoring design to its national requirements, the subsidiary can have its products reclassified by customs inspectors to lower rates of import duty, to meet local safety and engineering standards, to use local grades and types of raw materials, and to cater to local customer tastes.

Chapter 11. International Executive Development. Nationals will be employed in each subsidiary to the greatest extent possible, and only a few bilateral movements of managers will be planned. Nationals will be sent to headquarters to learn technical skills needed in their homeland. During their temporary absence, headquarters managers may fill their positions, but this will be limited by the shortage of qualified headquarters personnel, particularly as the corporation's products become more complex.

Geocentric Balance in a Matrix Organization

Most people probably feel that decisions should be responsive to national needs and simultaneously should maximize the efficiency of each product, that multinational corporations should satisfy acceptable aspirations for both nationalism and efficiency. A number of multinational companies already move products, managers, capital, and research around the world, adjusting the rates of flow to suit local environments. Their ideal is to be rational on a global basis. Some are organized by product but avoid ethnocentrism by very strong dotted-line relationships to each nation. Some are organized nationally but avoid polycentrism by strong product ties.

A matrix organization structure is frequently used to facilitate global rationality. Kramer (1981, pp. 80–81) has described the two characteristics of a matrix organization:

> *Structurally*, there is a dual rather than a single chain of command. Some managers report to two individuals rather than to the traditional single boss. . . .
> *Behaviorally*, there is lateral (dual) decision-making and a chain of command that fosters conflict management and a balance of power. . . .
> Matrix organizations usually contain three key positions, depicted in [Exhibit 1.4]. At the top is the *top leadership*, the general executive, who plays a role quite similar to the one he plays in traditional organizations.
> The *Matrix managers*, who share common subordinates, are located on the sides of the diamond. In an MNC's international operations, one of these is likely to be a product-oriented manager and the other an international, regional, or country manager. In a "pure" matrix organization, the two are fairly equal in power and importance. Jointly, they hammer out business plans and are responsible for meeting the goals set by the top leadership.
> The *two-boss managers* are each responsible for the normal functions of the business, such as general management, manufacturing, marketing, and finance, at the regional or country level. Thus, they are at the apex of their own pyramid, which they manage in traditional ways. Matrix, therefore, does not affect everyone in an organization; in fact, only a small number are affected. Matrix managers are usually found in upper or middle management. Two-boss managers also report to both of the matrix managers, which means they must learn to accommodate simultaneous — and sometimes competing — demands.

The course structure of a business school provides a helpful way to begin conceptualizing how a multinational matrix organization functions. In the classroom, a subtle distinction is drawn between salesmanship and

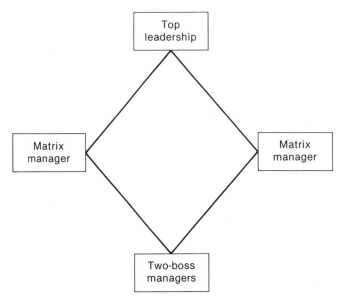

EXHIBIT 1.4
Matrix roles (from Kramer, 1981).

marketing, between shop floor industrial relations and production planning, between cost accounting and corporate finance. In small firms these activity pairs are blended together, but in a multinational multiproduct matrix organization these activities can take place in different nations.

The field salesman's task is to know his customer's needs well enough so that he can quarterback teams of product specialists, knowing the right moment to call them for help. In the global product headquarters the task of the marketing analyst is to understand the competitive position of his product in each nation and to envision, develop, and implement appropriate remedies to outmaneuver rivals. The sales organization is anchored by national customers; the marketing organization is anchored by global products. This itself leads to a matrix organization. Between these two anchored ends lie the product sales support staff; the wielding of power in the organization depends on whether these are closer to the national sales forces or to the headquarters product specialists.

The approach to the whole question of labor policy varies among nations, and therefore must be organized by nation. Similarly, subcontracting and purchasing should be organized by vender, which means by nation, regardless of where the product is destined. However, as will be seen in Chapter 6, the multinational ability to rearrange production globally means that the planners in headquarters, by scheduling the production for each plant, ultimately determine the scenario for future layoffs and for overtime at each subsidiary. If the political or union consequences of these layoffs are unacceptable in a nation, the production planners can change their cost functions for that nation to reflect these constraints in a quantitative manner. Integrity is maintained because restrictive cost functions for a layoff will now make that nation a less attractive site for future plant investment.

In summary, a matrix organization has the potential to resolve awkward dilemmas in multinational corporations. Yet the structure itself provides merely the ground rules within which power will be exercised.

A grid or matrix organization is intended to bring together expertise in the geographic, product, function, planning, and time areas. There are both structural and political ways to look at matrix management. From a structural point of view, decisions are made simultaneously by representatives of each national office and each affected function and product representative from headquarters. This implies both the glamor of task forces and the petty frustration of not being able to start a meeting until the last representative arrives. Unfortunately, matrix organizations require an expensive organizational superstructure. Some corporations have tried a formal matrix organization but, aghast at seeing the cost, they have then dismantled part of the matrix. In successful matrix organizations power is based on expertise rather than position or charisma. Because influence is widely dispersed, the matrix culture has the advantage of being adaptable, with groups, project teams, or task forces formed, reformed, continued, or abandoned. It is not a simple structure yet a matrix organization can be responsive, flexible, and sensitive to the environment or task. Simultaneously it demands of each individual both self-discipline and the ability to tolerate ambiguity.

In a matrix organization the intent is to push decision making as far down into the organization as possible and rely on group consensus to compensate for inexperience. Decision making must be flattened to avoid swamping the senior executives. The first requirement is that communication within the corporation be thorough and complete. A risk is attached to this: Sensitive information often must be distributed well beyond the executive suite, leading to the ever-present danger that some data will find their way out of the corporation. The second requirement is that those in charge of projects be able to understand and to use the available data.

Structural View of a Matrix Organization

Dow Corning has had a formal matrix organization since 1967. At first it was a two-dimensional matrix organization. Each major product line was a profit center. The cost centers were the functional activities (marketing, manufacturing, finance, etc.), which sold services to the profit centers. Later two additional dimensions were added. Geographic areas were incorporated because business development varied widely among areas. Each geographic area was to be considered both a profit and cost center since profit-center products could not be managed everywhere in the same manner. The fourth dimension, time, attempted to achieve congruence between short- and long-term decisions. The multidimensional organization is constantly changing, and thus long-term planning is an inherent part of its operation. Goggin (1974), as chief executive of Dow Corning, described his matrix management.

In Dow, Corning's matrix management there is a Business Board for each of the company's ten [product] businesses. The only full time board member is the manager of the business. His position in the organization is at once critical and tenuous. It is critical because his direct responsibility is the profit yield generated from the business he is charged with managing. It is tenuous because on paper he does not have direct control of the resources needed to accomplish his task. His operative body, his total resource is composed of representatives from the marketing, technical service and development, research, manufacturing, and economic evaluation/control functions [see Exhibit 1.5]. These are the Business Board members. They report directly to their functional group heads (vice president of marketing and distribution, director of technical service and development, and so on).

Organizationally, there is a strong dotted-line relationship running from the board member to the board manager. More important than organizational lines, however, is the clear understanding of where the profit responsibility lies. [Exhibit 1.5] illustrates the structure and communications pattern of a board. Its manager reports directly to Dow Corning's top management. His primary task — to generate

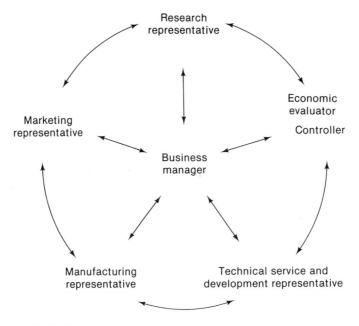

EXHIBIT 1.5
The business board.

profits — is accomplished through the total and combined support of his board members.

For most employees, life proceeds as it always does, regardless of the matrix. Davis and Lawrence (1977, p. 141) estimate that in a 50,000-employee corporation only 1 to 3 percent will have the dual reporting responsibility of a matrix. These few hundred managers work like epoxy resin that binds delicate glass fibers into tough fiberglass. It is more important that they function well than that they undertake the ritual ceremonies that have become associated with matrix management.

The Dow Corning structure has evolved from the original, drafted by Goggin. New product conceptualization and development has remained a U.S. activity, despite the president's hope that it would be global. In the geographic split of the corporation the United States is bigger than Europe, Asia, South America, and Canada. Because the regions are not equally sized, the smaller ones are much less powerful than the larger ones. A rarely discussed consequence of an open and organic structure is that there are fewer bureaucratic rules to protect the weaker regions, products, or functions.

Power View of a Matrix Organization

Goggin's view of matrix management presents the structural picture. Power relationships give clout to the structure. Both multinational and high-technology worlds require flexibility and dynamic adjustment, with individuals contributing skill, knowledge, and adaptability.

> Periodically, however, basic decisions must be made that inevitably involve hard choices among competing alternatives. The manifest content of planning discussions concerns projects and programs; the latent content involves power and position. . . . Planning is not synonymous with forecasting, not by any stretch of the imagination. Rather it is a dynamic process by which inside and outside interests arrive at a new balance of power — reflected in a new structure and new policy — designed to establish the parameters of executive decision making for some period of years, but not forever. (Sayles and Chandler, 1971, p. 42)

Power is a subtle creation. Mutually contradictory organizational strategies can be balanced against one another, with their coexistence acting as a means by which top management manages power. Simultaneously, and in mutual contradiction, top management of a multinational corporation should aspire to:

1. Increase the variety of relationships by inducing competition within and beyond the organization. . .
2. Improve cooperation in existing relationships by managing dependency. . .

3. Alter the nature of relationships to keep others involved and simultaneously create a self-enforcing "goldfish" system of control (Sayles and Chandler, 1971, pp. 113–116).

Competition can be created within a multinational corporation to stimulate the overall structure. For example, as long as there is any independence between the functions of marketing and production, a marketing subsidiary can receive products from whichever corporate factory or vendor offers the best terms. Such autonomy and internal competition are not compatible with clarity. Sapolsky (1972, p. 141) describes matrix management of the Polaris submarine development:

> Eleven different methods of ejecting a missile from a submerged submarine were said to have been simultaneously considered. . . . Similarly . . . two teams approached the problem of developing an inertial guidance system. Having control over the performance goals, however, provided the Admiral with the alternative of curtailing goals as well as trying parallel approaches to build a viable system. There are pressures to assign clear unambiguous missions to plants, laboratories and other organizational units, thus making the evaluation of managerial performance easier. . . . On the other hand, clarity of function is usually associated with greater specialization. In practice this means that expertise in a given field will be concentrated in a given organizational unit. This makes critical assessment of their plans and recommendations by upper management very difficult, since there are no comparably expert units to give testimony.

In his detailed study of corporate resource allocation, Bower (1970) emphasized that all top management can do with a capital expenditure proposal is assess the credibility of the managers who recommend it. In a multinational corporation this is an especially difficult problem. For example, consider an efficiency and effectiveness audit of how the corporation's Belgian treasury unit maintains its banking connections. Such an audit seems to call for expert judgment until one realizes that a Belgian treasury unit is in competition with the cost of getting funds to Belgium from elsewhere and is only one of many possible sources of funds for other subsidiaries. The conceptualization and evaluation of such competitive trade-offs can be facilitated by the kind of program outlined in Chapter 3. Top management power derives partly from the latent competition it can induce. Kramer (1981, p. 93) uses the phrase "nonconcurrence" for "latent competition."

> A European organizational consultant [advised] that since a matrix never establishes true equality, it is best to take this into account and design a structure whereby one matrix manager has divisional authority and the other has the power of advice and nonconcurrence. This means that the latter can go on record with the fact that he is not happy with the former's decision. In the event of nonconcurrence, the other matrix manager must bring the matter to the attention of their common boss, the top leader. Both matrix managers, therefore, will exercise cau-

tion regarding escalation to higher levels. While it is important to define the issues to which the power of nonconcurrence applies, it is likewise important not to define them too precisely. The more each circumstance is defined, the greater the temptation to build up staffs to address them — and hence the tendency to create a bureaucracy. The virtue of this system is that decisions can be made quickly without dispute or constant referral to higher line or staff authority.

Dependency.   The Nestle operations in each nation are each freestanding. On the other hand, the organizational units of IBM are highly dependent on one another. A simple example will illustrate dependency. Governments insist on "local content," yet simultaneously there are economies of scale in manufacturing. Thus if a product can be designed as two subassemblies, each can be manufactured in a separate nation. The result is that each subsidiary depends on the other.

Aiken and Hage (1968) developed an index of organizational interdependence. In a multinational corporation, since each unit is dependent on others for subassemblies, cash flow, and marketing concepts, even approximate interdependency indexes are alarmingly high. The objective of dependency management is to keep the participants' indexes in approximate balance, so that each unit that depends on others has some items on which others are dependent — as hostages for the bargaining process.

Improving the Interrelationship.   Lawrence and Lorsch (1972) recommend highly differen iated subunits connected by "integrators." The individual who is an integrator needs sufficient organizational stature, technical prowess, and personal charisma to gain entry into each subunit, and he must then contribute continuously to maintain that foothold. So much for the applicant qualifications. What does the integrator do?

Sayles and Chandler (1971, p. 208) compare an integrator to an organizational metronome. "Although it is rarely stated this way the [integrator] is primarily dealing with rates of time and organizational process, not technical variables. He cannot easily second guess the technical prowess of his line support groups. . . . In the long run he is dependent upon both the support and the technical judgment of the groups [he is to integrate]."

The integrator can control a group's technical contributions comparatively easily. What he must do is control organizational participation. This means making sure that the line or functional people do things such as the following:

1. Give problems their proper weight and context.
2. Tackle problems in the right sequence and at the right time.
3. Shift the decision criteria.

The integrator functions as a giant metronome which enables the diverse parts of a large organization — parts that would normally be responsive to their own internal group rhythms — to respond to the same beat. To do this he forces people to see the consequences of their actions. Using both visual and conceptual tools as well as oral and written directives he forces other managers to make commitments and decisions by affecting their trade-offs (e.g., schedule versus cost) and priorities. In shaping the response of his "team" to his centralized beat, he may also seek to change the resonance characteristics of the system. He can change the character of the system's response with a shift in organizational relationships. For example, he can insist that a group now report to Division B instead of Division A, or consult earlier, or more often, or must now give its consent before x, y, and z occur.

Textbooks say that managers plan, direct, and control. But Sayles and Chandler say that integrators bargain, cajole, intervene, coach, confront, and give orders. These six activities use information — prodigious quantities of both raw data *and* adroit studies. Yet the ideal is *not* to use these six activities but to have the personal discipline to avoid meddling, letting subordinates solve problems themselves.

Integrators are searching for *impersonal* means of achieving visibility for troubled areas. If a problem can be acknowledged simultaneously by all those people who are affected, its very visibility creates pressures for its solution. Sayles and Chandler (1971, p. 115) report that "managers in other countries have shown a similarly high degree of interest in the use of visibility-type pressures to pry out vital information. These become especially appealing to adopt in any society in which the normal desire to conceal failure is reinforced by heavy cultural stress on the importance of maintaining one's honor at all costs." Behrman (1970, p. 68) corroborates this view that control means thwarting the temptation to hide problems.

> Personal communication among officers was reported by one European-based multinational enterprise to be its most significant technique for central control. Outward evidences of control are few, but repeated meetings of 70 or 80 managers, functional officers, and technicians at trade fairs, conventions, technical conferences at the parent, on-the-road visits by its top managers (all five of whom make the tour annually), and daily phone contact, produce a type of consensus that avoids the necessity of tight control over operations. These communications are for persuasion, not dictation, for the company believes in "decentralization of operations and tactics but centralization of planning and strategy." This coordination is buttressed by probably the tightest budget control of any of the European companies. In addition to parentally approved annual budgets, affiliates must prepare 3-year, 5-year, 10-year, and 15-year projections, and the parent itself is working on a 30 to 50 year projection of the future market for its major products.

The product management dimension of a matrix is extremely important, for it is here that product strategy decisions are analysed. Usually these involve investments in intangible assets, such as product and process research, missionary marketing to consumer groups hitherto untouched, and decisions to wrestle market share from specific rivals for long-term reasons.

Usually the product management teams are suituated in the headquarters nation. Sometimes they are situated in other nations. When a subsidiary has a product management team within it, it is said to have a global product mandate.

Some global product mandates reflect natural comparative advantage. For example, Canada generates more hydroelectricity than any other nation except the Soviet Union, so engineers of Canadian General Electric have become expert in the design and service of waterwheel turbines. General Electric salesmen anywhere in the world who receive inquiries about waterwheel turbines work with the Canadian team that has the global mandate in waterwheels. As another example, northern Italy produces excellent and inexpensive appliances, so NV Philips of Holland moved its appliance management to Italy, from where it now controls a world network of plants.

Other global product mandates are actually part of world mandates that arose from government technical specifications. For example, standards of television transmission in Europe are different from those in North America. NV Philips turned over to its North American subsidiary the development, design, and manufacture of television receivers appropriate for North America.

A final kind of global product mandate is assigned to a subsidiary for strategic reasons. Black and Decker power hand tools use the same motor components in drills, sanders, jigsaws, and other tools. Economies of scale are substantial in manufacturing these products, but the Canadian market is so small that manufacturing costs exceeded U.S. manufacturing costs plus Canadian import duty. Instead of shutting down the Canadian plant, the headquarters executives assigned to Canada the worldwide sander production. The resulting volume cut unit costs not only of sanders but of drills and jigsaws also, with the result that all became viable.

Geocentric Planning Guidelines

In a matrix organization more complex planning guidelines for the nine problems of integration are possible.

Chapter 2. Exchange Management in a Multinational Corporation. No hedging will be done except for currencies with pegged exchange rates or to consume excess foreign tax credits that would otherwise expire. Headquarters will strive to achieve a balanced global portfolio of long-term positive and negative cash flows in each major currency.

Chapter 3. Maneuvering Liquid Assets. Dividends, intersubsidiary loans, transfer prices, and managerial fee payments will be considered to transfer liquidity to subsidiaries when they need it, in such a way as to minimize taxes paid to the world minus interest earned on liquid assets. After analysis, these options will be *implemented* only when they are preferable to normal banking transactions in each nation.

Chapter 4. Multidivisional Expansion to a New Nation. Diligent effort will be made to identify important stakeholders in each new nation and gauge their predispositions to the corporation. Product divisions will be introduced into the nation in a carefully orchestrated sequence. As the stakeholders' tolerance of the corporation increases, further divisions which may be more profitable to the corporation can be introduced.

Chapter 5. Logistics. The total product flow on some routes will justify the corporation's chartering its own vessels. These charters will be managed in such a way as to pressure rate reductions (or nonescalation) from liner companies on other routes.

Chapter 6. Production Smoothing. Demand for each item fluctuates in each market. One attraction of being multinational is the portfolio effect of a reduced fluctuation of total demand. This means switching markets from one factory to another and reswitching them as demands change.

Chapter 7. Multinational Plant Location. A multinational corporation has tremendous bargaining power and flexibility *until* it builds a plant. Once built, the plant may be a hostage. This suggests that there will be innumerable studies about possible plant locations, which therefore should be computerized.

Chapter 8. New Product Launch. A nation can be used as a test market for the world. This suggests grouping the nations to launch in stage 1, stage 2, and so forth. Nations grouped for the first stage must be selected to yield valuable and timely information. This can be used to cancel or advance the product's launch in other national markets.

Chapter 9. Pricing. Prices for the line of goods are determined in one benchmark country (e.g., the United States). Simultaneously an optimal markup factor is calculated for each nation by which the benchmark prices are multiplied to obtain local prices. This scheme is simple enough to permit central coordination, yet it is also responsive to overall market conditions in each nation.

Chapter 10. Product Design. Marketing considerations other than price lead to a proliferation of tailored designs as described in the section on polycentric organization. Production considerations tend toward a single design to be marketed throughout the world, as described in the ethnocentric section. The geocentric resolution is to modularize the design by subassemblies (and styling panels). Some modules should be standard around the world; others should be tailored.

Chapter 11. International Executive Development. Multilateral moves and the use of third country nationals must be analyzed. Because the number of foreigners a government will allow to hold executive positions in a subsidiary may be restricted, visas should be allocated with care. The emphasis on integration implies nurturing personnel who can tolerate the role ambiguity such a position implies.

Each chapter of this book describes a difficult integration and each outlines a computer model. The computer is an impersonal demander of information and an impersonal means of detecting exaggerations. The models are merely *tools* that can be used by powerful executives as part of their personal political processes, and thus every prospective executive should be aware of their existence and their possible uses.

Bibliography to Chapter 1

Aiken, Michael and Gerald Hage, "Organizational Interdependence and Intraorganizational Structure," *American Sociological Review*, Vol. 33 (1968), pp. 919-929.

Behrman, Jack N., *National Interests and the Multinational Enterprise: Tensions Among the North Atlantic Countries* (Englewood Cliffs, NJ: Prentice-Hall, 1970).

Bergsten, C. Fred, Thomas Horst and Theodore H. Moran, *American Multinationals and American Interests* (Washington: The Brookings Institution, 1978).

Blake, David H. and Robert S. Walters, *The Politics of Global Economic Relations* (Englewood Cliffs, NJ: Prentice-Hall, 1976).

Boston Consulting Group, *Perspectives on Experience* (Boston: Boston Consulting Group, 1970).

Bower, Joseph L., *Managing the Resource Allocation Process: A Study of Corporate Planning and Investment* (Cambridge: Division of Research, Harvard Business School, 1970).

Brooke, Michael Z. and Mark van Beusekom, *International Corporate Planning* (London: Pitman, 1979).

Channon, Derek F. and Michael Jalland, *Multinational Strategic Planning* (London: Macmillan, 1979).

Clee, Gilbert H. and Wilbur M. Sachtjen, "Organizing a Worldwide Business," *Harvard Business Review*, Vol. 42, No. 6 (1964), pp. 55-67.

Curhan, Joan P., William H. Davidson, and Rajan Suri, *Tracing the Multinationals: A Sourcebook on U.S.-based Enterprises* (Cambridge, MA: Ballinger, 1977).

Davis, Stanley M. and Paul R. Lawrence, *Matrix* (Reading, MA: Addison-Wesley, 1977).

Dundas, Kenneth, The Management of U.S. Subsidiaries in Canada, doctoral dissertation, University of Western Ontario, 1979.

Etzioni, Amitai, *Modern Organizations* (Englewood Cliffs, NJ: Prentice-Hall, 1964).

Fouraker, Lawrence E. and Sidney Siegel, *Bargaining and Group Decision-Making: Experiments in Bilateral Monopoly* (New York: McGraw-Hill, 1960).

Galbraith, Jay R., *Organization Design* (Reading, MA: Addison-Wesley, 1977).

Goggin, William C., "How the Multidimensional Structure Works at Dow Corning," *Harvard Business Review*, Vol. 52, No. 1 (1974), pp. 54-65.

Heenan, David A. and Howard Perlmutter, *Multinational Organization Development* (Reading, MA: Addison-Wesley, 1979).

Knickerbocker, Frederick T., *Oligopolistic Reaction and Multinational Enterprise* (Cambridge: Division of Research, Harvard Business School, 1973).

Kramer, Robert J., *New Directions in Multinational Corporate Organization* (New York: Business International Corporation, 1981).

Lawrence, Paul R. and Jay W. Lorsch, *Organizational Planning: Cases and Concepts* (Homewood, IL: Irwin, 1972).

Leavitt, Harold J., *Managerial Psychology* (Chicago: University of Chicago Press, 1972).

Martyn, Howe, *International Business* (New York: Free Press of Glencoe, 1964).

Menzies, Hugh D., "Westinghouse Takes Aim at the World," *Fortune*, Vol. 101, No. 1 (1980), pp. 48-53.

Olson, Bernhard E., *Faith and Prejudice* (New Haven: Yale University Press, 1963).

Perlmutter, Howard V., "L'Entreprise International — Trois Conceptions," *Review Economic et Social*, May 1965; a translation appeared in *Quarterly Journal of AISEC International*, Vol. 3, No. 3 (August 1967).

Robinson, Richard D., *International Management* (New York: Holt, Rinehart and Winston, 1967).

Rosow, Jerome M., "Industrial Relations and the Multinational Corporation: The Management Approach," in *Bargaining Without Boundaries: The Multinational Corporation and International Labour Relations*, edited by R.J. Flanagan and A.R. Weber (Chicago: University of Chicago Press, 1974), pp. 147-162.

Rutenberg, David P., "Organizational Archetypes of a Multinational Company," *Management Science*, Vol. 16, No. 6 (1970), pp. B337-B349.

Sapolsky, Harvey M., *Polaris Systems Development: Bureaucratic and Pragmatic Success in Government* (Cambridge: Harvard University Press, 1972).

Sayles, Leonard R. and Margaret K. Chandler, *Managing Large Systems: Organizations for the Future* (New York: Harper and Row, 1971).

Stopford, John M. and Louis Wells, *Managing the Multinational Enterprise: Organization of the Firm and Ownership of the Subsidiaries* (New York: Basic, 1972).

Vaupel, James W. and Joan P. Curham, *The Making of Multinational Enterprises: A Source Book Based on a Study of 187 Major U.S. Manufacturing Corporations* (Cambridge: Division of Research, Harvard Business School, 1969).

Vaupel, James W. and Joan P. Curham. *The World's Multinational Enterprise: A Sourcebook of Tables Based on a Study of the Largest U.S. and non-U.S. Manufacturing Corporations* (Cambridge: Division of Research, Harvard Business School, 1973).

Vernon, Raymond (ed.), *Big Business and the State: Changing Relations in Western Europe* (Cambridge: Harvard University Press, 1974).

Williamson, Oliver, *Markets and Hierarchies* (Englewood Cliffs, NJ: Prentice-Hall, 1975).

Zaleznik, Abraham and Manfred F.R. Kets de Vries, *Power and the Corporate Mind* (Boston: Houghton Mifflin, 1975).

PART ONE

Multinational Financial Management

CHAPTER TWO

Exchange Management in a Multinational Corporation

Introductory Note to the Case

Dozier Industries

Dozier is a small, high-technology business with no foreign experience. One might reasonably assume that the company would be averse to risk, either because of the chief financial officer's inexperience or because a bad review of this opening act could thwart Dozier's attempt to achieve multinational status. Nevertheless, try to predict the cost of "no action," even though it's a most unlikely alternative.

The first level of analysis for this case is to work through the two calculations comparing the use of the forward market, with borrowing pounds to repatriate immediately (pound receivable equals pound borrowing plus British interest). It is a very simple finance calculation once the correct interest rates are determined.

The second level of analysis is to outline procedures to follow in pricing future export orders. Currently, Dozier has excess capacity, so this U.K. order is making a substantial contribution to overhead.

The third level of analysis is to study Dozier's balance sheet, and think imaginatively about how to refinance some of its current and long-term liabilities. Bold international financing would probably not be appropriate yet for Dozier, but it should be evaluated to keep in mind later.

Exhibit 2.4 uses the terms Eurodollar and Europound. The prefix "Euro-" simply means that the currency is outside its home, and thus outside the direct control of its central bank. Thus at any moment in time the Eurodollar rate is the

*same everywhere in the world (outside the United States).
Similarly, the Europound rate is the same everywhere outside
the United Kingdom, and so in Exhibit 2.4 the Paris rate can
be listed as a United States rate.*

Dozier Industries

Richard Rothschild, the chief financial officer of Dozier
Industries, returned to his office after the completion of his
meeting with two officers of Southeastern National Bank. He
had requested the meeting in order to discuss financial issues
related to Dozier's first major international sales contract,
which had been confirmed that morning, January 13, 1976.
Initially, Rothschild had contacted Robert Leigh, a vice president at the bank who had primary responsibilities for Dozier's
business with Southeastern National. Leigh had in turn suggested that John Gunn of the bank's international division be
included in the meeting since Leigh felt that he lacked the
international expertise to answer all the questions Rothschild
might raise.

The meeting had focused on the exchange risk related to
the new sales contract. Dozier's bid of £425,000 for the
installation of an internal security system for a large manufacturing firm in the United Kingdom had been accepted. In
accordance with the contract, the British firm had transferred
by cable £42,500 (10 percent of the contract amount) as
deposit on the contract with the balance due at the time the
system was completed. Dozier's production vice president,
Mike Miles, had assured Rothschild that there would be no
difficulty in completing the project within the 90-day period
stipulated in the bid. As a result, Rothschild was planning on
receiving £382,500 on April 13, 1976.

History of the Company

Dozier Inc. was a relatively young firm specializing in electronic security systems. It had been established in 1963 by
Charles L. Dozier, who was still president and owner of 78
percent of the stock. The remaining 22 percent of the stock
was held by other members of management. Dozier, formerly

This case was prepared by Professor Mark Eaker of Southern Methodist University
and is reprinted with his permission and that of the copyright owners, the Board
of Trustees of the Leland Stanford Junior University.

a design engineer for a large electronics firm, founded his own company to market security systems for small firms and households. By 1966 Dozier had begun to concentrate on military sales and the company's growth paralleled the growth of U.S. expenditures in Vietnam. As the U.S. involvement in Vietnam and military expenditures in general began to decrease, Dozier's military sales slumped and the company sought increased business in the private sector. During the period of transition from being primarily a military contractor to relying on private sales, Dozier experienced severe reductions in revenue and profits (see Exhibit 2.1). In 1975 the company showed a profit for the first time in three years, and management was confident that the company had turned the corner.

By early 1976, military sales accounted for only about 20 percent of Dozier's total revenue. The company's management believed that the best prospects for future growth lay in sales to companies in countries that were experiencing terrorist activity. Therefore, in the spring of 1975 Dozier launched a marketing effort overseas. The selling effort had not met with much success until the confirmation of the contract discussed here. The new sales contract, although large in itself, had the

EXHIBIT 2.1
Dozier, Inc.

Sales and Income Summary

Year Ended December 31	Sales ($000)	Net Income ($000)
1963	314	28
1964	397	34
1965	521	43
1966	918	86
1967	2,127	179
1968	3,858	406
1969	5,726	587
1970	7,143	702
1971	9,068	857
1972	8,646	309
1973	5,471	(108)
1974	5,986	(16)
1975	6,427	82

EXHIBIT 2.2
Dozier, Inc.

Balance Sheet as of December 31, 1975

ASSETS

Current assets	
Cash and securities	$ 147,286
Accounts receivable	859,747
Inventories	1,113,533
Total current assets	$2,120,566
Properties, plants, and equipment	
At cost	$4,214,906
Less accumulated depreciation	1,316,702
Net plant	$2,898,204
Other assets	
Investment and loans	$ 225,000
Total assets	$5,243,770

LIABILITIES AND EQUITIES

Current liabilities	
Accounts payable	$ 467,291
Notes payable — bank	326,400
Total current liabilities	$ 793,691
Long-term liabilities	
Notes payable	$ 275,000
Common equity	
Common stock	$1,126,705
Reserves	313,622
Retained earnings	2,734,752
Total Equity	$4,175,079
Total liabilities and equity	$5,243,770

EXHIBIT 2.3
Dozier, Inc.

Bid Preparation

Materials	$414,250
Direct labor	208,410
Shipping	35,000
Direct overhead*	104,205
Allocation of indirect overhead	$ 50,246
Total cost	$812,111
Profit factor	48,726
Total	$860,836

Spot pound rate on December 3: 2.0255
Pound value of the bid: £   425,000
The International Monetary Market in Chicago reported on December 3 that March 1976 futures were selling at 1.996 and on December 2 the June 1976 futures were selling at $1.9710/£.

*Based on 50 percent of direct labor.

---

potential of being expanded in the future since the company involved was a large multinational firm with manufacturing facilities in many countries.

Foreign Exchange Risk and Hedging

During the morning of January 13, the day the bid was accepted, the value of the pound was $2.0320. However, the pound had been weak for the past six months (see Exhibit 2.5). Rothschild was concerned that the value of the pound might depreciate even further during the next 90 days and it was this worry that prompted his discussion at the bank. He wanted to find out what techniques were available to Dozier to reduce the exchange risk created by the outstanding pound receivable.

Gunn, the international specialist, had explained that Rothschild had several options. First, of course, he could do nothing. This would leave Dozier vulnerable to pound fluctuations, which would entail losses if the pound depreciated or gains if it appreciated versus the dollar. On the other hand, Rothschild could choose to hedge his exchange risk.

Gunn explained that a hedge involved taking a position

EXHIBIT 2.4
Dozier, Inc.

Interest and Exchange Rate Comparisons

January 14, 1976

	United States	United Kingdom
Three-month money*	5.125	10.22
Prime lending rate	7.00	11.50
Three-month deposits (large amounts)	5.00	10.16
Eurodollar three-month		5.375
Europound three-month		
(quoted by banks in Paris)	10.50	
Other key London rates		
91-day treasury bills		10.28
Local authorities three-month fixed deposit		10.50
Finance houses three-month fixed deposit		10 9/16

The spot rate for the pound: 2.0290
Three-month forward pound: 2.0032
*Prime commercial paper in the United States; interbank rates in the United Kingdom.

Source: *The Economist*

---

opposite to the one that was creating the foreign exchange exposure. This could be accomplished either by engaging in a forward contract or through a spot transaction. Since Dozier had an outstanding pound receivable, the appropriate hedging options would be to sell pounds forward 90 days or to secure a 90-day pound loan. By selling pounds forward Dozier would incur an obligation to deliver pounds 90 days after the transaction at the rate established on the day of the transaction. This would ensure that Dozier would receive a set dollar value for its pound receivable, regardless of the spot rate that existed in the future.

The spot hedge works similarly in that it also creates a pound obligation 90 days from the transaction. Dozier would borrow pounds and exchange the proceeds into dollars at the spot rate. On April 13, Dozier would use its pound receipts to repay the loan. Any gains or losses on the receivable due to a change in the value of the pound would be offset by equivalent losses or gains on the loan payment.

Leigh assured Rothschild that Southeastern National would

EXHIBIT 2.5

Historical Spot and Forward Pound Rates
in U.S. Dollars

Date	Spot	Three-Month Forward Rate
7/9	2.2020	2.1864
7/16	2.1855	2.1682
7/23	2.1800	2.1570
7/30	2.1650	2.1445
8/6	2.1360	2.1137
8/13	2.1075	2.0865
8/20	2.1100	2.0940
8/27	2.1105	2.0948
9/3	2.1120	2.0947
9/10	2.1120	2.0942
9/17	2.0830	2.1665
9/24	2.0550	2.0350
10/1	2.0430	2.0245
10/8	2.0470	2.0242
10/15	2.0560	2.0315
10/22	2.0780	2.0500
10/29	2.0730	2.0470
11/5	2.0660	2.0396
11/12	2.0640	2.0388
11/19	2.0430	2.0184
11/26	2.0330	2.0088
12/3	2.0255	2.0021
12/10	2.0240	2.0008
12/17	2.0240	2.0000
12/23	2.0225	1.9965
12/30	2.0250	1.9918
1/7/76	2.0350	2.0032
1/14/76	2.0290	2.0032

Source: *The Money Manager*

be able to assist Dozier in implementing whatever decision Rothschild made. Dozier had a $1.5 million line of credit with Southeastern National. John Gunn indicated that there would be no difficulty for Southeastern to arrange the pound loan for Dozier through its correspondent bank in London. He felt that such a loan would be at 1.5 percent above the U.K. prime rate. To assist Rothschild in making his decision,

EXHIBIT 2.6

Sterling. Going, going . . .

The prospects of a major recovery of sterling between now and Christmas are now so thin that they hardly exist. Since our last currency review in August, confidence in the pound has continued to decline. That decline in confidence has been masked to some extent by the renaissance of the dollar; when these trappings of disguise were whipped away during the recent reversal in the dollar's strength, the weakness of sterling stood out stark and clear as the effective rate breached new lows to nudge the 30% depreciation barrier.

It should decline further. The Labour Government, far from initiating the £1 billion cuts in public spending that were deemed necessary if overseas holders' confidence in sterling were to be maintained, have actually announced that they are not considering any major measures to cut government spending in the short term; there is a widespread conviction that they will not cut expenditure in the medium or long-term either, but it is the immediate future that concerns the foreign exchange markets.

In the immediate future the Government's policy of allowing the exchange rate to take the strain of keeping unemployment to a minimum is likely to become more obvious, a policy that is likely to show an increasing divergence from the views of the Bank of England. The Bank is displaying increasing signs of alarm over the scale of public spending and the public sector deficit, and so it should. It is widely believed that the government's borrowing requirement in the current financial year has risen by a third over last April's estimate of £9 billion.

The Chancellor of the Exchequer announced the Government's decision not to cut public spending during 1975 at the same dinner at which Governor of the Bank made it clear that the Bank is becoming increasingly concerned over public spending.

Sterling will be weaker against some currencies than others in coming months, but the British may find themselves celebrating Christmas with a currency worth less than $2 even if the dollar does not regain its strength. There is not much consolation in that.

Source: Fallon, Padraic, "Sterling— Going going . . .," *Euromoney* Nov, 1975, pp. 47–78.

Gunn provided him with information on interest rates, spot and forward exchange rates, as well as historical and forecasted information on the pound (see Exhibits 2.4, 2.5, and 2.6).

Rothschild was aware that in preparing the bid Dozier had allowed for a profit margin of only 6 percent in order to increase the likelihood of winning the bid and hence developing an important foreign contact. The bid was submitted on December 3, 1975. In arriving at the bid, the company had estimated the cost of the project, added an amount as profit, but kept in mind the highest bid that could conceivably win the contract. The calculations were made in dollars and then converted to pounds at the spot rate existing on December 3 (see Exhibit 2.5), since the U.K. company had stipulated payment in pounds.

Rothschild realized that the amount involved in the contract was such that an adverse move in the pound exchange rate could put Dozier in a loss position for 1976 if the transactions were left unhedged. On the other hand, he also became aware of the fact that hedging had its own costs. Still, a decision had to be made. He knew that "no action" implied that an unhedged position was the best alternative for the company.

Introduction

Management by objectives and the evaluation of managerial performance both require that someone distinguish between outcomes over which a manager has control and those over which he has not. In evaluating the performance of a manager in another nation, should the headquarters or the subsidiary take responsibility for exchange rate changes?

During the 1970s an American would say that the West German deutsche mark had appreciated, and that the British pound had devalued. Suppose a German-headquartered multinational kept U.S. $1000 in a bank account. Because it keeps its balance sheet in deutsche marks, the German corporation would record a foreign exchange *loss* on this asset. On the other hand, a British headquartered multinational, keeping a similar U.S. $1000 in a bank account, would record a foreign exchange gain on this asset. The German headquarters would take a dim view of the losses incurred by their American manager. The British headquarters would express delight at the strong performance of their American asset.

Evaluation is simple as long as the manager of the American subsidiary deals only in U.S. dollars. In a geographically organized corporation, managers of autonomous national subsidiaries might deal only in their local currency; if they did, their evaluation would be simple. Usually, however, multinational corporations undertake a worldwide flow of sub-assemblies, finished products, technology, and intersubsidiary loans. This means that while managers of subsidiaries are evaluated on the basis of their performance, its measurement usually involves several foreign currencies.

Let us see which exchange rate U.S. corporations use to evaluate their foreign subsidiaries. Pure trading cannot be planned and should be transacted only if today's spot exchange rate is right. Five percent of U.S. corporations both budget and evaluate performance at the spot rate (*Business International Money Report 1977*); presumably these are the trading corporations.

In 20 percent of U.S. corporations, the budget for foreign operations is approved at the then current spot rate. At the end of the year, performance is evaluated at the end of year spot exchange rate, which places the entire foreign exchange burden on the subsidiary. This type of subsidiary-management evaluation process is common in ethnocentric corporations.

Polycentric multinationals budget commitments using forecast exchange rates, then evaluate the performance of subsidiary managers at year-end spot rates. *Business International* reports that 50 percent of U.S. corporations operating abroad evaluate in this way. Although this evaluation process still renders the subsidiary manager susceptible to exchange rate risk, the foreign exchange burden he experiences is less than that of the subsidiary manager of an ethnocentric corporation.

Fifteen percent of U.S. corporations budget commitments at a forecast rate and also evaluate subsidiary managers at this same forecast rate (even if the forecast turns out to have been incorrect). Geocentric multinationals, which tend to employ this scheme, view the subsidiary more as a cost center than a fully autonomous profit center. The activities of the entire subsidiary network are rationalized, and the subsidiary manager's evaluation is based on his contribution to the corporation as an aggregate system. As such, the subsidiary manager is shielded from the effects of unforeseen foreign exchange rate fluctuations. Nevertheless, the subsidiary manager should be motivated to adjust his marketing and production decisions to take advantage of whatever exchange rate occurs.

A forward contract occurs when two individuals agree that on a specified future date they will exchange a stated amount of one currency for a stated amount of another. Usually one of the individuals is a bank. A bank active in forward markets keeps track of its exposure in each currency for each day of maturity. By the rates it quotes, it attempts to offset its purchases with its sales of each currency so as to control this exposure. As we saw in the Dozier Industries case, it makes little difference whether the corporation borrows abroad in order to repatriate now, or whether it enters the forward market. Either method allows it to avoid the risk of exchange rate fluctuations. In the commercial market one can obtain forward rates for 1, 2, 3, 6, and 12 months for many currencies and even longer contracts for a few currencies. As the Dozier case suggested, if a corporation has an exposed asset abroad, it can today borrow in that nation, in order to repatriate the proceeds immediately. This creates an exposed liability to offset the exposed asset. In this way the corporation can hedge for much longer than one year (Neave and Rutenberg, 1981).

		Evaluation of manager at year end	
		Actual year end spot rate	Today's forecast of the year end rate
Exchange rate used for budget forecasting	Today's spot rate	ETHNOCENTRIC	
	Today's forecast of the year end spot rate	POLYCENTRIC	GEOCENTRIC

EXHIBIT 2.7

The subsidiary's budget is set at the beginning of the year; performance is evaluated at year end.

As marketing and production managers have to make long-term commitments in several currencies, it seems sensible to insulate their marketing or production decisions from the *risk* of exchange rate fluctuations. Four psychological theories encourage such separation. First, *expectancy theory* (a model of perception) states that if effort leads to outcome, then the effort will occur if the outcome is desirable. Conversely, a manager will exert less effort if he perceives little link between his effort in marketing or production and the outcome that was swamped by an exchange rate change. Second, *operant conditioning theory* predicts that good efforts that are not rewarded will be extinguished; to extrapolate, therefore, a swing in exchange rates could reward and reinforce wrong production or marketing decisions. Third, a *general performance model* states that blocking path goals leads to frustration and stress, made manifest in passive withdrawal, active hostility, and depression. The corporation, facing an unfavorable exchange rate shift, does not want to cause this behavior. Finally, *dissonance theory* would be relevant if a conscientious manager undeservedly gained from a favorable change in exchange rates. If the manager had a low tolerance for this guilt, he might subconsciously sabotage his own marketing or production efforts the following year to "even the score."

For internal budget purposes, polycentric and geocentric corporations need a forecast of exchange rates. They obtain the short-term rates of up to one year from the data provided by the commercial market, but they also have the data with which to forecast long-run exchange rates for some currencies. The simplest conceptual model for forecasting is that of covered interest arbitrage. Just as Dozier Industries could borrow three-month Europounds, it could also have borrowed for a longer period, say five years.

Let us examine a five-year horizon. An investor has two options. The first is to invest in a five-year U.S. security at the five-year rate (r_{us}). At the end of five years, one dollar of investment would become

$$(1 + r_{us})^5$$

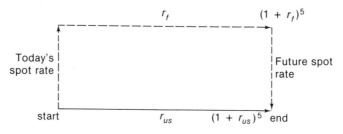

EXHIBIT 2.8

Covered interest arbitrage states that the two routes should be equally profitable.

The second option is to convert from dollars to foreign currency at today's spot rate, to invest abroad at the foreign five-year rate (r_f), and to repatriate the earnings at the future spot rate. One dollar of foreign currency would become

$$(1 + r_f)^5$$

Fundamental to arbitrage is the concept that there is a lot of smart money on the move, originating from many nations and moving quickly to the best deals. If the market feels that one route is more profitable, in the absence of inside information or peculiar tax situations, the resulting transactions will either increase the U.S. interest rate or decrease the foreign interest rate until the two routes are equally profitable. This means that the exchange rate five years hence is, in aggregate, forecasted to become

$$\text{Spot rate in 5 years} = \text{spot rate today} \frac{(1 + r_f)^5}{(1 + r_{us})^5}$$

Many money markets are efficient and this forecast is adequate. However, for some currencies other factors must be accounted for by the headquarters treasurer when forecasting rates. Most governments have, at some time in the past, imposed restrictions on the flows of capital out of their nation. A "blocked" currency is one with tight restrictions. Such restrictions allow the internal rates of interest to be lower than they otherwise would be in a world equilibrium. Foreign investors fear that such restrictions might be imposed, thus trapping their capital. To compensate for this perceived risk, the r_f must be higher than in the absence of fear, making the forecast future rate a bound.

The headquarters should forecast not just for a five-year maturity but for all future years in all currencies. Today's spot rates and the bond yield curves (Malkiel, 1970) for each national currency are all they need. Unfortunately, some countries are too unstable to have a bond market and an analyst must use his or her best judgment when estimating rates.

This introduction has dealt with the service that the divisions should expect from the headquarters treasury group: forecasting rates as well as budgeting and evaluating based on these rates. Marketing and production managers can get on with their work, with exchange rates taken into account. We will now study models that underlie the rate-setting process in polycentric, ethnocentric, and geocentric corporations.

Polycentric View of Exchange Management

A geographically organized multinational can be thought of as a geographically diversified portfolio of assets. Few American individual investors or mutual funds are internationally diversified. American investors achieve their international diversification by buying shares in U.S.-based multinational corporations. Errunza and Senbek (1981) calculate the positive relationship between international involvement and stock market premium.

Chen, Ricks, and Shawky (1977) found that the actual returns on the stocks of multinational corporations are affected by a world market index and an exchange risk factor. Investors are compensated for bearing both volatility and exchange risks. This implies that an investor forming a portfolio consisting primarily of the stocks of multinationals will gain from international diversification.

Fundamental to a polycentric view is the concept that many smart people are *trying* to profit in exchange rates. If a corporation has no more inside information than anyone else, it will sometimes gain, sometimes lose, and on average break even. No abnormal systematic gain can be expected if the prices move as a random walk. Giddy and Dufey (1975) showed that a random walk model adequately fits the spot movement of the currencies of Canada, France, and the United Kingdom for 1972-1974 data. Using a longer data base, Levich (1979) showed that for the currencies of Switzerland and Italy a random walk model is a good description of the data; for Belgium, France, and Germany the random walk model is a poor fit; and for Canada, the United Kingdom, the Netherlands, and Japan a random walk model does not fit, presumably because of erratic government intervention. Nevertheless, in none of these cases is the nonrandom pattern distinct enough or long term enough that trying to benefit from it will cover the transaction costs.

The polycentric headquarters views each subsidiary as a capital investment, the value of which is determined by the discounted value of its future repatriated revenue flows. The corporation lacks the organization to reallocate its assets once invested, in response to the changing states of the world economies. Only intermittent executive action will force redeployments. Although the headquarters decision to invest may have been based on a risk-return perception that was appropriate then, each national subsidiary of a geographically organized corporation pushes its own interest in new investment. Actually larger subsidiaries sometimes use their greater political presence within the corporation to block detailed studies that compare the financial risk of one nation with another.

The headquarters treasurer of a polycentric corporation tends to view fluctuating exchange rates as random events occurring with shifts in the world's economic and political structure. Such interest rate movements can rarely be forecasted or systematically reacted to by the corporation. Hence the polycentric attitude is to avoid wasting money on hedging fees.

Nevertheless, in two circumstances the headquarters treasurer may have the incentive to hedge. First, the treasurer could attain a higher return after taxes if on occasion he hedged to renew a tax credit. Second, he may decide to bet against a government that has chosen to peg its exchange rates.

If a corporation has paid more taxes abroad than it would pay at home on its global income, the U.S. government not only receives zero tax but actually grants the corporation a tax credit. Corporate tax credits in the United States may be carried forward five years and back two years. A corporation with unused five-year-old tax credits can either let them expire or find a way to "renew" them. Hedging provides a legitimate way. Suppose a U.S. corporation has a five-year-old foreign tax credit of $480,000. Liechtenstein imposes no tax on income derived as a result of foreign exchange fluctuations, so the U.S. corporation can have its Liechtenstein subsidiary hedge Italian lire by borrowing lire or by a forward contract, so that the corporation will gain $1 million if the lira rises and lose $1 million if the lira falls (numbers chosen to keep the arithmetic simple).

Suppose there is 50 percent probability that the lira will rise and that the corporation will gain $1 million. In that case, the corporation would have had to pay an additional $480,000 U.S. tax (marginal tax rate of 48 percent). However, by applying its $480,000 excess foreign tax credit, it can retain the entire $1 million. There is a 50 percent probability that the lira will fall. In that case the corporation will lose $1 million, and the unused old tax credit will expire at year end. However, the loss can be carried forward five years. Though the old tax credit expired, a new one lives onwards — until used to offset a profit.

The second occasion on which a headquarters treasurer *may* hedge is when he can foresee that a pegged exchange rate might be changed. Not all exchange rates fluctuate in a random fashion. Some governments intervene in the exchange market to support their currency. This is termed a "dirty float." The alert treasurer may decide to hedge when systematic government intervention occurs, even though he can act only within limits set by exchange restrictions of the foreign government.

"In many countries, even in those with convertible currencies, local companies are only allowed to enter the forward market to cover specific receivables and payables" (Chemical Bank, 1972, p. 14). For example, U.S. dollars can be converted into French francs and vice versa — they are both convertible. Anyone can easily convert U.S. dollars into Israeli sheckels, but it requires the permission of the Israeli central bank to convert sheckels to dollars in Israel. Conversion of sheckels in another country is viewed by Israel as a violation of Israeli law. The sheckel is not convertible. Freedom of entry into the forward market or the bond market for hedging purposes is rare when an exchange rate is pegged. Although the world's currencies are commonly believed to be operating in a general floating rate system, only a handful of them (admittedly among the most important) float individually against all others. Most of the others are tied to one of the key currencies or to a composite unit. The summary breakdown below from the *International Monetary Fund Survey*, February 20, 1978, illustrates the order within the apparently bewildering variety of the world's currency map. Each year a few governments change the grouping of their currency but the pattern remains.

Currencies Floating Independently. British pound, Canadian dollar, Italian lira, Japanese yen, Philippine peso, Mexican peso, Spanish peseta, Turkish lira, U.S. dollar.

Currencies Pegged on the U.S. Dollar. Bahamas dollar, Barbados dollar, Bolivian peso, Botswanian pula, Burundian franc, Republic of China's new Taiwan dollar, Costa Rican colon, Dominican peso, Ecuadoran sucre, Egyptian pound, El Salvadorian colon, Ethiopian birr, Ghanian cedi, Grenadan East Caribbean dollar, Guatemalan quetzal, Guyanan dollar, Haitian gourde, Honduran lempira, Indonesian rupiah, Iraqi dinar, Jamaican dollar, Korean won, kip of the Laos Peoples' Democratic Republic, Liberian dollar, Libyan dinar, Maldivian rupee, Nepalese rupee, Nicaraguan cordoba, Oman rial, Pakistini rupee, Panamanian balboa, Paraguayan guarani, Romanian leu, Rwandan franc, Somalian shilling, South African rand, Sudanese pound, Syrian Arabic Republic's pound, Thai baht, Trinidad and Tobago dollar, United Emirates dirham, Venezuelan bolivar, Yemen Arab Republic rial, Peoples' Democratic Republic of Yemen dinar.

Currencies Pegged on the British Pound. Bangladesh taka, Gambian dalas, Irish pound, Seychelles rupee, the leone of Sierra Leone.

Currencies Pegged on the French Franc. The francs of Benin, Cameroon, Central African Empire, Chad, Comoro, Peoples' Republic of the Congo, Gabon, Ivory Coast, Madagascar, Mali, Niger, Senegal, Togo, Upper Volta.

Currencies Pegged on the International Monetary Fund's Special Drawing Rights (SDR) (historically the U.S. dollar but now a weighted average currency): Burmese kyat, Guinean syli, Iranian rial, Jordanian dinar, Kenyan shilling, Malawi kwacha, Mauritius rupee, Qatar riyal, the dobra of São Tomé and Príncipe, Saudi Arabian riyal, Tanzanian shilling, Ugandan shilling, South Vietnamese dong, the zaire of Zaire, the Zambian kwacha.

Currencies in the European "Snake." Belgian franc, Danish krone, Luxembourg franc, the Netherlands guilder, Norwegian krone, West German deutsche mark. Each currency can snake between maximum margins of ±2.25 percent with respect to a weighted basket of the other currencies.

Currency Composite Other Than SDR. Algerian dinar, Australian dollar, Austrian shilling, Cyprus pound, Fiji dollar, Finnish markka, Indian rupee, Kuwait dinar, Malaysian ringgit, Maltese pound, Mauritanian ouguiya,

Moroccan dirham, New Zealand dollar, Singapore dollar, Swedish krona, Tunisian dinar, Western Somoan tala.

Currencies Adjusted According to a Set of Indicators. Argentinian peso, Brazilian cruzeiro, Chilean peso, Colombian peso, Portuguese escudo, Uruguayan new peso.

When a nation pegs its currency to a key currency, it must keep reserves of gold or key currencies to have something to sell while supporting the price of its currency when this is necessary. When the nation runs low in key currency, it can contact the International Monetary Fund to request a loan of the key currency to replenish its reserves for future sales. The nation can also request that the key currency central bank buy its currency on the open market. Thus economic pressure for a devaluation can be resisted for some months, and even years.

Folks and Stansell (1975) developed a discriminant analysis model to tally the factors that on average predict a devaluation. A treasurer must judge which are most relevant to the nation under consideration. He must project himself into the shoes of the finance minister of that nation, gauge the political pressures he is feeling, and determine their effect on his economic judgment. Sensitivity to inside information helps, and this information is more likely to come to the subsidiary than to the distant headquarters.

A central bank may be sustaining an exchange rate for political rather than economic reasons, and it may be quoting forward rates that are discrepant from those that the treasurer honestly anticipates. The government can sustain the pretense because access to the future market is usually denied to all except those with a "substantiated legitimate need." Therefore, the treasurer who is sensitive to impending devaluations can expect to gain. The amount of gain is limited; the exchange authorities allow a corporation to hedge no more than its exposure. Given that limit, the following decision rule is sensible. Either do not hedge, or hedge to the limit. This decision rule was developed by Shapiro and Rutenberg (1974).

It is now the beginning of period 0. We telex the exchange broker for the quoted rates of hedging different maturities, and then calculate the cost of hedging each period independently (cost of hedging to end of period minus cost of hedging to beginning of period). The hedging problem decouples into T separate problems, one in each time period. Let us first analyze period 0. Should period 0 be hedged? It depends on what we judge to be the possible extent of loss due to devaluation. Consider:

C_t = known cost of now hedging each separate period t (from broker's quotes) [For Dozier, the cost of hedging the three-month period beginning 1/14/76 was $\dfrac{2.029 - 2.0032}{2.029} = 1.27\%$ (see Exhibit 2.5).]

π_0 = probability of no devaluation during period 0

$1 - \pi_0$ = probability of a devaluation during period 0

d_i = one of several estimates for the extent of devaluation [For Dozier, d_1, d_2, d_3, may be 10, 12, and 15 percent.]

p_i = the probability of devaluation to level d_i, *conditional* on there being a devaluation, such that p_i = 1 (Possibly 75, 20, and 5 percent respectively, for Dozier.)

$p_i d_i$ = the expected extent of devaluation assuming a devaluation will occur (10.65% for Dozier.)

p_i	d_i	$p_i\, d_i$
.75	.10	.075
.20	.12	.024
.05	.15	.0075
		.1065

Therefore, the expected extent of a devaluation in period 0 can be expressed as

$$D_0 = (1 - \pi_0)\, p_i\, d_i$$

Should period 0 be hedged? If period 0 is not already hedged select the cheaper of:

1. Hedge at cost c_0
2. Expected loss D_0

If period 0 is already hedged, decide which of the following is preferable:

1. Sell the hedge to someone else for $c_0 - s$, where s is the spread between the buying and selling rate (preferable if $c_0 - s - D_0 > 0$).
2. Retain the hedge thereby avoiding devaluation loss (preferable if $c_0 - s - D_0 < 0$).

Suppose for Dozier π_0 = .3

$$C_0 = 1.27 \text{ percent}$$

$$D_0 = (1 - .3)\, 10.65 = 7.455 \text{ percent}$$

Since $D_0 > C_0$, Dozier should hedge period 0 now. Should period 1 be hedged now? At the beginning of period 0 a hedge of any future period 1, . . . , T can be looked at as a speculation in an option contract. That is, quite apart from our interest in hedging period 1, we are also interested in the *movement* in the cost of hedging period 1. Similarly, we are just as interested in a change in the cost of hedging periods 2, 3, . . . , up to T. Let us call a typical period t. Now, at the beginning of period 0, we have a quote c_{0t} as today's cost of hedging period t. From thinking about who will intervene in the market, and how and when they will act, we must anticipate what the cost quote will be at the beginning of the next period of hedging that same period t.

Decision models have been developed by Shapiro and Rutenberg (1974) to aid a treasurer with these questions. They have also been derived for more complicated situations where a multinational faces multiple possible devaluations or key events (such as an election), or when corporate policy is to never unhedge. A corporate treasurer should be adaptable as to when to hedge if he wishes to minimize the cost of devaluations to his firm.

The treasurer of a polycentric corporation may also recognize a profit by dealing with blocked currencies where the foreign central bank insists that all foreign exchange transactions take place through it. A corporation that needed funds to expand in a blocked nation could legally enter them through the nation's central bank, the usual gatekeeper of foreign exchange. However, the corporation might be able to get a better exchange rate by shopping around for another corporation that would like to repatriate funds from that blocked nation.

The deal usually works as follows. The local subsidiary of corporation A needs local currency now, which it can repay from profits in, say, four years. Local subsidiary of corporation B loans local subsidiary of corporation A the capital at whatever rate of interest is reasonable in that nation. Meanwhile, in the United States or some other nation, A loans B capital as security (if necessary), plus interest to cover the interest differential and the likelihood of exchange controls being tightened (the equivalent of a devaluation). These deals are conceptually similar to forward contracts. However, the "market" is a network of telephone calls. Within the eyes of the central bank of the local nation, these machinations violate the *spirit* of the law and were used in Peru as evidence against a corporation during expropriation decisions. So the expected profits from such back-to-back loans have to be balanced against the increased probability of expropriation multiplied by the assets (their real value in a confiscatorial environment) that might be lost.

Having established the exchange rate management policy of headquarters, we might wish to consider the interaction that occurs between the treasurer and the subsidiary manager. The subsidiary manager's performance is evaluated by a comparison of his year-end profits, measured at the spot rate, with his budget, which was established at the beginning of the period using forecasted exchange rates. The subsidiary manager may be rewarded or reprimanded because of a random discrepancy between the forecasted rates and the year-end spot rate. Thus the subsidiary manager has some mild incentive to help predict the exchange rate (to get approval for his projects). However, he has great incentive to adapt his marketing and manufacturing decisions as the exchange rate changes.

This scheme is appropriate for subsidiaries whose exchange rate floats. In such circumstances, the discrepancy between forecasted and actual exchange rates is likely to be small, and the subsidiary manager is pressured to adapt rapidly. In some corporations, such as Alcan Aluminium Ltd., each subsidiary keeps its accounts in local currency and is allowed to hedge if the subsidiary treasurer feels excessive risk. In theory, one subsidiary could be buying and another selling futures in the same currency. In practice subsidiary treasurers communicate, so they tend to agree as to which currencies are weak. Note that even if each subsidiary hedged to neutral in its local currency, commitments in the local currency would not be hedged, so the corporation as a whole would likely have exposure.

In summary, the headquarters treasurer of a geographically organized polycentric corporation will rarely hedge. Instead, he will passively absorb the risks that the subsidiary marketing and production manager contracted. Only in special circumstances, such as when old tax credits are renewed or when, for political reasons, governments intervene in the currency market, may the treasurer become involved with future contracts.

An Ethnocentric View of Exchange Management

Ethnocentric treasurers justify hedging on the grounds that the erratic appearance of exchange rate losses will depress the stock price of their corporation. By U.S. accounting rules, exchange rate losses have to be footnoted in the corporation's annual report, whereas the costs of hedging are buried in the aggregates of the profit and loss statement.

Corporate treasurers in the United States follow rules established by the Financial Accounting Standards Board (FASB), which in 1975 eliminated reserve accounts for foreign exchange fluctuation. To this end, FASB No. 8 defined "exposure" by stating which assets and liabilities are to be translated at current rates. As seen in Exhibit 2.9, a corporation's accounts receivable are said to be exposed (if denominated in local currency) but the value of a foreign warehouse is not, for its value is to be translated at historical rates. FASB-8 rules will be applied to foreign operations that represent extensions of the parent company operation (e.g., a marketing subsidiary abroad) as do most assets of an ethnocentric corporation. The Standards Board No. 52 states that the exposure of a relatively independent polycentric operation be based on the total net assets of this operation measured in its "functional currency." The functional currency in which a foreign subsidiary keeps its accounts is to be the currency of the "prime economic environment in which the entity operates and generates net cash flows." Where that functional currency has suffered from rapid

EXHIBIT 2.9

FASB's Statement of Financial Accounting Standards No. 8 and No. 52

	Exchange Rate for Translation	
	Current	Historical
ASSETS		
Cash on hand and demand and time deposits	X	
Marketable equity securities		
Carried at cost		X
Carried at current market price	X	
Accounts and notes receivable related unearned discount	X	
Allowance for doubtful accounts and notes receivable	X	
Inventories		
Carried at cost		X
Carried at current replacement price or current selling price	X	
Carried at net realizable value	X	
Carried at contract price (produced under fixed price contracts)	X	
Prepaid insurance, advertising, and rent		X
Refundable deposits	X	
Advances to unconsolidated subsidiaries	X	
Property, plant, and equipment		X
Accumulated depreciation of property, plant and equipment		X
Cash surrender value of life insurance	X	
Patents, trademarks, licenses, and formulas		X
Goodwill		X
Other intangible assets		X
LIABILITIES		
Accounts and notes payable and overdrafts	X	
Accrued expenses payable	X	
Accrued losses on firm purchase commitments	X	
Refundable deposits	X	
Deferred income		X
Bonds payable or other long-term debt	X	
Unamortized premium or discount on bonds or notes payable	X	
Convertible bonds payable	X	
Accrued pension obligations	X	
Obligations under warranties	X	

This table illustrates the exchange rates to be used for translating balance sheet accounts under the FASB's statement on translation accounting.

No !

inflation, the net assets will be restated on a price level adjusted basis. When the functional currency figures are translated into U.S. dollars at current exchange rates any apparent gain or loss in the exposure in this latest year will no longer be reported as part of the parent company's income for this year as required for ethnocentric extensions, but rather will be treated as a direct adjustment of the parent company's shareholders equity.

Few treasurers wait until the year's end to determine corporate exposure; they use pro forma balance sheets to forecast exposure, and they hedge if it appears excessive. A treasurer who is anxious about foreign exchange, as many in ethnocentric firms are, will do his best to bias the exchange rate forecast he quotes to divisions. The treasurer adds a spread between the buying and selling rates quoted for corporate use. He calls the spread a "risk premium," and treasurers are known to deviously adopt arguments of modern finance to justify the spread that induces operating divisions to reduce their exposure. Such treasurers never think that some foreign exposure might be desirable. (Beedles and Senchak, 1978; Errunza, 1977).

Transfer prices, budgets, and exchange rate information are biased by both headquarters and the subsidiaries, since neither wishes to be burdened with the risk of exchange rate fluctuations. The corporate atmosphere of ethnocentric firms is not conducive to the development of a cooperative and comprehensive exchange rate management policy.

Why do headquarters treasurers continue to hedge so ethnocentrically? Their reasons are both psychological and bureaucratic. One treasurer told me that his job is "like standing naked on a windy corner. Were you covered? If not, why not?" After we had discussed the accuracy of various exchange forecasts, another treasurer confided "I use Citibank so that when we take a loss we can blame them." One rarely meets an international treasurer in an ethnocentric corporation who feels that either his international or his treasury superior understands his work.

Ethnocentric corporate treasurers pay substantial hedging fees to undo diversification out of the "safety" of the home currency. The accumulation of hedging fees can be surprisingly large. For example, even though the British government formerly supported sterling futures, an internal Ford Motor Company study showed that, through the years 1946 to 1969, a policy of always hedging was appreciably more expensive than one of never hedging but taking losses when devaluation occurred. The spread between a buying and selling rate appears very low on a single 30-day futures quotation, but the accumulation of these monthly fees from 1946 to 1969 was surprisingly large (Kohlhagan, 1975).

Worse than the expense of hedging is the fact that the very definition of exposure is arbitrary. Exhibit 2.10 shows some of the different bases for defining exposure. As can be seen, the same foreign subsidiary could be perceived quite differently if its parent were American, Swedish, or Japan-

EXHIBIT 2.10

Different bases for defining exposure

Monetary Items Translated at Current Rate Non-monetary Items Translated at Historical Rate	*All Items at Current Exchange Rate*
Argentina	Denmark
Australia	Ethiopia
Brazil	France
Chile	Germany
Fiji	India
Jamaica	Italy
Kenya	Japan
Mexico	Malaysia
New Zealand	Netherlands
Nigeria	Norway
USA	Peru
Uruguay	Singapore
Venezuela	Switzerland
	UK

Current Accounts at Current Rate Noncurrent Accounts at Historical Rate	*Other Translation Rules*
Bermuda	Bahamas
Bolivia	Belgium
Canada	Greece
Columbia	Panama
Pakistan	Paraguay
South Africa	Philippines
Sweden	Ireland
	Rhodesia
	Spain
	Trinidad
	Zaire

ese. Even as the U.S. Financial Accounting Standards Board changes its definition of exposure it will have to change it to another standard for stewardship reasons. Consistent stewardship demands that there be a basis for valuing *all* subsidiaries. However, managerial *action* to take advantage of the rate change may not be congruent with the basis for valuation.

Attitudes toward exposure provide a clear test to distinguish between an ethnocentric and a polycentric (or geocentric) treasurer. Suppose a corporation has hedged a pegged currency, and there is a possibility of devaluation, although its probability is far from certain. Should the treasurer sell that contract (unhedge) if someone offers more than its expected worth? This frequently happens during the early stages of a run on a currency. The treasurer of some other ethnocentric corporation, desperate to say he was covered if a devaluation occurs, may be willing to pay up to the extent of the possible devalution. The ethnocentric treasurer, who would prefer that all divisions minimize exposure, acts as though the probability of devaluation were a certainty. From his bureaucratic viewpoint, this action may be prudent. In contrast, a polycentric treasurer views exposure as a constraint on his taking advantage of a market imperfection, and as such he can feel "not guilty" when he sells the forward cover just a few weeks before the devaluation may occur — as long as he profits from doing so over several crises. A polycentric treasurer would therefore prefer more exposure than his ethnocentric counterpart. His willingness to accept some exchange rate risk and the inherent flexibility of the polycentric exchange package reflect the superior information flows and the very different risk tolerance of the polycentric corporation.

The Geocentric View of Exchange Management

A truly geocentric multinational may best be described as a dynamic portfolio of risky assets. By the late 1970s it became conventional academic wisdom to believe that an individual investor is interested in a mean-variance efficient portfolio. Individual investors, perhaps operating through mutual funds, can diversify as they choose. Because individuals can diversify, they view a diversified corporation merely as a mutual fund. A polycentric corporation is a mutual fund. Yet a geocentric corporation is different because it has the ability to redeploy assets after shocks have occurred.

Stock market theory has been built and tested on single-period models. Consider the analogy to roulette. The investor lays out the money, the wheel of chance is spun, and only certain locations pay. The polycentric corporation has no influence over the odds, nor can it rearrange its chips after the wheel has stopped. A geocentric firm is different. Consider again the roulette analogy. After the wheel of chance has stopped, thereby revealing the favored locations, the geocentric firm has the ability to rearrange some of the chips. The justification for a geocentric headquarters is to allow the corporation to rearrange the sourcing between its plants, to alter the denominations in which to float new debt, and to retune its marketing efforts. And if perchance the wheel of fortune is jostled to a new position, the geocentric firm again has the flexibility to adapt. This book is concerned with models to guide coherent adaptation.

Given that the marketing and production managers should not have to bear the brunt of foreign exchange fluctuations, the treasurer's department seems the most appropriate corporate group to assume the risk. It must establish a transfer price, for exchange risk, to ensure a standard cost for the functional managers. The treasurer's office may or may not decide to hedge the overall corporation. If the treasurer's office does selectively participate in the commercial market, then it may even become a minor profit center. However, its main function is to absorb the exchange risk from operating decisions.

Options

Consider the problem faced by the corporation's marine division that wants one new vessel and is negotiating to have it constructed in a Japanese, or a Polish, or a Singapore shipyard. Negotiations are expected to last six months before the division signs a purchase order with the most suitable of these yards. If it is signed, there will be progress payments (at specified dates) and then a final payment, when the vessel passes ocean tests, payable in yen, zloty, or rupees. To chose from among these three shipyards, the marine division must know what its U.S. dollar commitments will be and hence should pay the treasurer at headquarters for an option on the specified number of yen and again for an option on zloty and again on rupiahs. The marine division can then negotiate with the three shipyards.

When there is an inadequate forward market, the options can flow *to* the treasurer's department. One U.S. lumber company was negotiating to purchase hardwood in Indonesia at a price specified in Indonesian rupiahs *or* U.S. dollars, with the U.S. company being able to decide which to pay. The hardwood buyers turned to their treasurer's department for advice on how hard to negotiate for this clause. The most credible advice is for the treasurer to quote a bonus to be paid the buyer to get such an option (Merton, 1973).

Real Assets

The risky assets and liabilities of the multinational corporation are not necessarily those that appear on the balance sheet, but are instead the future streams of different currencies. Accurate exchange rate forecasts are not possible, but the covariances between long-term exchange rate changes can be forecast (Shapiro and Rutenberg, 1976; Goodman, 1979).

The marketing plans yield a forecasted stream of revenue. Each established factory will require a stream of local currency for wages and domestic purchases; there are interest payments, scheduled debt repayments, and dividends. These flows must be forecasted on a few scenarios of exchange rates. A simulation of the cash flows of the corporation can then be prepared. Scenarios of possible futures (including exchange rates and restrictions) have to be written, so that each set of decision alternatives can be evaluated for robustness.

An example should help make this clear. Consider a multinational corporation, with an established market in Japan, about to develop an ore body in western Canada. (The mineral will be smelted in Canada, then shipped to Japan.) To finance the mine and smelter should the treasurer prefer to float bonds in Canada or Japan? Some treasurers would take a balance sheet approach and argue that the assets in Canada should be off-set by Canadian debt. Other treasurers would take a cash flow approach and borrow in Japan. In their eyes the mine will require a continual flow of Canadian dollars to pay for wages, maintenance, and local taxes, yet the corporation has no sources of Canadian dollars. On the other hand, it will have a continual stream of yen from the sales revenue, part of which can be used for bond interest and principal repayment. A geocentric executive would adopt this view and prefer to borrow yen. Specifically, from a portfolio model a geocentric transfer should be able to calculate the premium the corporation would be willing to pay to borrow yen. Despite this premium he might nevertheless borrow Canadian dollars if the government provided access to subsidized interest rates, or if the treasurer could foresee a possibility of nationalization in which Canadian bondholders would act as a local pressure group. Nevertheless, a geocentric treasurer's basic consideration is future cash flows.

With estimates of the total cash flows, the treasurer can determine the criteria for composing the corporate portfolio. There are usually hundreds of different capital investments among which to select. The risk return balance and the relationships between each investment and the existing global portfolio must be examined to determine the asset mix whose risk return level dominates all other combinations. At first glance it may appear that there is a bewildering array of possibilities. Most of the work of a corporate planning group is to screen out the implausible alternatives; only a few dozen decisions of financial importance are likely to emerge. For example, many nations stipulate that the proceeds of a local bond issue may be used only to build a factory in that nation. As another example, Swiss bankers appear to stipulate (collectively) the maximum debt they will float for each particular corporation. Even if a corporation tries to envision global alternatives, it confronts so many constraints on its viable financial options that their total is readily manageable. One such constraint is the minimum expected return the corporation expects before expanding into another market, on an efficient frontier between risk and return. For a prespecified expected return, the combination of activities which minimizes risk can be calculated by means of a quadratic program, rather like a linear program which has a more complicated objective function to handle the covariance terms (Lietaer, 1971).

The geocentric treasurer utilizes exchange rate information received from subsidiary managers as well as observation of imperfections in the currency market — such as those caused by systematic government inter-ference — to hedge selectively. Employing the decision rules established by the hedging model mentioned in the section on the polycentric view, the geocentric treasurer and managers occasionally participate in the futures market. The treasurer may use information from hedging practices as in-put into the portfolio of positive and negative cash flows in each currency.

A standard currency is required for operating a multinational accounting system. If erratic government intervention into a national currency makes it unsuitable as a base currency, then this also means that the currency is an unsuitable standard for multinational accounting, as appears to be the case with the Israeli scheckel. This does not necessarily mean that the physical headquarters has to be moved, but another currency may be more suitable. For example, the Canadian-headquartered multinationals Alcan, Massey-Ferguson, and Moore now keep their accounts in U.S. dollars.

In summary, the geocentric multinational will strive to maintain a balanced portfolio. The concept of the geographically diversified portfolio of the polycentric corporation is extended in the geocentric corporation to allow for the redeployment of the corporation's marketing and production facilities. The value of a risky asset to the individual subsidiary is adjusted to match the treasurer's interpretation of the effects of economic shifts and government policies on future income flows. The treasurer makes this adjustment by biasing the subsidiary's forecasted exchange rate. The portfolio's composition will change as the states of nature change.

Such a dynamic management practice as that pursued by the geocentric corporation is necessary in the sometimes hostile environment in which the corporation operates. Many nations where subsidiaries are located are antagonistic toward capitalist corporations, particularly multinationals. Because of the geocentric's rationalized production and marketing system, it is particularly susceptible: A breakdown in one nation caused by government policy or economic uncertainty may affect the entire network. Simultaneously, the geocentric's ability to redeploy assets means that a higher expected return and a lower variance of cash flow can be achieved than that which is possible in a polycentric corporation.

The polycentric corporation fits on the mean–variance frontier. The precise location may depend on assuming a fair amount of risk. Not so the ethnocentric corporation, whose costly financial constraints will also

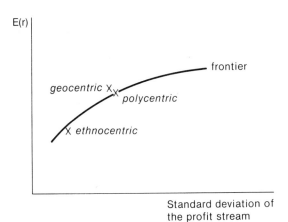

EXHIBIT 2.11
Risk-return space of the three corporate archetypes.

reduce its profitability below the frontier. The geocentric's ability to re-deploy assets to adapt to the state of the world may (if it is managed efficiently) allow it to be above the polycentric frontier of Exhibit 2.11.

Conclusion

The impact of exchange rate fluctuations on the multinational is twofold:

1. Short-term exchange rate fluctuations may be incorporated by head-quarters into the year-end evaluation of a subsidiary manager's profit performance. The subsidiary's earnings may be enhanced, or devalued, according to random currency movements, the rate at which the sub-sidiary's budget was forecasted, and the rate at which the subsidiary is evaluated.
2. Many marketing and production decisions involve long-term commit-ments by the organization, which causes the headquarter's treasury office to be starkly aware of the effect devaluation may have on the future income flows of those investments. Therefore, some multina-tionals use exchange rate forecasts or introduce risk biases into their decisions to commit resources.

If the morale of the subsidiary manager and the productivity of the workers are to be sustained, operating managers must be shielded from the effects of currency fluctuations. The degree to which the headquarters treasurer insulates the subsidiary manager from the effects of exchange rate fluctuations in evaluation procedures as well as the degree to which he offers incentives for the manager to react to current conditions in a manner that is most beneficial to the organization's total performance vary with the organizational archetype of the corporation. The exchange rate forecast and portfolio adjustment techniques employed by the trea-surer and the cooperation that he receives from managers will greatly in-fluence the long-term growth and profitability of the multinational.

The assets of the ethnocentric multinational are naively diversified; capital investments are based on strictly adhered to return on investment criteria. There is no mechanism by which to perceive assets as a coherent whole. The ethnocentric treasurer stodgily operates according to world-wide procedural guidelines. Subsidiary managers are evaluated in a manner that exposes them to the variable movements of currencies. On the home front, treasurers deplete corporate funds by hedging all foreign activities in their attempt to avoid all risk of currency devaluation. Given that hedging is the purchase of futures to protect against currency devalua-tions, it is not an activity designed to maximize profits but rather a cost incurred to avert a possible loss. Ethnocentric executives conduct their foreign operations in a guarded and pessimistic manner. Income streams are not maximized but merely maintained. The accumulated cost of the treasurer's hedging activities and the limited and rigid nature of the head-quarters–subsidiary communication lines contribute to the inefficiencies of the ethnocentric operating system.

Polycentric headquarters pursue rational and flexible investment policies, and thus are more efficient than their ethnocentric counterparts. Head-quarters examines potential portfolio acquisitions using historical data and relationships. The portfolio is periodically adjusted to reflect the changing states of various world economies and the evolving profit potential of various nations. However, no particular risk-return goal is maintained. The polycentric's corporate atmosphere breeds a competitiveness that encourages the headquarters treasurer to recognize inconsistencies in the environment. He has the flexibility, drive, and knowledge to grasp profitable opportunities. Although the fragmented state of the subsidiaries' production and marketing activities prohibits totally effective communication flows, subsidiary managers and headquarters treasurers have a mutual incentive to discuss foreign exchange rate information.

Geocentric headquarters view themselves in a two-stage process, in which they make long-term commitments with an eye to the flexibility this will allow in operations. The first-stage decisions involve long-term financing, nurturing major markets, and building core factories. These first-stage decisions can be made mindful of many scenarios that the future might bring (Garstka and Rutenberg, 1973) so that in the second stage the operating managers have recourse to adapt flexibly to whichever scenario actually occurs. As the chapters of this book will make clear, the great advantage of a geocentric corporation is the incredible robustness of its manufacturing, its marketing, and its short-term financial networks. Conversely, the expense of a geocentric headquarters can be justified only if it manages this robust flexibility to take advantage of (and not be hurt by) whichever particular circumstances arise. The resulting corporate *total* cash flow is more certain. However, the financial analysis of an individual project has to be performed by analyzing the performance of the global network with the project, and then reanalyzing it without the project. The with and without analysis has to be performed under each environmental scenario. In a geocentric corporation analysts think about the location of bond issues and new equity placements to make sure that these commitments to annual cash flows can be satisfied without creating local strains, by diverting currency flows needed for marketing or manufacturing. Exchange rates and inflation rates are forecast for the 2–5 year medium term, so that production redeployments and marketing emphases can be adapted to these forecast changes in real manufacturing costs and real marketing revenues.

The portfolio adjustment practices of geocentric firms surpass the description of multiperiod portfolio strategy provided by current financial theories. Current portfolio selection theory involves a one-period decision process. In contrast, the geocentric multinational's portfolio selection strategy is essentially a two-stage decision process, where the corporation has recourse to adapt in the second stage. Current states and forecasts of future states of nature can be reflected within the covariance matrix, a crude surrogate for the flexibility to redeploy cash flows. The geocentric's active subsidiary management procedures are discussed further in subsequent chapters.

Questions from Other Viewpoints

1. *Corporate Rational Normative Global.* You just covered this viewpoint in the chapter.
2. *Corporate Rational Normative Subsidiary.* Find a financial newspaper of 10 years ago. (Try the library.) Look up the 10-year bond interest rates of two or three nations. Also find the spot exchange rates that then prevailed, and predict the exchange rates for now. Contrast your predictions with current spot rates.
3. *Corporate Rational Descriptive Global.* For a business in your favorite nation, make up an income statement and start and end of year balance sheets in local currency. If the headquarters is in Japan or Canada or Brazil use actual exchange rates and the classifications of Exhibit 2.10 to translate your business into these three headquarters accounts.
4. *Corporate Rational Descriptive Subsidiary.* One of the consequences of foreign exchange fluctuations is that purchases and sales abroad keep changing price. What standard accounting systems are now used to facilitate rational decision making in environments of changing prices?
5. *Corporate Emotional Normative Global.* People often give up and plead uncertainty when asked to forecast exchange rates. How would you manage such a work situation?
6. *Corporate Emotional Normative Subsidiary.* Headquarters accounting systems usually monitor their subsidiaries in terms of headquarters currency. Managers are promoted and awarded bonuses on the basis of performance. The performance of a subsidiary manager depends on his efforts and luck on the exchange rate. Review (from prior courses and the library) the theories listed on page 48. Select the most relevant theory and summarize in two pages the emotional consequences of a reward system, one part of which depends on the individual's effort, but a major part of which is a random reinforcement.
7. *Corporate Emotional Descriptive Global.* To manage a corporation's foreign exchange requires intellectual skills and also a specific kind of personality. Describe the personal qualities, personal pressures, and personal satisfactions that this work probably entails.
8. *Corporate Emotional Descriptive Subsidiary.* What are the long-run

emotional pressures on the treasurer of a subsidiary who always has to think in a foreign currency and who feels that vestiges of ethnocentrism by headquarters still show in their view of his nation's currency and predicted money supply and inflation?

9. *Societal Rational Normative Global.* It is said that fluctuations in spot rates are bad, so central banks sometimes intervene in the spot market (this is called a dirty float). Suppose central banks were to stop intervening in the spot market but always stand ready to write long-term futures contracts. Would that tend to stabilize spot rates, or would it have no effect?

10. *Societal Rational Normative Subsidiary.* Most nations insist that every foreign exchange transaction involving their currency be done through their central bank. The governor of the central bank has many responsibilities, one of which is recruiting and supervising the bank's manager of foreign transactions. Write a job description for a bank's manager of foreign transactions that includes the criteria against which the individual's performance will be measured; assuming: (a) only one rate of exchange will prevail at a particular time; (b) there will be different rates of exchange for different classes of transactions.

11. *Societal Rational Descriptive Global.* In the days of fixed exchange rates, the International Monetary Fund had a definite role — to help sustain the rates or to counsel their change in an orderly way. What is the current role of the IMF? Study the IMF Annual Report and study its activities for the last two years as reported in the index of a major newspaper.

12. *Societal Rational Descriptive National.* Find the rates of domestic inflation for four major nations in 1970 and in 1980. Is there any evidence that before 1970, when exchange rates were generally pegged, ministers of finance felt pressure to dampen inflation?

13. *Societal Emotional Normative Global.* You have been assigned by your government to be part of your nation's delegation at the IMF Annual Meeting. Respond to a proposal that like nations of the world unite under one currency. Are you for or against? Outline your response. With each point create a phrase that will cause the emotions of the listeners to resound.

14. *Societal Emotional Normative Subsidiary.* For the benefit of a narrow-minded foreigner, explain why his profiteering in your nation's currency is immoral.

15. *Societal Emotional Descriptive Global.* Describe the kind of personality that would find most satisfaction in spending a lifetime in a government body working on international finance.

16. *Societal Emotional Descriptive National.* Select three instances of a nation suffering rapid inflation. (Either one nation in three periods or three nations in the same period.) In the library look up comtemporaneous newspaper or magazine accounts of the impact on peoples' lives. What were the similarities? What were the differences?

Bibliography to Chapter 2

Adler, Michael and Bernard Dumas, "The Long Term Financial Decisions of the Multinational Corporation," in *International Capital Markets*, edited by E.J. Elton and M.J. Gruber (Amsterdam: North Holland, 1975), Chapter 9.

Beedles, William L. and Andrew J. Senchak, "Indirect International Diversification Through U.S. Multinational Firms," Unpublished Working Paper 78-27, The University of Texas, Austin, 1978.

Black, Fischer, "The Pricing of Commodity Contracts," *Journal of Financial Economics*, Vol. 3 (1976), pp. 167-179.

Chemical Bank, *Foreign Exchange Exposure Management*, Multinational Cash Management Group, Chemical Bank, New York, 1972.

Chen, Andrew H., David A. Ricks, and Hany Shawky, "The Performance of Multinational Corporations' Common Stocks and the Efficiency of International Capital Markets," Unpublished Working Paper 77-74, College of Administrative Science, Ohio State University, 1977.

Errunza, Vihang R., "Gains from Portfolio Diversification into Less Developed Countries' Securities," *Journal of International Business Studies*, Vol. 8, No. 2 (1977), pp. 83-99.

Errunza, Vihang R. and Lemma W. Senbet, "The Effects of International Operations on the Market Value of the Firm: Theory and Evidence," *Journal of Finance*, Vol. 36, No. 2 (1981).

Folks, William R. and Stanley R. Stansell, "The Use of Discriminant Analysis in Forecasting Exchange Rate Movements," *Journal of International Business Studies*, Vol. 6, No. 1 (1975), pp. 33-50.

Garstka, Stanley J. and David P. Rutenberg, "Computation in Discrete Stochastic Programs with Recourse," *Operations Research*, Vol. 21, No. 1 (1973), pp. 112-122.

Giddy, Ian H. and Gunter Dufey, "The Random Behavior of the Flexible Exchange Rates: Implications for Forecasting," *Journal of International Business Studies*, Vol. 6, No. 1 (1975), pp. 1-32.

Goeltz, Richard K., "Managing Liquid Funds on an International Scope," Unpublished Working Paper, Joseph E. Seagram and Sons, Inc., New York, 1971.

Goodman, Stephen H., "Foreign Exchange Rate Forecasting Techniques: Implications for Business and Policy," *Journal of Finance*, Vol. 34, No. 2, 1979, pp. 415-427.

Kohlhagan, Steven W., "Evidence on the Cost of Forward Cover in a Floating System," *Euromoney*, September 1975, pp. 138-141.

Levich, Richard M., "Efficient Markets and International Financial Management," *The International Money Market: An Assessment of Forecasting Techniques and Market Efficiency*, Chap. 6 (J. A. I. Press, 1979).

Levy, Haim and Marshall Sarnat, "Devaluation Risk and the Portfolio Analysis of International Investment," in *International Capital Markets*, edited by E.J. Elton and M.J. Gruber (Amsterdam: North Holland, 1975), Chapter 5.2.

Lietaer, Bernard, *Financial Management of Foreign Exchange: An Operational Technique to Reduce Risk* (Cambridge: MIT Press, 1971).

Lloyd, W.P., "International Portfolio Diversification of Real Assets: An Inquiry," *Journal of Business Research*, April 1975. Vol. 3, pp. 111-120.

Malkiel, Burton G., *The Term Structure of Interest Rates: Theory, Empirical Evidence, and Applications* (Morristown, NJ: General Learning Press, 1970).

Merton, Robert C., "The Theory of Rational Option Pricing," *Bell Journal of Economics and Management Science*, Vol. 4 (Spring 1973), pp. 141–183.

Mueller, Gerhardt G., *International Accounting* (New York: Macmillan, 1967).

Neave, Edwin and David P. Rutenberg, "When to Hedge Successively," Unpublished Working Paper, Queen's University, 1981.

Roll, Richard and Bruno Solnik, "A Pure Foreign Exchange Asset Pricing Model," *Journal of International Economics*, Vol. 7 (1977), pp. 161–179.

Senchack, Andrew J. and Laura T. Starks, "International Diversification Through Listed Foreign Securities," Unpublished Working Paper 78-28, The University of Texas, Austin, 1978.

Shapiro, Alan H. and David P. Rutenberg, "Managing Exchange Risks in a Floating World," *Financial Management*, Vol. 5, No. 2 (1976), pp. 48–58.

Shapiro, Alan H. and David P. Rutenberg, "When to Hedge Against Devaluation," *Management Science*, Vol. 20, No. 12 (1974), pp. 1514–1530; reprinted in *International Capital Markets*, edited by E.J. Elton and M.J. Gruber (Amsterdam, North Holland, 1975), Chapter 5.1.

CHAPTER THREE

Maneuvering Liquid Assets

Introductory Note to the Case

Paisley S.A.

"Paisley S.A." is based on a major French company. Its subsidiaries have proceeded with their own financial plans in a polycentric manner – marketing problems have dominated, and finance has been viewed as a support activity. The sales and processing subsidiaries purchased chemicals from the French mother company. In the past these subsidiaries took such a long time to pay that their accounts payable to Paisley were a significant portion of their liabilities. This would be a smart thing to do if France were a cheap nation in which to raise capital, but it is not. Furthermore, as a government contractor in France, Paisley is presumably open to genteel government suggestions that it contribute more positively to French balance of payments problems this year.

Like any real problem this case has many layers. First, the cost (interest, tax, expected exchange rate change) of moving funds between three nations must be calculated. Second, the benefits of altering the dividend pipelines by having France own a holding company in a nation that imposes zero corporate tax, which would own all the foreign subsidiaries, must be sketched. Third is an analysis of the financial statements to estimate how much cash flow each subsidiary will need in 1982. Fourth, the financial flows that would satisfy their cash needs at minimum tax cost must be calculated. Finally, the morality of maneuvering liquid assets must be considered.

In a high-technology business such as Paisley the products are unique and changing rapidly. To an accountant this means that transfer prices and research and design royalties can be calculated in several different ways (the overhead expenses can be allocated according to different bases). In international business every nation calculates corporate income tax differently, thus allocations have different tax consequences. Keep an eye on worldwide after-tax income.

Paisley S.A.

Marc Chemenceau, assistant to Vice President of Finance Jean Lefevres of the Paisley company, was told to analyze an aspect of the company's financial policies. He was a recent MBA graduate of INSEAD the distinguished Graduate School of Business at Fontainebleau, where he had specialized in finance and international business. His vice president felt that Paisley's financial resources were no longer being utilized as effectively as they might be.

Paisley S.A.* was a French company that manufactured and marketed commercial fragrances, dyes, and chemicals worldwide. During 1981 foreign subsidiaries had substantially increased their accounts payable to the parent company; in 1982 they would want additional large increases. These increased demands on the parent company's financial resources coincided with an increase in its own needs for working capital and a drop in 1981 profits of the parent company. These internal pressures promised that 1982 would be a difficult year. Because of the high inflation rate at the time, the newly elected Socialist government had limited the amount of credit available to the economy; short- and long-term interest rates were increased, and foreign payments were rationed.

Paisley et Cie. had been established in 1935 by Mr. A. Begin to commercialize synthetic perfumes he had patented. Established perfume houses wouldn't touch his ersatz perfumes, so he manufactured dyes and then revived his synthetic perfumes as commercial air fresheners. An air freshener order from the Paris Metro finally launched the company. In 1960 his son, Robert Begin, assumed the presidency. He

This case was prepared by Lutz Holfield under the supervision of Professor David Rutenberg.
*S.A. (Societe Anonyme) means a stock corporation similar to an incorporated U.S. corporation.

reorganized the company into three parts: Paisley S.A., the parent operating holding company; French subsidiaries; and foreign subsidiaries. Paisley had always been research and development oriented, patents protected its high profit margins, and technical control was tight with much sharing of ideas on a global basis. To assure impeccable quality control, both Begins insisted that the French factory was to be the only source of raw materials, imported semifinished products, and imported finished products. No intersubsidiary shipments were permitted.

Subsidiary finances were not carefully monitored. Until now each Paisley subsidiary had developed its own budget within very informal guidelines from headquarters. In fact, once submitted, the subsidiaries' budgets were not discussed as long as sales and profit showed an increase over the previous year's performance.

This behavior accorded with A. Begin's view that the core skill of Paisley was to dominate a niche of the fragrance and dye market and to try to amortize the continuing cost of that research over more sales by being international. International finance and accounting were viewed as housekeeping functions. Executives rarely discussed the impact on the subsidiaries of different finance policies and accounting principles, of local environmental variables, or exchange rate changes. Thus top management pursued a consistent strategy of:

1. Research and Development: Between 6 and 9 percent of sales had been consistently allocated to R&D, including the testing that governments required. Over half the sales revenue was produced by products less than five years old.
2. Internationalization: Exporting and the creation of foreign subsidiaries were emphasized. The first, Paisley-Brazil, was created in 1938. By 1981, foreign sales were 60 percent of total sales. This policy of internationalization had proved to be extremely reassuring during periods of French instability as in 1968 and again in 1981. The contribution of foreign operations had been fundamental to Paisley's growth and profitability (Exhibit 3.1).
3. Diversification: The firm's R&D capabilities had led it into related specialty chemicals. In 1972 these chemical products were 12 percent of total sales; by 1980 they represented 25 percent.

The results of these three strategies had been a fast and

profitable growth, but a disordered organization. Total sales for the group grew tenfold between 1970 and 1980, while profits increased nine times and R&D expenses fifteen times. In 1981 sales were FF 196,000,000, profits were FF 10,780,000, and R&D expenses were FF 21,570,000. The financing of the growth had been achieved largely through retained earnings. In 1980 total debt was less than 28 percent of total liabilities and equity.

Vice President Jean Lefevres was wondering how to coordinate the financial policies of the foreign subsidiaries and the parent company to reduce the amount and cost of financing required for the group. He was concerned by the fact that he lacked financial control over these subsidiaries. His position at Paisley required that he manage the cash position and short- and medium-term financing of the parent company in France, but he felt he was merely responding to events.

The Organization

The operating holding company, or parent company, had three product divisions: fragrance, dyes, and miscellaneous chemicals. Each of these divisions was then organized on a functional basis.

The French subsidiaries reported directly to the top management of Paisley but also communicated widely with the corresponding product divisions of the operating holding company or with the R&D division. Their financial autonomy varied; some had an independent borrowing policy and others depended on the parent holding company.

All the Paisley foreign subsidiaries were owned by Genmarc holding company, incorporated in France. Direct exports were channeled through this company. In organizational terms, the product divisions of Paisley (or exporting French subsidiaries) had direct contact with the foreign subsidiaries. To have better access to certain markets Paisley had created several wholly owned sales subsidiaries. Some, like the subsidiary in Brazil, had set up limited manufacturing or packaging operations because of tariff problems, patent necessity, or governmental pressures. Genmarc had originally been responsible for these subsidiaries. The changing nature of the foreign operation from arm's-length export to limited manufacturing had made it necessary to establish additional links with the product divisions that sent goods to the foreign subsidiaries. Thus Paisley product divisions usually bypassed

Genmarc in their communications with the individual managers of the foreign subsidiaries. Genmarc received dividends and royalties from the subsidiaries and also could collect a markup on export orders.

Financial Policies

The large integrated foreign subsidiaries functioned as if financially independent of the parent company. Their high profitability and relatively low dividend to Paisley allowed them to finance their expansion from retained earnings. When external financing was necessary they dealt with local banks with which they had long developed relationships. This was especially true of the U.K. subsidiary, owned by Paisley since 1960.

The large subsidiaries reported to the parent company, but their reports were treated casually. Their forecasts were accepted as long as profitability and sales were growing. Clearly, no one at Genmarc or Paisley was particularly competent in international finance and accounting. No one systematically considered the impact on the subsidiaries of different financial policies and accounting principles, of local environmental variables, or of currency fluctuations.

The smaller subsidiaries were much more dependent on Paisley. They financed their growth by increasing their Genmarc accounts receivable. When additional financing was required they asked Paisley for longer credit terms or for a formal loan. Usually Genmarc and the Paisley product divisions approved their requests.

Conflicts had arisen occasionally about devaluation losses. Subsidiaries with large accounts payable to Paisley denominated in French francs were severely hit when a devaluation in the local currency suddenly increased the local currency value of these accounts. As a result, some subsidiaries had started to borrow in local currency while others had the burden of devaluation split on a 50:50 basis with Paisley.

By the end of 1981 both Vice President Lefevres and Marc Chemenceau felt increasingly uneasy about the financial needs for the coming year. The foreign subsidiaries' increase in accounts receivable was imposing a heavy financial strain on Paisley. The working capital requirements had also increased because of larger inventories as well as an increase in domestic accounts receivable. This was expected to continue well into 1982. Furthermore, price increases for finished products in France were viewed with disfavor by the government, but labor and material costs were increasing steadily. As a result profit margins in France for 1982 were expected to be less than in 1981.

Outline of the Memo

Marc Chemenceau felt that financial autonomy of the subsidiaries was detrimental to the group. He discussed this with Lefeveres, who was skeptical about disrupting profitable growing concerns. Chemenceau believed that some of the techniques he had learned at Fontainebleau could be utilized to restructure the relationships between the different subsidiaries and the parent company. For example, increased centralization opened the door for a more tax-conscious management of transfer prices. When approached with this idea, Lefevres authorized Chemenceau to prepare a report on his findings using two subsidiaries. This pilot study would give Begin and Lefevres a basis for more realistic decisions. Any move by Paisley to financial centralization would clearly have other consequences.

As Chemenceau researched his report he became increasingly aware of the complexity of computing gains from worldwide financial centralization. He therefore decided to make several simplifying assumptions.

1. Debt for the parent company and subsidiaries could be borrowed at the beginning of the year and repaid with interest at the end of the year.
2. Accounts receivable by the parent from foreign subsidiaries were in French francs.
3. Because he could not foresee foreign exchange losses or gains, he decided to ignore their tax implications, and consequent cash flows.

Using these assumptions Chemenceau worked to estimate the optimum financing for 1982 from simple forecasts based on cost figures for the end of 1981; thus he could calculate saving that might result from a centralized financial policy. To emphasize his point with Lefevres, he felt he should prepare actual after-tax calculations of the corporate cost of moving funds by means of dividends, transfer prices, and intersubsidiary loans. Specifically, he set out to calculate the cost of borrowing locally and whether to use dividends, transfer prices, or intersubsidiary loans to effect a transfer

EXHIBIT 3.1
Paisley S.A.

Financial Data, Foreign subsidiaries 1981 (FF thousands)

Country of Incorporation	Extent of Owner- ship (%)	Sales	Profit (Loss)	Dividends To Paisley	Purchase of Finished Products From Paisley S.A.	Purchase of Semi- finished or raw Materials	Royalties Paid to Paisley for R&D
Argentina	55	2,610	45			1,890	180
Belgium	100	1,800	72	54	540	1,350	54
Brazil	100	5,130	(180)			3,420	
India	40	360	(5)			54	
Italy	100	8,010	135	27		4,590	405
Japan	49	9,000	(252)		5,400	900	
Mexico	80	11,970	450			1,800	540
Peru	70	4,410	45	40		1,530	315
United Kingdom	95	52,200	3,510		810	2,970	2,070
United States	10	4,500	135	27		15	
West Germany	10	4,050	225		180	243	162
		104,040	4,180	147	6,930	18,762	3,726

Direct exports
to other nations
by Genmarc 16,200

120,240

EXHIBIT 3.2
Paisley S.A.

Balance Sheets of Selected Subsidiaries (FF Millions)

	1981	*1982 (forecast)*
UNITED KINGDOM		
Assets		
Fixed assets	27,810	29,520
Accumulated depreciation	8,640	9,090
Net fixed assets	19,170	20,430
Inventory	5,940	6,120
Accounts receivable		
Other Paisley subsidiaries	5,040	4,230
Others	6,570	6,750
Cash	1,890	1,080
Total assets	38,610	38,610
Liabilities		
Common stock	6,300	6,300
Retained earnings	18,990	21,060
Long-term debt	6,750	6,390
Short-term debt	4,410	2,700
Accounts payable	2,160	2,160
Total liabilities	38,610	38,610
BRAZIL		
Assets		
Fixed assets	159	218
Accumulated depreciation	17	22
Net fixed assets	142	196
Inventory	304	493
Accounts receivable	855	1,174
Cash	29	43
Total assets	1,330	1,906
Liabilities		
Common stock	72	72
Retained earnings	261	116
Long-term debt		
Paisley	145	247
Other	72	0
Short-term debt	99	130
Accounts payable		
Paisley	638	1,268
Other	43	73
Total liabilities	1,330	1,906

EXHIBIT 3.3

Paisley S.A. Subsidiaries

Sources and Uses of Funds
Anticipated for the year 1982, (FF thousands)

UNITED KINGDOM

Sources of funds

Accumulated depreciation	450
Accounts receivable from others	810
Cash[a]	810
Retained earnings	2,070
Total sources	4,140

Uses of funds

Fixed assets	1,710
Inventory	180
Accounts receivable subsidiaries	180
Long-term debt	360
Short-term debt	1,710
Total uses of funds	4,140

BRAZIL

Sources of funds

Accumulated depreciation	5
Long-term debt from Paisley	102
Short-term borrowings	31
Accounts payable to Paisley	630
Accounts payable to others	30
Total sources of funds	798

Uses of funds

Fixed assets	59
Inventory	189
Accounts receivable	319
Cash	14
Retained earnings	145
Repay long-term debt to others	72
Total uses of funds	798

[a]The U.K. treasurer has stated in another context that the minimum cash asset he could operate with is FF 600 million, so a further FF 880 million could be available.

EXHIBIT 3.4

Expected Real Cost of Borrowing

Country	One Year Borrowing[a] as of June 1981 (in local currency) (percent)	Treasurer's Forecast of Exchange Rate Change Over Coming Year (percent)
France	15.9	base for measurement
Germany	14.25	+ 5
United Kingdom	13.00	− 8
Brazil	129.5	− 120
Eurodollars	17.3	− 5
Luxembourg	17.5	0
Italy	21.5	− 9

[a]A subsidiary that knows it will have excess cash for a year can keep it on deposit with its bank and earn almost the borrowing rate. Because of differences in competition between banks, spread is lowest in the United Kingdom and highest in Brazil.

to the other subsidiary for each of the following three pairs of countries:

1. United Kingdom — Brazil
2. Brazil — France
3. United Kingdom — France

Lefevres asked Chemenceau to visualize increasing the local borrowing of one subsidiary by FF 1000, and then transfer it to the other subsidiary by whichever means were possible from dividends, transfer price adjustments, or changing intersubsidiary loans. The cost per FF 1000 of each of the three flows in each direction was to be calculated separately for each pair of nations.

In addition, Chemenceau decided to include a one-page appendix demonstrating the tax savings of establishing a holding company in Luxembourg, a tax haven. Genmarc would then be dissolved, for the foreign subsidiaries would be owned by the holding company. According to French law the profits of such a holding company would not have to be consolidated with the parent for tax purposes.

EXHIBIT 3.5

Reductions in Liquidity Caused by Taxes

	Corporate Income Tax	Foreign Tax Credit	Tax on Inter-Company Dividends	In Computing Taxable Income, Is Interest Expense Deductible?
France	50 percent	For with-holding tax	3.75 percent (effective)	Deductible if interest rate $\leqslant 2\%$ + Bank of France rate
Brazil[a]	30 percent 0% for export sales	Foreign income not taxable	0	Deductible
U.K.	52 percent	For all foreign taxes	0 within United Kingdom, 52 percent if from foreign subsidiaries	Deductible

Note: Import tariff is 11 percent into U.K. and 40 percent into Brazil for Paisley Chemicals.
[a]Accumulated surpluses greater than 200 percent issued capital is taxable at 15 percent.

EXHIBIT 3.6

Withholding Taxes Imposed by Host Government

HOST GOVERNMENT	DESTINATION	INTEREST (percent)	DIVIDENDS (percent)
France	Brazil	10	15
	United Kingdom	10	5
	Nontreaty	25	25
Brazil	France	10	15
	United Kingdom	25	25
	Nontreaty	25	25
United Kingdom	Brazil	34	0
	France	10	0
	Nontreaty	34	0

Ethnocentric — Introduction

This chapter is concerned with moving funds between subsidiaries. The purpose of such moves is to get liquidity to each subsidiary when it needs it, in a way that minimizes total taxes paid by the corporation.

Corporations differ in the guidelines they impose on subsidiaries for handling liquid assets, but three patterns predominate, each corresponding to one of the archetypes of headquarters–subsidiary relationships discussed in Chapter 1. Some headquarters feel uneasy about subsidiary managers holding liquid assets from year to year and insist on their declaring dividends to headquarters. This assures control of the foreign managers by the ethnocentric headquarters, although at a high cost in taxes. Geographically organized corporations tend to view each subsidiary as totally independent (which it legally is) and have little involvement in the management of liquid assets; this policy has the fewest negative behavioral consequences, although it results in a high level of total short-term assets. Between these two extremes, the geocentric corporation moves liquidity to subsidiaries when needed by manipulating transfer prices, managerial fees and royalties, dividends, and intersubsidiary loans in order to maximize interest received on liquid assets minus total taxes paid on a worldwide basis. As Robbins and Stobaugh (1973) noted:

> Make no mistake about it — even though these large enterprises seemingly are decentralized, their worldwide network of units and intercompany links are in fact controlled indirectly by their rule books, or "bibles" from headquarters. The "bibles" are in the form of standard procedures, sometimes consisting of several volumes, that specify such items as the limits of local borrowing, standard terms of payment of intercompany accounts, and standard rules for management fees.

Clearly, such headquarters intervention may weaken incentive systems built on the profit center concept. Whether maneuvering is worth the effort can be determined best by building a model; the difference between current and model after-tax profit provides a benchmark against which to judge the behavioral costs of headquarters intervention.

If deemed prudent, maneuvering liquid assets can enable a multinational to react to anticipated changes in exchange rates, currency controls, and other such risks and opportunities. The forecast exchange rates of Chapter 2 are a necessary input to the model explained in this chapter. Where several possible scenarios of the future environment have been envisioned, maneuvers for each can be evaluated.

Geocentric Model — A Generalized Network

The subject of this chapter is the optimal use of tax havens, bilateral tax treaties, nonuniform treatments of income received from abroad, and national differences in income tax rates, import duties, and border taxes. This is a partial analysis for tactical planning because it takes as given the planned operations of each national subsidiary, and hence whether the subsidiary is to be a net source or recipient of funds in each year.

Suppose there are N subsidiaries around the world, and the analysis will be carried out over T years. A real problem deals with all N subsidiaries; for simplicity, we deal with only three subsidiaries: i, j, and k. The analysis begins by forecasting the net cash surplus/deficit for each subsidiary for each period b_i^t, and by setting the safe levels below which bank deposits $K_i^{t,t+1}$ and other liquid asset holdings $G_i^{t,t+1}$ must not fall. From there, a linear program is developed as a guide to the optimal maneuvering of liquid assets between the subsidiaries. The linear program can be solved on a computer.

For each major product line or industry in a nation, a planner can plot the industry attractiveness (growth rate is the usual proxy) against the cash generation capability (related to market share) of the product line. Planners have generally adopted the Boston Consulting Group names for the four quadrants: cash cows, stars, dogs, and seedlings. In a growing industry an enormous (but estimable) amount of cash is needed to gain market share (to transform a seedling into a star). In a low-growth industry, an enormous cash flow can be generated for a few years by curtailing research, exploiting workers, and raising prices (which transforms a cash cow into a dog). Exhibit 3.7 is a tool used in many corporations to conceptualize cash flow over several years. This specific example is taken from the 1976 annual report of the Black and Decker Manufacturing Company.

Even within the strategic deployment of each product line in each nation, hard work is required to forecast the cash inflow requirements or cash outflow. Inflation of input prices must be forecast. Revenue must be estimated from pricing plans and market expansion intentions. The most probable rates of taxation must be forecast to yield after-tax income plus depreciation.

It is far more revealing to forecast *pro forma* cash flows and interest income in nominal, rather than what economists call "real," terms. Deflating these values with anticipated inflation obscures the possible conduits that can channel required liquidity to where it is needed at the most advantageous exchange rates. The forecast exchange rates from Chapter 2 are used in each year of the program. (Some nations employ different exchange rates for different kinds of transactions, and during the 1980s more nations will probably impose currency controls.)

Business unit	Company business (%)	Unit growth rate (%)	Relative market share
1. European Power Tools	38	14−15	3.2−4.0
2. U.S. Consumer Tools	20	7−8	2.0
3. McCulloch	14	10−11	0.6−0.7
4. U.S Professional Tools	10	5−6	1.25−1.75
5. Pacific International	10	26	0.3−0.4
6. Canada	6	10	4
7. Australia	2	4.5	5

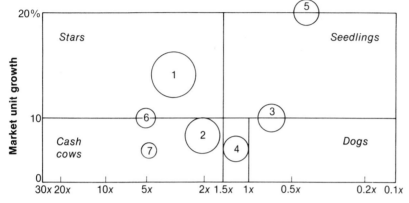

EXHIBIT 3.7

Product portfolio.

A peculiar feature of U.S. banks must also be considered. If any part of a corporation has obtained a loan from a U.S. bank, then the corporation will be required to keep on deposit in branches of that bank no less than a specified "compensating balance." If each subsidiary maintains a dollar account at one the branches of a U.S. bank, then the sum of these accounts can be used to satisfy the compensating balance requirement. Thus an aggregated compensating balance functions as an effective way to make intersubsidiary loans. The compensating balance requirement is depicted by the bunched parallel K arcs in Exhibit 3.8; the flow through these arcs must be greater than or equal to the compensating balance requirement.

Liquid funds can be held by a subsidiary from one year to the next. This holding is represented in Exhibit 3.8 as a flow through the arc connecting a subsidiary in one year to the same in the succeeding year. For example, $G_j^{t,\,t+1}$ funds are held by subsidiary j for the year t to $t+1$. If there is a significant term structure to the best interest rates that a subsidiary could obtain, then two-year arcs can be added to take advan-

YEAR t   YEAR t + 1   YEAR t + 2

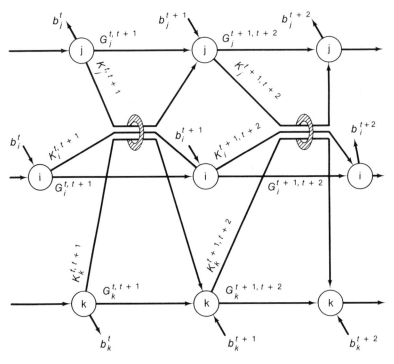

EXHIBIT 3.8
Inflows and outflows for subsidiaries i, j, and k.

b_i^t = capital generated across all product lines — planned expenditures

$G_i^{t,t+1}$ = amount of liquid assets carried by subsidiary i in the one year
period from t to $t + 1$, employed in the most profitable manner

$K_i^{t,t+1}$ = amount of cash held by subsidiary i (usually in a dollar account
in a U.S. bank) that can satisfy compensating balance requirements

tage of the higher interest rates obtainable on longer term loans. However,
to simplify exposition, we use only one-year arcs.

A feasible solution to the problem of maneuvering liquid assets is one
that gets funds to those subsidiaries that need them. Exhibit 3.9 presents the problem of maneuvering liquid assets in a multinational company as a network problem. Our objective is to minimize taxes paid to
the world minus interest received. The problem *sounds* very complicated.
Fortunately, all of these complexities can be handled within the problem
itself. Along the way from 0 to T we have to meet demands for liquidity.
In year T there will be some excess liquidity (assuming that the problem
is feasible). The more excess liquidity, the better our accomplishment

(less was lost to taxes, and more has been gained from interest). Hence the objective function of this linear program is to maximize the sum of liquid assets remaining after time T. These liquid assets are the three arrows flowing off the right-hand side of Exhibit 3.8.

For any given pattern of intersubsidiary ownerships, there are at least four ways to transmit liquid assets from one national subsidiary to another. These control variables are:

1. p_{ij} Adjust transfer prices on shipments between subsidiaries i and j.
2. f_{ij} Charge legal and managerial fees and royalties on technical knowledge supplied to subsidiary j by subsidiary i.
3. $l_{ij}^{t,t+1}$ Make new intersubsidiary loans and repay old ones with interest. Delayed invoicing is a loan.
4. d_{ij} Remit dividends from subsidiary j to its legal stockholder subsidiary i.

A linear program has constraints. Each node of the network represents a separate constraint. For node i in year t the flows of funds in minus

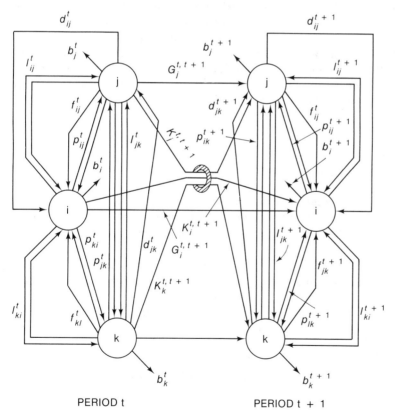

PERIOD t   PERIOD t + 1

EXHIBIT 3.9
The complete network.

the flows out must equal b_i^t. In each year, N compensating balances must be specified, as must $N - 1$ dividend flows, $N(N - 1)$ transfer price flows, and $N(N - 1)$ loan flows. The number of managerial fee flows will be either $N(N - 1)$ or $N - 1$, depending on whether fees and royalties have to follow the ownership pattern. Thus, at most, $T(3N^2 - N - 1)$ flows will have to be calculated. There are direct and indirect costs associated with each transfer, which decrease the liquidity of the corporation (even government irritation must be paid for with legal fees and "political contributions"). These are referred to as "factors of attenuation." The model aids to minimize these costs. The problem is a generalized network (also called weighted distribution, or machine loading problem). Dantzig (1963, Chapter 21) presents an excellent discussion of the generalized network problem. Extremely fast computer algorithms have been developed by Balachandran and Thompson (1975).

Because of the power relationships within a corporation, it is prudent to begin to implement control over liquid assets by modeling variables over which headquarters already has control (dividends and fees). Once a dividend and fee model has been proven in use, headquarters can proceed to model intersubsidiary loans and adjusted transfer prices and to implement the models in a prudent and consistent manner. We now consider each of the four transfer methods in detail. Although the power, control, and political implications of adjusted transfer prices are onerous, the data analysis is the most simple, hence we begin with this method. Conversely, to implement changes in the dividend policy is quite easy, but to analyze it is difficult; hence we will analyze dividends last.

Adjusted Transfer Prices $A(p_{ij}^t)$

Suppose subsidiary i manufactures certain subassemblies that are shipped to subsidiary j. Simultaneously, subsidiary j manufactures other subassemblies which it ships to i. From economic theory we know that if the transfer price is the marginal cost, then decentralized rational decisions will accord with the interests of the overall corporation. In Chapter 6 we calculate the delivered marginal cost of each item in monthly detail; an annualized figure, however, is adequate for maneuvering. It is on the basis of these low transfer prices that the b_i^t should be estimated.

To move funds from i to j we could raise the transfer price on items being shipped from j to i (transfer prices on items shipped from i to j are already on their floor and cannot be lowered). A change in the liquidity, $A(p_{ij}^t)$, is incurred by raising the transfer price on shipments from j to i:

$$A(P_{ij}^t) = \text{forecast exchange rate} \times \text{(any export tariff by } j$$
$$+ \text{ income tax rate in } j)$$
$$+ \text{ import tariff in } i - \text{income tax rate in } i$$

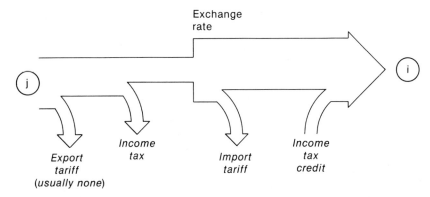

EXHIBIT 3.10
The factor of attenuation on transfer price manipulation $A(p_{ij}^t)$.

Suppose we have been shipping an item from j to i with a transfer price of $10. The tariff rate on items of this class is 10 percent, so the cost to subsidiary i is $10 + 0.10($10) = $11. The company now raises the transfer price to $11, which is an increase of 10 percent. The new cost to subsidiary i is the new transfer price plus the new import duty, which is now $11 + 0.10($11) = $12.10, which is an increase of 10 percent over the previous cost. Hence in Exhibit 3.11 the cost curve segments are linear.

All items being shipped from j to i should be ranked by their rates of duty, and their prices should be manipulated in sequence; that is, the price of the lowest duty item would be raised to its upper bound before the price of the item with the next highest duty would be raised. The upper bound has to be set subjectively, with an eye to avoiding investigations. Thus if a company has two items, one with a 10 percent rate of duty and one with a 20 percent rate, the price of the item with 10 percent duty would be raised first. Fixed (not *ad valorem*) tariffs do not change with the transfer price, so these items should be adjusted first. In Exhibit 3.11(A), each segment of the curve represents the cost of the transfer price adjustment to a different item — each item has a different tariff rate. Thus the first segment represents the costs associated with adjustments in transfer price for an item with tariff rate of 10 percent and the next segment represents items with tariff rate of 20 percent. It can be seen that the total cost of maneuvering assets is higher for items with higher tariff rates. (Export tariffs are rare. Where they exist the ranking of products should be by the total of the tariffs to be paid.)

Exhibit 3.11(C) represents the marginal cost curve corresponding to the total costs in Exhibit 3.11(A). The marginal cost of adjusting a transfer price could easily be negative — total costs would be reduced by raising the price of this item to its upper bound. To illustrate, suppose subsidiary j is shipping goods to subsidiary i. There is no income tax in j, but i has an income tax rate of 75 percent. The item being shipped is exempt from all import and export duties. If the transfer price of the item is raised,

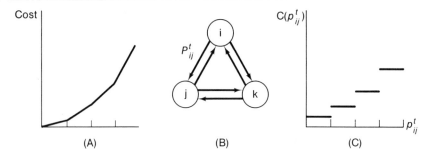

EXHIBIT 3.11

Maneuvering assets by means of adjusting transfer prices. (A = total cost of adjusting transfer prices on shipments from j to i; B = cash flows through the arcs; C = marginal cost of adjusting transfer prices.)

income increases in j (zero tax) but decreases in i (75 percent tax). This results in lower taxes paid to the world. Therefore the cost of flowing funds through the p_{ij} arc $A(p_{ij}^t)$ is decreased by increasing the transfer price when the marginal cost is negative.

If each subsidiary is a semiautonomous profit center, there is a possibility that cooperation among subsidiaries could give way to competition. A bilateral monopoly relationship is possible between i and j. When one manufacturing plant (monopolist) is the only source for one marketing outlet (monopsonist), the dynamics of transfer pricing from the manufacturer to the marketer frequently escalate so high that the marketer ends up charging his customers a price higher than that which a joint monopolist would charge. In other words, the consumers suffer, and the manufacturer and marketer divide a profit pie that is unnecessarily small. An imposed transfer price will work as long as producing-to-demand remains in the self-interest of subsidiary i. There are two internal indirect costs to flow through a P_{ij} arc.

One indirect cost lies in the profit forgone by subsidiary i as it tailors its promotional efforts to its cost of goods, which is partly the manipulated transfer price. (There is a temptation to do this in a polycentric corporation when each subsidiary is an independent entity and when it is evaluated on its return on investment.) Clearly the costs of acrimony over negotiated and imposed transfer prices are greatly reduced if unit sales and production quotas are set centrally.

The other external indirect costs arise from government inquiries. If the price is too low, both governments will intervene. The tax authorities of country j will see tax revenues forgone (in the United States, I.R.S., Section 482; see the 1967 Court of Claims case against Eli Lilly and Company). The import tariff commission of country i will see dumping. If the transfer price is too high, income tax will be forgone by country i. These external indirect costs have to be paid in the time and effort at investigatory hearings, additional advertising to counter ill-will, and actual settlements.

Several governments have tried to define a fair transfer price. The U.S. Treasury Department regulations specify that an arm's-length price be used. The Treasury Department lists four methods to be used in sequence:

1. Comparable Uncontrolled Price Method. Monitor the prices of sales between unrelated corporations and use those. Differences in the quantity sold, quality, terms, use of trademarks or brand names, time of sale, level of the market, and geography of the market may be grounds for claiming that the sale is not comparable. Gradation adjustments can easily be made for freight and insurance but cannot accurately be made for trademarks.
2. Resale Price Method. The transfer price equals the resale price minus a standard markup. There is considerable leeway in determining a standard markup.
3. Cost Plus Method. No definition of full cost is given, nor is there a unique formula for prorating shared costs over joint products. The markup over cost allows room for maneuvering.
4. Another Appropriate Method. The Treasury regulations explicitly state that while a new market is being established it is legitimate to charge a lower transfer price: "It is specifically provided in the regulations that goods may be sold, for a period, at a price which is below the full cost of manufacture in order to establish or maintain a market."

The North American concern with transfer prices, in the corporate income tax context, implies a concern that foreign companies bear their "fair share" of the tax. In Europe, revenue is raised by a value added tax, similar to a North American sales tax but applied on all intermediate transactions, not just on sales to the final consumer. Mathewson and Quirin (1978) note that the tax philosophies of the European Economic Community (EEC) countries differ from those of North America in an important respect:

> The basic thrust of Europe in tax legislation, at least in recent years, has been to define a tax base which is coextensive with the domestic population. This is most clearly seen in the application of the value added tax (VAT) in which export sales are exempt while VAT paid on all domestic purchases may be claimed as a credit against tax payable on domestic content of export sales from VAT. While the Europeans are willing to have foreigners contribute to domestic tax revenues via corporate income taxes on exports, one suspects that faced with a choice between the tax revenues and the exports, they would expect to find that the constraints imposed by E.E.C. members on transfer pricing involving exports from the E.E.C. to be of minimal significance.

One technique used in practice to increase transfer prices without inviting government reaction is to invoice the goods through a chain of subsidiaries, each of which adds its commission. For example, consider a load of lubricants shipped directly from the U.S. refinery of a large oil com-

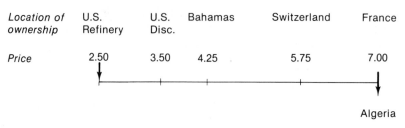

EXHIBIT 3.12
Chaining invoices to adjust asset flows.

pany to the company's marketing subsidiary in Algeria. The chain of invoices, however, might indicate that ownership flowed from the U.S. refinery through its Domestic International Sales Corporation to its subsidiaries in the Bahamas, Switzerland, and France, to the marketing company in Algeria, as in Exhibit 3.12. These increasing prices are of course the transfer prices of each paper transaction.

All shipments invoiced out of one country are charged the same price (hence there is no apparent discrimination), and the final subsidiary is invoiced from the link that delivers the transfer price deemed appropriate. Suppose the corporation also has a subsidiary in the Azores that would actually lose money if the transfer price were $7. The corporation might decide to avoid an Azores government investigation by allowing its Azores subsidiary a token profit. If the transfer price must be below $5 for a profit to be shown, the Azores would have to be invoiced from the Bahamas as shown in Exhibit 3.12. A corporation may have several branching chains of trading companies, usually following historical relationships, in order to give the chains credibility.

Fees and Royalties $A(f^t_{ij})$

Managerial advice, allocated headquarters overhead, and royalties on patents and trademarks are nebulous and difficult to price. Hence they can be suitable conduits through which to move funds. For example, a royalty, which is a fee for the use of patents held by headquarters, is charged to the subsidiary just as it would be to an arm's-length company. It could be determined on at least four different bases.

1. A specified number of cents per pound of output.
2. A specified percentage of the sales price.

3. A fixed sum per annum (perhaps together with 1 or 2).
4. The ongoing cost of the corporate R & D facility is allocated to all production units on the basis of their pounds of production.

If these royalties are a tax-deductible business expense in country i, then a tax saving will occur if the royalty is increased. Hence it may be profitable to consider the most suitable of these four bases for computing the royalties. However, fees and royalties may not be tax deductible, and some nations impose a withholding tax. If fees and royalties received from abroad are taxable as income in country j, then there is a tax cost. For example, in the Paisley case, the U.K. subsidiary is currently owned by Genmarc in France. Pursuant to the French–British tax treaty, the U.K. government would impose no withholding tax on the royalties. If the site of Genmarc were moved to Luxembourg, the French income tax would be saved but the tax on royalties would now become 5 percent.

There will likely be an indirect cost to any increase in fees and royalties. A Minister of Finance struggling to keep capital from flowing out of the country will be more likely to intervene if the announced formula is changed.

The computational procedure is as follows: For each subsidiary j, prepare a list of every conceivable fee, royalty, or allocatable expense of that subsidiary. Eliminate those that are not tax deductible in nation i or in nation j. For each fee, calculate the amount of funds that would flow each year. Also calculate the percentage tax cost (income and withholding taxes) and sequence the flows by total tax cost. Then resequence the flows in terms of the probability that their *omission* would be noticed by officials in either nation i or j, given that fees have previously been calculated on another basis. Where the use of one fee necessitates reporting another, combine these two and sequence them by their weighted average tax rate.

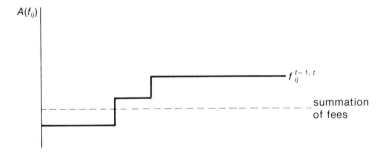

EXHIBIT 3.13
Summation of fees sequenced by their transfer cost.

The costs indicated in Exhibit 3.13 will be incorporated into the linear programming generalized network model. Once the network problem has been run, we can study the period-to-period variations in the fee flows. We can then adjust the fees and find the allocation methods that produce the flows that best fit those required by the model. We then rerun the program to fit the definition.

Intersubsidiary Loans $A(l_i^{t}, {}_j^{t+1})$

The most prevalent form of intersubsidiary loan is a speed-up or delay in invoicing shipments between a pair of subsidiaries. This may be done because normal terms of payment differ between the two nations, because of tax savings in some cases, or to bypass restrictions on remittances. In addition, actual shipping schedules can be accelerated in one direction and decelerated in the other so that one subsidiary carries inventory for both.

Most amounts due from affiliates on open account are generally required to bear interest after six months, unless zero interest can be shown to be a regular trade practice. Even within such bounds, the leading and lagging of the invoices on imports and exports can create a substantial loan. Where desirable, the company can institute a program of netting, whereby all intercorporate payables and receivables flow only to the net creditors of the corporate group. By netting, a company can:

1. Reduce its exchange purchases.
2. Provide a more flexible means of controlling its overall liquidity picture.
3. Allow for a more timely analysis of the company's foreign exchange exposure.

Exhibit 3.14 prepared by *Business International* provides a consolidation of the limits granted by major countries.

Unless there are specific laws to the contrary, one subsidiary has the right to grant a formal loan to a subsidiary in another nation and to be repaid with interest. Years ago, some corporations abused this right and had subsidiaries make zero-interest loans with no specified maturity. Such loans look so similar to dividends (but are not taxed) that tax authorities are now on the alert for "deemed dividends." Hence a loan must have a reasonable interest rate and a reasonable repayment date. Where there is leeway as to reasonableness of interest rate, the treasurer can select either the minimum or the maximum to minimize total taxes (we discuss taxes later in this section).

In determining the actual amount of funds a subsidiary will need to borrow each year, it is not sufficient to look only at the net cash deficiency of that year alone.

EXHIBIT 3.14

Limits on Leads and Lags and Netting in Major Countries*

(Periods Given Are Maximum Possible Terms.)

Country	Export Lag	Export Lead	Import Lag	Import Lead	Netting
Australia	180 days	Not allowed	180 days	Not allowed	Permission required
Belgium	180 days	90 days	180 days	90 days	Permission required but readily available
Brazil	Not allowed	Allowed-no limit	180 days	Not allowed[a]	Not permitted
Canada	Allowed-no limit	Allowed-no limit	Allowed-no limit	Allowed-no limit	Permitted
France	180 days[b]	Allowed-no limit	90 days[c]	Not allowed[d]	Permission required but difficult
Germany	Allowed-no limit	Allowed-no limit	Allowed-no limit	Allowed-no limit	Permitted
Italy	90 days	360 days	360 days	30 days	Not permitted[e]
Japan	180 days[f]	180 days[f]	120 days	120 days	Not permitted[g]
Mexico	Allowed-no limit	Allowed-no limit	Allowed-no limit	Allowed-no limit	Permitted
Netherlands	Allowed-no limit	Allowed-no limit	Allowed-no limit	Allowed no limit	Permitted
Spain	90 days	180 days	180 days[h]	Not allowed[i]	Permission required but difficult
South Africa	180 days	Allowed-no limit	Allowed-no limit	Not allowed	Not permitted except with special permission
Sweden	180 days	Allowed-no limit	180 days	Not allowed[j]	Permission required but readily available
United Kingdom	180 days	Allowed-no limit	Allowed-no limit	Not allowed	Permitted
United States	Allowed-no limit	Allowed-no limit	Allowed-no limit	Allowed-no limit	Permitted

*Based on information from local banking sources.
[a]Except with special authorization of exchange department of central bank for a maximum of 25% of value of imports; [b]but usually depends on terms of agreement; [c]except for raw materials, which have a maximum of 180–360 days' lag time; [d]except for 30% down payment on imported capital goods; [e]Italian exchange office of Foreign Trade Ministry can authorize exceptions. Offsetting debits and credits can be effected by banks only when two different companies are involved, except for oil companies; [f]but exporters can legally make use of 360 days for both leads and lags of exports less than $500,000; [g]except for so-called "invisible" items, such as trade-related expenses; [h]includes 90-day grace period and longer lags are permitted; [i]except with very special permission or when 25% down payment is required for placement of order; [j]except if over Skr50,000 if prepayment is in accordance with normal commercial practice.

An analogy will help clarify this statement. Suppose your parents loan you money to attend college and charge 10 percent interest. On graduation, principal plus interest totals $10,000. Intending to study for an MBA, you estimate that your need for additional liquidity will be $5,000 the first year and $6,000 the second year. Finally, suppose that your parents insist on one-year loans but grant new loans immediately. How big will each loan be?

0. Now, at year 0, you need to repay the $10,000 debt and obtain $5,000 more. So borrow $15,000.
1. At the end of year 1 you will need to repay the capital of $15,000, interest on it of $1,500, and obtain new liquidity of $6,000. So borrow $22,500.
2. On graduation at the end of year 2 you will need to repay the capital of $22,500 and its interest of $2,250. Assuming that you have a job after graduation you will not need new liquidity, but because you have not yet accumulated funds to pay off your debt, you need to borrow $24,750.

In this example your needs for liquidity flows of $5,000 and $6,000 had to be reconstituted into loans of $15,000, $22,500, and $24,750. After the maneuvering network is solved, a separate calculation will reconstitute loans from the liquidity flows calculated in the maneuvering network. Unfortunately the interest on intersubsidiary loans gives rise to taxes, which reduce liquidity.

Suppose in year 1 subsidiary j is due to receive interest income from subsidiary i. Nation i may impose a withholding tax on interest paid abroad. Nation j may impose a withholding tax on interest received from abroad. Both withholdings may be reduced by a tax treaty between nations i and j. If subsidiary j pays taxes (it won't if it experiences a loss or consumes unused tax credits), its revenue authorities may or may not tax interest income from abroad. Usually tax will be charged, but only partial credit (counting the time value of cash) will be allowed for the withholding taxes.

After the loans have been reconstituted from liquidity flows, and the tax implications detailed, we will have to deduct these taxes from liquidity and recompute the optimum. If there are several ways to reconstitute loans, select the one that minimizes global taxes. The maneuvering liquid assets problem is intended to be recalculated every quarter, or at least every year. The patterns of intersubsidiary loans (which determine tax rates) appear relatively stable, so repeated iterations are rarely needed.

Thus far we have talked about intersubsidiary loans as though the exchange rate were forecast to remain unchanged. Suppose A is to receive a loan and pay r_A interest if denominated in A's currency, or r_B if in B's currency. When the loan is made, the exchange rate is one unit of currency $A = e_{AB}^t$ currency B. From Chapter 1 we forecast that when the loan is repaid the exchange rate will be one unit of currency A $= e_{AB}^{t+1}$ currency B, with currency A expected to devalue so that $e_{AB}^{t} > e_{AB}^{t+1}$. If the loan is denominated in the borrowing currency A, then B will show a foreign exchange loss of $e_{AB}^{t} - e_{AB}^{t+1}$ per dollar loaned to A, and an interest income of $e_{AB}^{t+1} r_A$ rather than $e_{AB}^{t} r_A$. Subsidiary B will pay fewer taxes, and saving will be $(e_{AB}^{t} - e_{AB}^{t+1})(1 + r_A)(\text{tax}_B^{t+1})$. If the loan is denominated in currency B, then A will have to pay back the appreciation of both capital and interest. Subsidiary A's tax savings will be $(e_{AB}^{t} - e_{AB}^{t+1})$ $(1 + r_B)(\text{tax}_A^{t+1})$. Thus the choice of denominating the intersubsidiary loan in currency A or B depends on the tax rates and bounds on the allowable rate of interest. The choice does not depend on the extent of devaluation (though it would be reversed if a revaluation were forecast).

Dividends $A(d_{ij})$

If there are N wholly owned subsidiaries, the intersubsidiary ownership pattern is fixed, and $N - 1$ dividend arcs are known. The problem is to estimate the cost function $A(d_{ij})$ for each arc. The cost function (if nonlinear) and the restrictions on dividend flow depend on the tax base. It is presumed that aspects of the tax base internal to each country have been optimized so that in this formulation we need consider only intersubsidiary allocations.

First, the tax laws on dividends for three nations are discussed, starting with the uncomplicated tax laws of Liechtenstein. Though they will not be examined here, local taxes imposed by states, counties, and cantons are substantial enough that they should be included in the cost functions. Tax treaties between pairs of nations should also be studied, especially when a company operates with a foreign corporate charter, a branch, or a more unusual legal entity.

When planning a base company (a tax haven or financial clearing house) in the popular tax haven countries of Surinam, Panama, Liechtenstein, Switzerland, Cayman Islands, and Barbados, usually the most applicable laws are those of the corporate headquarters, the U.S. Revenue Acts of 1962 and 1976 for a U.S. corporation. The combination of these two Revenue Acts is so complicated that several chartered accountancy firms have prepared computer simulations of the tax position of their client corporations. The complications center around the "tainted income." We examine one example, Subpart F income.

Foreign Tax on Dividends $A(d_{ij})$

In Liechtenstein, corporations pay income tax (*Ertragssteuer*). Dividends paid by resident corporations are subject to a 3 percent coupon tax. This is never refunded or permitted to be credited as a cost of doing business. There is no tax on dividends received. No tax treaties that change these provisions currently are in force.

In Belgium, corporations pay income tax (*impôt des sociétés*; *Venootschapsbelasting*) at the rate of 30 percent, but income entering retained earnings is taxed at the rate of 35 percent when retained earnings are above BF5 million (model this as a 5 percent incentive for paying dividends until retained earnings drop to BF5 million. Dividends paid by a resident corporation are subject to an 18.2 percent withholding tax, which is never refunded or permitted to be credited as a cost of doing business (deduct this from the incentive for paying dividends). Of dividends received into Belgium (after any withholding taxes by the government of the sending country), the tax imposed by the Belgian government is 18.7 percent (15 percent Belgian withholding tax plus 30 percent Belgian income tax on 15 percent of the 85 percent that survived Belgian withholding tax). By tax treaty, dividends received from an Italian corporation are exempt from Belgian withholding tax.

West Germany imposes an income tax (*Korperschaftsteuer*) and business tax (*Gewerbesteuer*) on corporations doing business there. A 25 percent withholding tax is placed on dividends paid. Profits not distributed to shareholders are taxed at 51 percent for income tax and 13.5 percent for business tax. Profits distributed to shareholders, however, are taxed at only 15 percent income tax. Dividends received by a German corporation are given a credit against company business tax, but not income tax. The effective tax rate depends, as before, on whether these profits from abroad will be distributed to shareholders.

Let us review dividend taxation with an example. Let the parent company in Liechtenstein own a subsidiary in Germany, which has a subsidiary of its own in Belgium. Let us work up the ownership tree (Exhibit 3.15). The Belgian subsidiary declares a dividend of 100 units to its German parent. The Belgian government has a withholding tax of 18.2 percent, so that 81.80 units arrive in Germany and are converted from francs to deutsche marks. The German business tax, based on the entire dividend of 100, is 13.50 percent, so income net of business tax is 86.50. Company income tax is 15 percent of income net of business tax, that is, $0.15 \times 86.50 = 12.97$. (This rate assumes income will be destined for dividends;

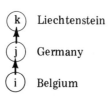

k Liechtenstein

j Germany

i Belgium

EXHIBIT 3.15
Maneuvering assets through dividend payments.

income retained within the firm is taxed at 51 percent.) Only at this point is credit granted for the Belgian withholding tax, so that German company income tax due is $12.97 - 18.20 = -5.23$ units. The Belgian withholding tax was 18.20 units, the German business tax was 13.50 units, and the German company income tax is -5.23. Their total is 26.47 units on a dividend of 100 units. That is to say, only 73.53 percent of the dividend gets through from the Belgian subsidiary to its German parent, and $A(d_{BG}) = 0.2647$.

The German subsidiary uses its dividends received from abroad and its own profits to declare a dividend of 100 units to its parent in Liechtenstein. But the government of Germany imposes a 25 percent withholding tax on dividends leaving Germany, so that 75 units arrive at the parent in Liechtenstein. That nation levies no taxes on dividends received from abroad, nor does it grant tax credits. Thus $A(d_{GL}) = 0.25$.

U.S. Subpart F Income

The United States taxes a certain kind of income earned abroad, even if it is retained abroad. Such Subpart F income consists of nonmanufacturing income (rents, royalties, licensing fees, dividends), and of income from services performed for subsidiaries outside the nation. Subpart F income is precisely defined in Internal Revenue Code Sections 951 (a) (1) (A) (i) and 952.

As long as some of the Subpart F income is repatriated as dividends, there is no Subpart F tax. The table of minimum dividends is set out in IRC 963 (b) (3). The lower the foreign tax rate, the higher the dividend rate must be. If the subsidiary tax rate is 35 percent, the minimum distribution of earnings and profits will be 63 percent. The U.S. government grants a tax credit for taxes paid abroad, so that the total tax does not exceed the U.S. rate of income tax of 48 percent. Unless a minimum distribution is made, the subsidiary's entire Subpart F income is taxed at 48 percent.

Exhibit 3.16 shows that for dividends in excess of the minimum distribution, the per unit cost is the slope of the total tax line. The figure applies to each year; if liquidity must be built up in a subsidiary, a sensible strategy would be to apply minimum distribution to a chain of subsidiaries so that the sum of dividend flows exceeds a prescribed minimum. Such a consolidation is permitted by 963 (c) (2).

The United States is not the only nation to impose such rules as Subpart F. In Canada, for example, rules are specified for Foreign Accrual Property Income (FAPI).

The tax laws of each nation encourage the incorporation of certain kinds of corporations. In the United States, there are corporations such as Domestic International Sales Corporations, Western Hemisphere Trading Corporations, China Trade Act Corporations, and Section 931 corporations which operate in Puerto Rico, the U.S. Virgin Islands, Samoa, and

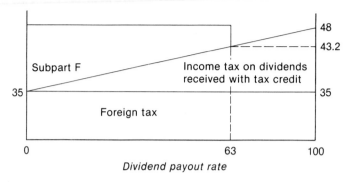

EXHIBIT 3.16
Total taxes as a function of dividend payout rate.

other U.S. holdings. Other nations have similar institutions. Such legal entities of every nation must be analyzed, for they can reduce taxes paid to the world. A corporation without such entities should consider creating them.

Local Loans

In each nation all possible sources of funds should be studied, including the assets that would have to be pledged as security, the amount that could be borrowed, the interest rate (augmented by the opportunity cost of restrictive covenents that bankers impose). Fixed assets such as factories and inventories in a nation are valuable, primarily to local bankers in that nation. Movable assets such as ships can be collateral in almost any nation, so the solution procedure is to guess where they will best be mortgaged and run the problem.

A local loan can be formulated very neatly within the network (Crum, 1974). In one year the bank makes money available. A year later that same amount of money plus interest will be siphoned out of the subsidiary's liquidity, as seen in Exhibit 3.17.

Foreign banks commonly grant loans on an overdraft basis, so that the borrowing company pays interest only on the amount of the granted loan it has in use. In contrast, a U.S. bank grants a line of credit for which it charges a commitment fee. The corporation can borrow up to the line of credit; the borrowing company pays interest on the entire amount of the granted loan (whether or not drawn down from the bank, though often a lower rate is paid on the amount not withdrawn) and furthermore must keep specified compensating balances on deposit in the bank. As the company has to keep transaction and precautionary cash, the compensating balance requirement is not as onerous as it would be in a deterministic world, though it should be reflected in a slight upward adjustment in U.S.

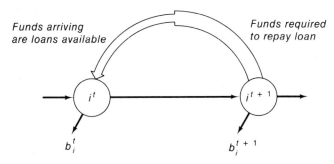

Interest represented in the factor of attenuation

Funds arriving are loans available

Funds required to repay loan

i^t

i^{t+1}

b_i^t

b_i^{t+1}

EXHIBIT 3.17
Local loan makes liquidity available in year t, but its repayment with interest reduces liquidity in year t + 1.

interest rates to make them comparable with foreign "overdraft" interest rates.

Accounts in U.S. dollars held in the bank by the many corporate subsidiaries around the world are generally considered to count toward the compensating balance requirement (depicted by the donuts in Exhibit 3.8):

$$\sum_{i=1}^{N} K_i^{t,\,t+1} \geqslant \text{compensating balance requirement in year } t$$

The sum of subsidiary balances permits the company to arrange a costless partial movement of funds between subsidiaries as the composition of the compensating balance is changed.

The Optimal Capital Structure of a Subsidiary

Accountants know how to consolidate the balance sheets of several subsidiaries into a single corporate consolidated balance sheet. If one subsidiary has borrowed from another subsidiary, the resulting liability of the first subsidiary and asset of the second cancel out in the process of consolidation. Thus the debt/equity ratio usually refers to a consolidated corporation. However, in a multinational corporation each subsidiary is in a different tax jurisdiction. Hence it becomes sensible to plan the debt/equity ratio of each subsidiary to reduce the total taxes paid by them all.

Many governments allow interest to be deducted from net income. Countries impose different withholding taxes on interest and dividends paid to foreigners. The recipient governments frequently differ in their taxation of dividends and interest received from abroad. In general, lowest taxes to the world are paid when the subsidiary's capitalization is mostly debt. Unfortunately, the interest payments on debt are a persistent, non-discretionary flow of funds. They are difficult to manipulate. Whenever the tax advantage of debt is low, headquarters will want to fund its subsidiary with equity in order to have the maneuverability of dividends. This theory suggests that it would be inappropriate to survey for average debt/equity ratios, because an average of a high and a low is not meaningful. Actually, most situations are less clear cut and the sensible approach is to formulate this maneuvering model and simulate different capitalization structures for particular subsidiaries.

Systems within Systems

In the eyes of a treasury official in a nation, one purpose of a corporation is to pay taxes. If the multinational's subsidiary shows no profits on which to pay taxes, treasury officials will probably suspect manipulation. For example, Swedish-owned petroleum companies operating in Sweden showed healthy profits during the late 1960s and early 1970s. The fact that British Petroleum, Gulf, and Esso showed minimal profits provoked the government of Sweden to start investigating these companies. Guilt was presupposed. Mathewson and Quirin (1978) discuss serious constraints on the extent of multinational manipulation. The sensible approach would be to notice such situations in the model's solution and then forcibly increase the amount of tax that would be reported in a particular nation. Many other adjustments take place in the model to meet this constraint optimally. We can then plot the trade-off between the corporate objective function and the amount of taxes paid to a particular country. The point at which to operate then becomes a subjective judgment, cognizant of the various stakeholders and investment decisions that are discussed in Chapter 4.

Maneuvering liquid assets reallocates revenue from high-tax-rate nations to the low-tax-rate nations. If this were all this model did, it would represent a dubious contribution to humankind's knowledge. Fortunately, the model can be run to evaluate the effects of people's ideas by simulating parts of a larger reality. Consider five areas of current interest to international managers.

Short-Term Loan Negotiations, Both Local and Multinational.   The model presented in this chapter is a linear program and therefore has dual variables associated with each constraint. The dual variable associated with b_i^t represents the value at time T of discovering one more unit of liquidity in subsidiary i in year t. The string of T of these dual variables for a given subsidiary can be translated into a term structure of interest rates from which the year-to-year value of additional money can be calculated. Specifically, the one-period interest rate $r^{t,t+1} = u^t/u^{t+1} - 1$, where u is the dual variable. These data provide a very clear guide for making short- and medium-term loans in that nation, even revealing the term structure for medium-term loans. This interest rate can be used as the cost of capital for investment decisions.

Some banks are themselves multinational. In one nation the bank may ration credit because of a high demand for loans within the permitted interest rate. In another part of the world the bank may be short of deposits as it strives to expand. In exchange for depositing money in one part of the bank, the multinational company can negotiate loan priority in another part of the bank. The rationale behind this is that most currencies are blocked and it *may* be easier for a company to move money than it is for a foreign bank. The merit of such induced-swap transactions can be evaluated with this model.

Raising Long-Term Capital. Long-term capital can be raised in most nations, usually after negotiations with the host government and promises that local investments will result. To support such negotiations, worldwide manufacturing models of the type discussed in Chapter 7 must be supplemented by worldwide financial schemes. Similarly, one can evaluate the effects of mergers and divestments.

Restructuring the Pattern of Legal Ownership. If the company has N subsidiaries, there are $(N-1)^2$ different patterns of intersubsidiary ownership possible even if each subsidiary is constrained to have just one legal parent. If one removes the restriction that a subsidiary have one legal parent the tax data required are forbiddingly more complicated and vague than for cases of complete ownership. In practice the model presented in this chapter should stimulate new patterns of intersubsidiary ownership by eliminating some of the drudgery. A subcalculation, about which tax lawyers are well informed, is the benefit of operating in nation i with a corporate charter granted in nation j — operating in Ireland with a Bermuda charter is one possibility.

Inserting High-Profit Products. The Swiss pharmaceutical companies prefer to produce their high-profit products in the nations where they incur their largest cash drains to research and dividends. This practice, a vivid example of Vernon's (1966) product cycle theory, reduces the need to flow funds between nations, though at a high production and transportation cost. Ideally, one would like to simulate the effect of inserting a high-profit product into any subsidiary technically sophisticated enough to manufacture it.

Competitive Analysis. When one corporation plans to overtake another, it usually undertakes a thorough competitive analysis. The competitor's annual report is usually a consolidation of real worldwide operations which the first corporation would like to disaggregate and understand. A corporation that has already created a maneuvering model of itself may consider creating a similar model of its competitor. Although most of the input information is limited to estimates, two kinds of publicly available information have been commercially compiled.

First, the financial statements of most subsidiaries are available. Many governments require publication of the financial statements of each business incorporated and operating in their nation. With diligent work one can collect the subsidiary financial statements of a competitor, and with diligence one can assemble these into a financial model. This work has already been done for almost 100 multinational corporations, in the Source of Earnings Report of the Buttles Corporation (Plandome, New York 11030).

Second, the dividend conduits are available from organization charts. Multinational corporations have frequently evolved numerous subsidiaries and branches in every nation. Verlag Hoppenstedt (D6100 Darmstadt, West Germany) provides a compilation of the percentage ownership between every legal entity, its capitalization, and line of business. U.S. Organization Chart Service Inc. (La Jolla, California 92038), provides organization charts showing not only titles and relationships but also names in over 575 U.S. high-technology corporations.

Implementing the Model in a Polycentric Corporation

To simplify the exposition, this chapter assumes periods of one year. A five-year plan would require five one-year periods. Actually it would be appreciably more useful to model a five-year plan with six periods, made up of two quarters, a half year, two single years, and a two-year period. The model remains as before, but interest rates on borrowings and lendings must be adjusted.

The implementation of a model for maneuvering liquid assets for a large multinational corporation is time-consuming and relatively expensive. The first step is to estimate *pro forma* income statements to determine b_i^t. The second step is for the tax lawyers to estimate the cost of dividends and managerial fees. At this point the model can be run, and the dividend and fee decisions implemented, for they have few organizational ramifications. The third step is to model intersubsidiary loans and each subsidiary's access to its local money market. This involves a centralization of the worldwide treasurer's function and will likely be resisted. Manipulated transfer prices, which strike at the heart of profit center autonomy, should be the last to be implemented.

From the very beginning, and continuing through each step, there must be a task force to set up the data base. This will be the most time-consuming aspect of model implementation. This task force will, of necessity, include tax lawyers, accountants, and financial analysts, as well as systems analysts.

During the early stages of implementation it will be sensible to solve the problem with a familiar linear programming code. Most corporate O.R. analysts are familiar with linear programs, but few have *used* generalized networks (an ordinary network does not include factors of attenuation). Each flow is an activity, and each node is a constraint. Once a "small" problem has been tested and *used* month after month, there will be a push to add more subsidiaries.

Unfortunately, computer costs will become substantial if every legal entity in every nation is modeled. Only at this point is it sensible to switch to a generalized network. The power of the Balachandran–Thompson algorithm is that its systematic parametric programming of the cost coefficients allows analysts to impose constraints that bind several flows. A network formulation is attractive not only because it can be visualized, but also because it can be solved faster than a general linear program. A simple maneuvering liquid assets model can be inexpensively developed. A full model representing 100 subsidiaries may cost $500,000 and require one to three years of task work.

Conclusion

In a multinational company there are many opportunities for maneuvers that take advantage of multinational status. Currently, these are used only rarely, for fear of causing confusion and computational chaos. However, there is a growing acceptance of the concepts considered in this chapter. Several corporations have developed models. For example, Mobil Oil Company in 1970 created a linear programming model called Gnome to handle intersubsidiary liquid capital flows. Gnome was developed to model just one year at a time and to focus on dividends, intersubsidiary loans, and bank loans of all varieties. It was extremely detailed and very useful.

Most of the models now in existence are deterministic and centralized. The additional accuracy of a stochastic approach might not be worth the considerable added cost and computational complexity. Decentralized asset management may be more viable organizationally because the information flows may be more efficient than the centralized approach of this chapter. The existence of differential interest and taxation rates around the world certainly suggests that a global view be taken in order to minimize such things as interest expense and taxes paid to the various governments; however, in a business that is very turbulent, decentralization may be preferable.

Questions from Other Viewpoints

1. *Corporate Rational Normative Global.* You just covered this viewpoint in the chapter.

2. *Corporate Rational Normative Subsidiary.* A subsidiary really has trouble predicting its cash flow. If you have run the model with a best estimate of b_i^t, how would you use the model to advise the subsidiary of the costs of inaccuracy in its forecasts?

3. *Corporate Rational Descriptive Global.* One of the problems with manipulating transfer prices is that decision makers in divisions, striving to maximize their own performance, make decisions as though the transfer prices were real. A solution is to keep two separate sets of transfer prices: one set that is official, the other set for managerial decision making. How would you proceed to investigate the costs and the benefits of two sets of books?

4. *Corporate Rational Descriptive Subsidiary.* What evidence, if any, is there that division managers actually do alter their output decisions because of small changes in some transfer prices?

5. *Corporate Emotional Normative Global.* The frequent revisions of standard operating procedures that are necessary to implement a system of financial maneuverings present two conflicting problems. On the one hand, the divisional managers should be informed of the reasons for the frequent revisions. On the other hand, the more individuals who have access to this information, the greater the risk that the company's tax avoidance schemes will be leaked. What steps can headquarters take to resolve these conflicting problems?

6. *Corporate Emotional Normative Subsidiary.* Radicals are picketing your plant with signs denouncing financial maneuvers. Write a memo to your employees, to be signed by the plant manager. If you deny activities you actually have engaged in, there is probability that someone will pass the word to the pickets.

7. *Corporate Emotional Descriptive Global.* How do you go about firing a manager for poor performance when he says you manipulated transfer pricing against him? If the manager is a woman or a member of a minority and protests the firing to the U.S. Equal Employment Opportunity Commission, what kind of a case could you present?

8. *Corporate Emotional Descriptive Subsidiary.* In polycentric corporations each subsidiary plans for and arranges its own liquidity, coping with all the uncertainty of an underdeveloped banking system. How are these feelings of uncertainty and anxiety different (for the subsidiary treasurer) if he is part of continual geocentric maneuvers?

9. *Societal Rational Normative Global.* The reader may have a sense that the maneuvers of this chapter are immoral. One societal response would be to make them illegal, establish large monitoring staffs, and

be willing to punish offenders. An alternate solution would be to reduce the incentive to maneuver. List and explain which disharmonies between nations would have to be reconciled if the incentives were to be reduced.

10. *Societal Rational Normative Subsidiary.* If a nation would like to increase its tax receipts, usually it would raise the corporate income tax rate. To show the limitations of this method, create an example of a corporation with two manufacturing plants (and no bounds on the transfer price) such that an increase in the tax rate will *reduce* the amount of tax revenue that the nation collects. For your example, plot tax revenue versus tax rate for the one nation, assuming that the other nation does not coordinate action. Under what conditions would there be an incentive for the other nation to coordinate tax policy with the first?

11. *Societal Rational Descriptive Global.* Select three nations (your choice) for which adequate balance of payments data are available. Make a four-by-four table, the column and row headings being your three nations and "other." In each cell list the national balance of payment items that cause funds to flow from each row nation to each column nation.

12. *Societal Rational Descriptive National.* Under what criteria would a nation choose to instigate an investigation and possibly prosecute multinational corporations suspected of maneuvering liquid assets? You might compare your measurement criteria with Fowler (1978).

13. *Societal Emotional Normative Global.* Draw an angry poster of a corporation maneuvering liquid assets. Alternatively, listen carefully to radio or television advertising jingles and adopt the tune of one to mock maneuvering liquid assets.

14. *Societal Emotional Normative National.* A country's reaction to an attempt to maneuver liquid assets will depend on the country's economic status and the way assets are flowing. What steps could a government treasury minister take to encourage the flow of liquid assets from his economically rich country to politically friendly developing nations, while discouraging asset flows to hostile nations? Under what conditions is it important that these steps either be unnoticed or appear consistent?

15. *Societal Emotional Descriptive Global.* Many people believe there is something vaguely sinister about Eurodollars, EuroYen, and the like. This feeling may have important repercussions if held by a Foreign Minister (Secretary of State, Minister of External Affairs). To have such an individual listen to your rational explanation, you must *first* address and satisfy his emotional doubts. Interview two students who are not majoring in economics or business and with their help list four sinister feelings about Eurocurrencies, two that you can answer and two for which you have trouble satisfying your emotional doubts.

16. *Societal Emotional Descriptive National.* Your nation is identified as a tax haven in the advisory newsletters written for multinational treasurers. You are Minister of Finance and your cabinet colleagues are always pressuring for expansionary programs that will require more tax revenue. Lately, the Minister of Education suggested expanding the national university. In your past encounters with him, he has never had any interest in economics. Describe the nonfinancial benefits your nation gains from being a tax haven. Draft a concise memo.

Bibliography to Chapter 3

Balachandran, Venkataraman and Gerald L. Thompson, "An Operator Theory of Parametric Programming for the Generalized Transportation Problem," *Naval Research Logistics Quarterly*, Vol. 22, No. 1 (1975). pp. 79–125.

Burns, Jane O., "Transfer Pricing Decisions in U.S. Multinational Corporations," *Journal of International Business Studies*, Vol. 11, No. 2 (1980), pp. 23–39.

Crum, Roy L., "Cash Allocation in the Multinational Firm: A Constrained Generalized Network Approach," Doctoral Dissertation, University of Texas at Austin, August 1974.

Dantzig, George B., *Linear Programming and Extensions* (Princeton: Princeton University Press, 1963).

Eiteman, David K. and Arthur I. Stonehill, *Multinational Business Finance*, 2nd ed. (Reading, MA: Addison-Wesley, 1979), esp. Chapter 11.

Eli Lilly & Company v. *The United States*, 372 F. 2d 990, 178 Court of Claims [No. 293-61, Decided February 17, 1967], pp. 666–733.

Fowler, D.J., "Transfer Prices and Profit Maximization in Multinational Enterprise Operations," *Journal of International Business Studies*, Vol. 9, No. 3 (1978), pp. 9–26.

Mathewson, J. Frank and G. David Quirin, "Economics of Fiscal Transfer Pricing in Multinational Corporations," A Study Prepared for the Ontario Economic Council, Toronto 1978.

Merville, L.J. and J. Petty, "Transfer Pricing for the Multinational Firm," *Accounting Review*, Vol. 53, No. 4 (1978), pp. 935–951.

"Multinational Corporations and Income Allocation Under Section 482 of the Internal Revenue Code," *Harvard Law Review*, Vol. 89, 1976, pp. 1202–1238.

Reier, Sharon, "IBM's Science of Simplification," *Institutional Investor*, Vol. 14, No. 11 (1980) pp. 219–220.

Robbins, Sidney M. and Robert B. Stobaugh, "Multinational Companies: Growth of the Financial Function," *Financial Executive*, Vol. 41, July 1973. pp. 24–31.

Rodriguez, Rita M. and E. Eugene Carter, *International Financial Management* (Englewood Cliffs, N.J.: Prentice-Hall, 1976); esp. Chapter 8.

Rutenberg, David P., "Maneuvering Liquid Assets in a Multinational Company: Formulation and Deterministic Solution Procedures," *Management Science*, Vol. 16, No. 10 (1970). pp. B671–B684.

Seghers, Paul D., *How to Do Business Abroad at Least Tax Cost*, Englewood Cliffs, N.J.: Prentice-Hall, 1964.

Shapiro, Alan C., "Payments Netting in International Cash Management," *Journal of International Business Studies*, Vol. 9, No. 2 (1978), pp. 51-58.

Shulman, James, "When the Price is Wrong — By Design," *Columbia Journal of World Business*, Vol. 2 No. 3, May–June 1967, pp. 69-76.

Vernon, Raymond, "International Investment and International Trade in the Product Cycle," *Quarterly Journal of Economics*, Vol. 30, May 1966, pp. 24-35.

Wentz, Roy A., "Corporate Transfers of Intangible Abroad," *Tax Executive*, April 1967, pp. 142-159.

Multinational Expansion to a New Nation

Introductory Note to the Case

Michelin Tires Manufacturing Co. of Canada Ltd.

Many different groups have a stake in the outcome when a foreign corporation contemplates a significant investment in a nation. To a corporate planner it is a useful, even necessary, exercise to stand in the shoes of each stakeholder and evaluate the impact of the investment. It's the first step to a game theory understanding of the problem.

In 1968 France was convulsed by riots. Many wealthy French families felt that France would turn Communist. Demonstrations opposing the Vietnam war took place daily in the United States, but in general North America appeared to be a relative haven for long-term capital, while short-term money went to Switzerland.

How much could a Michelin planner have known about the United States and Canada?

1. *The U.S. tire companies had been expanding aggressively in Europe, but to sell nonradial tires they had been forced to slash prices.*
2. *B.F. Goodrich had commercialized radial tires in 1963 but U.S. automakers insisted on having at least two suppliers for each purchased component and so had refused to buy. Goodrich had been left with severe overcapacity.*
3. *The U.S. and Canadian governments had signed an Auto Pact, allowing General Motors, Ford, Chrysler, and American Motors, the four automakers to treat North America as one production unit by eliminating import duties. The*

pact did not cover automobile components, batteries, or tires, although this expansion was contemplated by some officials.

Michelin Tires Manufacturing Co. of Canada Ltd.

In July 1969, the Compagnie Générale des Establissements Michelin of Claremont-Ferrand, France, announced that it would establish production facilities in Nova Scotia, Canada — its first such sortie in the Western Hemisphere. Initial output would be steel tire cord and steel-belted radial truck tires. It was expected that some 85 percent of the latter would be exported to the U.S. market while the rest would be slated for Canada, South America, and the Caribbean. Nova Scotian government officials and politicians were overjoyed at the news of the substantial planned investment and the creation of 1,300 jobs. Their happiness increased when, less than three years later, the company announced an intended $40 million expansion. This would add facilities for making passenger radials and would create another 1,300 jobs.

The Michelin investment in Canada was induced by major grants and other forms of assistance from federal, local, and provincial governments. In discussing the details, Nova Scotia's Finance Minister Peter Nicholson, said there was "nothing new or strange in this day and age for international companies such as Michelin to be given incentives of various types. Countries all over the world were offering incentives and few eyebrows were raised."

Nicholson failed to anticipate the reaction of the powerful American tire and rubber lobby. In February 1972 this organization initiated a complaint with the U.S. Treasury Department, which instituted an investigation to determine whether the Canadian government assistance to Michelin constituted a "bounty or grant" in violation of U.S. laws, deserving of tariff retaliation.

The Michelin Organization

Michelin took out its first patent on the pneumatic tire in 1891, regularly introducing innovations thereafter. The two

This case was prepared by Professor Donald Thain of the University of Western Ontario and is reprinted with his permission. Copyright by the University of Western Ontario.

most recent and most important were the radial tire in 1948 and the assymmetric tire for high-speed driving in 1965.

From the start Michelin had been a family company. One of its most obvious characteristics was secretiveness. For example, to maintain security during the erection of its Nova Scotia plants, Michelin had brought its own construction crews from France and had paid the Nova Scotian Federation of Labour a large amount — $250,000 by one report — to compensate for not hiring local workers.

The secrecy surrounding Michelin had not obscured its financial success, however. Although reported figures were inadequate for complete analysis, Michelin's operating margin appeared to be about 13 percent. In addition, the company had a record of steadily rising profits, unlike the four U.S. giants — Goodyear, Firestone, Uniroyal, and Goodrich — and also unlike its chief European rival, Dunlop-Pirelli. By 1969 Michelin's tire sales exceeded U.S.$1 billion in value. In Europe alone, where it ranked first in tire sales, it employed more than 70,000 persons. The Michelin group of companies was totally self-financing. In 1969, its internal sources of funds, including posttax profits and reserves, amounted to more than U.S.$120 million. These figures did not include Michelin holdings in the Citroen automobile and Kleber-Columbes companies, concerns independently managed and registered on the Paris Stock Exchange.

In its strategy, Michelin was known to stress quality control and market planning but was believed to give top priority to technical research, analysis, and development. Thus it was credited with "radializing" most of the world's tire markets outside the United States, while U.S. interest, too, was clearly growing. In August 1971, U.S. market trends were assessed as follows:

> Radial tires, long popular in Europe, are experiencing a wave of interest that could eventually lead to incorporation on most if not all U.S. cars. While this is not likely in the near future, some 5% of replacement tires sold in 1970 were of the radial type, and projections indicate that by 1975 over 10% of the replacement market and a somewhat larger percentage of original equipment (OE) will be of the radial type.

Regardless of the reason, the Michelin radial enjoyed a reputation as the world's premier automobile tire, and in 1971 it accounted for 80 percent of Michelin's production. Understandably, the company's early commitment to radials gave it an advantage over competitors, who faced the necessity of using an increasing proportion of their resources for conversion to radial production. In the United States, for example, tiremakers were said to fear that a change to radials might cost them as much as $600 million.

Michelin's decision to offer radials in the U.S. market through plants located in Nova Scotia was to touch off a series of complex interactions among governments, business, and labor in Canada and the United States.

The Canadian Operation

The story of Michelin's Canadian venture was one of quiet political maneuvering on an international scale. A central figure was Robert Manuge, executive vice president of Industrial Estates Ltd. (IEL), a Crown Corporation which was the industrial development agency of the Province of Nova Scotia. IEL had been organized in 1957 to induce secondary manufacturing to settle in Nova Scotia. It was empowered to lend as much as 100 percent of the cost of land and buildings and at least 60 percent on machinery, all at current interest rates. Up to 1971, IEL's clients had numbered 70 companies. Of this total, 17 had either sold out or ceased operations entirely, but 80 percent had survived. The biggest blots on IEL's record were investment decisions that had committed $20 million to a plant for hi-fi equipment and $120 million to a plant for producing heavy water. (These amounts included large cost overruns.) The disappointing outcome of these ventures was one factor disposing IEL to seek ways of recouping its position. As one Canadian paper later put it, "It was no secret that the Michelin deal might go some way in getting IEL management off the hook."

Following a chance airplane contact, in December 1967, Manuge wrote to Michelin setting out the advantages of a Nova Scotia location to serve both U.S. and Canadian markets. Michelin's reply stated that the company was interested, but that negotiations must be secret. In February 1968, Manuge began "Project Y," a series of negotiations involving over 40 trans-Atlantic flights. Few of his colleagues were aware of the real nature of this project, and all visits by Michelin officials to IEL were carefully disguised. At the same time, a New York lawyer was carrying on an investigation with IEL on behalf of an undisclosed client about the possibilities of locating in Nova Scotia. Much later, Manuge discovered that the lawyer had been retained by Michelin to establish IEL's veracity and competence.

On July 28, 1969, Frank H. Sobey, president of IEL, announced that the negotiations with Michelin had been successfully concluded. The company was to establish two plants in Nova Scotia: a steel cord plant in the town of Bridgewater and a truck tire factory in the town of Granton. The first was expected to cost $10 million and to employ 500 workers within three years. It would sell its output to the second, which was expected to cost $41.4 million and to employ 800 within a three-year span. (Cost overruns later brought these plant investment figures to $22.5 million and $62 million for Bridgewater and Granton, respectively. The value of the U.S. and Canadian dollars were then almost equal.)

By the time the new plants were announced, the story of Michelin's negotiations had already leaked to the press, having broken early in 1969, or shortly after Nova Scotia had approached the Federal Government for assistance. Two other provincial governments had also made advances to the company, and these were naturally much disappointed. The mainly French Province of Quebec had even tried a last-ditch effort to secure the Michelin plants for itself by appealing to French President Charles de Gaulle, but this effort had been without effect. According to a Quebec government source, François Michelin was so bitterly opposed to de Gaulle's love affair with Quebec that it was almost impossible for Michelin even to discuss a plant for Quebec.

The Agreements

Before completing their negotiations, Michelin and Nova Scotia had arranged for financial support from provincial, local, and national governments, as seen in Exhibit 4.1. Besides quantifiable loans and grants totaling about $85 million, Michelin would get three other kinds of assistance, the value of which could not be precisely measured. These three would come from the Federal Government and would be additional to the tabulated Federal grants, which were payable under the Area Development Incentives Act (ADIA).

Also provided under the ADIA was an accelerated depreciation, against income taxes payable, of the capital cost of land and buildings. The company could write off the building costs at 20 percent per year and the machinery at 50 percent per year, profits permitting.

Moreover, Michelin also would be allowed to import much of its manufacturing machinery duty-free, under tariff item

EXHIBIT 4.1

Support for Michelin

Source	Type of Assistance	Amount ($ millions)	Terms
Nova Scotia (IEL)	10-year loan	$34.0	6 percent interest
	18-year loan	16.0	6 percent interest
	Grant (capital costs)	5.0	—
	Grant (employee training)	2.6	—
Granton	10-year tax reduction from 2.1 percent of assessment to 1.0 percent	2.475[a]	—
Bridgewater	10-year tax reduction from 3.7 percent of assessment to 1.0 percent	16.794[a]	—
	Donation of site	0.001	
Federal Government	Cash grants		Payable on achievement of commercial production levels
	To Granton	5.0[b]	
	To Bridgewater	3.07[b]	
Total		$84.94	

[a]Assumes 100 percent assessment of actual $22.5 million cost in Granton and $62.2 million in Bridgewater. Ignores adjustments for present value and imputed interest on tax savings.
[b]Federal cash grants were payable under the Area Development Incentives Act of 1964. Amounts depended on the value of investment made and the number of jobs created. Areas eligible to receive the grants were designated on the basis of employment statistics, non-farm-family income, and income distribution.

427001–1 (the Machinery Program), provided such machinery fell within the scope of this tariff item and was of a type not available from production in Canada.

Finally, Michelin would be granted the right to import certain tires into Canada duty-free for a period of three years. The imported tires had to be of a type and size not produced by Michelin in Canada, and the offer was conditional upon the duty-free privilege not disrupting the operations of existing tire producers in Canada. In the absence of this provision, all Michelin tires imported into Canada would have been charged the normal rate of duty on tires, which was 17.5 percent. (For tires reexported to the United States, a duty-drawback was available, although of course such tires would be charged the U.S. duty, which was 4.0 percent.)

It was believed in some quarters that if Canada had not agreed to compensate Michelin for the amount of duty payable on imports, the company might have planned a different and less efficient product mix: It would probably have produced a lower volume and tires of a greater variety of types and sizes, which might have reduced the employment opportunities offered by the project as well as its efficiency. The government was attracted by the fact that this would be an industrial development project rationalized to meet the standards of world competition. Michelin would manufacture certain types and sizes of truck tires in Canada, and other types and sizes of truck, passenger car, and light commercial vehicle tires would be supplied from other plants. Michelin's Canadian market was of course not large enough to warrant manufacture in Canada solely for the domestic market, but the import provisions would allow long production runs, thereby assuring that the Nova Scotia plant would remain competitive on an international basis.

In seeking assistance, Michelin officials made it clear that they were not asking for special treatment or benefit; they would have no objection to the same arrangement being made with other Canadian tire manufacturers and they had no objection to the tariff on tires being reduced or removed. This latter course was unacceptable to the Federal Government, however, since time was lacking to assess its impact on the total industry.

As a rule, federal assistance in the form of ADIA grants, accelerated depreciation, and duty-free imports under the Machinery Program were available to all qualifying companies. Assistance in the form of tariff remissions was less common, but it had been granted for many years in circumstances where the government considered it appropriate. It was available, however, only by a special Order in Council. Michelin had been promised such an Order in a confidential letter, written by the Federal Government's Minister of Finance Edgar Benson, with the approval of his Cabinet colleagues. Although this letter was imprecise as to the date when the duty-free privilege would begin, it was implied that the time would be no later than the start of Michelin's Canadian production.

Production from the steel cord plant began June 30, 1971, and the first steel-belted tire rolled off the Granton line on October 28, 1971. At the time, the combined plants represented the largest secondary manufacturing investment ever made in the Western Hemisphere by a European company.

Industry Reactions

So far as the rest of Canada's tire industry was concerned, early news about Michelin caused little stir. For one thing, the company was concentrating on truck tires, a relatively small segment of the tire market. For another, competition had heard with pleasure of delays in Michelin deliveries and start-up troubles at the plants. Thus little serious thought had been given to the long-term implications of Michelin's arrival.

This complacency was to disappear in January 1970, when a Federal Government official informed the president of the Rubber Association of Canada (RAC) of everything the government was doing for Michelin. After listening in "stunned silence," RAC's President W.V. Turner asked some questions to ensure that he understood completely and then reported back to the industry. Company managements were said to be shocked: They saw the Michelin arrangements not only as a source of increased competition but also as a betrayal of the other tire companies by the government.

The Canadian Tire Industry

The Canadian tire industry was almost entirely foreign-owned: Of six major companies, five had U.S. parents and one had a European parent. These six foreign-owned subsidiaries were Goodyear, Goodrich, Firestone and Uniroyal of Canada, Mansfield-Denman-General Ltd., and Dunlop Canada Ltd. Among them the six had eleven plants, all but one located in the populous southeast central provinces of Ontario and Quebec. The eleventh plant was located in the Western province of Alberta.

Neither the government nor the industry reported much dollar data on tires. Rather, many published statistics lumped tires with the rest of the rubber industry, including rubber footwear and miscellaneous rubber products. Taken altogether, in 1972 the rubber industry accounted for about 0.85% of Canada's GDP ($888 million out of $104.8 billion). It also accounted for roughly 1.5% of Canada's manufacturing employees, wage and salary payments, gross output and value added.

Trade statistics available for tires showed that imports were larger and growing faster than exports in both Canada and the United States. In the opinion of industry spokesmen, the import threat was certain to increase. Canada was bound, as a signatory to the General Agreement on Tariffs and Trade (GATT), to a gradual lowering of her tariffs on a wide range of products, including tires and rubber products. This would create obvious difficulties for the Canadian tire industry, which had been created and developed behind a high-tariff wall.

Industry-Government Relations

As one company executive put it, by 1970 the Canadian tire industry was "sick of playing 20 questions with the government." Such an attitude grew from historical events. For example, the government had encouraged the tiremakers to work together for maximum efficiency during World War II, but in 1952, by bringing a successful price-fixing suit against the companies, it had effectively frightened them away from any future efforts at cooperation. Similarly, the government had encouraged the tiremakers to produce a full line of tires in Canada by setting tariffs at a high 17.5 percent, but during the 1960s consideration had twice been given to U.S.-Canadian free trade in tires. That is, two proposals had been advanced to include tires under the U.S.-Canada Automotive Trade Agreement, which in effect had brought the U.S.-Canadian free trade in motor vehicles — provided U.S. makers would produce an agreed proportion of their output in Canada. This agreement had permitted longer production runs on both sides of the border. It had also increased Canadian output: From under 50,000 in 1964, unit shipments of passenger cars had risen to 1.13 million in 1971, with Canada exporting about 428,000 more units to the United States than vice versa.

Besides the two proposals to put tires under the U.S. — Canada Auto Pact, in 1969 another disturbing proposal emerged in the course of discussions between the tire companies and officials in the Ministry of Finance. According to one executive who was present, officials had formed the opinion that the Canadian tire industry was poorly managed, lacking in a sense of direction, and fraught with bickering. The government was concerned about industry efficiency, and at one point the ministry officials had threatened to make the industry more efficient simply by lowering tariffs on all imports.

Even apart from such threats, Canadian tire industry executives were themselves concerned about efficiency. In 1969 talk about rationalization resumed under the leadership of RAC. Companies were fearful, however, lest their discussions leave them open to further antitrust proceedings. Thus they decided to take their problem to the newly formed Department of Industry, Trade and Commerce (DITC). Here it was agreed that a cost study should be made for industrial rubber products and that the companies would provide the necessary data, with the proviso that DITC would keep each company's disclosures confidential. After this study got underway, DITC further agreed to study the more specific topic of tire industry rationalization. Pursuant to this agreement, appointments were about to be set up between DITC and the tire company presidents. But suddenly DITC informed RAC's president that these discussions would have to be postponed. No explanation was given at first, but in January 1970 RAC's president was called to Ottawa and informed of the Michelin deal.

It was now up to the industry to decide on what course of action to pursue.

Industry–Government Negotiations

From the outset, Canada's tire industry spokesmen maintained that they had no objection to the government's loans and grants to Michelin — these being forms of assistance that were available to any company. Rather, the bone of contention was the remission-of-duty agreement. To the industry it seemed that this agreement meant that the government was not only bankrolling Michelin but was also creating an effective rationalization for the company — one such as they had been seeking, but one from which they would not benefit.

Based on this analysis, the industry's first hope was to get the government to back off from its duty-free concessions. It soon became apparent, however, that the government was fully committed.

The tire manufacturers then started meeting together in RAC to see if they could agree on what the government could do for them to compensate for the Michelin deal. This effort, too, soon ran into problems. According to RAC's President Turner, one reason was that all the companies had replaced their presidents in 1969 and 1970, and the new men did not have as good a relationship as the old guard. In addition, the companies had very different strengths and weaknesses and very different commitments to the future of their organizations. As a result, every suggestion that was favorable to one company met with opposition from another. The only tactic on which there was unanimity was to return to Ottawa with a demand that the Michelin agreement be rescinded.

Nevertheless, various proposals were examined, and one was actually put forward, only to be torpedoed. This proposal was similar to the U.S.–Canadian Automotive Trade Agreement in that it suggested that the Canadian tire companies be allowed to import tires duty-free, provided that they maintained certain production levels in Canada and that such production levels would increase proportionately with the growth of the Canadian tire market. Immediately after the proposal had been mailed, however, one company promptly went on record as opposing it. The agreement on a course of action did not last more than two days.

Discussions with the government and within RAC then continued for some months at a fairly low level. The issue came to a head again in late 1971 as Michelin came into production. At that time, spokesmen for RAC approached the government once more, only to discover that one member, Uniroyal, had made a proposal before they arrived. Uniroyal had asked the Minister of Finance for duty-free entry on radial steel tires and equipment when imported by that company into Canada. This break in ranks left RAC's spokesmen with a bad taste in their mouths.

Meanwhile, government officials had been meeting with the companies individually as well as collectively through RAC. The companies were asked to consider whether the opportunity to import a percentage of their sales volume duty-free would be an incentive for them to increase their efficiency by permitting them to specialize. In late 1971 this suggestion was expanded into four separate proposals, and the companies were invited to talk about them on an individual basis. These four proposals were as follows:

1. Duty-free entry of radial tires and equipment, when imported by manufacturers of radial steel tires in Canada.
2. Duty-free entry of radial steel tires when imported by manufacturers of tires generally.
3. Duty-free entry of radial steel tires and equipment by any company doing business in Canada.
4. A reduction of the tariff from 17.5 to 4 percent on a most-favored-nation basis.

All the Canadian tire companies said no to the third proposal since it would permit their customers to import directly from the United States. The fourth proposal was also very upsetting since it would mean a violent transition in the nature of Canadian production. If the tariff were to be lowered, the executives wanted it done on an orderly, long-term basis. Dunlop favored the second proposal, since it did not foresee producing its own steel radials in Canada. Firestone, however, had recently committed itself to an investment in Canadian steel cord tire production and it opposed any scheme that would destroy what it saw as a competitive advantage. Goodyear, the industry leader, did not want to settle for anything less than Michelin had received, although it maintained that a preferable strategy was to continue to press the government to drop the Michelin package.

The lack of industry consensus had been clearly demonstrated. Most of RAC's executive members returned home convinced that joint action was impossible and that their problems would have to be solved within their own companies.

By this time, Canadian government officials were beginning to be deeply worried about another problem — i.e., growing opposition to the Michelin deal in the United States. According to one tire company president, the Government had hoped to solve this problem by getting the Canadian companies to accept one of its four proposals, after which it expected the companies to try to dissuade their U.S. parents from opposing the Michelin deal. The Michelin threat in the two countries was, however, different in nature and degree, and it was unclear how persuasive such a company effort might have been.

The U.S. Industry and Its Responses

In the words of Mr. H. G. MacNeill, president of Goodyear Tire and Rubber Co. of Canada Ltd., "The Canadian problems with Michelin amounted only to a skirmish on the sidelines of an international economic battle."

For several years the U.S. tire industry had been facing economic problems that were usually attributed to low productivity, high labor costs, and outmoded production facilities. In addition, the U.S. industry had suffered a major marketing disaster when, in the mid-1960s, it had sought to replace its conventional four-ply tires with two-plies, only to have the latter rejected by consumers and auto manufacturers.

The growth of imports was still another problem for the U.S. tiremakers. From 1963 to 1970 imports had pushed their penetration from 1.8 to 10.6 percent of the total U.S. market, and they would have made further gains in 1971 were it not for a temporary 10 percent surcharge imposed on all imports during that year in defense of the U.S. balance of payments.

For U.S. makers, the tire import threat was three-pronged: first, imported cars with imported tires were taking some 16 percent of the market; second, Japan and other relatively low-wage producers were sending in millions of replacement tires mainly to sell on a price basis; and third, acceptance of high-priced, high-margin radials was growing. By the end of 1972 radials were capturing some 7 percent of the U.S. market, compared with 65 percent in Europe.

Although many U.S. tiremakers saw radials as the wave of the future, conversion to radial production had been slow. Those who were making them at all were producing only limited quantities, and no U.S. maker was fully committed to using the steel wire belting on which Michelin had built its reputation. Rather than converting to radial tires after their two-ply difficulties, the U.S. companies had instead opted for producing the so called bias-belted tire — one that combined traditional ply construction with a belt under the thread. Conversion to this type of tire had been relatively inexpensive compared with the $600 million that a conversion to radials might cost. Moreover, bias-belted tires had found good market acceptance: In 1972 they were expected to account for 85 percent of OE tires and 37 percent of replacements.

Under these circumstances, the U.S. tire industry raised a storm of protest about what it considered the unfair advantages given to Michelin in its Canadian operation. Since all the Canadian grants and loans were equally available to U.S. producers through their Canadian subsidiaries, the target of their charges was the remission of import duty. They did not, however, restrict themselves to this one point in their complaints to the U.S. administration, but rather attacked the whole incentive program of the Canadian government.

Remedy Sought

The remedy sought by the U.S. companies was a so-called countervailing duty. Under U.S. law, the U.S. Treasury must grant the industry's request should investigations show that the foreign government had set up a subsidy program to promote exports of the product in question. (It was not required that injury to U.S. producers be found, as in the case of antidumping actions.) The amount of the countervailing duty would be calculated to offset the foreign bounty or grant, and the duty would be added to the regular duty, which was 4.0 percent in the case of tires.

The U.S. industry was successful in getting the U.S. Treasury to open an investigation into this matter, and hearings were underway by July 1972. The Canadian position was that the Countervailing Duty Law was inapplicable since the Canadian grants were available to new industries whether they produced for export or not. In contrast, the U.S. industry noted that Canada's subsidies had gone to a plant that had been built in the expectation that "most" of its output would be exported to the United States rather than sold in Canada or elsewhere. Treasury officials were reported to attach importance to this latter argument. On the other hand, they conceded that to grant a countervailing duty in this case "would represent a new and stiffer interpretation of the U.S. law," since the United States had not previously invoked the law "against imports from countries providing tax incentives and other assistance to new industries."

Based on this novel but widely significant feature, the inquiry had attracted "considerable attention abroad." Even the decision to investigate had been expected to cause "additional friction" in U.S.–Canadian trade relationships.

Introduction

Risks are incurred when a multinational corporation expands to a new nation. Since most corporations are multidivisional, headquarters must choose which division to urge to move first into the new nation. Few headquarters executives are conscious of making such a choice. This chapter considers the selection of the most suitable division. The chapter is arranged into polycentric, ethnocentric, and geocentric sections; analytical models are presented in each.

Polycentric Process

Most polycentric corporations became multinational by a process of creeping incrementalism. Expansion to a new nation may have begun with an unsolicited export order. Slowly the export market expanded, with rarely any attention from headquarters. Headquarters attention was usually first drawn by a capital appropriation request for a warehouse in the new nation. Such requests are usually presented as part of ongoing operations, and are approved on the basis of return on investment (ROI) calculations, based on the conservative assumption of cost savings. There will rarely be a political forecast in the capital appropriation. The next step may occur when the local management wishes to begin manufacturing. In some developing nations, the government threatens to withhold import permits unless the corporation performs some assembly operations. The largest, though intangible, asset of the corporation in a nation is the present value of the expected stream of marketing revenue. Frequently, however, it seems to be the real asset (e.g., the warehouse) that becomes the hostage in executives' thinking. The weakness of a polycentric organization is that once it has expanded to a nation there is only a weak organizational mechanism available to redeploy its assets if this becomes necessary. Hence the initial decision must be sound.

Notwithstanding this concern, the essence of a polycentric corporation is that its executives perceive risk as though the corporation were a geographically diversified mutual fund. Modern stock market theory sees risk as having a price; financial risk can be bought and sold. A polycentric corporation feels that it should diversify broadly and thus pool risk.

In headquarters, the contact officer manning a national desk may experience ambiguity as to his role, as described in Chapter 1. His importance increases as corporate involvement within "his" nation is expanded from importing to systematic sales, to licensing, to a joint venture, and then to a wholly owned subsidiary. To the extent that self-interest in his career colors his business judgment, he will favor the subsidiary's incremental expansions and will have little motivation to perform adequate political intelligence. More specifically, it will be against his personal bureaucratic interests to pinpoint the stakeholders in the nation who are capable of impeding significantly the plans of the corporation.

When a national contact officer is pushed to make political prognostications, his usual inclination is to report "facts." But undigested facts are not enough.

> Ask a busy U.S. international executive how he copes with the world information explosion. If he is honest, he will point to a wastepaper basket filled with unread documents and explain that there just isn't enough time to get through everything, and besides, most of the material in that wastepaper basket is worthless. (Keegan, 1968)

Long-term political *analyses* should be tailored to the possible strategic decisions the corporation *must* make for that nation. This requires rare managerial consistency, overview, and insight. This is not likely to be attained in a polycentric corporation. The personal motivations are too great, and besides,

> people abroad [and at home presumably] are reluctant to commit themselves in writing to highly "iffy" things. They are not cowards or overly cautious; they simply know that you are bound to be wrong in trying to predict the future, and they prefer not to have their names associated with documents that will someday look foolish. (Keegan, 1968)

In the polycentric corporation the most promising manner to bring some structure to such highly "iffy" perceptions is for all concerned to acknowledge that there are some underlying patterns in social phenomena. Even though nobody can predict the future there can be agreement as to how mature a phenomenon is.

In the business of scanning the environment (Aguilar, 1967) the challenge is to avoid cluttering a decision maker with premature phenomena, which might die, or with phenomena that have become so entrenched as to be unstoppable. Hence an implicit agreement must evolve in an organization as to how developed a phenomenon must be to warrant free-form discussion at headquarters, and when it has sufficiently matured that it be assigned to an individual to be monitored.

A Facilitating Methodology

Task forces are used when deciding which divisions should enter which nation. The attention that a task force leader gives to "getting everyone on board" is an indication of the importance of establishing enough familiarity with and attendant knowledge of the alternatives. "Nonmetric scaling" could be used by this leader to bring some structure to vague perceptions of the decision problem. This methodology helps pinpoint important considerations and steers the company toward wiser investment decisions.

Step 1 provides input needed to produce a nonmetric scaling map of the perceptual space being used by each participant. From eight divisions there are 28 feasible pairs of divisions. Twenty-eight cards, each bearing the names of a pair of divisions, are given to each task force member. He must sort the cards so that the top ranked card shows those two divisions with the *most similar* priority for corporate funds in the nation (they should be closest to tying for the same priority regardless of whether the actual priority is high or low). Participants find it easy to decide which divisions were most similar and which were least similar; intermediate comparisons take longer. Each participant's deck of cards is run through the computer program for nonmetric scaling; the computer prints a two-dimensional depiction (as in Exhibit 4.2) of how the participant configures the eight divisions' priority for funds. After the data are plotted, each paper is trimmed into a circle to emphasize that the dimensions (the meaning of the groupings) are unknown.

In step 2, the leader of the task force studies the pile of paper circles, one by each participant, and groups them into a few somewhat similar clusters. (There are mathematical techniques for clustering that could be used.)

Step 3 is to articulate a rationale for the clusters.

Step 4 is to gather data on the disputed divisions and prepare exhibits that highlight *differences* between these divisions in a Delphi-like procedure (Mason, 1969).

Step 5 is to reconvene the task force and concentrate attention on the disputed divisions in an effort to clarify the true nature of the corpora-

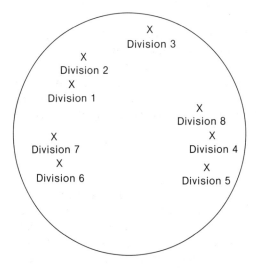

EXHIBIT 4.2
One participant's nonmetric scaling of divisions.

tion's strategy for the new nation. Following the spirit of Mason (1969), disagreements about the priority of various divisions will require the executives to articulate unique features of this corporation's strategy for the new nation.

In summary, in a polycentric organization there is no structure in which to perform rigorous analyses of commitment investments in a new nation. The methodology outlined in this section was designed to facilitate the interaction of a task force whose leader lacks definitive power. Once the task force is in reasonable agreement, it proves relatively easy to select a division to enter each nation.

Ethnocentric Process

To an ethnocentric executive, risk is to be avoided. Many real capital budgeting decisions are made *de facto* when a manager immediately rejects (screens out) a project as being unworthy of detailed examination. The ethnocentric top executive is haunted by the fear that once a nation gets mentioned on the agenda of things to investigate, a task force will be created. The executive knows from experience that such task forces are unstoppable. The task force will be beguiled by the natives; seeing themselves (or their protegees) as managers of the new national venture, they will usually report favorably. Thus the only way to suppress such risk-seeking profligacy is to control agenda creation and snuff out any mention of new nations.

An ethnocentric executive who feels uncomfortable about the foreigness of wholly owned subsidiaries of which he might lose control will feel even more anxious about joint ventures abroad in which he must share control with a foreigner. In order to understand the attitude of U.S. executives toward joint ventures and co-production agreements, Amariuta, Rutenberg, and Staelin (1979) conducted a mail questionnaire survey of the vice presidents (International) of U.S. corporations. Executives were asked how many joint venture proposals their corporations had rejected in the last three years and at what level. It was emphasized that the joint ventures could be anywhere in the world. The astonishing result was that most proposals were rejected *a priori*, with no analysis whatsoever.

Working from the right side of Exhibit 4.3 we see that formal capital appropriation analyses are used to help eliminate only the final 5 percent of all starting proposals. Yet the evaluation tools of finance deal mainly with such analysis. The second disturbing result is that so few proposals are eliminated by creating alternatives against which to compare them. To verify this, executives were asked to think about their most recent international joint venture and recall how many alternative host countries they had considered for this project. Over 77 percent had considered only the nation chosen. Of the 23 percent who had bothered to compare alternatives, each considered an average of three nations. Fewer than a

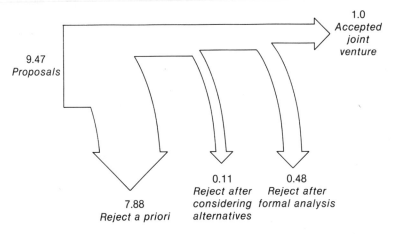

EXHIBIT 4.3
Severity of screening.

third had a strategy of actively searching for joint ventures. It is interesting to note that in those corporations without an active strategy, most of the proposals were never seen by the vice president-international. Subordinates had screened most proposals out as unsuitable.

Joint ventures in communist nations represent a special extreme for American executives who have been historically conditioned to react to communism. The governments of Yugoslavia, Hungary, Romania, and Poland allow equity joint ventures between their state enterprises and capitalist corporations. Usually the foreign corporation contributes technology and capital; the state enterprise contributes capital. Each government imposes its own methods of accounting (Brada, 1976; Price-Waterhouse, 1976) and the capitalist share is (usually) limited to 49 percent. Each year's accounting profits may be reinvested or paid out as dividends. The critical asset of the foreign corporation is the present value of the stream of dividends. A co-production agreement is similar except that one takes dividend payment not in cash but in output. If a joint venture terminates, its residual value is supposed to be divided between the two parties like dividends. In practice, one would have a basis for negotiation only so long as one is not withdrawing.

As shown in Exhibit 4.4, executives who were internationally more knowledgeable saw less risk in doing business in Eastern Europe and that, perceiving less risk, required a lower return on investment. This is to be expected, for lack of knowledge is closely linked to ethnocentrism. However, less knowledgeable U.S. executives anticipated significantly *less* trouble (red tape, endless negotiations) than did experienced executives. From a purely rational viewpoint one would expect that experienced executives could thread their way through bureaucracies faster than unknowledgeable executives. (In their ethnocentric way, less knowledge-

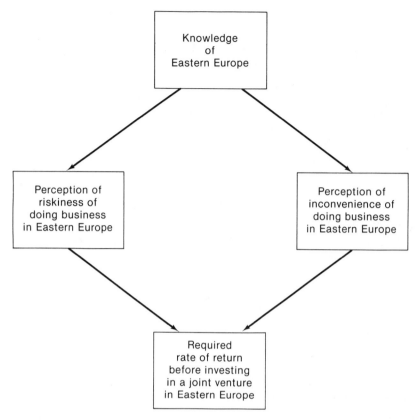

EXHIBIT 4.4
Paths between knowledge and threshold rate of return.

able executives saw more risk but were oblivious to the expensive work of negotiating and sustaining relationships in Eastern Europe.) Thus one danger of an ethnocentric attitude is that such executives do not realize that they have an enormous problem in coming to understand each nation.

Some theory will put this survey in perspective. Think of the corporation exposed to a stream of potential deals. Whereas a domestic executive can make commitments rather intuitively, theory would lead one to expect an international executive to be more systematic — the territory is less familiar, the range of opportunities is greater, and the number of proposed deals is much greater.

Because time taken to screen is expensive, we would expect executives to group proposed deals into:

1. Reject immediately.
2. Investigate further.
3. Accept immediately.

"Investigate further" means spend money to reach the next milestone in an investigation so that the project can be grouped once again. From screening theory, we know that the cutoff criteria ought to depend on the relative cost of rejecting a proposal that ultimately would have been shown to be profitable or mistakenly accepting a bad proposal. The same theory shows that the more one knows about a subject, the fewer proposals one need investigate before accepting a deal. For example, to accept two out of three proposals suggests either very clear decision criteria or that the cost of an investigation is very high. It is as though the surveyed multinationals saw investigation as costly and painful.

The Checklist

Several corporations have more than 100 product divisions, so many that even the corporate planning group has difficulty keeping track of the strategy of each. An important corporate planning task is to identify those divisions that should be encouraged to move faster to a worldwide position and those divisions that should be restrained from leaving the United States. The viewpoint is rather ethnocentric. The planners presuppose that attractive opportunities exist somewhere abroad and that no foreign government resistance will be met. In this section we examine a checklist used in the headquarters of a U.S. corporation to rank divisions as to their readiness to go abroad.

Checklists are used more extensively in corporations than business school teaching would indicate. They reduce the cost and pain of an investigation. Such lists remind subordinates of factors to be considered and they screen huge problems down to manageable size. The following checklist gives 15 factors to be considered. The first two factors eliminate a division. The next three factors limit the division's suitability. Eight factors positively propel the division. If a division scores in the final two factors, corporate planning begins an immediate analysis of its expansion abroad. For each division, each factor could be checked.

1. Current Domestic Divisional Problems Preclude Diluting Management Attention (Eliminating) Like the boy who ran away to sea to avoid facing unresolved problems at home, some managers of troubled divisions may want to escape by going international. If the origin of their problems lies in their own managerial ineffectiveness, the division should stay domestic. One possible retort could be that such a constraint is ethnocentric, that the domestic market for this product is cut-throat, and that if the corporation thought globally, it would expand abroad while shutting down the domestic operations. Such conceptual flexibility is viable only when the corporation has experience in performance evaluation and prediction based on years of experience in many nations. Until then, current domestic problems eliminate the division from the list of candidates.

2. Division Has a Domestic Orientation with Essentially Nontransferable Expertise (Eliminating) Some products and services sold to a narrow segment of one nation — the government, for example — are inappropriate abroad. Although the managers could conceivably accommodate another government, they have neither the energy nor the inclination to do so. Generally these divisions sell not a product but systems management expertise to facilitate the coordination of agencies of the government.

3. No Unique Technology or Marketing Skills (Limiting) Early in a product's life cycle, the division has a unique technology and may market it in a unique way. Later, however, there may be nothing unique to offer to the market and nothing to offset the cost of the cultural unfamiliarity of a foreign nation.

4. Domestic Technical Standards Differ Significantly from World Standards (Limiting) Not only would the corporation have little to contribute, but corporate control would be weakened.

5. Most Major Worldwide Markets Are Already Dominated by Competitors, Especially Multinationals (Limiting) When a corporation expands aggressively, its competitors react. From their knowledge of national markets they can cause the corporation serious losses. Poor performance by the subsidiary would affect the political position of executives in corporate headquarters, strengthening those who doubted the expansion anyway and allowing them to gain influence to squelch further expansion.

6. Divisional Profitability Is Over 10 Percent Real Return on Investment (Positive) A consistent ROI record of over 10 percent plus inflation breeds an attitude in divisional managers that makes them hard to stop, so the corporate executives might as well encourage them.

7. Technology (Positive) In some cases, the division's current technology is unique. In other cases, headquarters believes that a technological breakthrough is near, and that the division should acquire assets abroad cheaply and develop dealers and personnel to be ready for the new technology. Furthermore, the corporation should act before the national government realizes the implications of a seemingly modest initial purchase of assets.

8. Marketing Skills (Positive) The most pertinent aspect of marketing skill in high-technology industrial marketing is the tradition of communication and feedback between marketing and engineering design, so that the customer is helped to clarify his needs and design adaptations are made to meet these demands.

9. Strong U.S. Market Position (Positive) The larger one's market share, the greater is the likelihood that a diligent manufacturer can lower its cost of production. In manufacturing abroad, some of this expertise will be transferable. This assumes that the United States is a large enough market that a strong U.S. market position also means a large share of the world-wide market.

10. Real Market Growth Greater Than 5 Percent (Positive) For the division's product, worldwide market growth data can be adjusted for inflation. The quality of worldwide data is usually terrible, but it is good enough to determine whether real growth centers around 5 percent or around 10 percent. Growth is important if entrenched competitors are to accommodate themselves to a new entrant. A growth rate must be used to calculate the present value of a stream of future income.

11. Emerging Markets Abroad (Positve) Based on a belief in experience curves, the corporation desires a large share of the markets it enters. This is easier to achieve when the market is newly emerging and no competitors are entrenched.

12. Real U.S. Market Growth Greater Than 10 Percent (Positive) The industry containing this division is growing very fast in the United States and presumably it would grow fast abroad. If the corporation injects more capital into the division now, it can dominate the market worldwide. The real problem, however, is that managing such growth absorbs so much executive energy that overseas growth seems superfluous.

13. Accepted U.S. Industry Leadership Position (Positive) There is usually a leader in an oligopoly. If the division is the leader and wants to remain the leader, it should expand abroad before its competitors do, or it may forfeit leadership.

14. U.S. Marketing Position Threatened by Competitor's Sourcing Components or Products Abroad (Compelling) Another company can try to blackmail our corporation into not moving abroad, whenever our corporation is a customer of one division of a company and a supplier to a second division of the same company. If the second division plans to move abroad, the company may threaten to find another supplier. When such blackmail is threatened, headquarters (not the divisions) has a compelling reason to analyze the costs and benefits of moving abroad.

15. Markets Currently Served from the United States Are Threatened by Increasing Import Restrictions (Compelling) In a developing nation the threat of tariffs is familiar. In a developed nation, a national corporation may be selected by the government planners as the chosen instrument to supply this particular technology. If our corporation builds a manufacturing plant, it may be able to negotiate to avoid foreclosure from this national market.

These 15 criteria emphasize marketing (and, to a lesser extent, technological) leadership. Nevertheless, the criteria are crafted from an ethnocentric view that the attributes of the division should dominate the decision-making process; the criteria never question whether the corporation will be welcome abroad — this is assumed.

Geocentric Process

The geocentric ideal is to show explicitly how the corporation's choice of a division affects the various pressure groups in a nation. "Pressure groups" is perhaps too general a term; the word "stakeholder" emphasizes the stake these groups have in the corporation's decision. After listing typical stakeholders (these must be tailored to the particularities of each nation), we consider a model of the division selection decision. This can be a one-stage or two-stage decision. (A two-stage decision would begin with the introduction of one division to build up goodwill with particular stakeholders who would otherwise block introduction of the second division — a division more attractive to the corporation.)

In most of the literature on capital budgeting, risk is treated passively. To a geocentric executive, risk can be influenced. This is compatible with diversification. But whereas the polycentric view is that the risk exists as a constant quantity, a geocentric executive works to reduce the risk faced by his corporation by considering it in combination with other powerful forces in the societies of each nation and working to make the corporation invaluable.

The interesting difference between capital budgeting theory and corporate practice is that few top executives spend much time estimating probabilities. Instead they devote their energies to changing the probabilities. The more senior the executive, the harder he works to manufacture causal chains that will reduce the risk faced by his significant assets: physical, marketing, or human. He sees the world as a nonzero sum game, a view that allows him to think about the craft of coalition making.

At the negative extreme, the xenophobia within certain countries may lead to either a complete bar to foreign investment or to the expulsion of foreign companies, with confiscation of assets. At the positive extreme, there exists a real accommodation so that the foreign company becomes almost indistinguishable from national companies.

The majority of nation-states are somewhere in the middle range of this spectrum. This basic fact colors any consideration of multinational corporate performance. Foreign ownership implies differences in values and objectives as well as language and customs. These foreign birds have strange and different colors when they first migrate to new lands. Without any natural camouflage they may become fair game for the local hunters. Time and experience means a natural adaptation or ultimate extinction. (Rosow, 1974, p. 147)

Many articles and checklists measure *the* business climate of nations — as though each nation had only one business climate. Actually few societies are so monolithic as to have only one climate. Societies are pluralistic in nature, with several stakeholders — individuals or groups with enough power to block or facilitate a project. It is extremely important that someone in the corporation learn to differentiate the several stakeholders, "the local hunters" in Rosow's quotation, and to rank each stakeholder's preferences for one division over another. Behrman (1969, p. 114) presents a general list of possible stakeholders, to which I have added comments and examples.

1. *Private customers'* acceptance of the corporation's product performance.
2. *Customers'* (especially government agencies') perceptions of the foreignness of the corporation. Most countries support local industry, particularly if locally owned. However, in Romania, for example, the novelty of dealing with a foreign corporation may be an assist.
3. *National government* goodwill. This may be subdivided into the Ministry of International Trade and Industry, the Ministry of Finance, and any other government agency, if there are differences in their views.
4. *Municipal government* perceptions of the corporation as being either a good or an unstable employer. In India, it may be necessary to also consider the state government, because of its power to delay licenses.
5. The current and potential eagerness of *local managers* to adopt corporate goals as their own. Many U.S. corporations still fear that their Japanese managers are more loyal to Japan than they are to the corporation. The degree to which this division's products are in the national interest may ameliorate any conflict of loyalties.
6. *Workers' and trade unions'* perceptions of the prospect for adequate wages. This is generally an asset, as multinationals have a reputation for paying higher than average wages.
7. *Other executives'* opinions (pro or con) about the corporation.
8. *Public opinion.* In Hungary, the public is probably eager for contact with the West. An investment in some supposedly capitalist nations, however, may be viewed by that country's populace as exploitation by the multinational company.
9. *Corporate headquarter's* perception of the likelihood that the division's operation in this nation will quickly be a net cash producer and will grow steadily. An investment in Romania might also be seen as a foothold for further expansion in Eastern Europe.
10. *The financial community's* (including local banks) relationship with the corporation.

An international executive should prepare a similar list, tailoring it to the social structure of the particular nation under consideration. The challenge is to have these stakeholders in mind when deciding which division to move first.

Current corporate selection practice may best be described as a "confirmed hunch." A bright and hardworking executive tentatively selects the division intuitively. His staff works to validate or confirm that decision. If they uncover unforeseen problems, and if they are honest analysts, they will explain the problem to him; he can then select another division. Even under the best of circumstances, it is arduous to communicate about dimly understood preferences and perceptions. Frustration often leads to anger, which makes subordinates anxious. The decision then gets delayed. As other executives interfere, political gamesmanship clogs the process.

The models of this chapter provide a structure to help the analysis proceed. Strategic decisions will always depend on the most tenuous input. The challenge to an analyst is to reconcile every bit of this indistinct input. His output will usually be focused questions for more detailed subsequent analysis. In that different executives provide different insight, the analyst's task is to separate the points of agreement from points of disagreement and to present the decision implications of the disagreements. It is in this spirit that the next two models are presented.

One-Stage Selection

One-stage selection implies that a division (or several divisions) will be selected, moved into the nation, and left there to operate. The one-stage selection has three steps. They are most conveniently performed on a computer, with the questions posed on the computer screen (Saaty, 1977).

Step 1a determines the preferences of each stakeholder and thus determines the direction in which each stakeholder is likely to use its force. Consider each pair of divisions, and from the vantage point of the stakeholder express his preference, choosing one of the following categories for each pair:

Division rating	*Score in cell* ij
Division i is unquestionably superior to division j	5
Division i is superior to division j	4
Division i is much better than division j	3
Division i is somewhat better than division j	2
Division i is equal to division j	1
Division i is somewhat less good than division j	$\frac{1}{2}$
Division i is much less good than division j	$\frac{1}{3}$
Division i is inferior to division j	$\frac{1}{4}$
Division i is unquestionably inferior to division j	$\frac{1}{5}$

If there are d divisions there are $(d-1)\,d/2$ pairs of divisions. The computer can arrange the preference data into a square matrix of divisions (the diagonal cells are all one) and can calculate the eigenvector of the matrix. The eigenvector is merely a scale of preference, on a line 1 through 10, as in Exhibit 4.5. This vector is $d \times 1$ where there are d divisions.

Step 1b brings together the preferences of all the stakeholders. There is

	Matrix							Eigenvector			
Divisions:	*g*	*h*	*i*	*j*	*k*						

	g	*h*	*i*	*j*	*k*
g	1	5	4	...	
h	1/5	1			
i	1/4		1		
j	:			1	
k					1

yields

$$1 \underline{\hspace{5cm}} 10$$
$$\quad i \quad g \ j \qquad k \qquad h$$

EXHIBIT 4.5

Depiction of matrix and eigenvector output of the computer.

a separate eigenvector for each of the *s* stakeholders. Collect these eigen-vectors together as a (*d* × *s*) matrix.

Step 2 compares the stakeholders and determines their relative strength. Because each stakeholder has some power to block or impair the corpora-tion's move into this new nation, we must now assay the corporation's relative vulnerability. The view is that of a parallelogram of forces, with each stakeholder pushing in its own direction (that was step 1) and a strong stakeholder pushing harder than a weak stakeholder (step 2).

Input the list of stakeholders into the computer, and have it display each pair of stakeholders so that the executive can ponder the relative potential power and predispositions of each.

Stakeholder rating	*Score in cell ij*
Stakeholder *i* can mercilessly intimidate stakeholder *j*	5
Stakeholder *i* can slightly intimidate stakeholder *j*	4
Stakeholder *i* can strongly influence stakeholder *j*	3
Stakeholder *i* has some influence over stakeholder *j*	2
Stakeholder *i* is equally matched by stakeholder *j*	1
Stakeholder *i* has somewhat less influence than stakeholder *j*	½
Stakeholder *i* cannot influence stakeholder *j*	⅓
Stakeholder *i* is intimidated by stakeholder *j*	¼
Stakeholder *i* cowers before stakeholder *j*	⅕

As before, have the computer calculate the eigenvector of this matrix. This vector is (*s* × 1) where *s* is the number of stakeholders.

Step 3 combines step 1 with step 2. Have the computer multiply the (*d* × *s*) of eigenvectors from step 1b with the (*s* × 1) vector from step 2 to get a (*d* × 1) vector. Each element in this (*d* × 1) vector indicates the priority that should be given to that division.

Not only are the divisions ranked by priority, but the program shows how close the rankings are. This is a valuable indicator of how much further discussion time should be devoted to the select few divisions.

This procedure is simple enough to highlight the important subjective inputs. Because computer time is minimal, sensitivity analysis is easy, so that the analyst can evaluate the implications of differences between the executives' perceptions.

The weakness of the one-stage procedure is its assumption that "threat" is continual, not something that is triggered. We will now proceed to a two-stage selection procedure that allows for a finer differentiation of the process of threat. Even this procedure is merely a screening device to give voice to inarticulate feelings and perceptions. The best division may not promise enough profit to justify the risk.

Two-Stage Selection Procedure

In the preceding single-stage model each stakeholder was passive. The two-stage model adds three elements:

1. The stakeholder currently has a perception of the corporation (i.e., the corporation has goodwill with each stakeholder).
2. A stakeholder will block the corporation if sufficiently irritated. The stakeholder will be irritated to a different degree by each possible division and may move to block the entrance of a division so irritating as to exceed the stakeholder's goodwill to the corporation.
3. A stakeholder learns from the corporation's activities. The operation in his nation of each division has a different effect on the stakeholder's perception of the corporation. Actual operation will usually augment his goodwill.

For example, suppose the corporation manufacturing industrial products opens a repair division in a particular country. The irritation levels are low and the augmenting effect each year is attractive. This can be shown by estimating the reaction of each of the 10 stakeholders.

1. Customers frequently are frustrated enough to try any new repair shop and are delighted when it gives fast and reliable service.
2. There is little jingoism in repair work, and each year's operation of a successful repair network will lessen customer xenophobia.
3. Only a few national governments regulate service industries, and a repair division requires little import of capital or equipment. Once the corporation has established these operations in a nation, it is more likely to get government approval for other divisions.
4. A repair shop may run afoul of municipal government regulations, and the vagaries of repair work do not permit a very stable work force, so municipal problems may actually worsen (of course, if the shop is being used to train workers, municipal problems will be lessened).
5. Managers are not likely to be excited by a repair shop, nor will the operation be likely to capture the attention of potential recruits who want technical luster.

6. Workers and unions are sympathetic to the new entrant because multinational corporations are known to pay slightly higher wages than other firms.

7. Executives in other corporations would have little reason to block entry of a repair shop, and good service would rapidly build goodwill for the corporation.

8. Public opinion is unlikely to be inflamed when the repair division begins operation, and well-publicized appliance repair work could be priced as a loss leader to generate public goodwill if this is desirable for later divisions.

9. Corporate headquarters does not have to invest much capital; its main investment is in a cadre of experienced supervisors, who are recoverable if the venture fails. As the years pass, the repair division can be used as a staging ground for later divisions.

10. Few banking relations are involved.

The analyst can classify divisions into those that are currently candidates for expansion and those that are not. The repair division example illustrates a feasible division. Rather than starting with the feasible divisions, it is most productive to work backwards on this problem. List all the profitable but infeasible divisions. For each such division, find the least expensive combination of feasible divisions that will adequately prepare the nation for the desirable division. More than two stages may be required. Only at this point can the financial analyst begin applying standard capital budgeting formulas, not to individual divisions, but to the necessary set as a unit.

There may be constraints on the availability of likely first-stage divisions. Although most governments prefer to have research and development done within their nation, most corporations have such trouble managing their research and development that they do not want to break up their laboratories. They fear that if they put a small laboratory abroad, the precedent will have been set. Similarly, in many product lines, economies of scale are so great that only one plant can be built. Thus building in one nation precludes building in another. Another constraint is that of boycott lists. Constraints necessitate the simultaneous consideration of a multitude of combinations of states.

Closing Decisions

When a corporation wants to close down one of its product divisions in a nation, the corporation should expect pressure to be exerted on its other divisions. Major customers and suppliers of the remaining divisions, fearing that this closing will be the first of many, will cool their relationships, investing less in cooperative long-term work such as revising product standards. The same kind of stakeholder analysis that has been outlined provides a framework by which to analyze the indirect pressures that will be brought to bear.

Many multinational corporations set very tight financial controls and expect that plant and marketing operations will be miniature replicas of these in the headquarters nation. Nevertheless, they claim to be decentralized to the point of polycentrism. (One might describe them as ethnocentrics in polycentric clothing.)

With increasing worldwide price competition (aided by tremendous developments in quality standards) many of the miniature replica operations will become uneconomical, and many will be closed. In other cases, the shell of the plant will be maintained but old managers and old equipment will be replaced by new equipment, and the truncated plant will be operated as a satellite of a plant having responsibility for this product worldwide. As noted in Chapter 1, a few such miniature replica plants may themselves become the managerial plant, having a global product mandate.

During these transformations there is a disruption in the network of contacts that the subsidiary kept with its stakeholders. The new corporate operation will give slightly different weight to different stakeholders, and so it is prudent to manage the transition, rather than forgetting stakeholders and then trying to reestablish them later.

Bradley (1977) has done one of the remarkably few studies of the process by which a corporation loses viability in a nation. The extreme case, nationalization, is so fraught with emotion that the pain of analysis leads most businessmen to avoid formulating scenarios of how their business might slide toward nationalization. One rare example is Goodwin's (1969) analysis of how Exxon's International Petroleum Company of Peru came to be nationalized; the process is not as inevitable as a Greek tragedy.

Conclusions

All multinational corporations are inevitably faced with the decision of whether to enter a new nation. Sometimes the decision will be an easy one; more often, as in the case of Hungary, that decision will be complicated. A corporation's decision to expand its activities to a new nation is based on a multitude of factors; some act as constraints while others are stimulants. The purpose of this chapter is to develop procedures that will help a firm's management scrutinize its own decisions concerning international expansion. Attention has been focused on the divisional managers, because most large corporations — multinational or not; European, American, or Japanese — are organized by product division lines, and the divisional manager should be a key participant in such a decision; he alone can make it work.

The organization theories of Barnard (1938), March and Simon (1964), and Cyert and March (1963) emphasize search, especially search in the vicinity of existing practice. When Aharoni (1966) investigated how corporations decided to study and evaluate a nation, he found evidence of the notion that search is engrossing and that members of a task force appointed to evaluate a particular nation almost always favored that nation. What Aharoni only hinted at was that a task force usually consists of all the people in the corporation familiar with the nation, thus precluding any informed opposition.

Designing corporate policy includes articulating the objectives of the corporation, assessing its environment, and identifying corporate strengths and vulnerabilities. Environmental assessment can become a deeply felt commitment to ride with an environment. Searching a new environment seems to involve personal risk: "Get your feet wet" and "Get burned a few times" are common directives.

Strategic moves definitely arouse strong emotions. In such a situation it is difficult to find an appropriate problem analysis structure. Furthermore, if too much structure is imposed, interesting opportunities will surely be excluded. If too little structure is imposed, the magnitude of their task will engender feelings of anxiety that will overwhelm most analysts. (Their usual coping behavior is to ignore all but one small corner of a problem.) This chapter offers a sequence of analytical tools that provide some structure to the agonizing work of trying to help make strategy.

The models of this chapter are about as complicated as one can comfortably manipulate analytically. Reality is appreciably more complex. For example, the model is for one point in time and yet attitudes change (and at different rates). As Truitt (1970) noted, "In assessing risk . . . it behooves the foreign investor [and students of international business] to bear in mind that the host government will be asking, 'Yes, but what have you done for me lately?'"

Moreover, we've assumed that the stakeholders act in isolation, whereas in some societies particular coalitions of stakeholders are possible. One stakeholder without power to block a project may nevertheless work to become the catalyst around which a blocking coalition will coalesce.

Finally, the company's power to influence such coalitions has not yet been explored. Clearly, the corporation is bringing benefit to some sectors of the nation. Hence, with a well-planned program of public and government relations, it can become a force in its own right. The most perceptive model of corporate action may be the early days of the Tennessee Valley Authority. Actually (and ironically) the TVA was a government-owned enterprise whose early existence was threatened by private enterprise stakeholders. The chairman of the TVA, David Lilienthal, mastered a process of slowly coopting stakeholders, then systematically expanding TVA activities (Selznick, 1949).

Questions from Other Viewpoints

1. *Corporate Rational Normative Global.* You just covered this viewpoint in the chapter.
2. *Corporate Rational Normative Subsidiary.* What can a subsidiary manager do to monitor, in a systematic fashion, the attitude of stakeholders to the corporation and to each division?
3. *Corporate Rational Descriptive Global.* In an effort to reduce the probability that some future Brazilian government will nationalize the mine, the ownership of a vast iron ore complex in Brazil is being arranged as follows. The mine will be a joint venture, owned mostly by national steel companies, each in proportion to its consumption of iron. Since some nations that use iron ore may not want to own equity in the development, the development hopes to purchase equipment in those nations, financed by a loan from the national export assistance agency, so that those governments would be drawn in if nationalization occurs. From your understanding of nationalizations, will all this make much difference?
4. *Corporate Rational Descriptive Subsidiary.* This chapter on multi-divisional expansion deals with the corporation's goodwill with many stakeholders. Once the corporation has a subsidiary in a nation, it must nurture its relationships with each stakeholder, which suggests that the subsidiary manager's performance appraisal (and bonus) should include an audit of these intangibles. From your prior courses, review two articles that describe actual managerial evaluation to assess the kinds of measures that have evolved in other contexts and the maximum number of items on which an individual can be rewarded if he is not to get confused.
5. *Corporate Emotional Normative Global.* One way of looking at this chapter is that it presents a series of emotional props to help executives think about highly anxiety-provoking problems. From your knowledge of psychology, what other means could conceivably be used as an emotional buttress?
6. *Corporate Emotional Normative Subsidiary.* The notion that someday the corporation may want to expand with another division in a nation seems very long-term and tenuous. Tailor a set of criteria against which a subsidiary president could evaluate his divisional managers. How would these criteria be weighted differently in the following cases:
   a. Long before a new divisional expansion.
   b. During the expansion.
   c. After the expansion.
7. *Corporate Emotional Descriptive Global.* In headquarters you cannot do all the work yourself but must rely on the judgment of subordinates to identify stakeholders correctly and assess their importance.

If your subordinate distrusts the world, he will have an excellent ability to sense possible stakeholders but will tend to exaggerate their potency. Describe how you would go about calibrating the degree to which your subordinates exaggerate.

8. *Corporate Emotional Descriptive Subsidiary.* You manage a national subsidiary and have high hopes for its expansion. Some stakeholders in your nation expect a bribe, will be deeply offended if they do not receive it soon, and do have the ability to block your corporation's expansion. You have told headquarters of this need, and you have even used an ROI format because a bribe should rightly be viewed as a capital appropriation. Headquarters is dogmatic in what they call their corporate policy against bribes. Describe your feelings.

9. *Social Rational Normative Global.* One way to measure the efficiency or inefficiency of corporate capitalism is to contrast it with an alternative. One theoretical alternative might be centralized world-wide planning of all industries. Write one page of guidelines for such planning. Be explicit about the trade-offs you will make between further industrializing already industrialized nations and furthering the development of poor nations.

10. *Social Rational Normative Subsidiary.* This chapter has dealt with multiple divisions. Traditionally a nation is usually more concerned with vertical integration. For example, a government will persuade a corporation to build an assembly plant by threatening to withhold import permits. Make a list of each stakeholder, the objectives of the stakeholder, the sanctions it could impose, and whether it could apply pressure to one division to induce results in another division.

11. *Societal Rational Descriptive Global.* Think carefully to select an industry where output decisions are controlled by intergovernmental coordination agreements, yet the means of production are managed by corporations in at least some of the nations. Describe the process of intergovernmental coordination for this industry.

12. *Societal Rational Descriptive National.* How could an important stakeholder systematically investigate a corporation, rather than wait for the corporation to establish itself?

13. *Societal Emotional Normative Global.* During the 1970s numerous articles and books were written forecasting a bleak economic future for this world. Uncontrolled population growth and untrampled aspirations will cause a depletion of resources and a growth in pollution. In the mood of these forecasts, what guidelines do you think should be imposed on the industrialization of the world?

14. *Societal Emotional Normative Subsidiary.* The first division that moves into a nation has the deceptive appearance of a Trojan horse. You are an elected member of a state government (regional assembly, provincial parliament). Expand on this idea by writing the text of a five-minute speech opposing approval of a multinational corporation's overtures.

15. *Societal Emotional Descriptive Global.* If there were to be economic warfare between national governments, in what way would multinational corporations be viewed? Specifically, how could a subsidiary abroad become a hostage, influencing the actions of the headquarters government? In what way could a subsidiary abroad be a means of expressing the wishes of the headquarters government?

16. *Societal Emotional Descriptive Subsidiary.* The problem of this chapter is only a partial statement. There are many corporations that may be induced to compete to enter a nation. Select one of the stakeholders, and from that viewpoint write a one-page briefing memo on how to play corporations of different nationalities off against one another.

Bibliography to Chapter 4

Aguilar, Francis J., *Scanning the Business Environment* (New York: Macmillan, 1967).

Aharoni, Yair, *The Foreign Investment Decision Process* (Cambridge: Harvard University Press, 1966).

Amariuta, Ion, David Rutenberg, and Richard Staelin, "How American Executives Disagree about the Risks of Investing in Eastern Europe," *Academy of Management Journal*, Vol. 22, No. 1 (1979), pp. 138–157.

Barnard, Chester I., *The Functions of the Executive* (Cambridge: Harvard University Press, 1938).

Behrman, Jack N., "Some Patterns in the Rise of the Multinational Enterprise," Research Paper 18, University of North Carolina, 1969.

Bower, Joseph L., *Managing the Resource Allocation Process: A Study of Corporate Planning and Investment* (Cambridge: Harvard University Press, 1971).

Brada, Joseph C., "Markets, Property Rights, and the Economics of Joint Ventures in Socialist Countries," Working Paper 76-64, Graduate School of Business Administration, New York University, 1976.

Bradley, David G. "Managing against Expropriation," *Harvard Business Review*, Vol. 55, No. 4 (1977), pp. 75–83.

Charnes, Abraham, Frederick Glover, and Darwin Klingman, "The Lower Bounded and Partial Upper Bounded Distribution Model," *Naval Research Logistics Quarterly*, Vol. 18, No. 2 (1971), pp. 277–281.

Cyert, Richard M. and James G. March, *A Behavioral Theory of the Firm* (Englewood Cliffs, NJ: Prentice-Hall, 1963).

Fouraker, Lawrence E. and John M. Stopford, "Organizational Structure and the Multinational Strategy," *Administrative Science Quarterly*, June 1968, pp. 47–64.

Goodwin, Richard N., "Letter from Peru," *The New Yorker*, Vol. 45 (May 17, 1969), pp. 41–109.

Keegan, Warren J., "Global Intelligence: A Framework for Action," *Worldwide P and I Planning*, July–August 1968, p. 48.

March, James G. and Herbert A. Simon, *Organizations* (New York: Wiley, 1964).

Marer, Paul and Joseph Miller, "U.S. Participation in East-West Industrial Cooperation," *Journal of International Business Studies*, Vol. 8, No. 2 (1977), pp. 17–29.

Mason, Richard, "A Dialectic Approach to Strategic Planning," *Management Science*, Vol. 15, No. 8 (1969), pp. B403–414.

Meyer, Herbert E., "What It's Like to Do Business with the Russians," *Fortune*, Vol. 85, No. 5 (1972).

Meyer, Herbert E., "Why Business Has a Stake in Keeping Sovietology Alive," *Fortune*, Vol. 92, No. 3 (1975).

Meyer, Herbert E., "Why the Outlook Is So Bearish for U.S.–Soviet Trade," *Fortune*, Vol. 97, No. 1 (1978).

Molitor, Graham T.T., "The Hatching of Public Opinion," *Planning Review*, Vol. 5, No. 4 (1977), pp. 3–7.

Price-Waterhouse, *East West Trade*, (New York: Price-Waterhouse Information Guide, November 1976).

Rosow, Jerome M., "Industrial Relations and the Multinational Corporation: The Management Approach," in *Bargaining Without Boundaries: The Multinational Corporation and International Labor Relations*, edited by Robert J. Flanagan and Arnold R. Weber (Chicago: University of Chicago Press, 1974), pp. 147–162.

Rummel, R.J., and David A. Heenan, "How Multinationals Analyze Political Risk," *Harvard Business Review*, Vol. 56, No. 1, 1978, pp. 67–76.

Saaty, Thomas, "An Eigenvalue Method for Prioritization and Planning," *Journal of Mathematical Psychology*, June 1977, pp. 44–51.

Selznick, Philip, *TVA and the Grass Roots* (Berkeley: University of California Press, 1949).

Simon, Herbert A., "On the Concept of Organizational Goal," *Administrative Science Quarterly*, Vol. 9, No. 1 (June 1964), pp. 1–22.

Simon, Herbert A., George Kozmetsky, and Gordon Tyndall, *Centralization vs. Decentralization in Organizing the Controller's Department* (New York: Controllership Foundation, 1954).

Thompson, James D., *Organizations in Action* (New York: McGraw-Hill, 1967).

Truitt, J. Frederick, "Expropriation of Foreign Investment: Summary of the Post World War II Experience of American and British Investors in the Less Developed Countries," *Journal of International Business Studies*, Vol. 1, No. 2 (1970), pp. 21–34.

United Nations Industrial Development Organization, *Guide to Practical Project Analysis: Social Benefits—Cost Analysis in Developing Countries* (New York: United Nations, 1978).

The three finance chapters you have just read flow into one another to build successively. Although the topics were carefully selected to typify a short-, medium-, and long-term problem, these are merely a small sample of the variety of real finance problems in a multinational corporation. Consider a typical textbook in corporation finance. For each chapter think how that activity could be done in a multinational corporation. The guiding rule in most corporations is to decentralize an activity if possible, subject to two caveats. First, the *procedure* for performing the activity is often very centralized (for example, anyone can concoct a capital budget proposal, but headquarters specifies the format of the write-up, the mathematics of cash flow summarization, and the review procedure). The second caveat is that some decisions can be better made centrally. In essence, the justification for the expensive headquarters of a multinational company is to identify and make these profit-creating decisions. Chapters 2, 3, and 4 identify three such decisions.

The essence of the foreign exchange chapter is to say that exchange rate risk should not interfere with sensible business decisions. This does not mean that the risk is to be ignored; managers must adapt to whatever the rate is, while simultaneously providing guidelines for long-term planning — a tricky balancing act.

Maneuvering liquid assets provides liquidity where it is wanted, but the main motivation is that tax jurisdictions differ. Whereas a domestic firm is stuck with one tax environment, a multinational manager can exercise some discretion. This presents an awkward dilemma. Many people take a lifetime to gain a thorough understanding of the tax system of *one* nation. It follows obviously that a multinational executive cannot understand the tax systems of 50 or 100 nations. Faced with this challenge some managers give up and leave taxes to the tax specialists. Their decision analyses may be precise — but they will be precisely wrong. The essence of maneuvering liquid assets is that it is better to approximate taxes, to decide on the managerially desired action, and to have the tax specialists check it to revise the approximation. A normally operating company need take interest in only a few corners of the tax codes of the world.

Chapter 4 does not take risk as an exogenous given; some of the risk is what a corporation brings on itself by its actions and inactions. The essence of the chapter is that any corporation is in coalition with other powerful forces in a society. When a corporation suddenly grows or contracts or quits, it disturbs the equilibrium of these forces, and they may resist. National executives can manage these balances of force in an intuitive manner.

Multinational managers might better supplement their political flair with pedantic checklists and procedures. First, as a foreigner, the multinational executive lacks an intuitive feel for the situation. Second, the stakeholders lack sympathy for the problems of a foreign corporation. Third, the multinational's resources mean that its rate of expansion or withdrawal can be much more sudden than the natural rise or fall of indigenous companies. Finally, whereas an indigenous company has little choice but to accept the political reality of its nation, a multinational can choose where it wants to locate — and to choose well takes hard study.

PART TWO

Multinational Manufacturing

CHAPTER FIVE

Logistics

Introductory Note to the Case

Ascendant Electric of England, Ltd.

Internal company logistics account for about 15 percent of the cost of goods sold by a large multinational; import tariffs add perhaps a further 10 percent. It would be easy to reduce this 25 percent cost by building, in each nation, a miniature of the parent factory. To do so, however, would negate economies of scale.

The case that follows centers on a Los Angeles customer of an English company. The Californian company uses a dozen generators per day, which it now receives by ocean container once a week. The cost elements are detailed and provide a basis for comparing air and sea freight.

Fresh-cut flowers, live lobsters, electronic components, and jet engines are regularly shipped by airfreight, but ordinary generators don't commonly fly! Nevertheless, the long shipping route through the Panama Canal, combined with the charge for only backhaul airfreight may make airfreight viable for Ascendant.

Ascendant's director of physical distribution believes that there might be grounds for negotiating a rate. He needs to calculate the rate that would interest him in airfreight. If the airline cannot better that threshold, there would be no basis for further discussions.

But if the airline can better that threshold, his main task is to devise a negotiating strategy with the airline that will maximize the benefit Ascendant might realize.

Ascendant Electric of England Ltd.

John Larson, Director of Physical Distribution at Ascendant Electric of England, felt squeezed between a rock and a hard place. During the late 1970s the value of the British pound had risen because of North Sea oil and the government's tight monetary policy, so the cost of Ascendant's products had risen in terms of most world currencies. Simultaneously, from Ascendant's sales manager in America, its most important export market after Saudi Arabia, came request after request that the company lower its prices or it would continue to lose market share to Japanese competitors. In June 1980 Larson was asked by Ascendant's managing director to do whatever he could to reduce the logistics costs of shipping the electrical generators from Ascendant's plant in Rugby, England, to the U.S. West Coast.

The generators were transported by ship. Larson, while visiting London, found himself in a conversation about airfreight and had learned that Boeing 747 airfreighters are fully laden on their flights from California to Britain, but have excess space on their way back, for which airlines charge lower backhaul rates. Larson wondered whether it would be economical to airfreight Ascendant's generators to California, and what negotiating strategy he could use.

Cost Review of Supplying Los Angeles Customer by Sea

Ascendant's main California customer was in Los Angeles. The customer used a standard Ascendant generator in its diesel generator sets, which it sold as emergency power sources to hospitals, computer installations, and the like. This customer was forecast to purchase 3,157 generators in 1982, each weighing 195 kilograms (429 pounds) and occupying 15 cubic feet when packed on a base.

Sixty-four generators could be packed snugly into an 8 × 8 × 20 foot container (7 ft. 8 in. wide × 7 ft. 2 in. high × 19 ft. 4 in. long on the inside) and Ascendant shipped one container approximately every week. Generators were sent from the Rugby plant to a packing firm who installed a wooden base to each generator and packed them into an ocean container. This careful packing was designed to protect the generators from the shocks of loading, unloading, and handling. Larson collected the cost data on these shipments. Sometimes he used accounting standard costs, at other times he had to figure the cost himself:

Packing cost	$8.10 per generator
U.K. inland freight	$7.03 per generator
U.K. shipping terminal cost	$3.02 per generator

Vessels of the U.K. to U.S. West Coast Conference loaded containers at the Port of Felixstowe on the English coast, and passed through the Panama Canal before heading north to Los Angeles. The conference rate for electrical generators was $163/1000 kilograms, so the remaining out-of-pocket costs were:

Ocean freight cost	$31.78 per generator
Los Angeles terminal charges	$ 2.87 per generator
Out-of-pocket shipping payment	$52.80 per generator

In addition to this out-of-pocket cost, Larson decided to estimate the opportunity cost of inventory in transit. Within Ascendant, this was commonly called the "pipeline inventory." At the Rugby works generators were being assembled so rapidly that the once-weekly shipment to Los Angeles was only a fraction of one day's production. Hence, no additional inventory was ever accumulated at the Rugby plant, to be earmarked for Los Angeles.

The conference steamship company was using fast 24-knot vessels, and on first investigation it appeared that the inventory transit time via the Panama Canal was only four weeks. Subsequent analysis, however, revealed that the actual transit time was longer. Palletizing 64 generators and packing a container is not in itself time-consuming, but each job had to take its place in the queue of work. Once packed, the containers were held awaiting transportation to Felixstowe. The ships usually kept schedule, and in Los Angeles the containers were offloaded rapidly. But then they sat on the dock, sometimes for days, until the customer took delivery. The customer had to schedule the assembly of diesel generator sets into his other manufacturing work, and had fallen into the practice of taking delivery only as he needed the generators, thus deferring the payment of customs duties until he actually needed the goods.

Ten days after the container is landed portside the customer is supposed to be charged demurrage at $40 per day. However, the shipping companies did not charge demurrage to Ascendant for fear that they would lose its business. Nevertheless, there had never in the past been a need to negotiate the terms of sale around the question of precisely when the customer took delivery. Larson wanted to make sure that if the goods arrived in Los Angeles early, Ascendant would be paid that much earlier. He also was concerned that once accustomed to accepting shipments by air, the customer would suddenly specify that the shipments arrive by sea, and demand a price reduction equal to the difference between the *published* rates for airfreight and ocean liners.

Mindful of these points, Larson analyzed the pipeline inventory from Rugby to Los Angeles. The actual average transit time from Rugby to the customer's Los Angeles plant was close to six weeks. Ascendant's standard accounting costs of manufacture was $1,680 per generator and Ascendant's cost of capital was 25 percent per annum. Therefore, the pipeline inventory cost was $48.50 per generator.

Thinking about Airfreight

Larson reviewed these costs to determine which ones would no longer be incurred if Ascendant switched to airfreight.

The British packing firm that did such a thorough job of installing bases and packing generators into containers at $8.10 per generator quoted $12 per generator for packing on specially designed airfreight bases, each weighing 21 kilograms. To Larson this price smacked of gilding the lily. He felt sure that palleting could be developed that would be cheaper than ocean packaging.

Inland transportation to Heathrow Airport would cost $9.88 per generator. The goods would be flown directly to Los Angeles where they would clear U.S. customs and be available to the customer two days following shipment from Heathrow.

Airfreight was currently used as a means of transport only as a backup in case of production delays or when unforeseen orders had to be filled in a hurry — anything less than the six weeks' ocean transit time. Larson was therefore uncertain as to whether Ascendant's American sales manager would be able to ask for a higher price for generators delivered by air to Los Angeles. On the one hand, the customer would be able to reduce working inventory because a daily air shipment would replace a weekly ocean shipment. On the other hand, the lack of a backup service would obligate the customer to carry a larger safety stock of generators. Larson put this question aside temporarily, as he proceeded to structure his negotiating position with the airlines.

Boeing 747 freighters are loaded in the belly with many containers of standard sizes. Among the larger standard pallets is one 10 ft. 5 in. long by 7 ft. 4 in. wide and 8

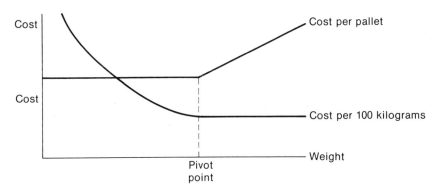

EXHIBIT 5.1
Pivot point between volume and weight charges.

feet high. A pallet can be rolled into the aircraft through its nose, and locked into place. So long as the pallet is packed with heavy items on the bottom, ordinary strapping is sufficient to hold the load.

The airline pricing system is to charge per pallet up to a "pivot point" weight, and to charge by weight thereafter. The pivot point density for wide-body jet aircraft is about ten pounds per cubic foot.

Through business friends in the freight business, Larson learned that from Britain to Los Angeles, air cargo density averaged only 4 pounds per cubic foot. Each Ascendant generator weighed 195 kilograms (429 pounds) and occupied 15 cubic feet, a cargo density of 28.6 pounds per cubic foot. Larson realized that Ascendant would have to use a freight forwarder to consolidate cargo. Ascendant's Los Angeles customer required approximately ten generators per day. If these were loaded onto one pallet it would weigh 4,290 pounds, and the engines would occupy 150 cubic feet. This would leave 560 – 150 = 410 cubic feet for general cargo which the freight forwarder could load on top of the generators on the pallet. The general cargo would weigh about 410 X 4 = 1,640 pounds. The weight of the generators plus the weight of the general cargo would therefore total 5,930 pounds, close enough to the airline's pivot point density of 10 pounds per cubic foot if the forwarder loaded lighter items.

Ascendant would negotiate a special deal with an established freight forwarder for whom this steady business would augment their existing airfreight flow sufficiently to negotiate with an airline for a reduction in freight rates.

Negotiating Strategy

Having collected this data, Larson needs to calculate the threshold airfreight rate that Ascendant could just afford to pay. Clearly, he wants to negotiate a much lower rate. Because Boeing 747s usually fly to California with space available, an airline's threshold rate would be determined by the marginal cost of fuel consumed by a very slightly heavier plane, approximately five cents per pound ($21.45 per generator) according to one unreliable source. The difference between these two threshold rates would be the benefits to be divided by Ascendant, the forwarder, and the airline.

Larson sits at his desk, calculating the ceiling rate that Ascendant could afford to pay. Now he paces his office, thinking out a strategy that will hold most of the benefits for Ascendant.

Introduction

Ask the manufacturing manager of a subsidiary to identify his most important problem, and he will likely respond by describing union relations and worker morale. These are *his* problems, not the problems of headquarters. From a headquarters viewpoint his job is to enhance productivity and meet schedules. He must notify headquarters when he is going to run the risk of a strike, when he has problems meeting quality, or when any other phenomena affect the global production network. If a subsidiary production manager is having trouble coping, the rest of the network can accommodate his erratic output, but it cannot solve his problems.

The three chapters of this section deal with the global production network as a system. The chapters build on one another, with logistics coming first. In a multinational corporation, the global logistics department is never large and is rarely powerful. The importance of logistics lies in the fact that if it is poorly managed the interaction between manufacturing and marketing will sour. The perfect logistics department is staffed by unsung heroes.

The three sections of this chapter are sequenced to accord with the Gruber, Mehta, and Vernon (1967) international product life cycle. During the first phase the newly developed product is exported from the home market. During the second phase the rate of product innovation slows (the product becomes more mature) and a network of plants can be built around the world. In the third and final phase for a long-established product, the inefficient plants (usually those where the product was first built) may be closed to rationalize production.

First Phase: Product-Centered View of Logistics (Ethnocentric)

During the first phase of a product life cycle, when exports are shipped from a central factory, foreign customers are usually charged for freight plus import duty. Actually the true cost of logistics between two points is the algebraic sum of 15 costs. Let us consider a manufacturer shipping by ocean liner. The logistics costs from factory to sales affiliate abroad is the sum of:

1. Extra inventory at the factory
2. + Packing
3. + Transport to dock and loading fees
4. + Paperwork
5. + Transportation charge of ocean liner or airline
6. + Inventory en route and waiting to clear customs
7. + Customs broker charge and other paper work

8. + Import duty
9. + Repackaging if necessary
10. + Inspection at the sales outlet
11. + Delivered inventory
12. - Export incentives
13. - Duty drawbacks
14. + Quotas
15. + Customer uneasiness about products imported from this nation

Between most pairs of ports the flow is so small that a corporation often signs a contract with a freight forwarder to take care of all the paperwork and to consolidate the shipments of several corporations into one container. An ocean container is a large box (8 × 8 × 40 feet or 8 × 8 × 20 feet on routes with more dense cargo) which provides good protection from both ocean spray and pilferage. Nevertheless, even if a freight forwarder issues one bill for all his services, the cost elements still exist. Therefore, the discussion will proceed as if the corporation handled its own paperwork, its own consolidation, and as if it is shipping on a regular schedule, say monthly.

Extra Inventory Inside Factory

There would be no need for extra factory inventory if this route were a minor share of factory output, if shipping were daily, and if deviations from plan never occurred in either the shipping schedule or the quantity shipped. Often the factory has to carry additional inventory to ensure the additional shipments and to accumulate enough product to fill a container. Capital is tied up in this inventory. The inventory carrying cost depends on cost of liquid assets of the subsidiary (discussed in Chapter 3).

Packing

Most cargo is packed into containers to reduce the cost of breakage, spoilage, or theft; most shipping charges are based on volume, not weight, unless the shipment is very dense. One of the advantages of standard container sizes is that it has become worthwhile to analyze how to package items so that you can squeeze the largest number of units into the container. Nevertheless, to pack 2,000 cubic feet of cargo into an 8 × 8 × 40 foot container is considered to be excellent packing.

Inland Transportation and Loading Fees

This cost can frequently be negotiated. As an export incentive, governments and transportation systems (both ocean liners and railways) frequently subsidize inland export shipments. Nevertheless, one gets the impression that so much executive time is spent on negotiating and renegotiating these concessions that the cost of executive time should be added into the inland fees. To reduce inland transportation charges a corporation can locate adjacent to container ports or airports.

Container port authorities have found that there are few economies of scale beyond 10,000 containers per month. However, the substantial economies up to that level result in relatively few container ports around the globe. If national subsidiaries of a multinational corporation are to specialize in producing just a few products (importing the balance of the product line using a large number of containers per month) new factories should be located at the container ports.

Export Documentation and Insurance

To many corporate export traffic departments, logistics means "almost four yards of forms simply to get a single export consignment out of the U.S." (Leach, 1969). In the past there has been resistance to the computerization of export form filling since the forms are constantly changing. However, now that computer form-setting languages are more flexible, computerization is increasing. The complication with export documentation is that it has to be done with an eye to maneuvering liquid assets, both altering transfer prices and making intersubsidiary loans by leading or lagging shipments and their payments.

The shipment must be insured. This provides a minor opportunity to maneuver liquid assets because coverage can be placed with an insurer in the exporting nation, in the importing nation, or in a third nation insurance center such as Switzerland or Britain. From Chapter 3 we know by how much the company's cost of capital will differ in each nation; if the insurance can be written in a currency other than that in which the premium is paid, it may be particularly worthwhile to consider where to place the insurance.

Transportation Charge

Liner conferences are price cartels. They originated when steam replaced sail and the overabundance of fast tonnage led to drastic price cutting in efforts to gain or retain customers. In 1875 shipowners on the London-Calcutta route agreed on rates for certain cargos so that they could all show a profit. Liner cartel pricing was and is encouraged by governments. The U.S. Justice Department exempts conferences from antitrust laws, and in many nations government-owned liners are conference members.

There are now more than 300 conferences. All have rules that provide for unified action to prevent outside competition, uniform rates for the various classes of cargo, and limits on internal competition.

In the past, when an outside shipowner challenged a conference with lower rates, he faced the menace of a "fighting ship." Such a ship, suboidized by conference members, would undercut the outsider, forcing him out of business. (However, when a well-financed outsider threatened to challenge the conference, the potential loss was so great that the outsider may have been urged to join the conference.) However, by the U.S. Shipping Act of 1916, fighting ships were barred from U.S. ports. American conferences now depend on loyalty agreements. In exchange for a 10 to 15 percent discount, the shipper agrees to send all of his goods on a conference ship. Nevertheless, the discount is repaid only after year end and should therefore be discounted by the cost of capital. During the 1970s the Soviet Union built up its merchant marine and shaved prices to attract more business. There was very little that the Western conferences could do to retaliate apart from warning of the dangers of becoming dependent on the Soviet Union.

Uniform rates per item are charged by each liner within a price cartel. But every item has a different rate because the conference is a discriminating monopolist, charging what the market will bear for that item. A cargo that has never been shipped before will be charged a very high rate because it is "not otherwise specified" or, in container terminology, it is "freight of all kinds." The shipper's traffic department must then petition for a reclassification and is usually expected to divulge what otherwise might be considered privileged information: the firm's incremental costs of manufacture, market forecasts, and the degree of price competition in the market area from local and imported goods. In other words, conferences set rates in accordance with marginal elasticities of demand for shipping space (Officer, 1971).

Cargo classifications proliferate because shippers differ in bargaining power. All shippers must be charged the same rates for a cargo classification. However, a skillfully written classification can exclude items of most other shippers.

> Particular shippers may be given special concessions, which are normally secret, either directly in the form of reduced rates or indirectly by classifying particular cargo items into a lower rate class than that prescribed in the tariff; for example, virtually identical cargoes from different shippers may be classified differently on the basis of slight differences in packaging or in technical description. (*Liner Conference System*, 1968, p. 45)

Attention to cargo classification is vital, as illustrated by Devanney (1972). "The Atlantic and Gulf/West Coast of South America tariff lists 14 different types of wax, each with a different freight rate, and six types of water (abrated, corn steep, distilled, mineral, toilet, and 'not otherwise specified') with rates varying from $51/ton to $186/ton." "Not otherwise specified" cargo pays the highest rate. To sustain such discrimination each commodity definition has to be precise, legalistic, and long—one conference's book is 300 pages long. And there are more than 300 conferences.

Internal competition is limited to speed and service. Writing about the

West U.S.A.–Japan Conference, Devanney (1972) explained that "the U.S. owners had fought the then very high speed (21 knots) of the Mariners on cost grounds, but the U.S. Navy insisted on this capability for defense purposes [subsidies were involved]. After putting the ships in operation the U.S. owners found they could attract the greater bulk of the trade. The Japanese responded with illegal rebates until they could place still faster ships on the service."

Internal competition in service occurred during the North Atlantic rate war when some companies gave illegal rebates such as absorbing inland rail cost in the name of "through service." This additional service was in response to the threat of competition by speed when Seatrain bought four huge 27-knot Euroliners, and Sea-Land ordered eight 33-knot SL-7s. This is not an example of admirable technological progress because cost rises as the *fourth* power of speed. Oil tankers, whose cargo is probably as valuable as general liner cargo, operate at only about 15 knots.

Because of the rising price of fuel, conferences are raising prices across the board through a fuel surcharge. A fuel surcharge is applied to all ships in the conference regardless of their rates of fuel consumption, so the gas turbine-powered Euroliners and SL-7s were mothballed and then sold as troop ships.

Inventory En Route and Awaiting Customs

Just as delivery of a surface parcel to another nation takes a surprisingly long time, so do shipments of goods. Loaded railway boxcars travel an average of 1 hour per day. At the port the cargo awaits its paperwork and its ship. As a deliberate nontariff barrier, customs officers may systematically delay clearance: in the late 1970s Japanese customs officers were delaying some imports for over a month. Shipments inland are said to get lost for ridiculous reasons — the address may be inadequate or the script indecipherable by the locals. During all this time the inventory holding cost accumulates.

Customs Broker and Other Paperwork

An unloaded cargo accumulates storage fees until all necessary paperwork is complete. The company hires a customs broker to expedite this paperwork. The broker's fees are usually charged on a value basis but the fee is rarely significant, perhaps 0.5 percent with a minimum of $15, to write documents for one item. Incentives for clearing customs more speedily appear rare.

Import Duty

Each item in the product line has a customs classification in each nation and hence a rate of import duty. For example, an item entering the

United States is classified into one of 45,000 generic classifications. Two implications follow. First, if the item is not specifically mentioned in one of the 45,000 classifications, then there is some room for debate as to the classification under which it should enter. Second, although the items in a product line are homogeneous in the eyes of a corporate designer, segments of the product line may be classified differently by a customs official, and differently again by a customs official in another nation. The classification has a great effect on the rate of import duty. If a product designer realized how his choices of materials and dimensions affected tariff classifications, he might want to alter his design slightly, in function or in aesthetics, to reduce total duty paid to the world. The difficulty is that time must be invested to transform the tariff classifications of the world into a form usable for the designer of even one product line.

For each corporation, each item produced has a unique part number, as does each subassembly, up to and including the finished product. With the corporate part number is a description of the part that establishes its customs classification and hence its rate of import duty. The corporation may find it worthwhile to rewrite some of these descriptions. The descriptions of parts do not necessarily have to accord with their final use. For example, the U.S. tariff schedule specifically classifies "plastic artificial flowers" and assigns them a 32 percent *ad valorum* rate. A "snap-on" flower would seem to be a "plastic artificial flower," but if the flower has not yet been snapped onto the stem, both may be classified as "plastic components," which enter at a 20 percent rate of duty. Nevertheless, that 12 percent duty difference would have been obviated if the designer had enlivened his flowers with any nonplastic material. The creative challenge is to develop a thesaurus which defines the components of artificial flowers as plastic components.

Of the 140 tariff systems in the world, all but India, Czechoslovakia, Canada, and the United States use the Brussels Tariff Nomenclature (BTN). The European Economic Community's common external duty was to be a simple average of the member nation's duty for each item. To implement that, each member's tariff system had to be translated into a single common nomenclature, an effort that required several years and was performed in Brussels. It is commonly thought that the BTN classifies items uniformly in all adopting nations. This is true only up to a four-digit identification number BTN xx.xx For example,

BTN   84.62   Ball, roller, or needle bearings.
BTN   84.63   Transmission shafts, cranks, bearing housings, plain shaft bearings, gears and gearing (including friction gears and gear-box and other variable speed gears), flywheels, pulleys and pulley blocks, clutches and shaft couplings.
BTN   84.65   Machinery parts, not containing electrical connectors, insulators, coils, contacts, or other electrical features and not falling within any other headings in this chapter.

The four-digit classifications are, in essence, standard worldwide and serve to prevent gerrymandering of descriptions. Within each four-digit classification each individual nation creates its own subclassifications to create its six-digit classification. Duty is imposed at the level of the *six*-digit classification. Hence uniformity does *not* exist and a company part number usually has a different BTN six-digit classification in each nation.

In addition to the corporate part number, its description, and its six-digit classification code into each importing nation, a corporation should also be aware of the exporting nation as there may be special tariff treatments such as:

1. Most favored nation treatment (almost all nations in GATT).
2. Common markets.
3. Common markets with quotas.
4. Duty drawbacks.
5. Local content or common market content requirements.

The multilateral tariff negotiations signed in 1979 resulted in a reduction in most import duties of most nations. Nevertheless, during the years of negotiations, government officials of all nations appear to have taught each other subtle nontariff barriers to trade.

Repackaging and Inland Transportation

This leg of the journey is uninteresting and few corporations bother to analyze it. Thus there is often a tendency for overcharging to occur.

Inspection at Subsidiary and Shrinkage

A persistent anxiety surrounds the inspection of import containers. In subsidiary after subsidiary, managers worry about receiving the wrong item and tell stories of having received spare parts for a different model, or equipment that had not been tropically treated. Little control can be exercised when such distances are involved: the subsidiary is dependent on the accuracy of the factory packers. Because of the delay between packing and unpacking, it is very difficult to set up an incentive system that provides meaningful feedback to the packers in the factory.

Shrinkage is a polite term for items stolen, smashed, or spoiled (by salt spray, for example). Containers have greatly reduced pilferage by dock workers, which used to be a problem with, among other cargoes, liquor shipments. Cargo can get smashed within a container just as eggs can crack in a carton. For example, compared to ocean transport, rail transport imposes more severe shock loads and vibration damage if there is severe shunting and poor road beds.

Inventory

The appropriate inventory models to use in the subsidiary are those that depict a stochastic lead time (a probability distribution between order entry and receipt of the goods). The amount of inventory held on average can decrease if:

1. The subsidiary sales are predictable and controllable.
2. Replenishment shipments are frequent.
3. The lead time is predictable.
4. Accurate packing is persistently expected.
5. There are several alternate factories producing the item, lest production at one be disrupted.
6. Airfreight could be used to expedite emergency shipments.
7. There are several possible suppliers within the nation lest import permits be suspended.
8. The subsidiary has enough managers who can spend time managing inventory.

Discretionary inventory is kept at both the factory and the subsidiary. Most inventory should be kept at the subsidiary. However, three offsetting factors are the interest cost on paying logistics charges earlier, the possibility that the corporation may suddenly quit this nation, and the possibility of having to reexport if a sister subsidiary has stocked out.

Export Incentive Programs (A Possible Deduction)

Most governments aid their exporters. Cizaskas (1976) described the export credit insurance and financing systems of the major trading countries. The French system provides an interesting example of a diversified credit program within a complex pattern of state participation and support. A French exporter may obtain insurance against political and commercial losses covering 80 to 90 percent of the credit he extends to foreign buyers of French goods. Unlike most other national export financing programs, the French system also provides for its exporters protection against specified exchange rate losses, reimbursement of inflationary price increases, and the availability of public "concessional" funds for large projects undertaken by French firms in developing countries.

An exporter usually wants total cash now. This cash is provided by the export development bank. The foreign buyer usually wants to stretch out payments. This the export development bank allows. For example, the exporter might receive FF4 million now, and the foreign buyer promises to make a specified sequence of payments, for example $200,000 per annum for each of the next 5 years. The exporter and foreign buyer can both be subsidiaries of the same multinational corporation. The corporation must focus on the sequence of cash flows received by the exporting subsidiary and paid by the importing subsidiary. The difference between the present values of these two cash flows (discounted using dual variables as discussed in Chapter 3) is the dollar export incentive to be deducted from this logistics cost calculation.

Duty Drawbacks (A Possible Deduction)

Some foreign subassemblies may be built into an export order. For example, think of U.S. components that were sent abroad for assembly and are now reentering the United States. (Examples include electronic assembly in Taiwan and American Motors Corp. having its engines assembled in Mexico.) The government charges duty only on the value that was added abroad. The U.S. Customs Service interpretation of Item 807.00 states:

> 1. Item 807.00 applies if no operation is performed on the exported U.S. components except for attaching them to other components to form the completed article; for example, by soldering (condensers attached to other components by soldering to form radios), by sewing (cut parts attached to other pieces by sewing to form garments), or by force-fitting, pressing, gluing, or similar operation.
>
> . . .
>
> 5. There is no restriction against using some foreign-made components and materials together with the U.S. components in the assembly process. However, *only* those U.S. components meeting all requirements of Item 807.00 are eligible for deduction under Item 807.00.

Each nation makes and administers its own rules on duty drawbacks. Such a duty drawback should be deducted from the logistics cost (after being reduced by the cost of the recordkeeping and paperwork and discounting the duty drawback because of the time lag from when duty was paid to the time the drawback is received).

Quotas and Local Content Laws (Use the Cost Equivalent)

Many nations select certain industries on which to impose import quotas, local content requirements, industrial benefits to offset military purchases from abroad, and the like. A quota is usually imposed to protect a declining industry. Local content requirements stimulate a growing industry by requiring that a percentage of the value added of goods sold in the country must be local. Exports create value added credits. Thus when there is 100 percent local content requirement, each import sold in that nation must be offset by exports whose value of local content equals the import. When a government makes a large purchase of sophisticated equipment (e.g., weapons) it frequently attempts to have some subassemblies made locally; items of an equivalent skill category which are exported may also be considered offsets.

Customer Uneasiness over Products Imported
from This Nation (Add Cost)

There are prejudices against (and occasionally for) imports from specific nations. Market research should be conducted in each nation to determine the price discount an item commands for each possible nation of origin.

Conclusion

The sum of these 15 costs divided by the quantity shipped equals the logistics cost from the factory to the sales subsidiary.

If the cost of capital is high, and if the corporation is comparing shipment from a nearby factory with shipment from a cheaper factory on the other side of the world, it may be worthwhile to compute the costs more precisely by including the time value of money. Thus there are two more considerations: the flow of actual cash outflows incurred in making the shipment and how long the journey lasts. With large, infrequent shipments, the interest accumulates on the inventory on the first day that it is sold. We would like to compute the total unit cost of the item.

First, on a time line as in Exhibit 5.2, mark all the actual expenditures incurred for this shipment. This pinpoints the costs relating to each shipment of inventory. Assume that the sales subsidiary keeps its inventory on a first-in, first-out basis. Work backwards through time to when the shipment cleared customs (mark on the time line when the duty actually had to be paid), and back to the time this shipment was manufactured. All those cash outflows on the time line, future valued to the day of first use, constitute the delivered cost of this shipment. Present value these costs to one datum point; the day of first use is most convenient.

In the geocentric section it will be seen that a company might consider chartering its own ships. If it does, a ship is so huge and the route between subsidiaries will have so many legs that the time value of money should be computed.

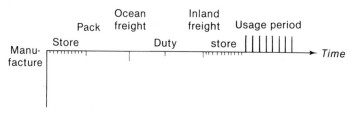

EXHIBIT 5.2
Cash outlays to present value.

Second Phase: Subsidiary-Centered View of Logistics (Polycentric)

During the second phase of a product life cycle, plants are constructed abroad. The marketing manager of each nation vies for a plant. In his striving, he is motivated to underplay logistics.

Let us stand in the shoes of a marketing manager who has spent the best part of his life building a loyal market he and his company can be proud of. Wholesalers and retailers know the company sales force and the standards it represents. Both company and customer resist temptations to cheat since they know the company is committed to stay. Let us pursue a medical image. A sales organization depends on products for its life support system. Only if the supply is adequate can the sales organization live. If the product supply fails, there is no way in which the company can avoid a depletion of goodwill through its entire channel of distribution. Furthermore, interruption of supply gives hostile competitors the opportunity to increase market share by signing up distributors.

One may reasonably predict that the sales manager abroad would prefer to have a factory in the safety of his territory. To this end he will convince himself and attempt to convince headquarters that his customers feel vulnerable without a local source of supply. All governments encourage local manufacture (import substitution), although the apparent seriousness of their urgings must be gauged with care. We might expect the sales manager to pass on to headquarters full reports of such urging. We might even suspect him of dropping involuntary clues to the government agency to state their requirements in the strongest diplomatic language. We might further expect the sales manager to magnify the significance of corporate errors. Of the thousands of containers he may receive in a year there will inevitably be errors in packing and in the delivery schedule. Instead of coping with these, we may expect him to exaggerate some of the difficulties.

It is said that every senior manager at one time or another has had to put his job on the line and threaten to resign unless his request is met. We may expect that the sales manager will time his threats to coincide with occasions when the corporation depends on his profit contribution. In the face of such pressures and in the absence of a strong analytical staff to assert cost analyses to the contrary, a polycentric corporation will have a proliferation of small local plants and hence international logistics will not be a major corporate concern. Those few items that are shipped between nations will be those on which no major sales commitment has been established and for which even a sales manager cannot deny the economies of centralized manufacture.

In a polycentric corporation, the logistics manager is under constant scrutiny. His every mistake is enlarged out of proportion by those who wish he did not exist. New plants are being constructed and so logistics flow patterns are being changed continuously. Worse yet, any delay in the scheduled start-up of a new plant means that logistics contracts have to be revised. In all this confusion some shipments get lost and hence it is essential that the logistics manager maintain personal contact with freight forwarders, shipping companies, customs brokers, and so on.

To cope with this detail it is common for a corporation to hire rate clerks from the carriers. A former clerk, hired for this expertise, tends to see his job as monitoring freight rates and tracking lost shipments rather than planning a logistics network. One might also predict that such individuals would use the mystique of detail as a protective shield for their jobs. Many export traffic departments are overwhelmed by paperwork, and their managers burden themselves by measuring their output in meters of forms. In order to cope it may be sensible to study how banks and stock brokers process paperwork, using ideas developed by industrial engineers to organize factory work flow.

Third Phase: Geocentric View of Logistics

In the final phase of the product life cycle, inefficient plants may be closed. Production will be rationalized. If several product divisions are shipping between two ports, it is advantageous to coordinate their shipments to keep a steady flow of full containers. Specifically, the corporation may be able to bargain with the carriers for a price cut or justify a staff study of cheaper means of shipping.

Planners in geocentric corporations foresee a substantial increase in intercorporate shipments of subassemblies and products. For decades governments of developing nations have required that multinationals build a local factory to produce part of their product line as the price of admission to their national market. Miniature plants still abound, but cost pressure is forcing corporations to build for economies of scale. The emerging outcome is a network of single-product plants, one per nation, each exporting most of its production while importing the rest of the product line from the network members. More intercorporate shipments imply a busier and more important corporate traffic department. Are traffic departments ready for the task ahead? Unfortunately not: Some tend to see logistics not as decision making but as paperwork.

Most corporations draw a sharp distinction between sales and marketing. Some salesmen have the wrong personalities for marketing. A similar distinction should be drawn between freight specialists such as the former rate clerks and logistics planners. A geocentric corporation needs a logistics planning staff. The staff has two tasks: to reduce costs between each pair of ports and to record these costs (current and projected) as a set of computer-based transportation tableaux (one per major product category) that link all plants to all markets.

First Task: Reduce Logistics Cost Between Each Pair of Ports

Corporate analysts are disturbed by the disparity between the traffic department's opaqueness as to why costs are so high and a consultant's claim that "a modern bulk carrier can transport one ton of cargo around the world at costs no greater than non bulk transport costs from New York to Philadelphia" (Jones, 1971). Perhaps the liners should be replaced and the corporation should charter its own general cargo vessels. A design engineer's viewpoint may be needed to cost estimate all the routes from a factory to a market. The first and most creative step is to envision all the *possible* routes from a factory to a market. Replace rail by truck or barge. Use a different port to evade a grasping carrier. Realize that the trans-Siberian railroad charges 40 percent less than ocean shipment (via the Suez Canal) between Europe and Japan. Consider daily airfreight to eliminate inventory. Consider a slight redesign of the product to better fit the classification categories of customs, ocean liners, or ground transportation. A corporation also needs a tough bargainer who can bluff his way to rate concessions.

Freight rates per ton mile vary so widely that imaginative planning may be highly rewarded. The rising cost of fuel will continue to raise the rates cited by Jones, but their relative magnitudes (and certainly their ranking) are persisting.

Mode	*Cost per ton mile*
Modern heavy trucks	0.80–2.00 cents U.S.
Railroad hopper cars	1.00–1.20
Unit trains	0.50–0.80
Inland tugs and barges	0.20–3.00
Liner conference vessels	0.10–1.20
Chartered bulk vessels	0.03–0.06

If the corporation is now using liner conference vessels, the logistics planning staff should consider other means. The first step is to consider a contract of affreightment.

A contract of affreightment is for a specified quantity of cargo to be carried, not on a named vessel, but on any vessel the carrier chooses. A corporation with adequate production plans (see Chapter 6) may be willing to commit itself to a certain flow of cargo, usually an annual flow with monthly maxima and minima. It then can shop among shipowners to find one or more who will contract to carry its shipments. Usually the minor shipowners who operate slow ships will be most interested. There are possible legal constraints (Manca, 1971), but there are also hundreds of variants to a contract of affreightment (Hill, 1974).

Fundamental to every analysis of ocean logistics is the need to translate risks and uncertainties into higher average inventory levels so that an analyst can estimate the cost of providing the same effective service. By signing a contract of affreightment the corporation receives a 15 to 30 percent discount from liner rates. On the other hand the less frequent affreightment service necessistates larger corporate inventories. Even safety stock inventory must be higher because makeup shipments sent by liners will not receive the customary 10 to 15 percent loyalty discount. The cost of lower flexibility, which is long term for a contract of affreightment, may be lower than it appears. By locating plants and assigning products, the corporation has implicitly committed itself to a predictable need for tonnage. Step 1 of the solution procedure is to analyze the liner/ affreightment service decision for every transportation route the corporation uses. For every pair of ports i and j make the liner/affreightment decision to calculate the total monthly cost of inventories, makeup shipments, and payments to the carrier.

If all divisions of a corporation combined have enough cargo on certain routes, the corporation can save money by chartering its own vessels. Several multinational manufacturers have taken this step. "The export orientation is dramatically underlined by Volkswagen's standing as a naval power: the company runs an armada of seventy ships with a capacity of over one million tons; the biggest private oceangoing charter fleet in existence" (Ball, 1972). Let us distinguish among the different kinds of charters (Chorley and Giles, 1980):

Bareboat Charters. In the case of a bareboat charter, a vessel is leased without a crew. The corporation bears all the risk of ownership but can subcharter if its demand estimates prove wrong. The corporation gets off-balance-sheet financing, and the bareboat hire is a current expense. Furthermore, there may be tax angles to consider.

Time Charters. These are the most frequently used method for chartering. The corporation leases the ship with full crew, and as with bareboat hire, it pays regardless of bad weather, port delays, or unavailability of cargo. The shipowner bears only the risk of keeping the ship running; it is "off hire" only when it cannot perform. Time charters, with durations of 3 to 20 years, are negotiated through brokers directly with the owners of the ship.

"Spot" or Voyage Charter. Vessels are constantly becoming available in almost every port, ready for instant employment. The shipowner supplies crew and fuel and takes the risk of the weather; the company provides the cargo and guarantees that loading and unloading will take no longer than the contracted "laydays." Voyage charter agreements are usually standard forms, but clauses can be added and deleted.

Charters of less than a year are commonly arranged through a market such as the Baltic Shipping Exchange in London. Both time and spot markets have been remarkably free of government interference, and worldwide communication is excellent.

The telephone is always — literally always at hand. In the car, the bathtub, at the exclusive restaurant with the permanently reserved table, the phone is the shipowner's lifeline . . . . "All I want is five minutes advance notice the first time the Japanese steel industry falls 5% short of its goal. Just so I can fix my fleet long term before the bottom drops out of the market." . . . This is a world in which a telephone commitment is a bond, a different, hard, calculating world. (*Forbes*, August 1970, p. 20.)

Charters, contracts of affreightment, or airfreight each might reduce logistics costs between two ports, but before this improvement can be implemented, two conceptual changes are necessary. First, as traffic departments receive larger capital appropriations they will have to be penalized for the cost of delays and errors in shipments. It is little wonder that subsidiary managers feel such anxiety at being dependent on imported subassemblies. Though vessels hit storms, and manufacturing plants are careless in what they pack, traffic departments should be motivated to exercise ingenuity and vigilance; real penalties may encourage them.

Second, vessels are designed with an eye to conference carriers who want maximum speed, subject to cost constraints. A corporate container ship may cruise as slowly as an oil tanker, but the vessel must keep on schedule in even the worst weather; this implies a hull designed for low drag in high waves, a propulsion system with reserve power, and a reliability analysis of optimal maintenance.

For purposes of production smoothing (Chapter 6) and plant location (Chapter 7), analysts need forecasts of logistics costs. Whether the corporation owns or has long-term charters on its vessels, the logistics department always has the option of spot chartering. Hence the price it quotes should be this month's spot price, and an estimate of what the spot price will be in each future period. Like a term structure of bond interest rates, one can estimate the spot rate five years from now by comparing five-year with four-year charter quotations for equivalent vessels.

Airfreight. Some flows may justify the chartering of vessels; other flows may be better handled by airfreight. However, airfreight costs per mile vary widely. The highest cost comes from the cost of an airfreight company operating jet freighters on this route and returning empty. The low cost occurs on routes with a large passenger volume. Wide-body passenger aircraft carry airfreight containers if their revenue exceeds the incremental cost of fuel (the additional fuel caused by the heavier load). Both these bounds are easy for an experienced analyst to estimate. Furthermore, the bounds can be forecast to vary as the cost of jet fuel varies.

Actual airfreight rates vary between these bounds, occasionally rising above what is considered the upper bound when a world crisis prompts the utilization of all airfreighter capacity available, and the price is bid higher temporarily.

If all cargo on a route went airfreight all the time it would be easy to estimate the total of the 15 costs, and the service would also be relatively easy to manage. It is much more usual to reserve airfreight for emergencies. To have an airfreight backup allows a reduction in safety stock inventories. Unfortunately, most human beings find it much more difficult to manage with contingency plans of this kind. They demand resolution.

Second Task: Transportation Tableaux

The second task of the logistics group is to maintain computer-based transportation tableaux. These will be used in Chapter 6 and Chapter 7. Whenever two or more factories can produce an item, the logistics planning group has the problem of deciding which markets should be supplied from which factories. The objective is to meet demands at the lowest total logistics and production costs. The decisions to be made are the output of each factory and the choice of factories to supply each market.

On a sheet of paper, lay out a tableau with factories listed down the side of the page, and markets across the top of the page. From each factory (call it i), to each market (call it j), the 15 logistics costs have been analyzed. The total logistics cost is c_{ij} per unit (using Chapter 3 dual variables, expenditures in each currency have been converted to one standard). List at the bottom of each column the latest demand estimates d_j for each market, for this item.

Each factory has a normal production rate for this item, p_i. The cost of production is usually analyzed with fixed and variable components. If the factory must produce faster than normal, the *variable* cost per unit will usually be a little higher than it would be if production were below normal. Only a certain rate of production above normal may be possible.

The transportation problem is a classic of operations research sketched in Exhibit 5.3 as a reminder. Huge problems involving 10,000 markets and 500 factories can be solved in a minute of computer time. The solution is a list of the amount to be shipped from each factory to each market which minimizes the global production costs plus the logistics cost. In other words, the computation cost is negligible compared with the cost of thinking and establishing the logistics costs. Systematic data management is needed because there is a separate transportation tableau for each major item, solved using a separate forecast for each period into the planning future. Keeping these updated with the latest estimates of costs and demands allows the headquarters logistics group to give quick responses to the daily problems and emergencies that arise, and to have a consistent basis for planning.

The transportation tableau is a tool that will be used over and over again throughout the rest of this book. In Chapter 6 the transportation tableau will reallocate markets to plants as demands fluctuate. In Chapter 7 cost minimizing reallocations will cost out each possible new plant site. In Chapter 9 a needed input is the incremental landed cost at each market. This comes from the transportation problem, where it is the dual variable associated with that market demand (averaged over the time periods).

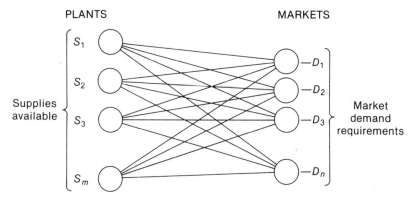

PLANTS   MARKETS

Supplies available

Market demand requirements

Network for Transportation Problem.

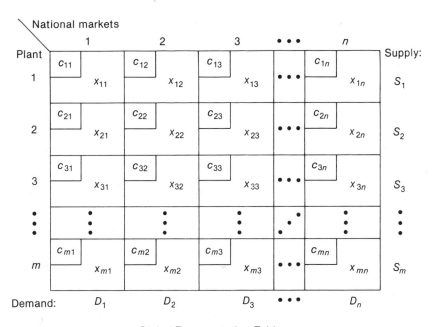

Global Transportation Tableau

EXHIBIT 5.3

Each logistics network can be solved by computer as a transportation tableau.

169

Conclusions

The logistics function in a multinational corporation is rarely large, nor is transportation cost more than a small percentage of product cost. Nevertheless, neither of these observations should beguile one into underestimating the usefulness of a well-managed logistics department. The profitability of some multinationals depends on their ability to separate marketing from manufacturing. To do so with calm assurance necessitates a reliable and responsive logistics system.

It is more common to see the logistics function scattered over several rival jurisdictions within the corporation, staffed by former rate clerks who have never been motivated to see the whole logistics cost. The unfortunate consequences are that too many small plants are built, sensible export markets are never launched, and periodic stock-outs allow rivals to gain a larger market share. The payoffs in logistics management are as asymmetric as they are in ambulance care. Improve a good ambulance service, and the gain is hardly noticeable. But many ambulance services are poor, and what a damnable waste that is.

Questions from Other Viewpoints

1. *Corporate Rational Normative Global.* You just covered this viewpoint in the chapter.
2. *Corporate Rational Normative Subsidiary.* If a corporation managed its own vessels rather than using liners, what adjustments would be required in a subsidiary's inventory policy?
3. *Corporate Rational Descriptive Global.* Find the names of some manufacturing corporations that charter vessels to transport their own products.
4. *Corporate Rational Descriptive Subsidiary.* It appears to be common practice for a subsidiary inventory manager to hold a high "safety stock" inventory. Suppose a headquarters team is on its way to audit your subsidiary's inventory practices. What information will they probably request? Think of a way to present your analysis of the information to highlight the unreliability of supply.
5. *Corporate Emotional Normative Global.* The impression one gets is that shipowners engage in a high-risk business and are compensated by a high return. What emotional problems arise in a corporation in which different divisions face very different kinds of risks?
6. *Corporate Emotional Normative Subsidiary.* Shipping experts are specialists in a difficult art, the mathematics of which would be formidable if rational analysis were attempted. Shipping experts can be emotionally committed to their subsidiary or can withdraw

(passive resistance) into their esoteric language and customs. Describe how you would work to assure a climate of supervision so that these vital specialists would not feel the need to withdraw.

7. *Corporate Emotional Descriptive Global.* Viewed as an investment, a logistics department may yield an attractive long-run return but the variance is high. Shipping has an esoteric language, its own traditions, even its own legal system. So if corporate executives suspect that something is being mismanaged within their shipping subsidiary they cannot easily move in a new executive to straighten it out. Give two examples of other such investments, and discuss how the corporate executives manage them.

8. *Corporate Emotional Descriptive Subsidiary.* You are the ocean traffic manager in a subsidiary of a polycentric corporation. From headquarters comes word that the corporation may charter a few ships, and will certainly start pressuring the steamship conferences. Describe your *feelings.*

9. *Societal Rational Normative Global.* What social good comes from there being *both* liners and chartered vessels? Develop your argument tightly enough to be able to predict whether the system could exist (wouldn't come unraveled) if one nation refused to enforce the requisite commercial law. How about two nations?

10. *Societal Rational Normative Subsidiary.* Sometimes a government feels that the liner conferences are overcharging to the point of affecting its export trade. A commonly proposed remedy is that the government buy ships and become a member of the conference so as to share in its profits. Assume that the profits of the government conference ships are devoted totally to subsidizing the exporters. Under what conditions might the exporters gain more than they would if the rates were reduced until the conference ships ran at cost?

11. *Societal Rational Descriptive Global.* In your nation, when was the most recent major government investigation into shipping conferences? To find out, use the index of a major newspaper such as *The New York Times.* Read about the conduct of the investigation. Write a summary of the negotiating points on such topics as the supply of vessel space, rate stability, import duties, and national security.

12. *Societal Rational Descriptive National.* A container port is a very expensive investment, usually paid by a government or government agency. Is there any evidence that any container ports are built as a result of rational analysis?

13. *Societal Emotional Normative Global.* The motto of IBM World Trade is "World Peace through World Trade." Under what world conditions would this happen? Are there any conditions under which war might be made more likely by trade?

14. *Societal Emotional Normative Subsidiary.* Your nation exports raw

materials and imports finished manufactures. Per ton freight rates on raw materials are low and on manufactures are high. Denounce this exploitation. (Be emotional with pinpoint focus by anticipating the responses from shipping conferences and rebutting each with scorn.)

15. *Societal Emotional Descriptive Global.* Why do some people find romance in ships and shipping?

16. *Societal Emotional Descriptive National.* Many nations have an airline as a "flag carrier." Imagine you are chairman of such an airline. Select four problems whose solution is confounded by your being a flag carrier. Select those that would cause you most anguish, and describe the emotional content of each. (Do not go out and interview anyone.) Feel free to use your powers of empathy and imagination.

Bibliography to Chapter 5

Ball, Robert, "Volkswagen Gets a Much Needed Tune Up," *Fortune*, March 1972.

Chorley, Lord and O.C. Giles, *Shipping Law*, 7th ed. (London: Pitman, 1980).

Cizaskas, Albert C., "French Exporters Are Backed by Diversified Credit Program," *IMF Survey*, June 7, 1976, p. 162.

Cuffley, C.F.H., *Ocean Freights and Chartering* (London: Staples Press, 1962).

Devanney, John W., III, V.M. Livanos and R.J. Stewart, *Conference Rate-Making and the West Coast of South America*, Technical Report 72-1, Commodity Transportation and Economic Development Laboratory, Massachusetts Institute of Technology, 1972.

Goss, Richard, "Shipping Conferences," *Journal of Transport Economics and Policy*, Vol. 5 (May 1971), pp. 173-183.

Gruber, William H., Dileep Mehta and Raymond Vernon, "The R & D Factor in International Trade and International Investment of United States Industries," *Journal of Political Economy*, Vol. 74, No. 1 (1967), pp. 207-215.

Hill, C.J.S., *An Introduction to the Law of Carriage of Goods by Sea* (London: Stanford Marine Press, 1974).

Jones, Roger M., "Imagination in Bulk for the Seventies," Jones, Bardelmeir, Clements and Co. Ltd., Nassau, Bahamas, 1971.

Leach, Rodney, "International Freight Transport Enters a New Era," *McKinsey Quarterly*, Vol. 14 (Winter 1969), pp. 3-47.

Manca, Plinio, *International Maritime Law*, European Transport Law, 19, Justikiestraat, Antwerp, Belgium, 1971 (especially "Affreightment" in Volume II).

Metaxas, Bas N., *The Economics of Tramp Shipping* (New York: Oxford University Press, 1971).

Officer, Lawrence H., "Monopoly and Monopolistic Competition in the International Transportation Industry," *Western Economic Journal*, Vol. 9, No. 2 (1971), pp. 134-156.

Terpstra, Vern, *International Marketing* (New York: Holt, Rinehart and Winston, Inc., 1972).

"The Billionaire Sealords," *Forbes*, Vol. 116, August 1, 1970, pp. 20–23.

The Liner Conference System, Report by the Secretariat of the Conference on Trade and Development (UNCTAD), United Nations, New York, TD/B/C.4/38 (1968).

The Liner Conference System, Report by the Secretariat of the Conference on Trade and Development (UNCTAD), United Nations, New York TD/B/C.4/62 Rev. 1 (1970) (Sales No. E70.70IID.9).

Williamson, Oliver, *Markets and Hierarchies* (Englewood Cliffs, NJ: Prentice-Hall, 1975).

CHAPTER SIX

Production Smoothing

Introductory Note to the Case

Ford Motor Co. Ltd.

For years business schools and consultants have been analyzing inventories to reduce the amount of unnecessary investment. Perhaps inventories now are too low. Certainly one gets the impression that they were maintained at too low a level during the merger of Ford's operations in West Germany and the United Kingdom.

This case clearly poses a warning. A polycentric production process will find ways to resist central coordination. The lesson of the case is to expect this difficulty, plan for it, and move deliberately but with carefully anticipated contingency plans. A reorganization can be perceived as a capital investment.

This case describes Ford's European car. Ford now markets a world car, with many subassemblies identical even though made at different factories around the world. The kinds of problems described in the case will always exist. How they are anticipated and managed determines the benefit that can flow from global production smoothing.

Ford Motor Co. Ltd.

To hear officials of some multinational companies talk, there is a surefire success formula for any large corporation with

By William M. Carley, *The Wall Street Journal*, February 20, 1974. Reprinted by permission of *The Wall Street Journal*, © Dow Jones and Co., Inc., 1974. All rights reserved.

global facilities. First of all, they say, the multinational should unify its product lines around the world to obtain mass production efficiency. Second, it should make its parts wherever such manufacturing is most economical. Third, it should focus its sales efforts on countries where markets are growing fastest. The result, say the formula's proponents, is a maximization of profits.

If all this sounds reasonable, not to say obvious, one might consider the fact that Ford Motor Co. has been following just that formula in recent years and is finding that the scheme isn't as surefire as it seems. This by no means implies that the giant automaker is thinking of abandoning its integrated approach; however, it does mean that Ford is finding some major flaws in the approach — a finding that is emphasized by talking to Gerd Maletz, an owner of one of the biggest Ford dealerships in Germany.

"Take spare parts," Mr. Maletz says. "An engine for one Ford model now must come from Britain, and we may wait months for it. And if the British workers are on strike — and they're always on strike — we wait and wait and wait. We could get a German engine in a couple of days."

Nor does Mr. Maletz think much of the quality of the cars produced by Ford's integrated manufacturing plants in Europe. "If you buy a new Granada (the top of Ford's European line), for the first 10,000 kilometers it seems very quiet, smooth and solid," he says. "But then there's a rattle here, and something goes wrong there, and you begin to run into all kinds of problems. We're having trouble selling the car."

In short, the integration of international operations can bring a host of problems along with the benefits. For Ford, integration in Europe has meant some huge cost savings. At the same time, however, the move has meant snarled production lines, soured labor relations, quality and delivery problems and, in some countries (especially Germany), a major decline in market share.

And the experience has had a major impact on the totality of Ford Motor Co. Last year, Ford's European operations accounted for about 25 percent of the company's worldwide production of 5.7 million cars and trucks. Ford's two principal European subsidiaries, Ford of Britain and Ford of Germany, together accounted for 20 percent of their parent's 1972 revenues of $20.2 billion and about 14 percent of the company's profit of $870 million. If it weren't for all the problems in Europe, these percentages, especially the contribution to profit, would have been much larger.

De that as it may, many multinational companies around the world still favor integrating their far-flung operations, and this is particularly true of those American multinationals that went on a shopping spree for foreign companies in the 1960s. "We have no choice," says a vice president of one American company that plans to follow Ford's footsteps in integrating European operations. "We have to have common products so we can go for cheap mass production. It's too expensive to manufacture on a country-by-country basis—you can't do that much longer without going broke."

A Matter of Economy

This vice president, as well as other officials connected with American multinationals, would do well to take a close look at the experience of Ford, which decided on integration in 1967. At the time, the company's rationale for so doing seemed sound indeed: Integration would avoid unnecessarily duplicating the amount—some $100 million—that it costs to engineer and produce a new auto model. "There's no sense spending that a dozen times or more for each country in Europe, when you need spend it only once," explains Gordon Guthrie, general sales manager of Ford's German subsidiary.

So Ford decided to produce just one European line in place of the completely different cars that used to be turned out by its British and German plants. And the single line began to reduce costs in another way, since the company began to buy parts in bigger volumes—meaning lower prices—from its outside suppliers.

Along with its integration of production, Ford also moved to shift its marketing emphases from countries like Britain, where auto sales were languishing in the 1960s due to government credit controls, to countries like France and Italy, where sales were growing. "In countries where markets were static, we had some of our strongest and most imaginative management teams; in other countries where the opportunities for expansion were greater, we had much smaller resources," Stanley Gillen, then chairman of the integrated operation (called Ford of Europe), told a company management meeting in 1971.

The Early Stages

To achieve integration, Ford began to weave a complex manufacturing web that stretched from its big plants in

Britain and Germany to its smaller units in Belgium, France, Ireland, the Netherlands, and Portugal. It was planned that some units would make parts, some would assemble finished autos, and some would do both, with the entire operation being directed from Ford of Europe's headquarters in Warley, outside of London.

But even in the very early stages, there were problems. One Ford executive, an American who moved from Detroit to Britain to help set up Ford of Europe, says he quickly ran into nationality differences. "It was easy to get our British people to agree (to a plan), but five minutes later they were always back questioning it," the American recalls. "It seemed almost impossible to get the German Ford people to agree to anything; but once they did they just kept marching even if they were marching right off the end of the earth."

The first all-new auto launched by Ford of Europe was a medium-sized car called the Cortina Mark III in Britain and the Taunus in Germany. The launch, which began in 1970, was a disaster, and the after effects are still plaguing Ford. "There's no question who screwed that one up," Mr. Guthrie conceded.

The fiasco stemmed partly from British experience with the metric system. For British workers had just converted to that system, long used by Germany and other continental countries; but, says one of the British workers, "we were still thinking in inches." As a result, the British and German parts often didn't mesh. "The doors didn't fit, the bonnet (hood) didn't fit, nothing fit," says Arthur Nestlor, a metal finisher in Ford's Dagenham, England, body plant.

It has been argued by British workers that some of the German-designed parts were too precise. "Our men often work with a one-sixteenth-inch tolerance, but on the German engine-suspension system, we had to work down to two- or three-thousandths of a bloody inch," contends Joe Macrae, a union shop steward at Dagenham. "The Germans wanted an engineering job done on the production line, and that's impossible."

Because of all the snafus, the Cortina-Taunus assembly line in Dagenham barely moved along. By January 1971, when some kinks had been ironed out, the line was speeded up — much to the displeasure of some workers, Mr. Macrae says. Coincidentally, Ford's wage contract was expiring at the time; and on January 29, 1971, unions struck Ford in Britain, halting production for nine weeks. It wasn't until September, nearly a year after initial production of the new car began, that Dagenham hit peak production. Ford says the peak should have been reached in two months.

But the problems attendant to the Cortina-Taunus launch have had an even longer-lasting impact in Germany. First of all, of course, there were the immediate effects of the British strike. "Britain struck, our plants went down and we fell flat on our tails," says a former executive of Ford's German operation. "Our dealers were crying for cars and they couldn't get them." But even after the strike was over, production problems led to quality problems, and consumer tests in Germany showed that the public thought the Taunus rated low on quality.

To avoid a second fiasco, especially in quality-conscious Germany, the launch of Ford's next new car was delayed until April 1972, six months later than had been planned. This car was the top-of-the-line Granada (a less luxurious and somewhat less powerful version of the same car is called the Consul), and the delay, if necessary, was nonetheless costly. For one thing, four months prior to the Granada's debut, General Motors Corp.'s German subsidiary, Opel, came out with its new Rekord line, which quickly snatched sales from Ford. But another damaging factor was that by delaying mass production until April, Ford of Germany missed the peak springtime selling season.

As a result of these problems, a Ford official concedes, "the Consul-Granada never has picked up sales momentum." Underscoring his words is the fact that the Consul-Granada production line in Germany was closed for a week last December due to slow sales.

Five Years, Five Chairmen

Ford of Europe has also been entangled in organizational problems, one being leadership. There have been five chairmen of Ford of Europe in five years, making continuity of policy difficult. (The current chairman, William Burke, previously headed Ford's Asian and Pacific operations.) Creation of Ford of Europe has also meant that some British executives have had to move to Germany and vice versa, which sometimes hasn't pleased all the executives. "They called me the 'slave trader,'" says a former Ford man who ordered some transfers.

The new layer of bureaucracy, which was felt by some Ford executives in Britain and Germany to have reduced their access to corporate decision makers in Detroit, has also created ill-will. And there have been bitter fights over pricing, with Ford of Europe pushing higher prices to maximize profits at the same time that some operating companies were trying to price their cars lower to be more competitive in the market.

In fact, Ford of Europe, which was supposed to improve communications, has instead created some bottlenecks of its own. "Everything, including hiring a single worker, has to go to Warley (Ford of Europe headquarters) for approval, and it can take forever," says Heinz Allrup, who represents workers at Ford of Germany plants. He cites the case of a foreman who died six months ago. "We just got permission to fill his job," Mr. Allrup says.

Another example: One day last year a Ford of Europe man walked into a German plant and announced that a department employing over 100 men would be closed. A worker's representative got on the phone to Hans-Adolf Barthelmeh, then chairman of Ford of Germany, and asked what was going on. It was the first time Mr. Barthelmeh had heard of the closing. (The shutdown was later rescinded.)

"General Animosity"

Hans-Adolf Barthelmeh is no longer with Ford of Europe, nor are several other executives who chafed at the integrated operation's various communications gaps and arbitrary transfers. But integration has also caused disaffection at nonexecutive levels. "There is a general animosity toward Ford of Europe," says Mr. Allrup, the German workers' representative. The reasons for this animosity are multifaceted. German workers, for example, are angry over layoffs stemming from British strikes. (Ford's Cologne plant recently said it would lay off 4,450 workers in the weeks ahead, with one of the cited reasons being the British three-day workweek.) British workers, on the other hand, are fearful of losing jobs to Germany.

But Ford of Europe's problems go beyond its work force. Take, for example, the case of its marketing plans. The German subsidiary was to have fed cars into France and Italy; however, Ford officials say they have found it difficult to sell in France, since they are competing against government-owned Renault, which doesn't need to make any profit and can thus cut prices to the bone. And Ford says it's also difficult to sell in Italy, where Fiat, which specializes in the tiny cars preferred by Italians, holds a massive 60 percent of the market. Another hurdle: The German mark has gained in value against both the franc and the lira, making the German-made Fords more expensive in both France and Italy. In any case, Ford's share of the European market has declined since integration — from 14.5 percent in 1965 to 11.7 percent in 1972.

Ford's integration in Europe hasn't had any clear-cut impact so far. More than anything else, profits seem to react to such factors as strikes and the presence or absence of credit controls. Earnings of both Ford of Britain and Ford of Germany have shown wide fluctuations; and Ford of Germany's profits since integration have never equaled its preintegration peak year of 1966, when the company earned $70.9 million (in 1972, it earned $58.5 million).

With all these problems, does Ford still feel that integration was the right choice? The answer seems to be a resounding yes — if only because of the cost savings attained by integrating. "We're still one of the most profitable auto operations in Europe," says Walter Hayes, vice president of Ford of Europe, "and we're still No. 2 in auto sales (behind Fiat), so we must be doing something right." And he adds that a lot of Ford of Europe's problems — such as communications and labor strikes — would have existed even without integration.

In the end, Mr. Hayes believes, the prime value of Ford of Europe's integration may prove to be more flexibility in management and operations. "We aren't thinking like Texans in Texas anymore," he says. "We're thinking like Americans who consider all the states as their market, and this will help us do better in the future."

Questions

1. It would appear that the launch of the Taunus in Germany should have been delayed one year. What explicit business plan might have been followed to launch it in 1972?
2. One gets the impression that Ford bit off more than it could digest in 1969 with this single-stage integration. Lay out a two-stage integration; state the activities you would put in stage one and how long it would last.
3. In the years since this article was written, Ford has systematically resolved most of these problems and is now accruing the benefits of European rationalization. Assume that the confusion of reorganization would take three

years, followed by two years of breakeven, followed by higher annual profit. Visualize the benefits as an annuity starting in year 6. What operating losses caused by turmoil and changes could Ford sustain in these first three years to counterbalance (present value) the stream of benefits? Specifically, for every dollar of benefit from year 6, how many dollars loss could Ford sustain in years 1 to 3? Plot dollars of loss against discount rate for $i = 2$, 10, and 25 percent.

4. Certain components manufactured in England are also manufactured in the United States. Explicitly how would the continental European inventory safety stock of Ford U.K. parts be set, given this option to bring in U.S. parts?

5. You're negotiating with Mr. Hansen, the English worker's representative, and he hurls at you the accusation that elsewhere in the Ford network one of the flexible plants is gearing up to produce critical Ford U.K. parts. Under what circumstances will this fact increase or decrease the probability of his calling a wildcat strike today?

6. The text of this chapter identifies four kinds of plants. Rank their suitability for the United Kingdom and justify your ranking. Do the same for Germany.

Introduction

The buffer that stands between marketing decisions and production decisions is a good logistics network and well-positioned inventories. Marketing and production executives depend on one another; only the logistics/inventory system separates them. Not only must their interface function efficiently, but it also must have the resiliency to absorb market mistakes and factory errors.

In a multinational corporation the logistics/inventory system is complex. A factory does not know with certainty where its products are destined to be used. A national marketing manager cannot be sure where his next shipment will come from. A telex from a marketing manager may be understood by him but incomprehensible when received at a factory in another nation. And worst of all are the messages that the recipient *thinks* he understands when he doesn't. Given the infrequency of shipments, a marketing manager may wait more than a month before his orders arrive, the containers are opened, and the error is realized. If factories transship subassemblies, then a strike in one factory will strain, and can impair, the worldwide system.

In each nation, production-smoothing problems and opportunities are different. A unique feature of a multinational corporation is that headquarters can alter the flows of products between nations to smooth production. The subject of this chapter is the reallocation of markets to factories to achieve optimal production smoothing for a multiproduct, multifactory corporation. We will follow the three stages of an international product life cycle. In the first phase, perception of the problem is dominated by technical considerations so that a product focus should be expected even if carried to ethnocentric extremes. Later the corporation will build plants in many nations, each of which will be operated somewhat independently. Finally there will be enough confidence and cost pressure to encourage geocentric rationalization.

Ethnocentric Production-Focused Production Smoothing

To a typical production manager, a well-designed factory is one with machines to replace simple laboring tasks. If the production rate is cut back, only a slight reduction can be achieved in total factory cost. Because domestic demand fluctuates, any excess production can be exported, although these export sales will be erratic. Exports are best handled through independent wholesalers, who handle many vendors and hence would not be hurt if the corporation could no longer supply them. In general, it is best to segregate nations into those to which the corporation will commit a permanent sales force and well-nurtured brand name and those to which it considers export not a permanent commitment.

Some products are extremely difficult to manufacture. New petrochemicals, pharmaceuticals, and integrated circuits pose incredible production engineering problems. After the production process has been explored in a pilot plant, the design engineers scale up to a commercial plant. Unfortunately the first plant rarely works as designed. A carefully designed sequence of test runs is needed to identify all problems, and subsequent debottlenecking takes anywhere from a few months to several years. After systematic test runs have been performed, the results can be analyzed to give the design engineers more accurate parameters for their next plant design. This means that the design of the early plants will unavoidably become obsolete. In most plants there are substantial economies of scale. Hence the planning dilemma is how large to dare design the early plants, knowing that obsolescence will cut short their economic life. In terms of a trajectory of total plant capacity through time, there is a critical rate of capacity growth. A multinational that builds faster than the critical rate will accumulate obsolete large plants.

A diffusion of new and innovative products — products that customers are learning to use — is underway. Nobody should expect new product diffusion to be predictable: Any demand forecast is little better than a guess. If the product is good, sales will rise, but erratically. If sales rise so rapidly they exceed plant capacity, stockouts will occur. Stockouts during the launch of a product have two consequences. First, stockouts will slow the subsequent diffusion by raising in the minds of potential customers doubts about whether to take the trouble to adapt. Second, stockouts during the launch phase of a product invite competitors who can get a free ride atop the accumulated goodwill of the innovator's advertising and missionary sales effort. In summary, capacity should not be built faster than the critical rate of growth. Actual demand should be built up more slowly because sales forecasts are inaccurate and stockouts are expensive.

In this situation, the great advantage of a multinational corporation is that it maintains a reserve of markets in which it has not yet launched the product. When a giant new plant proves itself on stream, the corporation can utilize any excess capacity by selecting appropriately sized nations in which to launch the product. To tailor demand to fit the capacity available, the most suitable national markets are small but well developed, and hence the product can rapidly achieve its sales potential. After each major plant proves itself, the corporation can select a few more markets in which to use whatever capacity is available. One suitable decision display is a graph showing the ultimate sales potential of the product on one axis and the percentage penetration of the market within one year on the other (Exhibit 6.1). Each nation is a point on this graph. Confidence bands drawn around the estimates of sales and penetration transform the point estimate into a rectangle of plus and minus one standard deviation.

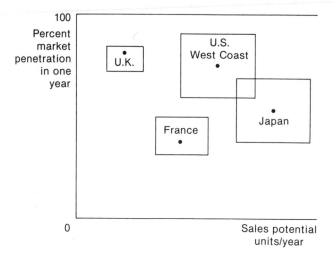

EXHIBIT 6.1

Sales potential versus market penetration indicates which markets are small and predictable enough to fill a plant.

In this product-centered view, demand has to adapt to available production. Because this is a new product, nobody yet has data on which to estimate the market responsiveness to management variables such as price, advertising, and sales force. By delaying exports until domestic demand fails to grow as fast as forecast, the multinational corporation has a great advantage over a domestic rival. Ethnocentric production smoothing means adapting demand to capacity.

Polycentric Nation-Focused Production Smoothing

Each region has its own factory; how its factory is operated is of concern only to the management of the region. The corporation has the ability to adapt to its environment. This means meeting demands with few stockouts, avoiding worker layoffs, and modulating overtime. Harmonizing these actions in the face of fluctuating demand is the generic production-smoothing problem. A polycentric attitude is most viable for a line of established products (for example, the stochastic coordination of a product launch just described in the ethnocentric section of this chapter requires headquarters power that the polycentric corporation does not have).

This section draws from and supposes familiarity with standard texts on production planning. Rather than redeveloping the mathematics of those models, we instead augment the variety of policy options and (preparing for the section on geocentric production smoothing) stress that one output of the analysis is the incremental cost, in each time period, of each item being manufactured.

The essence of a production-smoothing problem arises because demand is both cyclical and erratic through time. If plant capacity were equal to the highest peak demand, the last increment of capacity would be sitting idle most of the time. It is cheaper to build a smaller plant and invest part of the capital savings in inventory.

The model is developed through an incremental analysis by assuming that one more unit of demand occurs in a particular period. If there is excess capacity in that period, demand for an additional unit can be satisfied by immediate production, so its incremental cost will simply be the cost of production in that period.

Inventory

Now consider an extra unit of demand arising during the peak period. The plant is already producing at capacity, so the unit will have to be produced during a non-busy time and carried in inventory until needed. Thus the incremental cost will be the inventory carrying cost back to the production period, plus what then was the cost of manufacture. If an earlier period has a lower cost of manufacture, it may be economical to produce earlier, even though the inventory carrying cost is higher. Inventory carrying costs differ in each nation.

Overtime

Inventory costs may be reduced by working overtime. A minimum cost balance should be sought between these two smoothing techniques. However, overtime is expensive with higher wages and lower productivity caused by worker fatigue. The cost and capacity of overtime also depends on the plant's relationship with its union. If the wage level of workers is already high, workers may be unwilling to work much overtime. If the company insists, labor disputes and ill-will could ensue. On the other hand, some plants maintain a good working relationship in which they can ask the employees to work longer hours at peak demand, repaying the workers with favors such as extra time off during slack periods. Overtime is usually less of a problem if there is local unemployment, wages are low, or union–management relations are based on joint problem solving rather than the primitive method of confrontation.

Layoffs

Although layoffs are an immediate solution to production smoothing, the attendant problems and costs can be great. Sometimes it is preferable to await workers retiring, being fired, or quitting to reduce the work-force. Retirement need not be automatic at 65; workers over the formal retirement age often continue at the pleasure of the corporation. These workers are generally more receptive to layoffs.

Layoffs are legal in the United States and a few other nations. In most nations, however, government constraints are such that workers may be laid off only in cases of dire emergency. Since any layoff has potential political significance, it is prudent to consider the stakeholders discussed in Chapter 4.

Unions also play a large role in the cost of a layoff. Unions will push for tight controls written into contracts to prevent layoffs, and they usually insist that workers with the least seniority be laid off first, regardless of their productivity. Sometimes there are several branches in the "bumping" chain. Team-work relationships that have painstakingly developed can be destroyed by a layoff. Unions will often push for higher wages after a layoff to enable workers to better endure a future one. Layoffs therefore should be avoided if possible.

Once a probationary period has passed, a newly hired employee becomes an employee for life. He or she represents a huge asset: the capitalized present value of the worker's earnings until the worker quits or retires. Thus, in the face of demand uncertainty, it is prudent to use overtime and other means of production smoothing to minimize predicted peaks in employment. In the United States, high turnover is viewed as undesirable because of the cost of training replacements. Yet in a government- and union-constrained environment, systematic turnover reduces the risk that the corporation will be left with excess workers. This suggests setting higher target rates of planned turnover in nations with tighter regulations against layoffs.

Subcontracting to Family Vendors

The essence of the production-smoothing problem is the trade-off between the cost of carrying inventory and the time-varying cost of manufacturing one more unit. Although large corporations may be tightly constrained about layoffs, small family businesses are nonunionized and receive more exemptions from government regulations. "Small" usually means below 10 employees. During a boom these subcontractors get rich; at other times they lay off.

The production-smoothing challenge is to search the product line for items and subassemblies whose engineering tolerances are so sloppy that they can be manufactured on simple machinery. The administrative challenge is to maintain information on all possible subcontractors, build an organization that can keep contact with them even when there is little business, and have the compassion to help family subcontractors selectively in hard times. The advantage of an explicit study of production smoothing is that one can estimate the benefits of the fixed cost of maintaining contact with each potential subcontractor.

Maintenance

Operating managers tend to underinvest in maintenance; thus common corporate practice is to set up a maintenance fund for each machine. Every unit of output pays a bounty to the fund. The maintenance fund must be spent by the end of the fiscal year or else the budget authorization expires. This practice assures that maintenance is accomplished, yet the practice is highly dysfunctional from a production-smoothing viewpoint. During a boom year it makes little sense to shut down the plant for an overhaul simply to prevent the money from reverting to headquarters. Conversely, during a slack year the fund is too small for a major overhaul, even though production will not be missed and the quality and alacrity of contracted help is superior. It is therefore imperative to lengthen the cycle of each maintenance fund from one year to a full business cycle, so that maintenance is scheduled for slack periods. To do this requires study of the cost of delaying maintenance, in essence an analysis of how near to flat the cost curve is in the region of the optimum maintenance schedule.

Marketing

Usually sales departments receive goods at the standard accounting cost. However, the current actual cost of each item fluctuates through time. Were sales to receive goods at their fluctuating actual cost or its forecast, the sales department would have an incentive to delay or advance the promotion of sales. This would ease production-smoothing peaks, even though it complicates the analysis.

Mathematical Techniques

Most real production planning models are large linear programs that embody the cost of having workers switch from one manufactured item to another. A mathematical model of production smoothing requires as input a forecast of each month's required shipment of each item. The model computes the lowest cost of achieving this output. Furthermore, its calculations generate the incremental cost of producing each item in each period. This incremental cost is the cost of augmenting the quantity demanded of one item in one month leaving all other demands unchanged; all inventories, overtime, maintenance schedules, and so on, are adjusted. The incremental costs will be needed in geocentric production smoothing.

Geocentric Production Smoothing

As a corporation enters new markets and builds production facilities, it will expand its product line. This will satisfy other needs of the new markets and use recently built excess production capacity. Product divisions existing within the corporation ensure organizational control and coordination. The blend of product and national management provides the matrix framework in which geocentric production smoothing can occur. If several nations have at least one product in common (Exhibit 6.2), geocentric smoothing can allow for flexibility in both marketing and production of all products. For common products, markets can be reallocated from busy to slack plants. This reallocation in turn eases the multi-item production-smoothing problem within each plant.

Some sales territories are on a border between plants. If a marketing manager's sales territory is between two or more plants, the marketing manager may be able to act entrepreneurially. Assuming the item is identical from each factory, he can buy from the factory that will deliver more cheaply. Since production planning cannot begin until demand has been estimated, it might appear that the border marketing manager's entrepreneurship would complicate production smoothing. However, the border marketing manager and the headquarters production planner have a strong basis for agreement. From a corporate viewpoint, plants that are busy should withdraw from border territories, leaving those sales to plants with excess capacity. If a plant is operating near capacity, overtime will be required for incremental production, raising the per unit real cost. Each plant can deliver to the border at its incremental production cost plus the logistics cost analyzed in Chapter 5. This sum of logistics plus incremental production cost provides a clear guide for redistributing markets to plants.

Requiring that some items be of standard design to allow smoothing does *not* mean that production methods and plant layouts must be standardized. Quite the contrary. In sports, different positions on the

	Nation A	Nation B	Nation C	Nation D	
Item 62	X	X		X	geocentric smooth
Item 101		X			
Item 102		X			
Item 117	X		X		geocentric smooth
Item 120			X		

EXHIBIT 6.2

An item produced in two or more plants can be smoothed simultaneously.

same team all share the same "goal"; it is their methods of accomplishing that goal that differ. Similarly, the corporate ability to smooth production is enhanced if there are four distinct types of factories: lowest unit cost, flexible multi-item, seasonal, and stockpile sites. Producing an item in several of these factories simultaneously allows great flexibility. The bulk of worldwide demand for a long–life cycle product can be produced by the lowest unit cost factory, while the peaks and valleys of the demand curve are satisfied by seasonal plants (Exhibit 6.3).

National labor forces differ significantly and it may be sensible to match the labor force to the type of factory. The four types of factories are operated in very different styles. The selection of plant managers, the design of incentive systems, and the production process itself all depend on the type of plant necessary and the workers available.

Lowest Unit Cost Factory

Set up as a pure assembly line, a lowest unit cost plant is designed to produce at full capacity, with all attention focused on reducing product costs per unit. Engineers and labor management are continuously streamlining operations and improving productivity by overcoming production bottlenecks and training the workforce to greater efficiency. Experience curves can be used to predict the decrease in standard unit costs.

The use of a lowest unit cost factory precludes flexibility. A new item will frequently go through several design changes before it can be standardized. Only after an item has gone through this process should it be assigned to a cost-focused factory. Once demand for the item, whether it be a subassembly or a finished product, has been predicted through the *long* run, its production can be moved to a lowest unit cost factory.

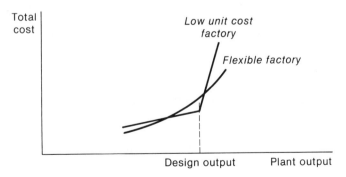

EXHIBIT 6.3

A comparison of low unit cost factory and flexible factory.

Lowest unit cost plants generally take one of two extreme forms:

1. Highly automated, perhaps with government subsidized capital.
2. Labor intensive, where wages are *very* low.

The design of a capital-intensive plant is primarily an engineering job. The equipment must be correctly situated, installed, and adjusted to run at a coordinated speed, usually at full capacity. A cut in production would raise the unit cost of overhead and capitalization. Highly automated plants are located near their primary market, usually in an industrial nation. Since the investment is long term, political and economic stability must be considered. Surprisingly, local wages and union practices do not play a vital role in plant location because the amount of labor required is small; however, the availability of trained mechanics and craftsmen is crucial. A well-established source of materials and manufacturing infrastructure is also important.

The United States is perhaps the most popular country in which to locate a capital-intensive factory. The domestic market is large yet easily accessible through a sophisticated distribution network. Although unions are powerful and wages are high, highly skilled mechanics and engineers are readily available. Labor relations are improving, with the number of industrial disputes leveling off and the number of lost working days dropping. The United States is politically and economically stable, with the risk of nationalization minimal. Many multinational corporations' headquarters are in the United States, shortening lines of communications between them and their large production facilities, thereby ensuring adequate supervision of major investments.

For a labor-intensive low unit cost factory, the level of wages is a crucial determinant of plant location. High labor intensity normally dictates a location in an underdeveloped nation with very low daily wages. The levels of industrialization and employment as well as the trend of social reform within the country are important, because historically, wage level rises as a country becomes more developed. The relatively low capital investment required is at risk only if the payback period is long; usually it is short.

Once the criterion of low wages is met, other characteristics of the labor force must be examined. The strengths and practices of local unions are important. For example, a low unit cost factory could work well within a stable, well-defined relationship with a trade union. On the other hand, if a union were too powerful, wages and productivity might be managed to the detriment of the company.

A labor-intensive lowest unit cost factory poses different challenges in design and management. Labor management in a labor-intensive assembly line factory places a great emphasis on worker productivity. Incentive systems and steady employment reward those who produce. Hence, for motivational reasons, it is not prudent to carry a large inventory of finished items at the plant. Because most jobs will be long term and routine, the company has to invest in worker training. To minimize the risk of losing a trained employee, turnover and layoffs must be avoided. A normal production load of one shift allows flexibility to work systematic overtime when extra output is needed for production smoothing.

As one example among many, the Philippines appears to be an attractive location for a labor-intensive low unit cost factory. Although nearly 50 percent of the working population is employed in primary industries, the manufacturing sector accounts for over 11 percent of workers and is growing. Philippine workers are mostly literate and so can adapt to manufacturing work. Productivity per employee has been rising rapidly. Wages in the Philippines averaged $50 per month in 1975 and are rising moderately. Unions exist and have the right to collective bargaining, but recent changes in the government have made both strikes and lockouts illegal. Compulsory arbitration is provided for, if no agreement can be reached. Layoffs require severance pay and permission of the government but are not impossible. Overtime is not difficult to arrange. These factors combine to create a favorable situation for a labor-intensive low unit cost factory that is a stable employer. In the Philippines martial law was declared in 1972. The political situation within the country and throughout the area has worsened since. A large capital investment in this area might be unwise, but a low capital cost factory that would take advantage of the low wages would have a short enough payback period that the corporation could ignore long-run uncertainties.

To build a low-cost factory, the corporation has to make a substantial investment — whether in automated machinery or in worker training. When the factory is asked to phase out a declining product and phase in a new one, the investment becomes vulnerable because managers and workers of a low-cost factory have had little need to develop transitional skills. Headquarters may have to send patient and sensitive experts to help each transition.

Flexible Factory

Visualize a job shop. A flexible factory is a multi-item operation, with flexibility of material flow, general purpose equipment (perhaps numerically controlled), and a completely literate work force managed with an emphasis on job enrichment. The challenge of managing a flexible factory is that there cannot be a tight cost control system. For example, a standard costing system provides a very reasonable ceiling above which cost should not rise. But the attempt to minimize accounting cost is incompatible with the need to change schedules and even interrupt production runs — after all, the flexible factory was built to ensure tight *time* control.

Labor management in a flexible factory also has to be run without tight control. Each worker has to be creative and imaginative in developing transitional skills. Cultural values and social status in many nations accompany the individual's creative pride in knowledge of a craft. Participative management can flourish in this type of atmosphere. Since a great deal of autonomy must be granted, it is essential that each worker know his own and his fellow group members' productivity. Worker selection and probationary review are crucial to keep slackers from contaminating the work atmosphere. This requires that the foremen and superintendents have the integrity and self-discipline to dismiss workers for poor performance. The corollary is that although there may be dismissal for cause, there should be no layoffs once workers have passed probation, except under the most adverse circumstances.

All new items are produced in a flexible factory. All unforeseen difficulties or problems are referred here. Although not all items would be produced in a flexible factory, the factory has the capability to begin production of any item within a short start-up time. Such standby capability has its cost. The benefit is that the corporation can then dare to build low unit cost factories in some of the impoverished and unstable nations of the world. Then if a risky plant is lost anywhere in the world the combination of the output from the flexible factory, stockpiles, and global overtime can meet customer needs until a replacement plant can be rushed into production.

A flexible factory requires a variety of skills and high degree of training; thus one can best operate in a country with an established manufacturing base and a well-educated labor force. The manufacturing base can provide purchased components and material, and the educated labor force will ensure adaptable and competent workers. For example, Ireland and Japan both provide ideal environments for flexible factories, but for different reasons.

The Republic of Ireland has a moderate but rapidly expanding manufacturing base, and it is within the European Economic Community tariff barrier. Although the Irish domestic market is small, bulk transportation is readily available to the United States and Europe. Irish workers have been ready to learn, and pockets of skilled labor throughout the country have been developed through apprenticeship and training programs. Over 20 percent of the labor force is in the manufacturing sector, with the rest scattered between primary and service industries. The Irish government provides capital grants and loans for the building of factories and the training of employees. The government imposes a system of levy grants whereby a company receives a refund for training workers. Since training is a major expense in setting up a flexible factory, Ireland provides an attractive opportunity.

Union membership is entirely voluntary, and over 50 percent of the Irish workforce is unionized. In turn, 95 percent of Irish unions belong to the Irish Congress of Trade Unions (ICTU). In the early 1970s, unions began to push for protective legislation and a more formalized approach to collective bargaining. The ICTU was the main proponent of this change, and it now actively negotiates its members' contracts and policies. For example, the ICTU has differentiated between an "all out" strike, which calls for other unions' support, and a "particular" strike, which is confined to the unions directly involved. In 1975 a surprising 30 percent of industrial disputes were caused by dismissal for cause or layoff as demand fell, and another 25 percent were caused by transfers and reorganization. These figures illustrate the critical nature of job security. Unemployment exceeds 12 percent, which encourages a low turnover of employees. Wages are equivalent to those in most industrialized countries and below those of the United States.

Japan has a highly developed manufacturing base suitable for flexible factories. Japanese labor is ideal because the level of vocational training and education is high, and the Japanese philosophy of hard work and company loyalty creates a good atmosphere. Japanese industry operates on a tenure system of lifetime employment so layoffs are not allowed. Hardly any workers quit to work for a competitor, so corporations can dare to train their workers. Promotion is based primarily on seniority. Because status and salary are not directly tied to job assignment, labor mobility within the plant is enhanced. Hence Japanese workers have no reason to object to new machinery, innovations, or retraining. Unions are organized on an enterprise basis, which also allows for labor flexibility. Overtime is worked as needed, but total Japanese wages (including benefits) are extremely high.

Seasonal Factory

Because it hurts to lay off workers, managers are tempted to delay action by biasing upward the sales forecast. Since such delay results in an even deeper layoff, it seems psychologically sensible that the layoff decision should not be made in the factory itself. The scapegoat has to come from outside — from a foreign headquarters, for example.

When several factories produce the same item, some can avoid a layoff if others lay off more frequently and/or cut deeper. Can there be a layoff factory designed for intermittent production? It would be socially more acceptable if this were a seasonal factory. Whenever the corporation has some items with a seasonal demand, it is worth evaluating a seasonal plant. Such a plant is designed to be operated only a few months of the year, frequently using rented equipment and old tools, dies, and assembly jigs. The location criterion is to find a community accustomed to seasonal work, whose pattern would be complemented by this plant. In poor years the plant can be operated for only a month or so (though to maintain a work force it is crucial to open the plant annually). In good years the plant can be run with large overtime for several months or up until the community's next season. The personnel policies must accord with this pattern, with overtime and layoffs commonplace.

Communities such as fishing villages, which are accustomed to seasonal work, are easy to find. Finding a country in which seasonal labor is a national phenomenon is a bit more difficult. One such country is Finland, where both men and women participate in the labor force, with 24 percent in manufacturing. However, due to the weather and the product and trade structure, there are strong seasonal fluctuations in the demand for labor, especially in northern Finland. The labor supply also fluctuates, dropping on average 10 percent during the winter. Labor disputes are on par with other European countries, but workers, especially in the north, are in a weak bargaining position. Because seasonal work is both socially and economically accepted, unions are less likely to press inflexible contracts.

The Finnish government, like many other governments, tries to replace temporary or seasonal work with more permanent occupations. Seasonal work, however, provides an opportunity to smooth out the peaks and valleys of unemployment. It is in the interests of both the government and business to offer seasonal work when unemployment is at its peak. Therefore, although seasonal work may not be encouraged by a country's manpower policy, it could complement it.

Stockpile Factory

A careful study of the income tax and property tax laws of every nation will reveal that some governments subsidize stockpiles, so that a subsidiary could have a low inventory holding cost. For example, in Denmark the capital component of the inventory carrying cost is 88.9 percent of the corporation's cost of capital. This pleasant result comes about because the tax authorities allow a deduction of up to 30 percent of the total inventory value in computing taxable income for any year. Given a Danish tax rate of 37 percent, the savings is 11.1 percent of the inventory value. The allowance deducted in one year must be added back to current taxable income in the following year. In other words, part of the corporate tax is deferred one year. In Sweden the incentives are even greater. With a write-down of 60 percent allowed and a tax rate of 40 percent, the inventory carrying cost is reduced to only 64 percent of the corporation's cost of capital. Other governments provide free warehousing and subsidized loans against inventory. Negotiations are always possible because most governments believe in full employment.

Tax incentives are only one part of the cost of carrying inventory. The multinational has some of its own capital tied up in inventory. As discussed in Chapter 3, a corporation's cost of capital may be different in different nations but tax costs restrain the corporation from moving the funds. These funds are nevertheless available for inventory. Exhibit 6.4 shows that if inventory is to be held longer than the break-even time, it would be preferable to accumulate the stockpile where holding costs are lowest.

A stockpile factory may be very small. Consider a factory that produces one-tenth of the corporation's worldwide demand for an item. Suppose that on average the corporation keeps two months of inventory. The factory would spend almost two years stockpiling its production before the corporation would double its normal world inventory. Hence, like a lowest unit cost factory, a stockpile factory should be assigned no near-obsolete or faddish items.

Purchasing

It is unfortunate that the world view of most corporations is dominated by the *export* orientation of sales managers and that most purchasing is done domestically. A very different evaluation of national risk and opportunity for the corporation would emerge from a global purchasing perspective.

Great savings are possible by the systematic and skillful use of international purchasing. For example, most centrally planned economies require an inordinate amount of red tape before goods of a capitalist corporation can be imported. Exports are quite different. In centrally planned economies there are sporadic national shortages of key currencies, at which times a capitalist corporate purchasing manager could negotiate a very attractive deal.

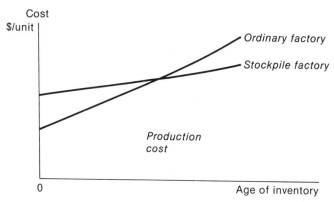

EXHIBIT 6.4
Production cost plus inventory holding cost.

The relationship of a corporation to its vendors is similar to its relationship with its factories. Just as there are four factory types, so there can be four vendor types.

Low Unit Cost. When it finds the right vendor, the corporation may be willing to negotiate long-term purchase agreements, with high penalty costs for default of the contract by either party. Furthermore, the corporation may support the vendor's acquiring specialized equipment, perhaps guaranteeing bank loans with the equipment mortgage as collateral. Nevertheless, mutual trust is necessary because even the most thoughtful cost escalation clauses sometimes fail to foresee all contingencies. Such long-term contracts should be written only for items whose design will be stable.

Inventory Source. If government stockpile programs are limited to domestically owned firms, it may be sensible to negotiate purchase agreements in those nations. The difficulty is assuring the vendor that the multinational corporation will honor its purchase contract. The vendor may fear that the contract will prove difficult to enforce, particularly in nations whose legal system is based on the Napoleonic Code wherein *force majeure* clauses allow a contract to become void if fundamental conditions change, a far more frequent occurrence than the analogous "Acts of God" clauses of Common Law.

No Vendor Dependency. A large vendor will take small orders to keep his shop busy. He has the men and equipment to deliver on short notice and will if the price is right. The multinational corporation may well decide to maintain relationships with a list of such vendors by systematically awarding each at least one small order a year. (Systematically nurturing small family vendors, as considered in "Nation-Focused Production Smoothing," should be continued, though such vendors are usually so small they can supply only their own nation and hence would rarely come to the attention of the headquarters purchasing department.)

Seasonal Orders. Instead of the multinational corporation owning plant and equipment that sits idle most of the year, it may be preferable to search for vendors who experience seasonal fluctuations. The multinational can receive a good price and service if it systematically orders during the seasonal low. The size of the multinational's order may vary widely from year to year, but even a small order should be placed each year.

Integrating Sources and Markets

This great variety of possible sources of an item provides a great opportunity to orchestrate production smoothing on a global basis. But by what mechanism might such orchestration occur? One might fantasize a monthly market, held at a medieval market town near a modern airport. Marketing managers from around the world would fly in to deal with production schedulers from factories around the world. They would haggle over price and quantity. Such an open market would encourage initiative and autonomy.

Unfortunately, the first problem with such monthly markets would be the travel expense. The second problem is the possibility of deals that are not optimal to the corporation; unless a factory were forced to charge the same price to all customers (f.o.b. the factory), a factory would tend to charge higher prices to close markets (protected from distant factory competition by their higher logistics costs). This would upset comparative accounting systems and could lead to a harmful split between marketing and production managers. Furthermore, if only one factory supplied a particular product, the pricing relationship would be similar to bilateral monopoly. To avoid these problems, it is prudent to computerize the market and thus to standardize policies with a production-smoothing program that allocates production to plants in an optimal manner (within certain bounds).

Computer Model

Headquarters is interested in two cost components: the worldwide logistics cost (developed in Chapter 5) and the production costs totaled over all the factories. For any given production allocation, the sum of these two costs gives the total cost of output.

Let us first look at just two factories. Given a worldwide demand in 100 markets, each with a different logistics cost to each plant, how should we allocate production to the two plants? Exhibit 6.5 shows how total cost can be minimized if Plant A produces 60 percent and Plant B produces 40 percent of production. The following paragraphs will explain how these costs are estimated and how the smoothing can be done by computer for many plants.

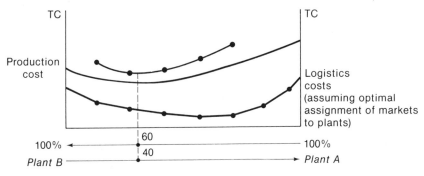

EXHIBIT 6.5
Production smoothing for two plants.

Logistics Costs. At headquarters, the planners use the logistics model that was developed in Chapter 5 for each group of products and for each month. At each iteration the factory availability will be set to the last iteration's proposed factory shipments. To allow flexibility, we will allow the program to increase or decrease total shipments from any factory up to an upper bound (say 10 percent). In later iterations the bound will be reduced.

Production Costs. In the transportation tableau of Chapter 5 we modeled factory flexibility as a *positive slack* (producing below current levels) and a *negative slack* (producing above current levels), each constrained within certain limits. The cost coefficient attached to each of the two slack variables depicts the value of flexibility for that factory or vendor. From each factory's individual production-smoothing model, the marginal cost of producing an incremental unit of the item in any month can be determined. In general, in a month the marginal cost of an item rises with the amount to be shipped. Each of the four kinds of vendors has its own ability to respond to changes in ordered shipments.

For each factory's marginal cost curve, assume the following:

1. We know the marginal cost at the last iteration.
2. We know the shape of the curve is convex (from theory).
3. For each of the four different kinds of factories we can estimate the percentage drop in marginal cost if shipments dropped by, say, 10 percent, and the percentage cost increase if shipments rose by 10 percent. Suppose these are 3 percent and 4 percent.

This information is fed into the transportation tableau at headquarters. The negative slack on factory flexibility is assigned a cost of 104 percent of the marginal cost. The positive slack on factory flexibility is assigned 97 percent of the same marginal cost. The quantity available for shipment is entered into the right hand side of the transportation tableau (Exhibit 6.6). If there are F factories, I groups of items, and T time periods, then there will be FIT marginal costs known from the production-smoothing models.

In French, a sequence of tentative bids and acceptances is called a *tatonnement* process. The computational scheme outlined in Exhibit 6.7 similarly requires several iterations of tentative bids and acceptances that converge toward a corporate optimum. It is easier to have each factory's production-smoothing program at its site, polling it for information only as needed, rather than trying to manage a huge centralized model. Nevertheless, the shipment quotas remain a headquarters's prerogative.

Step 1: Headquarters Logistics Program. A separate logistics problem has to be run for each production allocation in each time period to determine the optimal logistics route. Use the known marginal costs to estimate the cost coefficients for the positive and negative slacks, solve each of the IT

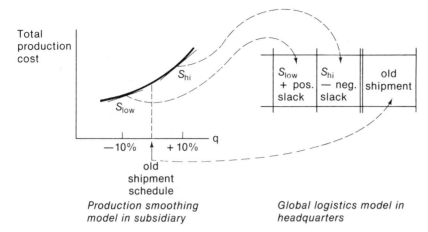

EXHIBIT 6.6
Marginal costs are transmitted from each manufacturing subsidiary to headquarters.

transportation tableaus, and for each factory

new shipment = old shipment + negative slack – positive slack

Enter the *FIT* new shipments into the right-hand side of the transportation tableau and begin a new iteration.

Step 2: Back to Each Factory. Telex the *IT* new shipments to each factory, and ask that each run its local production-smoothing model. A factory can use a linear program, a linear decision rule, a quadratic program, or an intelligent cost accountant — as long as the solution to the model yields marginal costs (the change in total cost if all other shipments remained unchanged except the incremental change in the one shipment under review).

The factory then telexes its *IT* marginal costs to headquarters. It supplements this telex with possible warnings about limits on the extent to which shipments could be increased, buttressing its argument with data on what the marginal costs would become.

Step 3: Back at Headquarters. In each transportation tableau, update the availability figure (to the tentative shipment schedule that emerged from Step 1) and the costs on the positive and negative slacks (to the marginal costs from the factories, add and subtract a little, as in Figure 6.6). Solve the *IT* transportation problems.

After a few iterations as described here, the *tatonnement* process stabilizes. Specifically, both slacks will be zero for all items, signifying that no changes in shipments appear indicated. At this point reduce the tolerances on the slacks (say from 10 percent, as in Figure 6.6, to 5 percent) and correspondingly reduce the estimated alteration to the marginal cost.

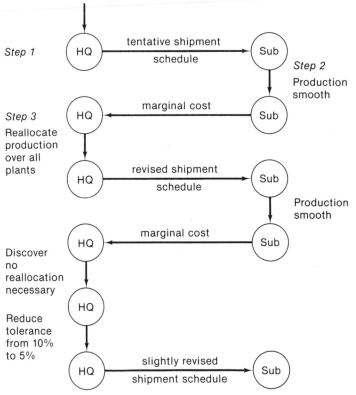

EXHIBIT 6.7
Computational scheme.

The Stopping Criterion

The medieval market closed at sunset. In computerized models there is always a temptation to iterate too long. Yet each telex to a factory is expensive because of the disruption it causes. Hence headquarters should try to achieve a monthly plan with as few as two iterations to each marketing manager and factory. Unless there is something immutable about a monthly update, it may be preferable to lengthen or shorten the period for analysis as conditions become more or less stable.

The solution to a transportation problem yields dual variables on the demands, which gives the marginal cost of one more unit produced. Each marketing manager needs this estimate of the unit cost of the item landed in his territory. So for each item in each territory, telex the marketing manager a forecast of landed cost month by month (lagged for transit time from each factory). The marketing manager can then revise his sales forecasts and so telex headquarters with this revision.

Human Problems

Massey-Ferguson had a problem with integrated logistics because marketing managers persistently inflated their forecasts of demand in the interval from two to six months in the future. Their long-run forecasts were unbiased. Their one-month forecasts were very accurate. But their intermediate forecasts were persistently optimistic. At Massey-Ferguson this became known as a "bow wave" forecast. The bureaucratic remedy would be that headquarters scale down the received forecast. The economic remedy would be that the marketing manager be charged a penalty for changes he makes to his forecast, the charge being greatest for the near term (the appropriate charges can be found by rerunning the production-smoothing problem).

Some markets are appreciably less predictable than others. To accommodate that randomness the marketing manager is encouraged to keep a local inventory (and bear its carrying costs) so that shipments are first in, first out (FIFO) for that inventory. To compute the target size of that inventory, an analyst needs, as input, the penalty for changes to the forecast. Thus the penalty charge intended to avoid "bow wave" forecasts also gives the value of more accurate marketing research, and of marketing methods to stabilize demand.

The final adjustment may be required in logistics. From each factory to each market, sum all items of all the product divisions to be shipped in each month. Add needed flows of subassemblies. With these total logistics flows, estimate the logistics costs on each route. If a chartered vessel now has an uneven carrying pattern, it may be necessary to revise the logistics costs in certain transportation tableaus and reiterate the problem.

At this time let us mention problems of administration.

First, if some subsidiaries are late in responding with their marginal costs, the headquarters can nevertheless proceed to rerun logistics with whatever partial information is on hand.

Second, some subsidiaries, curious to learn how to game the system, may report back false marginal costs in an effort to get the shipments they want. To thwart this, the headquarters computer can store for each factory its past history of *IT* shipments and *IT* marginal costs. The statistical analysis of these data can give headquarters estimates of changes in marginal cost if shipments are higher or lower, a basis for conducting exploratory staff analyses without disturbing the factory, as well as a means to detect possible errors in the cost feedback from the factories.

Finally, if one factory's marginal costs become very high because of high wage settlements and currency revaluation, the factory will be asked to make fewer shipments. Unless headquarters is planning to phase out the factory, local management must improve productivity. To this end, they need an *explicit* target of unit costs toward which they must aim. This analysis provides a basis for setting explicit targets.

Conclusions

In summary, certain markets will be flip-flopped between factories to ease production smoothing. Rather than identify them ahead of time, we allowed them to be identified on economic grounds. Think of the border that divides the districts of each plant. In each period we may move the border because it is defined as the point at which it is equally expensive to deliver from either adjacent plant. The purpose of production smoothing is to respond to fluctuating demands for items. The advantage of being explicit about the cost of absorbing demand fluctuations is that it makes explicit the advantage to adjust other parts of the global system.

Governments are concerned with employment stability and are aware of all layoffs. The foreignness of a multinational means that its layoffs will attract all the more attention. Thus any multinational must administer layoffs with an eye to the long-run stakeholder concerns discussed in Chapter 4. Offsetting this vulnerability is the fact that a multinational can choose *where* to make the layoff. Demand fluctuations mean that production-smoothing activities will be done somewhere. The essence of geocentric production smoothing is to orchestrate where to do which activities. In some nations the corporation will disquiet some stakeholders, but in no nations should it cross their irritation threshold.

Questions from Other Viewpoints

1. *Corporate Rational Normative Global.* You just covered this viewpoint in the chapter.
2. *Corporate Rational Normative Subsidiary.* Assuming that corporate headquarters uses geocentric production smoothing as a form of control, illustrate how headquarters could induce cost-cutting competitiveness in a subsidiary whose costs are forecast to become excessive. Make use of the neutral persuasion of an algorithmic forecast.
3. *Corporate Rational Descriptive Global.* Try to think of a product which a multinational corporation supplies your nation from more than one foreign factory.
4. *Corporate Rational Descriptive Subsidiary.* Report on government constraints altering each production-smoothing cost for one nation.
5. *Corporate Emotional Normative Global.* The individuals in head-

quarters who are assembling and computing the production plans have a frightening responsibility. Their calculations determine who will feel the grip of layoff and which divisional managers will have their relationship with their community damaged by a layoff. Is it better that the headquarters production planners be cool technocrats or that they blister in the emotional ravages of their acts?

6. *Corporate Emotional Normative Subsidiary.* You are the production manager in one of the subsidiaries where costs are such that employment levels vary widely. You have only a few products, so there is no hope of transferring workers between products. For these products the corporation builds a new plant somewhere in the world about every two years, and so you have been experiencing a two-year sawtooth cycle to your shipments in addition to the random fluctuations of the world markets. Individuals who were foremen have been demoted to workers and individuals who were workers have been laid off. Write a one-page letter that job applicants can take home with them, explaining these facts of life. Be aware that a strong union could end your practice, and that although there is currently no government legislation giving workers tenure after six months, there is a national sentiment that workers have a loyalty to their employers and employers should have a reciprocal loyalty to their employees.

7. *Corporate Emotional Descriptive Global.* Describe the kind of team managerial policies you would expect to see if the production planning team appears competent, engrossed in their work, and seemingly effective.

8. *Corporate Emotional Descriptive Subsidiary.* You are a production manager in a developing nation, struggling with all the problems this entails. Someone at headquarters sends you this chapter, with the implication that you will be included in the grand production smooth. Identify accomplishments that may be undermined by such inclusion. For each, how would you feel?

9. *Social Rational Normative Global.* As long as there is fluctuating demand there will have to be some forms of production smoothing (including rationing). List each of the cost coefficients for the one-nation problem. Beside each coefficient indicate whether the social cost coefficient is greater or lower than the corporate cost coefficient. If there is fluctuating demand, from a social point of view which kinds of nations would be least harmed by the fluctuations in employment?

10. *Societal Rational Normative Global.* Suppose a national government reduced the corporation's cost of carrying inventory in that nation (for example, under the motivation of an oil stockpile, the government loans money at low interest against warehouse receipts of all kinds of energy-using product, broadly interpreted). Would the indirect effect be to stabilize or destabilize employment?

11. *Societal Rational Descriptive Global.* Select a pair of close trading partners (two nations, A and B). On one sheet of paper plot 10 years of unemployment rates of A and of B, and plot exports from A to B and B to A. Is there any apparent serial correlation such that one of the four graphs is a leading indicator and another a lagging indicator?

12. *Societal Rational Descriptive National.* Compare and contrast the unemployment benefits of two different nations.

13. *Societal Emotional Normative Global.* Write a political tract about the wrongs of capricious layoffs, and the need for an intergovernmental "layoff fund" so that the work week can be cut when there is a glut, but workers' take home wages will remain unchanged — so as not to reduce demand.

14. *Societal Emotional Normative Subsidiary.* Why should your citizens be laid off merely because some imperial power 10,000 kilometers away has such a debauched society that it is in economic recession? Your forefathers died to fight off political imperialism; rally again to fight off economic serfdom. As head of trade unions of your nation, call a strike.

15. *Societal Emotional Descriptive Global.* Describe some actual bilateral agreements and consultative procedures that are intended to dampen international oscillations of unemployment.

16. *Societal Emotional Descriptive Subsidiary.* In a society where the government requires lifetime employment for those who have passed a probationary period, corporations tend to work their employees overtime until they are very certain that they can afford to create another position. Though most workers enjoy some overtime sometimes, one might expect an employee's relationships with his family, friends, and community to suffer. Outline different methodological approaches a sociologist would take to detect and describe these overtime-induced sufferings.

Bibliography to Chapter 6

Bergstrom, Gary L. and Barnard E. Smith, "Multi-Item Production Planning — An Extension of the HMMS Rules," *Management Science*, Vol. 16, No. 10 (1970), pp. B614-629.

Comanor, William S. and Thomas A. Wilson, "The Effect of Advertising on Competition: A Survey," *Journal of Economic Literature*, Vol. 17 (June, 1979), pp. 453-76.

Crowston, Wallace B., Warren H. Hausman, and William R. Kampe II, "Multistage Production for Stochastic Seasonal Demand," *Management Science*, Vol. 19, No. 8 (1973), pp. 924-935.

Holt, Charles, Franco Modigliani, James Muth, and Herbert Simon, *Planning Production Inventories and Work Force* (Englewood Cliffs, N.J.: Prentice-Hall, 1960).

I.L.O., *Yearbook of Labour Statistics* (Geneva: International Labour Organization, 1976).

O.E.C.D., Reviews of Manpower and Social Policies, *Manpower Policy in Japan, Vol. 11*, 1973; *Manpower Policy in Ireland, Vol. 15*, 1974; *Manpower Policy in Finland, Vol. 17*, 1977.

Topkis, Donald M., "Optimal Ordering and Rationing Policies in a Non Stationary Dynamic Inventory Model with n Demand Classes," *Management Science*, Vol. 15, No. 3 (1968), pp. 160–176.

Welam, Ulf Peter, "Multi-Item Production Smoothing Models," *Management Science*, Vol. 21, No. 9 (1975), pp. 1021–1028.

Yuan, John S.C., Jeffrey H. Horen, and Harvey M. Wagner, "Optimal Multi-Product Production Scheduling and Employment Smoothing with Deterministic Demands," *Management Science*, Vol. 21, No. 11 (1975), pp. 1250–1262.

CHAPTER SEVEN

Multinational Plant Location

Introductory Note to the Case

Bell GmbH

At the time of this case Europe was still divided into a European Economic Community (EEC) and a European Free Trade Area (EFTA), but merger negotiations were well along, so that the 9.6 percent tariff from the United Kingdom to the EEC was about to be eliminated. Bell's products, plastic boxes for the cosmetic industry, cost about one-tenth of a deutsche mark each. Empty plastic boxes are bulky, so the cost of transporting them to the filling plants of the cosmetic companies is not insignificant.

The sales growth of 20 percent per year in countries such as Greece, Portugal, and Spain was occurring partly because citizens there were purchasing more cosmetics, but also because the cosmetics companies were starting to move their filling operations to these countries. Nevertheless, at that time, Greece, Portugal, and Spain were not members of the EEC and so faced the EEC tariff. Currently, Bell is not dependent on any one cosmetic company, because even the largest takes only 10 percent of its output.

Plastic boxes are made of petrochemicals. As the cost of their raw material increases all manufacturers, including Bell, will charge higher prices; the boxes are only a small element in the cost of a finished cosmetic item, there is no convenient substitute, so industry demand will hardly be affected.

Different students emphasize different aspects of this case. Some focus on the engineering costs; others focus on industry rivalry. Yet others study the cosmetics industry so as to forecast when particular products will likely be moved to low labor cost areas. Finally, there's usually someone who wonders whether Bell shouldn't stay in Germany but change its corporate strategy to "hard to manufacture" plastic products, and quit making cheap cosmetic boxes. All except the last viewpoint will be analyzed in the text of this chapter.

Bell Schönheitsprodukte GmbH

The management of Bell Schönheitsprodukte GmbH decided in January 1972 to give serious consideration to undertaking a major plant expansion outside of Germany. The year 1971 had seen the formal revaluation of the once-floating German mark to a parity of U.S. $0.3106. This revaluation represented an increase of 13.6 percent in the value of the deutsche mark (DM) over the DM/dollar rate of May 1971. The year 1971 had also seen an increase in the wage bill (including social benefits) at Bell GmbH of nearly 15 percent. As Bell exported over 60 percent of its rather labor-intensive German production, these events threatened to greatly reduce the firm's profitability.

Internationalizing Bell's sources of production appeared to be the most interesting route out of this predicament. A U.S.-owned competitor which had previously been producing most of its output in Germany had just opened a plant in France and had proceeded to start a price war. Wages in France were on the order of FF5–6 per hour. Wages in Germany were DM6 per hour. The unanswered question, however, was "Where should Bell put the new plant?"

The Company and Its Products

Bell Schönheitsprodukte GmbH was a German, family-owned company with a total Europe-wide turnover of DM22 million in 1971. The product line consisted entirely of special opening, closing, sliding, and spring packagings for the cosmetic industry. Among Bell's over 200 customers were several very large multinational companies such as Unilever, Colgate-Palmolive, and L'Oreal. The single largest customer purchased 10 percent of Bell's sales.

This case was prepared by Professor Lawrence G. Franko of Centre d'Etudes Industrielles, Geneva, and is reproduced with his permission.

Bell's American name derived from the fact that its product line was produced under an exclusive license of an American company, Bell Industries, Inc. The American licensor, however, had no ownership position in Bell GmbH. Although Bell GmbH was a relatively small firm, it had already opened a plant in Great Britain in the mid-1960s. The United Kingdom plant had a capacity of 25 million units as compared to the 200 million unit capacity of the main German plant, located in Hanover. Both plants ordinarily produced at 90 to 95 percent of capacity. About DM18.8 million of sales came from the German plant's production; the remaining DM2.3 million was accounted for by U.K. production. Because of the 9.6 percent EEC common tariff, U.K. production went only to the United Kingdom. All other European markets (including other EFTA markets) were supplied by Germany. Indeed, the U.K. plant had been set up only because of the 9.6 percent ad valorem EFTA tariff facing German output. The U.K. plant employed 30 people, compared to 120 in Germany. Of the German personnel, 90 were women workers who assembled and decorated packages. The remainder consisted of administrative personnel plus technicians who designed and built much of Bell GmbH's machinery and who handled the very important (indeed critical) quality-control aspects of the business. None of Bell's employees were union members. According to management, "We are too small to have attracted the attention of the unions."

Sales were made in all countries of western Europe and in Yugoslavia. Under the terms of its American license, the company was restricted to selling in Europe and the socialist countries. Exhibit 7.1 shows the total 1971 European and U.S. markets for the kind of special cosmetics-packaging products produced by Bell. Given normal economic conditions, that is 4 to 5 percent yearly growth in GNP, management expected 20 percent per year sales growth in countries such as Greece, Portugal, and Spain.

Competition and Prices

Bell GmbH's competitors have the characteristics shown in Exhibit 7.2. Bell's management suspected that the two small Italian firms, D and E, were secretly backed by their government—all the more so since the Italian price level was 10 to 15 percent lower than that elsewhere in the EEC. Firms D and E had tried to export part of their produc-

EXHIBIT 7.1

Market Size for Closable Cosmetic Packaging, 1971

	Millions
United Kingdom	150
Germany	360
France	200
Benelux	90
Greece	5
Italy	150
Scandinavia	60
Spain	25
Portugal	5
Switzerland	40
Austria	10
Yugoslavia	5
Total Europe	1,100
United States	2,400

---

tion, but their quality standards were apparently not as high as those of Bell, A, and B. Moreover, their plants were unionized and subject to occasional strikes. Thus they had a poor reputation for meeting delivery dates outside of Italy. Still, they totally dominated the local market. Bell had once had 30 percent of the Italian market and was well known there. With practically nonexistent margins, however, Bell found it increasingly difficult to compete in Italy. Nevertheless, in late 1971, just as the Italian situation began to look really hopeless, the president of Bell, Herr Kahler, had received a letter from two former managers of Italian competitor E suggesting that Bell start up a plant in Italy — under their direction, of course.

With the exception of the Italian situation, prices elsewhere in Europe were relatively uniform: Bell charged all customers in the EEC the same price — DM100 per thousand at its factory. Competitor B, which had started the price war that had recently pushed prices down to DM95 from a previous higher level, also billed in deutsche marks. Competitor A, which billed in francs because of its dominant French position, by and large charged a similar price once value added tax adjustments were made. According to one Bell manager, "We tend to react immediately to what A and B do, and vice

EXHIBIT 7.2

Output of Plants by Country, 1971

Competitor	Ownership		Output (%)
A (large)	U.K. group	France	80
		United Kingdom	15
		Italy	5
B (large)	U.S. company	Germany	65
		England	30
		France	5
C (small)	U.S. (recently acquired)	Germany	100
D (small)	Italian	Italy	100
E (small)	Italian	Italy	100

versa. Everyone tries to differentiate their product other than by price, but finally, one packaging is like another."

Exhibit 7.3 summarizes estimates for the market share of Bell and its competitors in France, Germany, England, and the whole of Europe.

Alternative Courses of Action

In the face of competition, unfavorable exchange rate movements, wage increases in Germany, and the Italian proposal, management felt that action would be needed soon. Herr Kahler had received a phone call from Competitor A suggesting that they try to counter B's price cutting by an "arrangement." The virtues of such an arrangement from Bell's point of view, however, seemed questionable. Competitor A, after all, was sitting with 80 percent of its production in France, where wages were favorable and devaluation more often the rule than not.

Putting up a new plant in France, of course, seemed a most tempting possibility — all the more so since the French government offered very interesting incentives in certain parts of the country. In addition, some technical and design tasks could eventually be performed in France since indigenous skills were available. Ninety percent of the components needed would be supplied initially from Bell's usual outside suppliers in Germany. However, by the second year of operations, perhaps 30 percent could be obtained locally, and, if necessary, all materials could be obtained locally after the

EXHIBIT 7.3

Comparative Market Shares (in percent)[a]

	Bell	Compet-itor A	Compet-itor B	Others	Total
Europe total	19	35	25	21	100
France	7	70	20	3	100
United Kingdom	15	30	45	10	100
Germany	22	30	30	18	100

[a]Rough estimates. No one in the industry publishes sales figures.

third year. Finally, in regions such as Alsace, French technicians and workers generally were fluent in German. Thus there would be few language difficulties during the plant start-up. But management could not help wondering whether the French wage and exchange rate situations would remain as favorable to exports in the future as they had been in the past. Moreover, the investment incentives picture had recently been altered by the EEC agreement to limit incentive grants to 20 percent of project costs as of January 1972. And what if France were to suffer another social upheaval like that of May 1968?

In some ways, adding 25 or 50 million units of capacity to the U.K. plant seemed about the easiest thing to do. A plant and trained people were already in existence. Incentives might be available. The pound might be devalued again. And perhaps wages would not increase as fast as elsewhere in the now expanding EEC. As in France, local components could eventually be substituted for German-made goods. Still, the United Kingdom might be less attractive for the time being because it would probably take five years before tariff barriers would finally disappear between the United Kingdom and the EEC.

The request from the Italians reminded Bell management that a local plant might well help it to capture back its once 30 percent market share. Technical skills and components would be as easily available as in the United Kingdom and France. Moreover, Italy could conceivably provide a relatively low wage base for exports. And the lira had depreciated against the mark in recent times. But could any country that had taken 23 ballots to elect a president in 1971 be a stable place in which to invest?

One final alternative that appeared interesting to Herr Kahler and other members of Bell's management was that of setting up a plant in Spain. Perhaps such a move might give the company a much greater and longer lasting competitive advantage than would the other possibilities. Whether or not components could ever be obtained locally was simply unknown. Still, wage rates were thought to be low enough to easily compensate for the EEC common tariff. Although a 10 percent duty might have to be paid on components imported from Germany, it seemed probable that a rebate arrangement for reexported components could be negotiated with the Spanish authorities.

The plant sizes that appeared most interesting for Italian, Spanish, United Kingdom, or French operations were either 25 million or 50 million units per year. Factory buildings could be leased for very similar yearly rentals throughout Europe. Details of the capacity and cost alternatives considered are given in Exhibit 7.4. The necessary machinery would either be made at Bell's main plant or purchased in Germany. Tentatively, it was thought best to finance a for-

EXHIBIT 7.4
Bell GmbH

Capacity and Cost Alternatives

	Alternative 1	Alternative 2
Annual plant capacity (million units)	25	50
Space requirements	600 m^2	1000 m^2
Approximate yearly rental cost for leased plant[a]	28,000 DM	48,000 DM
Cost of machinery (to be purchased in Germany)	300,000 DM	500,000 DM[b]
Working capital requirements	100,000 DM	220,000 DM
Components cost (per million units)	46,000 DM	46,000 DM
Direct labor (per million units produced in Germany)	7,000 DM	7,000 DM
General administration and overhead (per year)	100,000 DM	150,000 DM[b]
Transport costs	2% sales price	2% sales price

[a]similar in all countries.
[b]For plants above 50 million units, machinery and overhead costs are roughly proportional to capacity.

EXHIBIT 7.5

Exchange Rates, Money Supply, and Prices, Selected European Countries 1965–1971[a]

	1965	1966	1967	1968	1969	1970	1971
Italy							
Rate of exchange (lira per dollar)	624.70	624.45	623.86	623.50	625.50	623.00	581.5
Money supply (1963 = 100)	125	142	164	184	213	273	
Cost-of-living index (1963 = 100)	109	112	115	117	121	128	
France							
Rate of exchange (francs per dollar)	4.902	4.952	4.908	4.948	5.558	5.520	5.116[b]
Money supply (1963 = 100)	118	127	133	145	146	157	
Cost-of-living index (1963 = 100)	105	108	112	118	124	131	
United Kingdom							
Rate of exchange (pound per dollar)	0.357	0.358	0.415	0.419	0.416	0.418	0.383
Money supply (1963 = 100)	113	118	131	140	144	157	
Cost-of-living-index (1963 = 100)	109	114	116	123	129	139	
Germany							
Rate of exchange (marks per dollar)	4.006	3.977	3.999	4.000	3.690	3.648	3.223
Money supply (1963 = 100)	117	119	131	142	150	165	
Cost-of-living index (1963 = 100)	107	109	110	113	116	120	
Spain							
Rate of exchange (peseta per dollar)	59.99	60.00	69.70	69.82	70.06	69.72	64.47
Money supply (1963 = 100)	139	155	178	198	229	250	
Cost-of-living index (1963 = 100)	123	130	138	142	147	157	

[a]Year end.
[b]Commercial rate.
Source: IMF, *International Financial Statistics*, January 1972.

EXHIBIT 7.6

International Financial Data, Selected European Countries (in $ millions)[a]

	1965	1966	1967	1968	1969	1970	1971 (Nov.)
Italy							
Official reserves	4,800	4,911	5,463	5,341	5,045	5,352	6,431
Balance on goods and services[b]	1,883	1,779	1,273	2,336	2,013	679	
Trade (goods) balance only	646	331	−21	1,048	542	−340	
France							
Official reserves	6,343	6,733	6,994	4,201	3,833	4,960	7,494
Balance on goods and services[b]			732	−238	−971	1,148	
Trade (goods) balance only			356	−158	−1,223	726	
United Kingdom							
Official reserves	3,004	3,099	2,695	2,422	2,527	2,827	5,572
Balance on goods and services[b]	378	801	−115	−118	1,613	1,911	
Trade (goods) balance only	−664	−204	−1,446	−1,543	−338	7	
Germany							
Official reserves	7,430	8,029	8,153	9,948	7,129	13,610	17,371
Balance on goods and services[b]	−86	1,593	3,970	4,554	3,780	3,225	
Trade (goods) balance only	248	1,878	4,116	4,485	3,902	4,024	
Spain							
Official reserves	1,422	1,253	1,100	1,150	1,282	1,817	3,104
Balance on goods and services[b]	−846	−983	−907	−709	−959		
Trade (goods) balance only	−1,759	−1,992	−1,781	−1,574	−1,871		

[a]End of year.
[b]Not including transfer payments.
Source: IMF, *International Financial Statistics.*

214

EXHIBIT 7.7

Wage Increases Related to Output Increases in Industry, Selected European Countries[a]

	1966	1967	1968	1969	1970	1971	(forecast) 1972[b]
Italy							
Percent increase in industrial output	11.3	8.5	6.3	2.9	4.0	−2.6	8.0
Percent increase in wages[d]		5.2	3.6	7.5	21.4	14.5	15.0
Ratio of output to wage increases		(1.64)	(1.75)	(0.36)	(0.14)	(0.19)	(0.53)
France							
Percent increase in industrial output	4.3	2.6	4.1	12.7	5.6	2.5	5.0
Percent increase in wages[d]	5.9	6.0	12.4	11.3	10.5	11.1	10.0
Ratio of output to wage increases	(1.24)	(0.43)	(0.33)	(1.13)	(0.53)	(0.22)	(0.50)
United Kingdom							
Percent increase in industrial output	1.8	−0.9	5.3	3.4	1.6	0.8	3.5
Percent increase in wages[d]	6.7	4.0	6.8	9.2	9.6	12.1	12.0
Ratio of output to wage increases	(0.27)	(−0.22)	(0.78)	(0.37)	(0.17)	(0.07)	(0.29)
Germany							
Percent increase in industrial output	1.8	−1.7	12.3	12.5	6.3	3.2	0
Percent increase in wages[c]	7.3	3.9	4.3	9.1	12.8	13.3	6.5
Ratio of output to wage increases	(0.25)	(−0.44)	(2.9)	(1.4)	(0.49)	(0.24)	(0)
Spain							
Percent increase in industrial output	15.0	6.2	6.5	14.5	7.9		6.6
Percent increase in wages[c]	16.0	15.0	7.0	9.0	17.0		12.0
Ratio of output to wage increases	(0.94)	(0.42)	(0.93)	(1.61)	(0.47)		(0.55)

[a]Calculated from OECD, *Main Economic Indicators*, various issues.
[b]Eurofinance-Vision Projections, *Vision*, January 1972, p. 38.
[c]Hourly earnings.
[d]Hourly rates.

215

EXHIBIT 7.8

Wages in Manufacturing (All Industries) in Local Currencies, Selected European Countries

	Austria per month Schilling[b]	Belgium per day Male B. Franc[b]	Denmark per hour (M & F)[a] Ore[b]	France per hour Francs[c]	W. Germany per hour (M & F)[a] D. Mark[b]	Italy per hour Lira[b]	Spain per hour Pesetas[b]	Switzerland per hour Sw. Fr.[b]	U.K. per hour Male s.d.[b]
1965	3,141	359.0	923	3.00	4.12	386	21.57	5.20	8/9
1966	3,514	389.7	1,040	3.18	4.42	401	25.13	5.58	9/3
1967	3,781	414.2	1,128	3.37	4.60	426	28.81	5.94	9/8
1968	4,018	438.7	1,283	3.79	4.79	445	31.16	6.24	10/4
1969	4,263	474.1	1,407	4.21	5.28	489	34.69	6.64	11/2
1970	5,074	—	—	4.56	5.77	—	—	—	—

[a]Male and female.
[b]Earnings.
[c]Rates.
Source: ILO Yearbook of Labor Statistics, 1970.

EXHIBIT 7.9

Indices of Industrial Capacity Utilization, Selected European Countries

Year[a]		Belgium	France	Germany	Italy	Nether-lands	United Kingdom
1965		95.3%	91.7%	92.1%	86.8%	89.7%	
1966		90.6	90.0	85.8	88.5	87.6	93.6%
1967		90.2	87.0	86.7	89.4	86.7	
1968		90.6	96.8	93.0	80.0	91.2	96.9
1969		94.2	94.7	97.3	79.1	93.2	95.8
1970		92.8	95.6	94.0	87.3	94.0	94.5
1971	(1)	94.7	96.1	97.1	86.1	96.5	93.6
	(2)	92.2	93.2	95.4	82.1	94.8	94.2
	(3)	92.9	95.5	93.1	79.4	93.6	93.4

[a]Year end 1965–70, and first three quarters 1971.
Source: "Wharton Indices of Industrial Capacity Utilization in Europe," *Wharton Quarterly*, various issues. (Available from The Wharton School, University of Pennsylvania, Philadelphia, Pa.)

eign plant by an equity stake equal to the cost of machinery. Working capital requirements could be met either by local borrowing or by the extension of account payable terms (for components) to the foreign plant.

As Bell management was preparing to draw up pro forma economic forecasts and cash flow projections for the French, United Kingdom, Spanish, and Italian alternatives, Herr Kahler reminded his colleagues of a letter he had received in November 1971. He suggested that this letter should stimulate Bell to examine the German economy a bit more carefully, too. The letter was from a Yugoslavian company that was soliciting Bell's participation in a joint venture whose aim would be to export back to Europe. Herr Kahler rejected serious consideration of such an alternative for the time being on the grounds that Bell was too small to enter into protracted negotiations with a prospective partner in a venture that might end up competing with already existing wholly owned facilities. Still, he felt it might be useful to look at the medium-term outlook for Germany and the competitiveness of the headquarters plant. If a firm in a country like Yugoslavia were to enter into the packaging business, perhaps continued German revaluations and steep wage increases could make the position of the main 200 million unit capacity plant less and less tenable over the years.

EXHIBIT 7.10

Bell GmbH

Sample Cash-Flow Projection for an Italian Investment[a]

Projected Cash Flows: Italian Investment in 50 Million-unit Plant

INVESTMENT

Machinery	500,000 DM	
Working capital	220,000	
Total	720,000	
Less: 70% debt	(504,000)	
Net investment	216,000 DM	

ANNUAL CASH FLOWS	Before Devaluation	After 10% Devaluation
Sales revenue		
(95 × 50,000 DM)	4,750,000 DM	4,750,000 DM
Expenses[b]		
Building rental	48,000	43,000
Components	2,300,000	1,970,000
Direct labor	170,000	153,000
General overhead	150,000	135,000
Transport costs	75,000	68,000
Interest (5%)	25,000	23,000
Net cash flow	1,982,000 DM	2,358,000 DM

[a]Showing results assuming: (1) no devaluation and (2) a 10% devaluation.
[b]Major assumptions:
  1. All components supplied locally.
  2. Income tax holiday provided by Italian government
  3. All production is for export.
  4. Depreciation not included in overhead charges.

Up to this point, it had been assumed that German production would still account for most of Bell's sales, even after the new plant was added. It was true that the German stockholders might not want to shift a lot of Bell's current production to a foreign country, but efforts at automation could only go so far. Bell had reduced the number of its women workers from 150 to 90 between 1970 and 1971 while increasing output. However, productivity increases could not be obtained at this rate in the future. Would some existing German plant capacity eventually have to be transferred elsewhere?

Questions

1a. "The product line consisted entirely of special opening, closing, sliding, and spring packagings for the cosmetic industry" sold to over 200 customers of which the largest purchased 10 percent of Bell's sales. Based on your understanding of the manufacturing technology and the cost of transportation approximately how many plants would it be rational for Bell to have?

1b. Given the total market size for the cosmetic packaging industry as a whole in Europe, estimate approximately how many plants would minimize the sum of logistics and operating costs.

2. From the viewpoint of Firms A and B, in which nations would Bell's next plant least threaten them, and how might they react to the Bell move that you are recommending?

3. Lay out the skeleton of the cost/benefit analysis that would be done by the Spanish or Italian government.

4. It is mentioned that "Kahler had received a phone call from Company A suggesting that they try to counter B's price cutting by an arrangement." What ulterior motives might A have had and from what actions would it want to restrain Bell?

5. Compared to the German norm, how many additional months of inventory would it be prudent to carry in customer nations to compensate for the probabilities of supply interruptions if the new plant were to be built in (a) Yugoslavia, (b) Italy, and (c) Spain?

6. Analyze Exhibit 7.4 to calculate the economies of scale in the cost of (a) constructing and (b) operating a packaging plant.

7. Extrapolate the data in Exhibits 7.5–7.10 to predict the equivalent of Exhibit 7.4 in 1980 in each of the nations.

8. Based on your analysis of the case in the preceding questions which models of the chapter would you recommend to Bell's management? What budget should they authorize for an analysis and what deadline should be established before committing the next plant?

Introduction

Until it builds a factory in a nation, a corporation has the flexibility to consider supplying the market from any one of a dozen different nations, playing governments off against one another for incentives. Once built, however, the factory becomes a hostage by which the national government can and does influence the corporation. Anticipating this reversal of the relationship means that the political forecasts needed by a multinational corporation should be more detailed than those needed by a domestic corporation in the same nation. After all, the domestic corporation *must* build a factory in the nation if it is to supply its growing market — there may be questions of capacity, timing, layout, and unionization, but the location decision is a foregone conclusion. Because a multinational corporation has more options, its executives need to be able to choose among them; political information is a vital input.

How Governments Perceive Factories

The fact that nations measure gross national *product* rather than gross national *consumption* suggests that they perceive the wealth of their nation as being its productive capability. Most politicians have the view that a nation of industrial workers is better than a nation of glad-handed salesmen. A ranking of work by worth might be:

1. Manufacturing.
2. Repair of plant equipment.
3. Agriculture.
4. Sales.
5. Consumer service.

This ranking suggests a mercantilist concept: Exports are good and imports are an undesirable necessity. National development plans are invariably written in terms of manufacturing plants rather than well-employed sales forces. There is a sense that a factory from abroad brings worker training and a diffusion of technology, whereas a sales manager from abroad brings glibness tailored to the pampered rich.

National prestige used to play a role in justifying steel mills and national airlines. Today, the ultimate symbol of achievement seems to be the manufacture of equipment in the commanding heights of technology — computer peripherals, solar cells, and the like. The statement "it all boils down to jobs" is too gross a simplification for the diverse goals and constraints under which most governments operate. As a general rule, it is prudent for a corporation to prepare a cost/benefit analysis of how the plant will contribute to the national well-being, expressed in terms of the national development plan, and weighted for the kinds of jobs created, whether for laborers or research scientists, using weights appropriate to that nation.

Social Cost/Benefit Analysis

Social cost/benefit analysis (Wells, 1975) is simply an attempt on the part of the host government to ensure that the multinational acts in the host nation's interest by putting resources to their proper use. In a classical economic world, the "invisible hand" would ensure that what is good for the multinational is good for the country. Input prices would reflect the value of the inputs to the economy, product prices would reflect value to the user, and competition would be such that excess returns would not exist. In many developing countries, however, weak competition and/or government intervention in the marketplace may have distorted price signals; projects profitable to the corporation may squander resources for which there is a greater social use elsewhere; and socially desirable projects may be unattractive to the investor.

Social cost/benefit analysis attempts to set the prices "right." The government official evaluating the project will estimate the cost to the economy of obtaining the same kind of benefits from the best alternative source that might be used. This then becomes the social price of the project's output. Similarly, prices of the inputs purchased by the corporation will be adjusted to reflect what they would yield in their next best use. For example, if the host country has a persistently high level of unemployment, an economist would say that the next best use of the worker's time is unemployment and therefore the "shadow wage rate" is near zero. Of particular interest to multinationals is how the inflow of capital is evaluated in such analyses. Actual payments to foreigners of dividends and interest are real costs to the host country and become cost items in their calculations. If the exchange rate is managed, the government would not use the legal exchange rate in these calculations but would use the "shadow exchange rate," a government economist estimate of the black market rate.

In addition to using social prices in calculating the effects of a project, most analysts will try to include "externalities" — costs and benefits to the economy that are not reflected in the company's income statement. For example, if a proposed plant holds promise of attracting other beneficial factories to a region in need of investment, some credit will be given to reflect these subsequent additional benefits. If the corporation knows its plant will be subject to a cost/benefit analysis, prudence would suggest that the corporation track the government analysis with its own calculations.

Most national governments would prefer indigenous industrialization, both to achieve self-sufficiency of the managerial process and to avoid being dependent on the world. As a bridge between now and the advent of managerial self-sufficiency, some governments give incentives to attract *selected* foreign corporations, while other governments impose requirements that manipulate the corporation into conforming. In other words, governments influence corporations with both incentives and penalties.

The Carrots of Government Incentives

Incentives are given by each level of government — national, state, county, and city. Examples include the following:

1. The right to establish a 100 percent subsidiary, rather than a minority joint venture.
2. Free rail, road, sewer, water, and power connections. Low-cost electric power, and guaranteed priority when excessive demand leads to localized brownouts.
3. A government will build the factory and lease it to the corporation at minimal rent for 99 years.
4. The corporation has the right to raise capital from the national development bank at subsidized rates of interest.
5. Factory equipment may be imported duty free.
6. Grants will be given for factory equipment.
7. A special school will be established to train workers, and their first month's wages will be paid by the government.
8. The anti-layoff laws will be waived for a certain period.
9. The county and city governments will grant a property tax holiday for, say, 10 years.
10. The national government will grant an income tax holiday for, say, five years.

These and other incentives are subject to negotiations. To aid those negotiations it is important that the corporation clearly evaluate the after-tax *present value* of each. Such a present value calculation is possible only if the corporate analyst understands how this plant will fit into the world-wide manufacturing network. For example, a five-year income tax holiday is meaningful only if the corporation can anticipate that by the fifth year, income will exceed losses carried forward. To take advantage of a tax holiday, the corporation can reduce production elsewhere so as to fully load this plant, and can set transfer prices and fees (Chapter 3) to show a profit on which to escape tax.

The Stick of Requirements

Some governments prefer the direct action of requiring that a corporation act in ways it prefers. These requirements are always specific by industry and frequently discriminate among corporations. In other words, not all corporations stand equal before national development boards.

A local content law sets a minimum requirement on the percentage value of an item that must be manufactured locally. There is frequently room for negotiation of the percentage and how value is to be calculated. The corporation can also negotiate how broad a product line can be defined as one item. The corporate negotiator can couch this discussion in terms of gaining credits by exporting part of the line to offset imports.

Governments and government agencies are major purchasers in most nations. They can discriminate by giving selective preference to certain corporations (or by excluding others from a list of approved vendors), thereby "suggesting" that a corporation manufacture locally.

Governments frequently impose price controls. A corporation usually has to take the initiative to request a price increase. The price commission considers the request for a time and then issues its ruling. The government may pressure a corporation to build a factory by stalling the importing corporation's price increase request for months or years and then rejecting it.

Most governments control imports. They impose tariffs and may require import permits. Sometimes a government will play competitors off against one another by promising that whoever builds a plant first will suffer less import competition while the others will face reduced quotas and/or higher tariffs.

Plant Location Decisions in a Geographically Decentralized Corporation

The manager of each national subsidiary *aspires* to have a separate plant in each nation. In an extreme form of polycentrism, the multinational corporation would locate its plants just as though it were a group of domestic companies. In essence, a polycentric executive has made the political assessment that each national government will insist that the market and factory are inseparably united. Frequently the symbolic value of a factory cannot be ignored, hence it should be analyzed.

That a factory can have symbolic value is attested to in several ways:

1. When a market is served by imports, the first corporation to build a plant usually gains market share. A local plant is perceived as a commitment of permanence by customers, especially dealers, and even by the corporation's own sales force.
2. To spur industrialization, some governments have encouraged import substitution plants by promising to raise import tariffs, restrict quotas, or delay the permit of a second entrant for a specified number of years.
3. In the struggle for worldwide market share, oligopolistic rivals fear

being foreclosed from a market, and thus build a small factory. A small nation may become the site of too many plants, none of world scale. In Canada this phenomenon is called the "miniature replica effect."

Let us work through the situation of two rival corporations exporting to a market. With increased market demand and/or a rise in unit cost of importing, a corporation could justify the fixed cost of a local plant. However, suppose the market is still too small for either rival to warrant incurring the cost of a plant. Nevertheless, each firm knows that its market share will suffer as soon as its rival builds. Many executives, experienced in such situations, know that a firm with a local plant has a competitive edge over one that does not. By building first, a firm can hope to increase its market share, especially its share of new customers. Only by building a catch-up plant can the preempted rival stop the erosion of its market share. The longer it waits, the greater the permanent erosion of market share. Of course, if both firms build too early, the resulting capacity glut will reduce industry profits. Scherer et al. (1975) provide an excellent discussion of the complex issues of competitive capacity expansion. From the date of construction of the first plant until the catch-up plant comes on stream, the firm that builds second loses market share to the leader, as shown in Exhibit 7.11.

Some corporations keep thorough and systematic track of each of their rivals. Most find it more prudent to conduct *ad hoc* analyses. In the United States, the first legal means of competitor analysis is the reports a corporation must file with various government agencies. Pursuant to the Freedom of Information Act, several Washington firms specialize in obtaining these reports for clients. Similar intelligence is available in other nations.

The second legal means is to interview the rival's managers and engineers. The usual practice is to contract with a medium level executive search

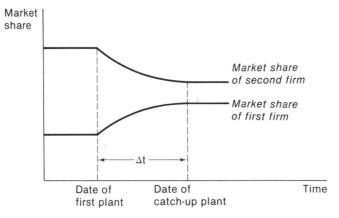

EXHIBIT 7.11
Market share and sequence of construction.

firm to prepare a slate of candidates. The more an interviewer knows, the more sense he can make of the interviewee's indiscretions. Some corporations counter this by sending trusted employees on interviews, not only to willfully mislead, but especially to sense issues from the interviewer's questions.

Knowledgeable competitive analysts describe their task as fitting together a jigsaw puzzle for which the most productive start is to attempt to stand in the competitor's shoes and see what would seem rational to him. A thoughtful competitive analyst can duplicate the staff work being prepared in the rival firm. Let us assume an active role in this process.

If we intend to build a plant in a certain period, we must anticipate when our rival will respond with a catch-up plant of his own. His effect on our market share means that only after anticipating his reaction can we calculate our cash flow from our plant. The first step is to draw our version on Exhibit 7.11 and estimate the attrition of market shares.

The second step is to stand in the rival's shoes and anticipate his reactions to our every move. One might visualize a conflict between the sales manager and the comptroller. If we build prematurely, the rival's comptroller will delay construction of their plant until the market has grown enough, even though this means sacrificing market share in the interim. We can stand in the shoes of the rival and estimate his monthly cash flows from now until he builds, his cost of construction, and his cash flows afterward. Use a computer to calculate the present value of this sequence of cash flows, thus simulating the rival's reaction timing, and find the reaction best to him. Usually we would have other information about the process by which the rival makes decisions, so we could predict more accurately when he would react to our initiative.

Our monthly cash flow, depicted in Exhibit 7.12, critically depends on when the rival reacts. Assuming that we can manage to be the first to build, our profitability is the present value of the Exhibit 7.12 cash flows.

For every month in which we could conceivably build the first plant, we must predict the rival's reaction so we can calculate our cash flows. For

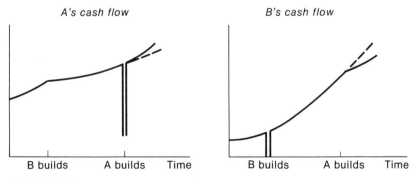

EXHIBIT 7.12
Best cash flow to A for given date of B's building.

each date of our building the first plant, we can calculate the present value of our future cash flows and those of our rival.

Half the problem has been solved. Now, standing in the shoes of the rival, and for each date at which the rival builds the first plant in the nation, calculate when *we* would respond. For each date of the rival's building the first plant, calculate the present value of cash flows to the rival and the present value of our cash flow.

The important date is when the first plant is built. Call the two corporations A and B. In Exhibit 7.13 the first graph shows the present value of cash flow to corporation A, one line if it builds first, the other line if it builds second. Note that after a certain date the market has grown so large and market share counts so much that the corporation will build a plant as soon as its rival does; after this date it shows the same cash flow whether it builds first or second.

The posture of each firm toward the other varies through time (Rao and Rutenberg, 1979). We can delineate five zones or intervals that characterize the growth of demand in the new market (Exhibit 7.13). The first is a *premature zone* when both firms find it profitable to import rather than

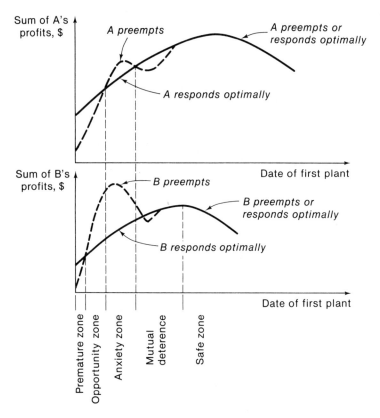

EXHIBIT 7.13
The dynamics of rivalry.

build a new plant. In the next interval, one firm has an opportunity to preempt its rival and thereby gain a stronger market position in terms of higher market share. This is the *opportunity zone*. Subsequent to this is the *anxiety zone*, an interval when each firm can preempt the other "advantageously," but only if the other does not build simultaneously. This is the prisoner's dilemma. It is followed by an interval of mutual forbearance, where neither firm finds advantage in preempting; each is deterred by knowing that the other will respond by building simultaneously because the market has grown large enough and market shares have become more valuable. This we call the *zone of mutual deterrence*. Finally, at some time one firm will find it so expensive to continue to import that it will build a local plant. The other firm will respond by building simultaneously to protect market share. This is the *safe zone*. As can be seen, in each zone the value for competitive information is quite different.

Everything else being equal, we would expect a large firm to build a plant first. However, the firm that has the *higher* import cost may be presented with an opportunity. In a competitively adverse situation it pays not to catch up but to initiate; intelligent leapfrogging can actually result in gains. But such opportunities occur only occasionally for a small firm.

In practice, the delineation between the opportunity zone and the anxiety zone is crucial, whether it is delineated by argument or calculations. Most executives have felt extremely anxious about the real possibility of excess industry capacity. "Some damn fool is going to trigger a round of capacity expansions" is frequently repeated. The first reason for clear delineation is that, in the anxiety zone, rivals can cope by choosing two nations, both ripe for a plant, and each rival can build a plant in one of the nations, sized adequately to supply the marketing needs of both corporations. If the product is homogeneous (gasoline or liquid oxygen, for example) this *twinning* of transactions is called a *swap*. However, there is no reason that the products must be identical (factories commonly produce private label brands). The twinning is essential so that each company holds the other hostage. Thus each of the two firms may build in a different market first and then exchange their outputs locally rather than incur shipping costs. In this way, not only is excess capacity avoided but efficient production networks are achieved. Scherer et al. (1975) discuss the prevalence of such practices. In the anxiety zone, both parties will welcome government intervention to prevent both from building a plant. The second reason for clear delineation is that corporate planners must make an argument for new plants early enough to arrange capital appropriations. It is vital to forecast the opportunity zone correctly, and to communicate the opportunities to superiors and subordinates. An inability to seize opportunity might lead managers to swapping arrangements, or worse, capacity expansions that result in excess industry capacity.

In summary, governments pressure corporations to build factories to replace imports. In each nation competitive dynamics also lead to early plants. In a polycentric corporation there will be many small plants.

Ethnocentric Plant Location to Minimize Cost

A global product manager displays his ethnocentrism by the assumptions he makes. He assumes that his task is to satisfy market demands of all nations, doing so at minimum *total* cost. The focus is on the economics of cost minimization.

Six kinds of input data are required:

1. A time horizon (say 10–20 years) over which to plan.
2. A demand forecast over the time horizon for each market:
   (a) Demand might depend on the presence of one's plant. For now, assume plant locations are given, estimate the demands, and proceed to calculate the plant capacity and operations.
   (b) The quantity demanded depends on the price, which in turn depends on the delivered cost. Output from this calculation gives the time trace of the delivered cost in each market. After studying the cost forecast, each marketing manager may choose to revise his sales estimates. The plant location model can then be rerun. If the marketing managers are confident enough to specify an elastic demand curve, Erlenkotter (1978) shows how to calculate plant sizes accordingly.
3. The logistics costs discussed in Chapter 5 extrapolated as far into the future as the planning horizon.
4. A thorough understanding of why there are economies of scale in each plant. Design engineers commonly assume a "0.7 rule," which describes cost function:

$$\text{plant cost} = \text{constant} \times \text{capacity}^{0.7}$$

In other words, a plant of double capacity will cost $2^{0.7}$, or 1.6, times as much. Engineering data show that the exponent is usually between 0.6 and 0.8 resulting in cost curves shaped like those in Exhibit 7.14. Nevertheless, after government incentives and local particularities have

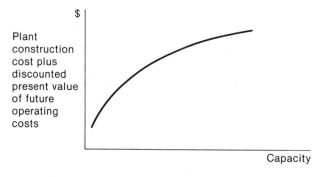

EXHIBIT 7.14
Economies of scale.

228

been incorporated into the cost function a wider range of exponents is possible.

5. Discount rate. One-time capital expenditures are to be balanced against streams of operating and logistics costs. For valid comparisons, all future expenditures must be discounted to the present. A discount rate is therefore needed (see Chapter 3).

6. Constraints on plant sequences and/or dates. Decisions to build plants are rife with political jockeying, both between power factions within the corporation and within governments. The ambiguity of such considerations may drive an ethnocentric manager to demand that someone state definite constraints as to plant sequences and deadlines. Within these constraints he will optimize. The model to be explained can be run several times to cost out each different set of sequence constraints and deadlines. These cost differences will be valuable feedback for the geocentric executive, as will be discussed in the next section.

These six inputs will be processed to minimize the discounted present value of cash flows over the time horizon. The solution of the plant location problem yields the plant capacities, construction dates, and operating load. The fact that these have cash flow consequences implies rerunning the Maneuvering Liquid Assets model of Chapter 3. That model yields precise discount rates. The plant capacity and timing decisions may then be improved by recalculation.

Improving Timing

Solve the logistics problem at time zero (using the market demands, logistics costs, and the plant's capacities available at time zero). The solution gives one point in Exhibit 7.15. In the transportation tableau allow the demands to grow with time (use Srinivasan and Thompson [1972] operators to keep the transportation tableau optimized). The total of lo-

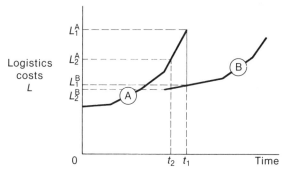

EXHIBIT 7.15
Logistics cost on all routes at each point through time.

gistics plus plant operating costs will rise as demands increase as shown in curve A of Exhibit 7.15. The upper end of line A occurs at t_1 when demand has risen to fill all available plants.

As soon as a new plant is built, it will supply local markets, so the sum of the logistics costs drops from L_1^A to L_2^B dollars per month in Exhibit 7.15. This desirable drop is offset by the interest on the plant investment. If the interest charge is less than the drop in logistics and operating costs, then it will be profitable to build the new plant earlier. How much earlier to build depends on the logistics cost, so with the new plant available, run the transportation tableau backward in time to calculate the lower logistics curve B. Stop working backward in time as soon as the difference between the logistics curves equals the interest cost on the plant. In Exhibit 7.15 this time occurs at t_2, when the logistics savings is $L_2^A - L_2^B$.

Timing reoptimizations can be done one at a time, starting with the first new plant. The calculations of Rao and Rutenberg (1977) show that this simple retiming can be very profitable. Constructing a plant earlier than needed has two side benefits. The excess capacity is available in case demand picks up or some other plant fails. Furthermore, as analyzed in the polycentric section, having the plant means that capacity overhangs the market, thereby preempting rivals.

The Optimal Plant Size

To decide to change the capacity of one of the intended plants we need to compare the cost of the increment of capacity with the benefits from that increment. The *slope* of Exhibit 7.14 provides the cost. The dual variables on the logistics problem through time provide the benefits.

In a transportation tableau, the dual variable associated with a plant measures the value of an additional increment of plant capacity. As the demand and logistics costs increase through time, keep an eye on the dual variable. For one plant, plot how the value of the dual variable alters through time. In Exhibit 7.16 the periods of zero value occur when this plant has excess capacity. Whenever a new plant is built, production will

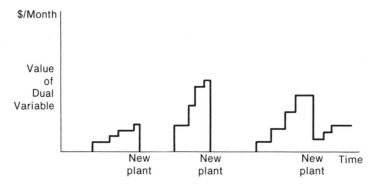

EXHIBIT 7.16
Time trace of the benefit of expanding the plant by one unit of capacity.

be reallocated, and some established plants will have excess capacity. The exhibit is plotted in terms of dollars per month. Using the discount rate for this nation, compute the present value of this stream of benefits. Compare the cost of an increment of capacity with the present value of the benefit, and make a small adjustment to the capacity to bring the values toward equality.

Recall that the polycentric corporation was pressured to build a factory in each strong national market. Healthy economies generally have natural resources and/or high labor productivity. Their exports usually exceed imports such that their exchange rate need not fall as fast as domestic inflation rises. It is difficult to export from such nations, because plant productivity improvements tend to be offset by the rising exchange rate. In contrast, the hardheaded production approach of an ethnocentric corporation is to convert national balance of payments analyses into U.S. dollars. In nations whose currencies are forecast to devalue faster than domestic inflation will rise, a multinational will face a falling real cost of wages and local supplies. To this end the corporation should select nations that lack natural resources and have an adequate but fragmented manufacturing base. Often these are the nations who give the largest incentives to get world-scale manufacturing plants.

Geocentric Perspective on Plant Location

Many governments perceive a multidivisional corporation as a single entity. List the divisions of a corporation down the side of the page and various nations across the top. If the division has a plant in a nation, mark the appropriate cell. During the next decade, some national governments are going to insist that the corporation open a plant, below the column of each such nation mark a 1 for one plant. During the same decade the world growth expected by certain products will necessitate new plants for some of the product divisions. For each such division, mark the number of new plants in the far right of its row.

The question to be explored by the geocentric headquarters is which product plants to assign to which nations. Involved is a delicate trade-off. The product division has probably done a global network analysis to calculate exactly which one or two national plant locations will result in the lowest global cost to the product division. Unfortunately, in a multidivisional organization it is likely that all the product divisions will be attracted to only a few nations. Staff in headquarters generally prepare lists of nations suitable for investment. This information is then used by the product division managers, who interpret the lists as revealing the preferences of the headquarters capital appropriations committee, and hence they tend not to consider other nations. Yet the real challenge of creative plant location is to search for nations that match the idiosyncratic needs of the particular product divisions.

Refer back to the table of nations and product divisions. For each product division determine the best location for the new plant. Then evaluate locating the new plant in each of the other nations. Optimize logistics, timing, and plant size so as to determine the additional cost that would be incurred if political pressures necessitated this location. The table of nations and product divisions, with each cell completed with the "additional cost," becomes the "payoff matrix" to the corporation. If each nation insists on a plant (without specifying which product), then the corporate staff can compute the least cost assignment of plants to nations as an orthodox assignment problem from operations research.

If governments prefer certain divisions to others (as they will if they perform cost/benefit analyses), then the government's payoff matrix will be different from the corporation's. It turns out that this problem can be formulated as a weighted distribution (machine loading) problem where each government has a goal of benefits that must be satisfied. With computers doing the drudgery of calculations, the analysts can work to refine what these solutions really are in the eyes of the corporation and in the eyes of each government.

Negotiating

The first and most important step is to stand in the shoes of the national planning agency and, as recommended earlier in this chapter, perform a cost/benefit analysis of the plant. Despite the aura of precision implied by a cost/benefit analysis, much of the input data are necessarily subjective. Part of the company's negotiating strategy can be to discuss with this government reasonable ranges for the input data that are particularly subjective.

The second step is for the marketing manager to work through the exercise of withdrawing from the nation and estimate the recoverable value. Even though the probability of disinvestment may be low, the exercise sets a bound beyond which corporate negotiators will not be pushed. Furthermore, the executives gain an awareness of clauses in supply contracts (both local and within the corporation) that may need to be broken.

The third step of preparation is to rehearse. Rehearsal requires that two people spar with one another, then reverse roles and spar again to test their negotiating arguments. The vital thing to realize is that the corporation has the upper hand only until it builds a factory, and thereafter the factory is a hostage. Hence most of the rehearsal should consider incidents that might arise after the factory begins operation. Qualitative aspects of emotional differences and bad strategies will be exposed.

Robustness in the Face of Risk

Many impoverished nations in the world are so desperate to industrialize that they will negotiate substantial capital, training, tax, and wage concessions. But such nations usually present risks, and corporate headquarters frequently eliminates risky nations without serious evaluation. Thus it is common for an ethnocentric headquarters to create for its product division managers a list of approved nations. Product division managers are encouraged to build in the approved nations; by strong implication, factories proposed in other nations would be rejected and hence are rarely proposed.

One approach to evaluating national risk is to try to express probabilities of disaster. The other approach is to calculate the threshold of risk within which a factory could be justified in this nation. Those who fathom political risk are then forced to gauge whether forecast risk is within this threshold.

Before proceeding further, it will be helpful to differentiate between balance sheet risk and supply risk. Many balance sheet items can be insured. Governments of exporting nations compete in granting long-term low-interest loans for factory equipment to be exported to underdeveloped nations. With the loan the corporation can usually obtain insurance against both expropriation and damage caused by civil disturbance. The corporation's entire balance sheet risk could be protected by insurance. In that case, from the viewpoint of risk analysis (though not equity appreciation possibilities) the factory might as well be totally owned by the local government but run by the corporation under a management service contract. But even if balance sheet risk is zero, supply risk remains.

The risk of interrupting the supply of goods to customers is most worrisome. Many multinational corporations have built their marketing strategy around a consistent supply of consistent products. Their brand carries the implication of an assured supply. The potential penalty in the face of the risk of supply interruptions must be analyzed *within* the corporation, because this penalty cannot be transferred to a government insurance agency. The corporation needs contingency plans. If a plant is lost, or if a transportation route is closed (the Suez Canal, for example), how can the corporation adapt? There may be several combinations of disasters and opportunities to consider. Each combination is usually called a scenario. For the purposes of developing a plan it is sensible to select just a few scenarios. Once the plan has been developed, it can be validated (checked for robustness) against many less likely scenarios.

The analysis has three stages. The first stage occurs as soon as supply is interrupted and production stops at one plant; all other plants producing these items must step up production (by increasing shifts, delaying maintenance, and so on). The second stage may involve starting to produce the items in one of the large, flexible factories. The third stage is to expedite the next plant opening, perhaps moving its site to a different nation to rebalance the production network.

Stage 1 In the immediate aftermath of a supply interruption the corporation faces a production-smoothing problem of working overtime, adding shifts, and delaying maintenance until the replacement plant is brought on stream. This increased production by other plants plus the amount of initial inventory will determine whether it is possible to satisfy demands until the replacement plant comes on stream. List a matrix of scenarios down the side of a piece of paper, and list possible production shut-down dates across the top. The starting inventory stockpile is that inventory on hand in the global system as of the loss day. Analyze operations until replacement day. For each scenario and loss day determine the value of just one more unit of stockpile. For each loss date, average these unit values with the probability of the scenario occuring (in the scenario that nothing bad happens, the unit value of another item held in stockpile until the scheduled next plant will be negative). Adjust the stockpile levels in each period until the weighted cost is zero of one more unit of stockpile.

The stockpile does not have to be kept at factories. Actually the system would be less vulnerable to strikes if a large part of the stockpile were kept with marketing affiliates.

Just after a new plant comes on stream, the stockpile level is low — there is sufficient plant capacity available at all factories to handle the shortage until the replacement plant is built. At an intermediate date the rising demands of the global markets require that the stockpile of inventory should be larger because if the system loses a plant now, it may take two years, or longer, to design and erect a replacement plant, even if the process is expedited. Later on, the imminence of the next scheduled plant coming into production means that less stockpile need be carried. If the corporation expects some warning before losing a plant, then it can proceed with lower stockpiles, planning to step up production and exports whenever the alarm sounds.

Stage 2. If the plant loss occurs at an intermediate date (when the stockpile would be highest), it may be economical to start temporary production in one of the corporation's flexible factories. Temporary production can be started only after a time lag. This lag could be reduced if tooling were available. Perhaps critical tooling for the next scheduled plant could be purchased and stored. The holding cost (adjusted for inflation) of tooling should be compared with the holding cost of the stockpile.

In summary, the markets need an assured supply of product. As long as this can be arranged from inventory, overtime, and from an expedited next plant, the corporation can dare to build in risky nations that are desperate to industrialize. Contingency plans are necessary. (In actually performing the calculations for Stage 2, one must first calculate Stage 3.)

Stage 3. We need analyze only the time interval between now and the scheduled on-stream date of the next plant. Obviously we will expedite the construction of the new plant. The only question is whether we should move the site.

At some sites a plant could be erected more quickly than at others, and some sites better rebalance the production network. Several sites should be analyzed. For certain scenarios one site will appear best, but for others another site will be preferable. At selected sites it may be worthwhile to begin site preparation—especially obtaining permits—early. Awkward problems arise if one plant is lost just before a scheduled construction of a new plant, and the scheduled plant would no longer fit suitably into the global production network. In summary, for each loss scenario, occurring in each time period, decide where the replacement plant would be built. Also estimate the expediting cost of opening the plant a day earlier.

Reducing the Probability of Nationalization

The text of this chapter began with a discussion of cost/benefit analyses that national governments make. Unfortunately cost/benefit analyses are static. A politician will ask what benefits the corporation has provided *lately* and can be expected to provide while he is still in power. Each of the stakeholders discussed in Chapter 4 must be considered in the corporate efforts to reduce the probability of nationalization. Currently, executives work mostly by intuition and judgment.

Plant location analysts get involved in at least three ways, which are helpful but not major.

First, plants are generally designed to be expanded, and there are rules of thumb and economic analyses (an inventory model of excess capacity) that suggest how large (and infrequent) the expansions should be. In nations where the corporation must make political statements frequently, it may be sensible to design for many small expansion phases. An analyst can calculate the additional cost (present valued) of such a strategy.

Second, in some circumstances it may be sensible to purchase equipment in nations whose governments grant long-term export incentive loans and also are significant in the eyes of the local government. If the local government nationalizes this plant, it automatically entangles itself with other governments. Fear of this entanglement may deter nationalization slightly.

Third, there are two extremes in plant specialization. If the plant supplies only the national market with all its broad range of products, then the plant may be a more tempting plum to nationalize, but it does not affect the global manufacturing network. On the other hand, if the plant specializes in only one component of the corporation's product line, the corporation as a whole is vulnerable to this nationalization; however, nationalization is less likely to occur because an overspecialized factory is worthless to the government (Bradley, 1977).

Questions from Other Viewpoints

1. *Corporate Rational Normative Global.* You just covered this viewpoint in the chapter.
2. *Corporate Rational Normative Subsidiary.* From an analytical model, a headquarters planner could compute the threshold cost curve of a plant in your particular nation. If a plant could be built below that cost, it would pass the headquarters ROI threshold. Explicitly how would your knowing the headquarters' guideline help you search for a plant site in your nation?
3. *Corporate Rational Descriptive Global.* Find checklists used by corporations to evaluate plant sites. Try *Business International*, Carl Heyel's *The Encyclopedia of Management*, or any other source. What emphasis do you see in these checklists? What factors do you see as ignored?
4. *Corporate Rational Descriptive Subsidiary.* Some national governments offer tax incentives to entice foreign-owned factories. Other national governments threaten to withhold import permits unless the corporation builds a factory or expands its factory to meet local content laws. Please generalize by describing the characteristics of each of these two groups of nations.
5. *Corporate Emotional Normative Global.* Whenever a task force gets involved in investigating a factory site, they have a tendency to get so involved in their work that they hate to say no. How would you manage such a group so that their inevitable identification with the site is used to the corporate advantage?
6. *Corporate Emotional Normative Subsidiary.* Think about the town or city that you are now in, paying attention to the style and climate of work. Suppose a foreign multinational corporation has selected your town or city as a *possible* plant site, because the economics look right. As an employee of your national subsidiary, you have been sent to your town to do an on-the-spot assessment to complement all the data that headquarters has on the town. Select an industry that is economically viable for your town, but whose style would not suit it at all. Write a tightly argued two-page memo to headquarters explaining the lack of fit.
7. *Corporate Emotional Descriptive Global.* Describe the emotional problems of a team of factory location analysts who make endless studies, none of which are implemented because the corporation successfully resists pressures that it build more plants.
8. *Corporate Emotional Descriptive Subsidiary.* Describe some of the nonquantitative, rather emotional factors, that actually affect factory location.
9. *Societal Rational Normative Global.* If an industry were ruled worldwide by one monopolist (or one planning commission), would there

be fewer or more *factories* than would rationally emerge from competition between several corporations? Would fewer or more *nations* have factories?

10. *Societal Rational Normative National.* Most nations have underdeveloped regions. Frequently incentives are provided to corporations to locate in the underdeveloped regions. The incentives often are expensive economically and embarrassing politically to the governments concerned both if the venture fails and if it succeeds magnificently. Suppose a government has operated such an incentive for 20 years. To calculate the benefits, it needs an estimate of the plants that would have been built in the region had there been no incentives. What approaches might you take to providing this estimate?

11. *Societal Rational Descriptive Global.* Find a source of automobile production data, such as *Ward's Auto World* or the *UN Statistical Yearbook*. List the top 10 nations in automobile production. Rank the 10 nations by their rate of growth in automobile production. When do you predict that each of the existing top 10 will change rank?

12. *Societal Rational Descriptive National.* What evidence is there of the extent to which tax incentives actually affect and alter plant locations?

13. *Societal Emotional Normative Global.* There are economies of scale in infrastructure, particularly of highly trained workers. This means that the advanced industrialized nations get the factories for advanced industrialized products, because only they have enough skilled and adaptable workers. Carried to the extreme this would lead to a world consisting of just a few pinnacles of prowess in electronics, or in chemistry, or any field wherein experts can excite one another to even greater heights of accomplishment. Write a brief essay either praising this process or damning it.

14. *Societal Emotional Normative National.* In many nations there are regional disparities, and industry is spread very unevenly. Why is this so in your nation?

15. *Societal Emotional Descriptive Global.* Why are there worldwide fashions in the laws regulating the operations of factories? For example, by the mid-1970s pollution control laws appeared on the books of most nations. Have "pollution havens" appeared?

16. *Societal Emotional Descriptive Subsidiary.* When the first foreign factory moves into a medium-sized town, what effect will it have on the social structure of the town?

Bibliography to Chapter 7

Bradley, David G., "Managing Against Expropriation," *Harvard Business Review*, Vol. 55, No. 4 (1977), pp. 75–83.

Doz, Yves L. and C.K. Prahalad, "How MNCs Cope with Host Government Intervention," *Harvard Business Review*, Vol. 58, No. 2 (1980), pp. 149–157.

Erlenkotter, Donald, "Plant Location: Where Demand Is Sensitive to Delivered Cost," *Management Science*, Vol. 24, No. 4 (1978), pp. 378–386.

Gaeteno, Lombardo and Richard C. Norris, "Facility Location — Some Practical Applications," paper presented at the 45th Joint National Meeting of ORSA/TIMS, Arthur D. Little, Inc., Cambridge, MA., 1974.

Knickerbocker, Frederick T., *Oligopolistic Reaction and Multinational Enterprise* (Boston: Division of Research, Harvard Business School, 1973).

Lent, George E., "Tax Incentives for Investment in Developing Countries," *IMF Staff Papers*, Vol. 14, No. 2 (1967), pp. 249–321.

Rao, Ram and David P. Rutenberg, "Multilocation Plant Sizing and Timing," *Management Science*, Vol. 23, No. 11 (1977), pp. 1187–1198.

Rao, Ram and David P. Rutenberg, "Pre-empting an Alert Rival," *Bell Journal of Economics*, Vol. 10, No. 2 (1979), pp. 412–428.

Rummel, R.J. and David A. Heenan, "How Multinationals Analyze Political Risk," *Harvard Business Review*, Vol. 56, No. 1 (1978), pp. 67–76.

Scherer, Frederick M. et al., *The Economics of Multi-Plant Operations: An International Comparison Study* (Cambridge: Harvard University Press, 1975).

Srinivasan, Venkataraman and Gerald Thompson, "An Operator Theory of Parametric Programming for the Transportation Problem I and II," *Naval Research Logistics Quarterly*, Vol. 19, June 1972, pp. 227–252.

Wells, Louis T., Jr., "Don't Overautomate Your Foreign Plant," *Harvard Business Review*, Vol. 52, No. 1 (1974), pp. 111–118.

Wells, Louis T., Jr., "Social Cost/Benefit Analysis for MNC's," *Harvard Business Review*, Vol. 53, No. 2 (1975), pp. 40–50.

International trade theory builds on the concept of gains from trade. For a variety of reasons such as raw material availability, climate, and attitude of workers, the relative costs of producing two or more products differ in different countries. That being the case, it makes sense for each country to specialize in the products in which it has a relative advantage, trading with other countries for products in which the others have a comparative advantage.

Gains from trade can be achieved within a multinational corporation, because dealing with a sister subsidiary within the multinational is more sure than dealing with a foreign stranger. Furthermore, each marketing affiliate of a multinational corporation can provide the manufacturing network with its market forecasts and market research in a way not possible under arm's-length conditions.

Chapter 7 shows the further gains to trade that occur when there are economies of scale in plant construction and operation. Economies of scale cause such specialization that some corporations find it most efficient for a high-technology division to have just one plant supplying the whole world. Economies of scale persist, but at an ever reducing rate, as plants are designed larger. The essence of the problem lies in the trade-off between economies of scale in plant and logistics costs. Logistics costs is a phrase that includes tariffs and quotas as well as shipping costs.

When an item (a finished product or a subassembly) is manufactured in two or more plants, the logistics and plants can be viewed as a network. It is easier to manage such a network by pretending it does not exist, and keeping permanent the assignment of markets to factories. But it is more profitable to allow some of the border markets to get their product from whichever factory is cheaper. Production costs vary from month to month as demands fluctuate and strain available capacity, as breakdowns occur, as production lines are reconfigured, and for hundreds of other reasons. If a factory can accommodate to these changes by shedding or taking on customers from a sister factory in the network, then it makes sense for headquarters to allow the two factories to be designed differently. If one is designed for steady output, its network sister can be designed to accommodate fluctuations.

Like sinews that allow the body to flex, logistics allows the manufacturing network to flex. Therefore an entire chapter is devoted to logistics. The chapter explains that costs can usually be reduced if all relevant costs are considered simultaneously. The essence of the chapter, however, lies in putting these costs together as entries in a transportation tableau which can be solved for production smoothing and plant location decisions. For such purposes, forecasts of future logistics costs are required.

PART THREE

Multinational Marketing

CHAPTER EIGHT

New Product Launch

Introductory Note to the Case

Philip Morris International

Good brand management is not allowed on the balance sheet of a corporation. We know how significant it is, yet we can measure and describe brand management only in indirect ways. So the best way to learn is to work as an assistant deputy brand manager, and slowly work up. Nevertheless, the intuitive flair of an energetic brand manager brings with it the potential ethnocentricity of believing that customers in all nations ought to be alike, and thereby underestimating market risks.

Multinational brand management is particularly challenging, because there is a desire for coherence so that the brand means about the same thing around the world. It is usually helpful to think of a brand as a person, with its own personality. Parliament Cigarettes have a personality in the United States, and one difficult question was whether Parliament would have the same personality in Canada, particularly in the province of Quebec, where French is the predominant language. These personality questions are a poetic way of speaking about market segmentation and niches in anticipation of competitors' responses.

The questions at the end of this case focus on the economics of the launch—it is a large, speculative investment, even if the competitors do nothing. Its being a speculative investment means that the data are vague and subjective.

Postscript: Parliament actually was launched across Canada as an American cigarette. Sales started slowly and were un-

responsive to increased advertising. Parliament was withdrawn slowly.

When the medical effects of smoking became a cause for public alarm, Canadian cigarette producers agreed on a code of conduct that required a warning on each pack, no television advertising, and restrictions on print advertising. Fines concerning the latter are imposed as a reduction in the offending brand manager's advertising budget.

Philip Morris International

In late 1961, executives of Philip Morris International were considering the introduction of a new cigarette brand into the Canadian market through their Canadian affiliate, Benson and Hedges (Canada) Ltd. Philip Morris had purchased virtually all of the outstanding common stock of Benson and Hedges (Canada) Ltd. in 1958 and were anxious to increase the business of Benson and Hedges in Canada. The company was successfully selling Trump cigars, but did not have an effective entry in Canada's cigarette market. Philip Morris executives were contemplating employing their second most popular U.S. brand, Parliament, using identical blend and packaging. They reasoned that changes were unnecessary because "awareness" studies had indicated that Canadians were cognizant of the brand name, Parliament, through the overlap, through U.S. media, of Parliament advertising into Canada.

The Canadian Market

Canada is the second largest country in the world (next to the Soviet Union) but is greatly underpopulated relative to other countries. Population as of June 1960 was 18 million with approximately 80 percent of this stretched in a thin line within 100 miles of the Canada–United States border. Officially, the country is bilingual and bicultural, but most of the French-speaking population is concentrated within the province of Quebec where they constitute about 85 percent of the province's approximately 5 million persons.

Canada is usually ranked either second, third, or fourth

behind the United States in terms of income per capita, vying with Sweden and Switzerland (all have approximately $U.S.2100 per capita GNP figures). Average hourly wages in Canada usually run about 15 to 20 percent behind those for comparable jobs in the United States except for certain industries such as automobiles where wage parity is only a few years away.

Canadians are often characterized as a cross between people from the States and the British, and indeed many institutional forms, such as government, exhibit characteristics of both countries. While Canadians display many traits similar to U.S. citizens and Britishers, they consider themselves unique, being more reserved and more conservative than people of the United States yet less cautious than the British and possessing a much more socially mobile society, in the U.S. manner. French-Canadians exhibit many of the characteristics of their European forefathers, being more volatile than English-speaking Canadians, yet in many ways quite different from their European counterparts. Both main groups in Canada seek to retain and foster a peculiar identity — the English-speaking against the culturally and economically dominant neighbor to the south; the French against the superior numbers and economic strength of English Canadians within the country.

The cigarette market in Canada has exhibited rapid growth since 1920 (see Exhibits 8.1 to 8.3). Sales of cigarettes in-

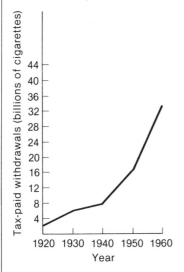

EXHIBIT 8.1
Tax-paid withdrawals of cigarettes for consumption in Canada, 1920–1960 (billions of cigarettes)

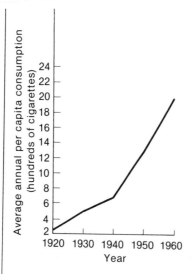

EXHIBIT 8.2

Average annual per capita Canadian consumption of cigarettes, 1920–1960 (hundreds of cigarettes)

creased from about 3 billion in 1920 to over 34 billion in 1960. Consumption per capita rose from 250 cigarettes to just under 2,000 cigarettes over the same period. The most pronounced growth in recent years has been exhibited by the filter and king-size varieties. In the 1957–1961 period filter cigarettes' share of the total market increased from 29 percent to over 50 percent. After the introduction of king-size cigarettes into Canada in 1957, the market share for this type of cigarette soared from zero to 15 percent by the end of 1960. The rapid acceptance of the filter and king-size cigarettes (see Exhibits 8.4 and 8.5) was one of the most significant developments to occur in the Canadian cigarette market in this period.

All advertising and sales promotion was provided by the manufacturers themselves. National advertising campaigns were implemented via a full range of print newspapers. Segmented campaigns were implemented via magazines, many of which were American. Electronic media (radio, television, via two national networks) and various specialized media such as billboards were also available. In addition, the manufacturers' selling organizations promoted distribution by systematically visiting wholesalers and retailers and encouraged sales by point of sale displays.

EXHIBIT 8.3

Average Annual Canadian Per Capita Usage of Cigarettes, 1924–1963

Year	Per Capita Usage of Cigarettes	Year	Per Capita Usage of Cigarettes
1924	275	1944	1036
1925	304	1945	1255
1926	341	1946	1209
1927	392	1947	1207
1928	451	1948	1236
1929	507	1949	1252
1930	493	1950	1252
1931	437	1951	1118
1932	353	1952	1234
1933	404	1953	1415
1934	446	1954	1447
1935	485	1955	1565
1936	508	1956	1679
1937	602	1957	1817
1938	613	1958	1901
1939	630	1959	1939
1940	663	1960	1925
1941	746	1961	2012
1942	879	1962	2083
1943	953	1963	2110

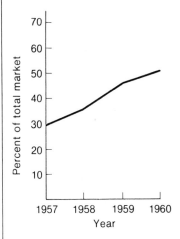

EXHIBIT 8.4
Filter cigarettes as a percentage of the total Canadian cigarette market, 1957–1960

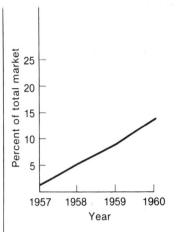

EXHIBIT 8.5

*King-size cigarettes as a percentage of the total
Canadian cigarette market, 1957–1960*

The Competition

The cigarette industry in Canada was a classic case of an
oligopoly market. As of 1960, there were only five major
firms in the marketplace, with two of them holding a combined 80 percent share. These two firms, Imperial Tobacco
Company of Canada, Limited, and MacDonald Tobacco
Company, never held less than 70 percent of the market
since Imperial was incorporated in 1912. In 1960, Imperial
held a 54 percent share and was the acknowledged market
leader. MacDonald, with a 27 percent share, seemed to be
content with a defensive strategy and spent relatively little
on advertising and promotion. (MacDonald's was established
in 1857.) The Philip Morris affiliated company, Benson
and Hedges (Canada) Ltd. had a negligible market share.
Rothmans of Canada Ltd. was considered an up-and-comer.
Since entering the market in 1957, the firm quickly got the
reputation as a company in a hurry. Rothman engaged in
marketing practices, according to some observers of the
Canadian industry, that the old-time companies considered
quite rough, tough, and even nasty. They were spending
heavily on advertising and promotion and had introduced
the first king-size cigarette, Rothman's King Size, to the
Canadian market — it was doing extremely well.

Imperial Tobacco was recognized as being the price leader
much as R.J. Reynolds was in the United States. Competition, as in the U.S. market, was not waged on price grounds,
but was instead concentrated on advertising, promotion, and

packaging. Interestingly, however, it was generally agreed
that as late as 1957 the Canadian cigarette market was very
badly "underadvertised" by U.S. standards. Canadian manufacturers were spending between 7¢ and 15¢ per 1000
cigarettes in 1956 while by 1959 this level had jumped to
25¢ to 45¢ per 1000 cigarettes.* Much of this spending
change was due to the entry of Rothmans into the market.
The new entrant had managed to usurp some of Imperial's
leadership functions.

Although the rapid growth of filter and king-size cigarettes
underlined the dynamic nature of the Canadian cigarette
market, executives within the Canadian cigarette industry

EXHIBIT 8.6

Cigarettes, Cigar, and Tobacco Sales
by Type and Number of Outlets, 1960

Type of Outlet	No. in Canada	Sales	Percent
Confectionary stores	—	na	na
Fruit & vegetable stores	—	na	na
Grocery stores (no fresh meat)	21,683	$ 25.4	3.8%
Grocery stores (fresh meat), beer	—	na	na
Variety stores	1,081	18.6	2.8%
Combination stores (groceries & meat)	9,340	109.1	16.8%
Combination stores (with beer)	—	na	na
Eating places	—	na	na
Eating places (with alcoholic beverages)	—	na	na
Eating places (other merchandise)	—	na	na
Department stores	74	21.7	3.4%
General stores	7,739	23.0	3.5%
General merchandise stores	702	25.6	3.9%
Drug stores (no soda fountain)	4,630	44.6	6.8%
Drug stores (soda fountain)	154	2.5	0.4%
Tobacco stores & stands	2,702	92.0	14.2%
News dealers	—	na	na
	44,175	$654.71	100%

*According to *Advertising Age*, September 16, 1968, Philip Morris spent 70¢ per
thousand on Parliament advertising in 1959. In 1959 most U.S. brands were between the Canadian figure of 15¢ per thousand and Parliament's high figure of
70¢ per thousand.

could also point to the high brand loyalty displayed by
Canadian smokers as evidence of the stability of the market.
Of 29 new brands introduced from 1957 to 1960, only four
survived. For example, in spite of the relatively low advertising and promotion budgets employed by the MacDonald
Tobacco Company, its two "Export" brands maintained a
sustained combined 23 to 28 percent market share.

The president of Philip Morris International and the president of Benson and Hedges (Canada) thoughtfully reflected
as they considered the Canadian market that it was typical of
markets around the world in that it exhibited in some areas
rapid change and, in other areas, considerable stability. How
would Canadian smokers react to the Parliament cigarettes?
Clearly, they were different from the standard Canadian
cigarette. Canadian cigarette tobacco was a straight Virginia-
type flue cured by Burley tobacco without added flavorings
to affect taste. The standard Canadian cigarette package
was a slide-and-shell box. This package, which was popular
in Canada, was a cardboard box shell which contained a sliding box that packed two rows of 10 cigarettes one on top of
the other with a foil paper between the two 10-cigarette
layers. Parliament with a recessed filter was an American-
type cigarette made from Virginia-type tobacco blended with
darker colored Burley tobacco and packaged in a soft package
or flip-top box. The distinguishing characteristic of the
tobacco in the American-type cigarette, including Parliament,
were the sugars, humectants (moistening agents), and flavorings (licorice, sugars, and alcohol) added to the tobacco,
giving the cigarette a characteristic flavor and taste. Another
distinguishing characteristic of Parliament and other American cigarettes was that they were less tightly packed than
Canadian cigarettes. The American soft package was crush-
able, and the flip-top box a cardboard container with a top
that flipped open exposing 20 cigarettes packed in two rows
of seven and one row of six cigarettes.

On the other hand, Parliament was Philip Morris's number
two brand in the United States and was doing quite well in
the extremely competitive U.S. market (see Exhibit 8.7).
Awareness studies had shown that Canadians were cognizant
of the brand name, Parliament, as a result of the overlap of
U.S. media into Canada. *Advertising Age* estimated that in
1960 Philip Morris was spending almost $40 million per
annum on advertising, and it was estimated by one Philip
Morris International executive that perhaps 5 percent of this
expenditure was exposed to Canadians, not to mention any

EXHIBIT 8.7

Philip Morris U.S. Sales by Brand (billions of cigarettes)					
		1961 est.	*1960*	*1959*	*1958*
Marlboro	(filter)	24.10	22.0	20.40	20.70
Parliament	(filter)	9.40	8.90	9.00	6.50
Alpine	(filter)	2.50	2.60	1.00	—
Philip Morris (king)		3.80	3.80	3.80	4.40
Philip Morris (regular)		4.60	5.50	6.60	7.80

EXHIBIT 8.8
Philip Morris International

Final Report — Canadian Copy Claim Report

A test of two copy claims was devised for Philip Morris International. The procedure was to have each smoker "test" a cigarette from a plain white package, and to react to the cigarette with various attitudinal words or phrases. Three groups of 800 people each were used in these tests. The first group, which we call the control or base group, smoked unmarked Parliament cigarettes from completely blank white packages and expressed their attitudes toward the cigarette. The second group smoked identical unmarked cigarettes from packages which had the phrase "American Type Cigarettes" printed on the package, while the third group smoked cigarettes from packages labeled "Cigarettes Blended with the Darker Colored Burley Tobacco for Better Filter Smoking and Lower Tar Delivery." The phrases were written in English on one side of the package and in Canadian French on the other side.

Results
1. The claim "Cigarettes blended with the darker colored burley tobacco for better filter smoking and lower tar delivery" was an ineffective claim.
2. The cultural difference between French- and English-speaking Canadians seems more significant than difference in sex, age, income, or type of cigarette usually smoked.

Discussion
The purpose of these tests was to determine what change would occur in smokers' attitudes toward cigarettes which were designated as "American Type Cigarettes" as opposed to "Cigarettes blended with the darker colored burley for better filter smoking and lower tar delivery." After smoking one cigarette the people were asked to select one word or another from each pair of words to describe their attitude toward the cigarette. For example, "mild" or "strong," "cool" or "hot."
  Since one group of people smoked unmarked cigarettes in a blank package, we have a base point against which we can measure any increments or decrements of the number of people associating a particular attitude with cigarettes smoked from the "test" packages which bore

the claims. We then concern ourselves with responses to the test cigarettes which received either a statistically significant higher or lower percentage of responses than were given to the blank package or control cigarettes. In other words, when an association is classified as significant, it means that in 95 out of 100 repetitions of the study the results would not be reversed.

While there were 14 such associations made toward each cigarette, the strongest pair of attitudes on the list is for a person to say "For me" as opposed to "Not for me." The following table shows two things. First,

Percent of Total Favorable Responses

Language Spoken	Blank	American-Type Cigarettes	Cigarettes Blended with the Darker Colored Burley Tobacco
English	67	63	69
French	64	76	68

the French-speaking people were not more favorably disposed toward the cigarettes used than were the English-speaking smokers when there was no claim attached to the cigarettes. Second, the claim "American-type cigarettes" significantly reduced the "For me" responses among the English-speaking people and significantly increased the number of responses of "For me" among the French-speaking sample. The "blended . . . burley . . . low tar" claim failed to increase the associations with "For me" among either the French or the English sample.

Percent Responding with "For Me"
As Opposed to "Not for Me"

Language Spoken	Blank	American-Type Cigarettes	Cigarettes Blended with the Darker Colored Burley Tobacco
English	46	38	49
French	57	66	55

No other breakdown of the sample, such as men vs. women, young vs. old, showed significant differences on the "For me" item.

A second method of looking at the association data is to analyze the total number of favorable associations as opposed to the total number of unfavorable associations expressed as a percentage. In other words, if every smoker selected each favorable association from each of the 14 pairs, we would have 100 percent favorable associations. In a sense, the total favorable percentage is a rough average of the percentage of people associating any one favorable word with the cigarette.

The following table shows that the overall reaction to the American-type cigarette claim was more favorable among the French-Canadians than among the English-speaking people and that the claim was also more effective than the "blended . . . burley . . . low tar" claim.

We could caution the reader that the individual items taken singularly can often be misleading since there is a tendency for consumers to generalize their liking for a product over a series of items. As we have already stated, we feel that the critical item is whether people say "For me" or "Not for me" about the cigarette. Thus the French-Canadians liked the "American-type cigarettes" and attributed significantly higher associations on rich tobacco flavor, good, slow burning, effective filtration and nonirritation, high-quality tobacco, well made, and desirable.

The "blended . . . burley . . . low tar" claim was ineffective among the French-Canadians. There were increases in associations with high-quality tobacco, effective filtration, and slow burning, but the taste and flavor connotations were not increased. One other item which did show a significant increase over the blank package cigarettes was costly as opposed to cheap.

In summary, then, to the French-speaking people the "American-type cigarettes" had flavor, filtration, and quality without being costly. The "blended . . . burley . . . low tar" cigarettes had filtration, quality, and expense but lacked an increase in flavor associations.

To the English-speaking smokers, the "American-type cigarettes" were associated with significant decreases in association with clean, desirable, and for me. It appears that the English-speaking Canadians rejected the "American-type cigarettes" purely on an emotional basis.

While the English-speaking smokers rejected an "American-type cigarette" even though it was given most of the same qualities as was the blank package, the "blended . . . burley . . . low tar" cigarettes were given some increases in qualities but no increase in preference over the blank pack cigarettes. Associations with good flavor, high-quality tobacco, slow burning, desirable, and well made were all increased for the "blended . . . burley . . . low tar" cigarettes; but even with these quality increases, the copy claim failed to draw an increase in the critical "For me" association.

To summarize the results of the English-speaking Canadian sample, they appear to have simply rejected the idea of an "American-type cigarette," and although the "blended . . . burley . . . low tar" cigarettes showed increased associations in taste, quality, and desirability, the concept was not sufficiently enticing to have an increase in acceptance of the cigarette.

---

exposure resulting from Canadian travel in the United States.

It was felt that the great similarities between the American and Canadian people in terms of culture, language, personality, and so on, would assure acceptance of a brand that was a major factor in the United States if it were made available to Canadians. Moreover, U.S. brands had been introduced in Australia and had done very well, and it was felt by Philip Morris executives that there was considerable comparability between Australia and Canada.

There was some reason for caution, however. A "Copy Claim Study" in Canada (see Exhibit 8.8) raised some questions about the appeal of U.S.-type cigarettes in Canada. In addition, similar research showed a preference for a hard, slide-and-shell package rather than the American soft cup variety. Further, it was known by Philip Morris executives that Canadians often exhibited a strong sense of nationalism in their consumer goods buying regardless of the product. Yet, as the president of Philip Morris International, Mr. Weissman, stated: "I can't believe that Parliament will sell well right up to the border and not within Canada. I've travelled in Canada since I was a boy, and those people are just like us."

Questions

1. Estimate the fixed cost of launching Parliament in (a) Quebec, (b) Ontario, and (c) all of Canada.
2. How should Philip Morris evaluate the spillover in Canada of Parliament advertising from border television and radio stations?
3. What competitive reactions should Philip Morris anticipate from Imperial, MacDonald, and Rothmans? Is there any sense that the competitors could preclude Philip Morris if it does not act precipitously?
4. What changes would you recommend to the product and packaging in response to the "American-type cigarette" report?
5. "I can't believe that Parliament will sell right up to the border and not within Canada. I've travelled in Canada since I was a boy, and those people are just like us." Express this belief as a covariance between 0.0 and 1.0 of American and Canadian sales.
6. In view of Mr. Weissman's position what risks to his career is he exposing himself to by launching Parliament in Canada? Once Parliament is launched how low would its market share have to be for Philip Morris to order it withdrawn? What organizational moves would you expect Mr. Weissman to make to shift the blame?
7. In dollars, how valuable is the Claim Report at this time?

Introduction

Most of the marketing and sales functions of a corporation should be done near the consumer. In a multinational corporation, this means that the first priority is to build competent marketing and sales forces in each nation. Once competence has been achieved, some centralization may be considered.

During the late 1960s advertising agencies scrambled to become global so they could offer corporate clients the possibility of one advertising theme with which to cover the world. Unfortunately, countries are different, and the attempts of ethnocentric corporations to impose a straitjacket on their operations caused them to offend national stakeholders and to fail to adapt to many opportunities.

The following three chapters deal with central coordination of marketing to increase profits. Chapter 8 focuses on the decision to sink cash into launching a new product in the markets of the world.

Regrettably, most newly launched products fail and the launch investment is squandered. On the other hand, if the product succeeds, one regrets not having launched it earlier, thereby realizing profits sooner and preempting competitors. This anguish is usually the result of an unsystematic decision-making process that precedes the launch decision. Executives rely on will-o'-the-wisp rumors, a few data, hope, and the belief that this product will succeed if only everyone will *work*. Emotions run high. It is not the purpose of this chapter to squelch the emotions that attend a product launch but rather to provide analytical boundaries within which the intuitive power of these emotions can be directed.

The Philip Morris case just analyzed represents a stable product with a lot of support data. Furthermore, the product is well established in the United States, from which advertising spills over into Canada. Finally, the corporation was rich enough that it could afford market research studies in Canada, although the ethnocentrism of the executives caused them to misinterpret the results they obtained. The launch of Parliament cigarettes failed in Canada.

Ethnocentric Similitude

Ethnocentric corporations develop, test, and market a new product in their home nation first. In essence, they are using the home market as a test market for the world. If (and only if) the product is successful at home, it is released to the international division for sales worldwide, and plants are constructed abroad. In the long run this leads to the closing of the home plant and the domestic market is supplied by the lower cost foreign plants, the familiar international life cycle of (a) export from the home nation, (b) foreign production starts, (c) foreign production becomes competitive in export markets, and (d) import competition begins.

To introduce a new product abroad, whether it be aimed at consumers or industrial customers, requires a major expenditure. The promotional theme and advertising campaign must be developed. The dealers should be oriented and trained. Warehouses should be leased. Overseeing these activities requires a substantial managerial effort with costly wages, travel, and secretarial support. The total of all these expenditures, which we will call k, is the fixed cost of launching the product.

It is this entire fixed cost k (usually several hundred thousand dollars per nation) that is at stake when the product is launched. The variable cost of the product may be low enough to allow a comfortable profit margin, but a break-even analysis shows the unit sales necessary to recoup the prelaunch expenditures.

This familiar break-even analysis of Exhibit 8.9 gives the unfortunate illusion of certainty. Little could be further from the truth in the launch of new products; it is risky, and this will be considered later in the chapter. In the United States, over 80 percent of new products fail and are withdrawn from distribution; many of the remainder limp along covering their variable cost of manufacture but never recovering the fixed cost of their launch. Sales cannot be forecast with certainty, but only to a probability distribution. The distribution is skewed, with a slight probability of exceptionally high sales. As in Exhibit 8.10, we will assume that the skew distribution is log normal; that is, if Exhibit 8.10 plotted the logarithm of sales it would be shaped as a normal distribution.

Given the task of predicting sales of a new product in an alien nation, an ethnocentric marketing manager feels helpless. To master his feelings he may turn to surrogate measures such as "telephones per 1,000 people"

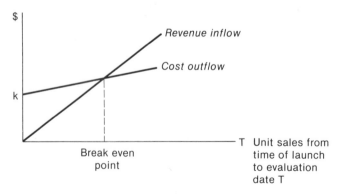

EXHIBIT 8.9

Break-even analysis may appear certain, but forecast unit sales are stochastic.

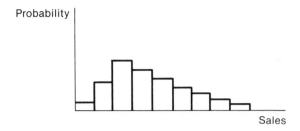

EXHIBIT 8.10
Probability distribution of sales is log normal.

or "automobile registration per capita," trying to discern patterns of similarity. The usual methodology is regression analysis. In interpreting the results of regressions, he focuses attention on the *mean* estimated unit sales, and only later will he analyze the risk envelope within which sales are being predicted.

With more experience, the marketing manager will group nations. Terpstra (1972, pp. 183, 185) describes the procedure, which now can be done easily given modern statistical packages:

> A large American electronics company was doing correlation studies on foreign markets, comparing company product sales with various data on the countries. What emerged very distinctly was a threefold grouping of all the firm's foreign markets. (In terms of a scatter diagram, there was not a single line to fit the data but three roughly parallel lines.) Further analysis corroborated the validity of the threefold grouping. As a result, the firm revised its method of planning marketing strategy in foreign markets. Instead of preparing annual marketing guidance on an individual-country basis, the company began preparing guidance for the three groups of countries, with a brief appendix for each market to cover whatever peculiarities it had. This approach needs to be taken with care, but it seems better than the alternatives of doing no research at all or carrying out high-cost research in all 77 countries. The arguments for and against such an approach would apply to any use of stratified sampling techniques.
>
> A further justification of country groupings and comparative analysis in international marketing lies in the current practices of multinational companies. In interviews with international executives, a recurring theme was the emphasis on the importance of experienced personnel over formulas or techniques for problem solving. Of course, the value of experience is that the experienced person is carrying over to a new market or situation something learned in a previous market or situation; that is, the experienced person is making his own comparative analysis. We suggest that such comparisons can be made more general, formal, and explicit. This is in line with the trend toward more scientific decision making which is receiving such emphasis in domestic business management.

Consumer goods can also be analyzed in the same way. The 1979 Annual Report of The Seagram Co. Ltd. discusses predictable similarities and unique differences in customer tastes for Seagram liquors:

> With increased earnings comes more disposable income, and the more frequent enjoyment of spirits and wines is traditionally an integral part of a higher living standard. In some countries — Brazil is a prime example — fostering a growing middle class is an avowed government policy. In other areas — Africa, for example — Seagram still is the only major company in the industry to have established a modern marketing organization. In both areas sales have multiplied over the decade past and are virtually certain to do so again in the 1980s.
>
> But capitalizing on such opportunities is easier said than done. Perhaps the primary prerequisite of major success is true appreciation of the very real differences in any given area.
>
> "Marketing programs in Africa have to start with the realization that each country here has different characteristics and therefore presents a separate challenge," says Jacob R. Scott, Seagram's top marketing man in Africa since 1971.
>
> The same point holds for vast Latin America, where there are at least as many differences as similarities. Brazilians react quickly to trends. Flavourful vodka-based drinks are currently a stylish destination for consumers who have left the local spirit, cachaca, and moved on from rum. Brandy has never been much of a factor in Brazil but is a mainstay in Mexico. Locally made champagne is a familiar aperitif in Argentina, virtually alone among the Latin American countries. And Argentinians, who prize old ties with Europe, have long been fond of Scotch, as have consumers in Venezuela.

Nevertheless, in an ethnocentric corporation "risky" countries are rarely analyzed, and are usually eliminated. When individuals confront uncertainty for which they lack cognitive models, they withdraw to more familiar problems. To control launch costs, the manager prefers to introduce the product in those nations most resembling his own. In an effort to avoid uncertainty he will cautiously "stage" their entry by grouping the nations in the order of familiarity.

Stage 1 — The Home Market. Even the most comprehensive market research (Green and Tull, 1978) can present only fragmentary glimpses of reality. Most market research is little better than in the Philip Morris case. An executive born into the culture is a better choice to integrate market research into a decision than an executive born elsewhere. After all, a product is the artful combination of design, price, promotion, and presence.

Stage 2 — Familiar Nations. Because the product is a whole package, the cost of a thorough reconfiguration would be excessive. Fortunately there are familiar nations where the corporation has launched similar products in the past and knows which elements definitely need to be reconfigured.

Stage 3 — Similar Nations. Ethnocentric managers may have no reason to reconfigure the product, believing that certain nations are similar to their own. Hence they launch the product as is. After the locals collect actual sales data and present an adequate case, the corporation could consider limited remodeling of the product.

Stage 4 — Alien Nations. Perhaps the easiest way to deal with alien nations is to export the product, allowing indigenous channels of distribution to assume the risks. No corporate decisions should be altered by these Stage 4 sales; they are a free bonus — not cash to be depended on.

Once a corporation has tentatively staged the nations, analytical executives may wish to be more explicit in their analysis of the risks of each national market, thus broadening their chances for success.

Four elements are required for each nation:

1. The estimation of the launch cost k.
2. The profit contribution per unit π.
3. The probability of breaking even — that sufficient sales will occur by a set date T, such that the total profit contribution will cover the launch cost.
4. The expected sales E and standard deviation σ of the sales rate d units per time period T. Because only a few products usually succeed and the majority limp along, when running regression analyses of sales data it is customary to use the logarithm of the sales rate d, and to fit a log normal distribution to it.

Launching the product in this market is a business decision so the E and σ of sales must be translated into a probability distribution of net cash position at the end of T. For the product to break even on evaluation day, the total profit contribution $Td\pi$ must exceed k. The price of the product is fixed, so cash inflow varies directly with total sales. Although *expected* sales may be way beyond break-even sales, there is concern for the probability of failing to break even. From the probability density function of total sales one can read the area of the probability of breaking even. The ethnocentric appendix at the end of the chapter continues the analysis in more mathematical detail.

Polycentric Production Smoothing

Polycentric corporations may launch a new product in all nations simultaneously. This simultaneity means that the fixed costs of all the nations must be incurred before any revenue is generated and the burden of production is heavy. If the product is successful in one market, it is more likely to sell well in several of the other nations also (positive covariance), thus overtaxing the company's limited resources. On the other hand, if the product fails, the corporate financial condition may be impaired.

Actually, sales managers will adopt a new product with varying degrees of alacrity. Those eager for a product like this one will adopt it immediately (they may well have been the driving force behind its development). Others decide to wait and see. And other national managers view the product as unsuitable in its present form. These laggards save the corporation from the cash drain that would arise if all subsidiaries launched the product simultaneously. The task of production smoothing (Chapter 6) is also simplified. Unfortunately some new products look so good while still under development that, long before the public announcement date, most subsidiaries have committed themselves to a launch.

An Example

In 1963 the Eastman Kodak Co. launched its Instamatic camera simultaneously in 28 nations. *Business Abroad* (1967) commented:

> The Instamatic system of photography has clicked internationally beyond the wildest expectations of marketing executives at Rochester. Overseas sales of the Instamatic topped domestic sales during the first year following its global introduction, the first time in Kodak's history that one of its cameras sold more internationally than in the domestic market. After two years, almost five million Instamatic cameras had been sold outside the United States. Four million were sold in Europe, including about a million in Germany and 750,000 in the United Kingdom.
>
> How did Kodak achieve this marketing coup abroad? Preparations for a worldwide market introduction began about 18 months before Instamatic finally rocketed onto the photographic horizon. Kodak officials had deliberated at length on making such a move. One point in Kodak's favor was the fact that the company had a unique saleable package (film, cartridge and camera). Kodak also was ideally set up to pull off the feat. It has associate companies, including wholly owned subsidiaries, in 46 countries. Six of the companies (United Kingdom, Canada, France, Germany, Australia, and Brazil) are major manufacturing facilities, while the other 40 provide marketing and technical services. In addition, Kodak has distributors in virtually every country and territory in the Free World.
>
> After deciding to make the Instamatic a global project, Kodak organized an informal ad hoc committee to coordinate introduction of the system abroad. The 10-man group included two representatives from each of the key manufacturing companies in England, France, and Germany; a representative of Kodak's general management; a member of the international sales division; another from the international advertising division; and the amateur camera sales manager. In the early spring of 1962, the newly formed international committee, whose members had been selected as the logical, interested parties in the launching of a new product overseas, went into action. For the next six months, it was to meet in London, Paris, Stuttgart, Rochester, and other cities around the world for discussions of anticipated marketing problems. Charles Fitter, amateur products coordinator in the international markets division, and a member of the *ad hoc* committee, recalled some of the ticklish decisions that had to be made.
>
> "We had to determine how much inventory was needed before the actual introduction of the Instamatic," said Fitter. "We even had to consider the needs of Kodak's photo-finishing customers. For example, they would need equipment to break open the film cartridges. Another consideration was the type and timing of the dealer presentations."

Initially, all Instamatics and Kodapak film cartridges were manufactured in Rochester. By 1964, Instamatic cameras were being manufactured in Kodak's associate companies in England, Germany, and Australia, and the Canadian company was assembling the cameras. Film cartridge production began in the United Kingdom, France, and Canada in early 1965 and in Australia a year later.

"The mass market abroad likes simplicity," said William P. Lane, assistant vice president and general manager of Kodak's international markets division.

Despite market research, previous sales history, consumer patterns, and other market estimating tools, demand exceeded supply during the first year. "Our sales estimating department, which has been doing this sort of work for 50 years, came up with what it thought was the most realistic estimate," said Lane. "In a sense, it's kind of a guessing game. This was a unique situation, and each market has its own peculiarities that have to be handled individually. It takes a tremendous effort to launch a product world wide from a standing start in terms of inventories."

The Instamatic system has helped change camera customs abroad. European women are using the Instamatic because of its operational ease. Historically, photography has been the domain of the European male, who prides himself in his camera ownership and in his ability to master its complexities.

The gadget-conscious Japanese market presents different problems. "The Japanese have a tradition of buying a camera as a camera and not as a picture-taking device," said Fitter. "Cartridged film is also much lighter because of import restrictions."

"Sales of Instamatic cameras abroad at the end of 1963 exceeded our original estimates fairly substantially," said Lane. "When we called in our overseas managers, their first estimates had doubled ours. Yet, that first year even exceeded their forecasts. In some overseas areas, particularly Europe, we had to cut down on our advertising until the camera supply caught up with the demand."

Some Mathematics

Sales are forecast before a product is launched in a market. After the launch the actual sales can be compared to the forecast, and the difference plotted. As in Exhibit 8.11 the majority (the mode) of products are slightly disappointing. On the other hand, offsetting these are those

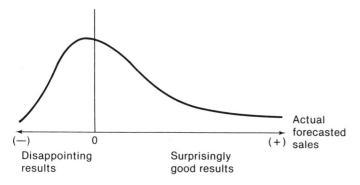

EXHIBIT 8.11
Distribution of forecast error.

few products whose sales greatly exceed expectations. The distribution is skewed.

In this chapter we will assume that the data fit a log normal form. Replotted on log paper, this distribution would appear to be a normal distribution. Hence, later in the chapter, the mean and standard deviations of the sales forecast will refer to the logarithms of sales.

The difficulty faced by Kodak was that sales exceeded expectations in almost all markets *simultaneously*. If one nation yields surprising results, what is the probability that each other nation will? For example, if actual sales are 20 percent higher than forecast in one nation, by what percentage do you raise forecasts in other nations?

An important distinction must be highlighted. In "Ethnocentric Similitude" the similarity between markets focused on similarity of per capita sales. The focus was on the mean, not the standard deviation, and certainly not the covariance.

Here we are assuming that the sales managers in each nation have made reasonable sales forecasts, which the headquarters analysts have improved upon by their regression analyses, similar to the ethnocentric executives. But, in addition to estimating the means, the polycentric analysts are vitally concerned with covariances, consistent patterns in the forecast error. If a product takes off in one country and sales exceed expectations, then the forecast error will be positive. If two countries are alike, the forecast error in the other country is likely to be positive also. (In this context, "likely" implies a positive covariance that is usually less than 1.)

An established multinational corporation has launched many items worldwide. On a worldwide basis some exceeded expectations; others fell short. These data are valuable when transformed into covariances (Staelin and Turner, 1973). Consider nations B and C. In nation B item i was forecast to a mean whose logarithm was E_B^i, whereas the actual sales were d_B^i. In nation C the same item i was forecast to a mean whose logarithm was E_C^i, whereas actual sales were d_C^i.

The new item seems more similar to some past items than it does to others. Comparing the new item with each previous item i, express the similarity by subjective weightings W^i such that $\Sigma\, W^i = 1$.

In other words, each of these similarity weightings will be used in place of a probability measure, in the formulas for variance and covariance as explained in any statistics text.

$$\text{Var} (\log d_B) = \Sigma_i\, W^i\, (\log d_B - E_B)^2$$

and

$$\text{Cov} (\log d_B)\, (\log d_C) = \Sigma_i\, W^i\, (\log d_B^i - E_B^i)\, (\log d_C^i - E_C^i)$$

This example is of two nations, but to prepare for the problems of real corporations, important formulas will be stated in terms of M markets. Thus:

$$\text{elements } BC \text{ in the correlation matrix} = \frac{\text{Cov }(\log d_B)\,(\log d_C)}{[\text{Var }(\log d_B)\,\text{Var }(\log d_C)]^{1/2}}$$

In the Kodak example, total worldwide sales exceeded plant capacity. To plot a probability distribution of worldwide sales use the covariance matrix plus the sales manager's latest estimates of expected sales in each nation. The methodology is identical to portfolio theory in finance where attention is on the dollar return of a diversified portfolio. Here attention is on the total sales from simultaneous sales campaigns in many nations.

If all the covariances were low, the corporate product management could relax in the expectation that forecast errors would cancel out. Optimistic forecasts for some nations would, on average, balance against pessimistic forecasts in other nations. If sales forecasts are done locally, each variance is higher because of inconsistencies in the forecasting procedure, but lower covariances result. The danger of centralized forecasting is that *all* nations are perceived optimistically (or pessimistically). In essence the covariance is a measure of consistent biases in the way the corporation's marketing team perceives the national markets.

If there was a reorganization in the way market forecasts were made, early forecasts should be given lower subjective W^i weights. Similarly, old data for one nation should be given much less weight if a nation is undergoing social change. The change may be subtle. Consider this statement by Geoffery Noyes of Oneida Silver Ltd., manufacturers of fine cutlery (Personal letter, 1976).

> In Australia we surveyed 120 stainless steel flatware patterns with a thousand women and we picked the designs to range from American style to Scandinavian modern style to British traditional style to Spanish Mediterranean style. There were about 8 to 10 patterns in each of these design clusters. Every one of the British traditional style patterns was at the bottom of the choice list. At the top were usually the American style or rather avant garde Mediterranean Spanish style patterns. When we researched the cause of this British rejection further, we found out that that is just what it was: the Australians were actively rejecting anything that had a cultural connotation of the old country. What a disaster it would have been if we had taken the advice of some of our older executives and simply shipped patterns from our U.K. factory into Australia.

Geocentric Launch

Geocentric corporations launch new products in an *adaptive* sequence. For years, Unilever has used Belgium as a detergent test market for the world. The detergent product manager uses the repurchase behavior of Belgian consumers to convince other national subsidiaries to launch the product. If the detergent is successful in *several* nations, remaining subsidiary managers find it harder to resist. Each manager knows from hard experience how to interpret sales data from sister subsidiaries. In a similar manner, when United Brewing of Copenhagen decided to market Carlsberg in North America in 1974, they contracted with Canadian Brewing to test market the beer in Alberta. Actual sales in Alberta were so positive that Canadian Brewing went national with Carlsberg as a premium product. Pharmaceutical corporations also launch their new products adaptively: Their sequencing decisions are imposed by the testing requirements of government drug agencies of each nation. Kemp (1980) describes how Japanese computer makers such as Fujitsu launch first in Japan and second in Australia:

Australia has indeed been a good target for Japanese products. The country, with a sparse population of 14 million, has accepted technology more readily than some larger and more advanced nations. The Japanese, too, have learned, through keeping in close touch with this market, that the Australian arena is a comprehensive microcosm of outside world requirements.

The full story on how and why the Australian axis is enabling Japanese makers to pry their electronic consumer goods out of their own cloistered region to compete in foreign-dominated territories may never be told. The Japanese themselves tend to be inscrutable and coy on the subject, never revealing why Australia has consistently been one of the first countries to receive their new products.

One Australian computer distributor, Gary Blom, is more forthcoming. Blom says this about the Japanese junction: "In effect what the Japanese do is develop a machine for their own markets, and then we modify it for an individual or possibly an international requirement. The Japanese respond quickly in giving us anything we want, whether it is in operating systems or in some structural detail, such as larger keyboards."

"There are many more [types of computers] than the Japanese can see at home," Matts [another Australian dealer] says. "They may send technicians out here to study them, or we can take machines like Digital Equipment or Data General to pieces and ask them to build revisions into their operating systems." They can then, he points out, "come back very quickly with these revisions to make their products more powerful and competitive."

The brash and entrepreneurial approach of medium-sized companies such as TCC has benefited Japanese suppliers of small- to medium-size business equipment. But in the past, there were too many uncomfortable failures of individual operators and small systems houses which exploited the market and could not support the hardware or software they sold.

Today the ground rules are tougher. The Japanese appreciate and work well with Australian inventiveness, particularly in software.

The Australian supplier, however, has to play with a full hand, which may include such things as paying in advance for goods or showing proof of a substantial customer support service.

Fujitsu's shrewd assessments and predictions of the Australian market have made it the bane of IBM Australia. The clever company has filched about a dozen installation sites away from the mighty mainframer, and it continues to present a strong challenge.

Facom [another Australian distributer] sends about 20 engineers each year to Fujitsu for training in advanced technology, so that the local company retains its high degree of autonomy and independence toward users. Support services are backed up by MART (Maintenance Assistance by Remote Telecommunications).

Throughout the industry there is little doubt that, especially in the formative years, the close working partnership between Australian entrepreneurial marketers and the patient and skillful Japanese adaptation of technology contributed significantly to the incursion of Japan's electronics goods into expanding world markets. While today Japan clearly does not depend on the support of any particular country, its computer makers may still pay homage to the adage that it pays to have a little bit of help from friends.

The important idea of the ethnocentric section was that the fixed cost of a launch should not be undertaken unless the risk is low enough. From the polycentric section the important idea was that of a covariance matrix.

Before launching the product in a market, a marketing manager has estimates of expected sales and of the variance about that mean. As soon as the product has been launched in a first market, and actual sales data are gathered, the manager can update the sales estimate of each of the other markets (only if the covariance between markets was zero would there be no value in this information). Nations in which the product is launched serve as test markets for the remaining nations.

It is desirable to preempt competitors by being first to launch a product in a nation. Thus, the decision rule of *when* to launch in a market should incorporate P_m^t, the *expected* profitability of market m if it is launched at time t. To calculate P_m^t the reaction of each significant competitor has to be anticipated. First, some competitors monitor globally while others have surprisingly parochial headquarters. Represent this assessment as a matrix of markets and competitors, in which each cell entry is the subjective probability that launching in that market will alert a competitor to prepare a rival product. Second, use this relationship to estimate market shares expected after the introduction of rival products. The market shares usually decrease with launch sequence, one reasonable assumption being a linear relationship between log market share and log sequence; the slope of the linear relationship varies between markets. Third, from competitive intelligence assess each corporation's current state of product development and the resources it is likely to devote to competition on this product. From this, gauge how quickly the competitor will respond once he learns of a launch, and how vigorously he will buy market share despite being eclipsed by the initial launch. All of this is required to estimate P_m^t .

Once the product has been launched in one market, the longer the corporation waits to launch it elsewhere, the more likely a competitor will be to preempt the next market. Therefore, the longer the innovator waits, the lower are its expected profits. The rate of drop-off in expected profits depends on the nation since nations differ in the speed at which the structure of a new industry is established.

Advertising spills over national borders. Direct spillover is exemplified by U.S. television commercials seen in Canada, Radio Luxembourg heard in Holland, and British magazines read in Bermuda. Indirect spillover occurs when tourists abroad request familiar products or return home wanting products they sampled abroad. This spillover is apparent when an advertising agency quotes its costs for two nations at less than the price of two; whichever is launched second should be charged only the incremental cost. Advertising spillover from earlier launches reduces the fixed cost of later launches.

Some characteristics of those nations suitable for the first stage of the launch are:

1. The international product managers stationed in the "first-stage" nations should be familiar with these countries so that they might better interpret and use the emerging sales figures (or market researchers should be accessible).
2. The nations should have well-established channels of distribution.
3. The nations should be small enough that the sum of their launch costs k remains within the budget.
4. Sales within these countries should have high correlations with other markets so that a given plant capacity yields the most information.
5. For first introductions, the launching corporation should look for markets to which competitors are blind so that few will get excited.
6. Customers vary by nation in their loyalty to "first launched" brands. It would be an advantage to enter those nations that form quick brand loyalties; however, these are frequently those customers who are slow to try a new product. Hence there is a tradeoff between competitive and informational objectives.
7. It is desirable to avoid those nations with a high advertising spillover. Customers affected by the spillover may be annoyed at their disadvantage of not being able to purchase the product. The advertising theme would no longer be new or as effective once these customers were approached and the spillover could give competition a head start.

A "real-sized" problem concerns perhaps 25 nations, of which the larger ones, such as the United States, might be subdivided into regions, to a total of say 30 markets, with several million different combinations of launches possible. To find a good solution, we will use a linear program. (Details are in the Geocentric Appendix.) The advantage of a linear program is that most of the pertinent considerations can be considered simultaneously. Furthermore, the opportunity cost of adopting a politically more acceptable solution can be calculated explicitly.

Finally, the solution to a linear program yields a dual variable to each constraint. There is a separate constraint for the initial variance of the sales estimate in each market. Hence the dual variable to each of these shows the value of incremental information about the market. Borrowing information from neighbor nations is only one way to reduce the variance of a sales estimate. More conventional means of market research are to create consumer panels, to interview dealers, and to test market in selected cities. These methods are costly. The dual variables provide an upper bound on how much to pay.

Ethnocentric Appendix

Instead of fixating on breaking even, let G be the net cash position (at the end of T). If G is negative, think of a line G units below "cost outflow" in Exhibit 8.9. We can calculate the probability of achieving at least a net cash position of G.

A product manager has a certain amount of discretion. Specifically, he can lose a certain amount of money on a product failure without serious reprimand. Rarely is it an explicit statement, but a person aware enough to be a product manager may sense that he can lose, say, a million dollars ($G^* = -\$1$ million) but a greater loss will seriously endanger his job. This threshold implies that he will launch the market only if:

$$\text{Probability (net cash at end of } T \geqslant G^*) \geqslant \alpha *$$

and where α^* is a subjectively set safe probability such as 0.9. In other words, he is willing to launch the product if there is a 10 percent chance of its failure costing him his job.

In Exhibit 8.12 main attention should be given to the chance constraint.

$$\text{Probability (net cash at end of } T \geqslant G^*) \geqslant \alpha^*$$

which is

$$\text{Probability } (T\pi d - k \geqslant G^*) \geqslant \alpha^*$$

The axes of Exhibit 8.12 are net cash G and probability α, so the chance constraint is depicted as a rectangle.

With 100 percent probability sales are going to be 0 or greater, so there is a 100 percent probability that the net cash position will not be worse than $-k$, the fixed cost of the launch. The point $-k$ anchors an end point for a family of possible net cash lines.

The net cash at the end of T is $T\pi d - k$, of which d is the only stochastic variable, and is known to expected sales E and standard deviation σ of a log normal distribution. Hence there is a different net cash line for each (E, σ). In Exhibit 8.12 the solid net cash line is for the (E, σ) of this market. This market fails to satisfy the chance constraint set by G^* and α^*. There are two ways to express the fact that this market fails to satisfy the chance constraint:

1. At the threshold probability α^* the net cash flow is $G^* - G_{gap}$.
2. Sales d are forecast. For the same expected sales E, there is a standard deviation σ_{goal} that would just satisfy the chance constraint. The net cash line (E, σ_{goal}) is shown as a dashed line.

Both of these expressions are depicted in Exhibit 8.12. Let us develop the mathematics for Exhibit 8.12 by following part of Charnes et al. (1968) DEMON, but with a final net cash position of G instead of 0.

The constraint from Exhibit 8.12

$$\text{Probability } (T\pi d - k > G) \geqslant \alpha$$

can be rewritten as

$$\text{Probability } (T\pi d \leqslant k + G) \leqslant 1 - \alpha$$

Focus on the inequality in parentheses. Divide both sides of the inequality by $T\pi$, take logarithms, subtract E, then divide by σ to get

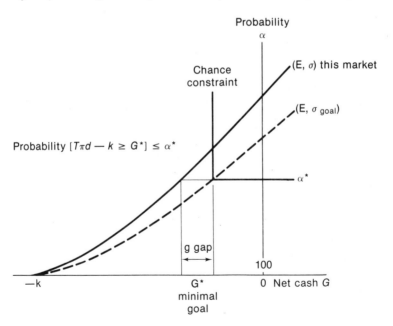

EXHIBIT 8.12

Market forecast (E, σ) transformed into probability α^* of achieving net cash position G.

$$\text{Probability}\left[\frac{\ln d - E}{\sigma} \leqslant \frac{\ln (k + G/T) - E}{\sigma}\right] \leqslant 1 - \alpha$$

If the distribution of d is log normal, $\ln d$ is normal. Hence $(\ln d - E)/\sigma$ is normal with mean 0 and variance 1. Let $P_{1-\alpha}$ be the $(1 - \alpha)$ percentile of this $N(0, 1)$ normal distribution so that

$$\frac{\ln (k + G/\pi T) - E}{\sigma} \leqslant P_{1-\alpha}$$

where $P_{1-\alpha}$ is negative, for it depicts downside risk. After cross-multiplying,

$$E + P_{1-\alpha}\,\sigma \geqslant \ln (k + G) - \ln \pi - \ln T$$

This equation is presented in Exhibit 8.13

The product manager has a certain aversion to risk, which sets α^*; hence the slope $P_{1-\alpha}^*$. If he launches prematurely, while the market forecast is known only to an excessive standard deviation, he can warrant that α^* probability of only the G read from Exhibit 8.13.

All the current information about the market is contained in (E, σ). Market research or launches in similar nations could add information that will revise both E and σ. But now, before the information comes, our *preposterior* estimates of the revisions owing to market research (or launches in similar nations) will be a reduction in standard deviation to σ'. No change in the mean E can be forecast (we guess it will rise or fall but do not know which). The difference between the G contour through (E, σ) and the G contour through (E, σ') is the value of this market research information. For example, in Exhibit 8.12 the value of market

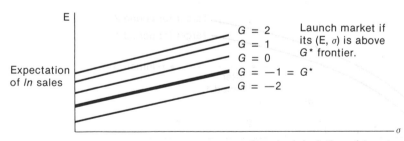

EXHIBIT 8.13
Parameterizing on net cash position G with threshold probability α^* held constant.

research to reduce the standard deviation from σ to σ_{goal} can be read as G_{gap}.

The probability that the market will ever be launched is usually less than 1. The expression $[E - \ln (k + G^*) - \ln \pi]/\sigma$ is $N(0, 1)$ a normal distribution with mean 0 and variance 1. Because E is the best current estimate of expected sales, the expression $[E - \ln (k + G^*) - \ln \pi]/\sigma$ percentile of $N(0, 1)$ is the probability that sales will ever cover the fixed cost k and achieve G^*. This expression approximates the probability that the market will be launched, so as a first heuristic, we could rank m markets by their value on this expression to get a preliminary sequence for the launches. The geocentric appendix gives a superior procedure, for instead of considering national markets in isolation it shows how to take advantage of the interconnection that actual sales data improve the forecasts in other markets.

Geocentric Appendix

Because we are dealing directly with the covariance matrix $\mathscr{C}$, we will calculate using variances rather than standard deviations. Exhibit 8.13 is transformed into Exhibit 8.14.

Each time period of delay reduces the months remaining to T, and hence raises the target. We will include the lateral movement of the target into a constraint in a linear program. Other launches in each time period yield information that reduces the variance of all markets including this one. The vector of launches x and covariance matrix $\mathscr{C}$ results in

$$\text{Reduction of variance} = x'\mathscr{C}$$

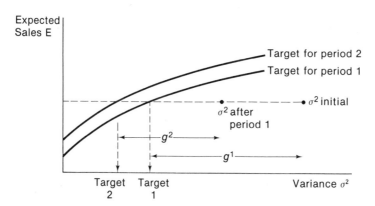

EXHIBIT 8.14

G contours showing the cost of excessive variance.

Actually, this presupposes that all the information for a market becomes instantly available. Realistically only the fraction f_m^1 of the information could be collected in market m and processed by market research within one period of the launch, a further f_m^2 within the second period from the launch, . . . , subject to $\Sigma_t\, f^t = 1$. Thus

$$\text{Actual reduction in variance} = x'\,(\mathrm{f}\mathscr{C})$$

Our concern is with the variance "gap." Thus the first period's equations are simply

$$
\begin{matrix}
\text{gap during} \\ \text{period 1}
\end{matrix}
=
\begin{matrix}
\text{initial} \\ \text{variance}
\end{matrix}
-
\begin{matrix}
\text{target variance} \\ \text{for period 1}
\end{matrix}
$$

$$g^1 = \sigma^2_{\text{initial}} - \text{target}$$

The second period equations include both the insight from first period launches and the movement of the target:

$$
\begin{matrix}
\text{gap during} \\ \text{period 2}
\end{matrix}
=
\begin{matrix}
\text{gap during} \\ \text{period 1}
\end{matrix}
-
\begin{matrix}
\text{immediate} \\ \text{insight from} \\ \text{first period} \\ \text{launches}
\end{matrix}
+
\begin{matrix}
\text{displacement} \\ \text{of the target}
\end{matrix}
$$

In other words,

$$g^2 = g^1 - x^{1'} f^1\mathscr{C} + \text{target 1} - \text{target 2}$$

which will be rearranged to

$$x^{1'} f^1\mathscr{C} - g^1 + g^2 = \text{target 1} - \text{target 2}$$

Similarly, the third period equations appear as

$$x^{1'} f^2\mathscr{C} + x^{2'} f^1\mathscr{C} - g^2 + g^3 = \text{target 2} - \text{target 3}$$

In Exhibit 8.15 the group of equations whose right-hand side is 1, constrains to 1 the probability that a market gets launched. The group of equations whose right-hand side is 0 assures that a market pays a G cost if it launches in that period, but not otherwise.

The inequalities should not be necessary but are merely a prudent caution that would flag attention and simultaneously avoid preventing earlier launches in case some error in $\mathscr{C}$ should accumulate to a negative variance.

Production limitations are frequently important, as they were in the Instamatic example mentioned previously. The capacity of each plant scheduled to come on stream establishes a constraint against which to model the buildup of market demand through time since the product was first launched. Note that in these equations we should use a *high* estimate of demand, for this is what an operations researcher classifies as a newsboy problem in which the cost of being short has been balanced against the opportunity cost of holding excess capacity. In a like manner, a capital constraint on the net expenditures for plants and national launches could be added if necessary.

The objective function contains a trade-off between return and risk. Tangent approximations may be taken to the summation of nonlinear terms $x_i^t G_i (g_i^t)$. If market i is launched prematurely, g_i^t depicts the units of variance it is expected to be short of the target when launched.

These equations can be put together as a mathematical program with linear constraints (Exhibit 8.15.) Let x^t be the vector of markets launched in period t. The linear program will compute the optimal launch dates. For example, $x_i = 0.6$ means 0.6 probability that market i is to be launched in period t. In period 1 we need definite answers as to which markets to launch and thus must find the best integer solution for the period 1 decisions.

Maximize

Subject to

x^1	x^2	x^3	x^4	g^1	g^2	g^3	g^4		r.h.s.		
				I				$\geq$	Initial variance	—	Target 1
$f^1 c$				—I	I			$\geq$	Target 1	—	Target 2
$f^2 c$	$f^1 c$				—I	I		$\geq$	Target 2	—	Target 3
$f^3 c$	$f^2 c$	$f^1 c$				—I	I	$\geq$	Target 3	—	Target 4
I	I	I	I					$\leq$	1		
I			—I					$\leq$	0		
	I		—I					$\leq$	0		
		I			—I			$\leq$	0		
			I				—I	$\leq$	0		

EXHIBIT 8.15
Sequencing as a mathematical program.

Questions from Other Viewpoints

1. *Corporate Rational Normative Global.* You just covered this viewpoint in the chapter.

2. *Corporate Rational Normative Subsidiary.* Evaluate the suggestion that a corporation should test market in a few cities of a nation as part of staging nations for a new product.

3. *Corporate Rational Descriptive Global.* Read and summarize the analyses of a product life cycle contained in Louis T. Wells, ed., *The Product Life Cycle and International Trade* (Boston: Division of Research, Harvard Business School, 1972) or Louis T. Wells, "Test of a Product Cycle Model of International Trade: U.S. Exports of Consumer Durables" *(Quarterly Journal of Economics,* February 1969) or William H. Gruber, Dileep Mehta, and Raymond Vernon, "The R&D Factor in International Trade and International Investment of United States Industries" *(Journal of Political Economy,* February 1967).

4. *Corporate Rational Descriptive Subsidiary.* What methods can be changed to speed the flow of accurate reports on actual customer sales which are needed for market staging?

5. *Corporate Emotional Normative Global.* Most of the "data" for this problem are subjective impressions. What mathematical and organizational weight would you give to these subjective impressions, in that each "expert" knows only some nations and some products, and that experts differ in their expertise?

6. *Corporate Emotional Normative Subsidiary.* All the discussion of adaptive sequences, or keeping the sequence the same but advancing or delaying launch dates, has implications for a subsidiary. Specifically, the subsidiary sales managers do not know when or whether they will have to launch the product — predictions are constantly being redated. Hence when called on to act they will have to do so with little notice. Suppose you are the subsidiary marketing executive. Lay out a specific program of preparing your sales managers. Be specific about the state of psychological readiness in which they should hold themselves.

7. *Corporate Emotional Descriptive Global.* Many historians of World War I have commented that declarations of war became irreversible once mobilization had been ordered. Railroads had been scheduled to converge troop trains, weapons, ammunition, food, horses, and feed, all from different origins, and these schedules were too intricately interconnected to change. Suppose someone "solved" the launch problem for you. Describe the rules you would enforce that would modify the schedule to make it more ready for the unexpected and simpler to manage.

8. *Corporate Emotional Descriptive Subsidiary.* Describe the emotional

problems of maintaining a high state of readiness to launch a new product when you have no control over the launch date and you fear that competitors will move first.

9. *Societal Rational Normative Global.* The early adopters of a product are guinea pigs for mankind — they incur certain risks and frustrations in using unproven products. If you believe that the rate of introduction of new products is excessive (due to oligopolistic competitors striving to eclipse one another), devise an "insurance" system by which a government could slow the rate of introduction. If you believe that research ideas are stifled in laboratories, and that the rate of introduction is socially inadequate, devise an incentive scheme that would research the early adopters without distorting their purchase decision (and therefore distorting the information content of their decision).

10. *Societal Rational Normative National.* You are Minister of Industrial Development in a nation that is committed to improving the environment and opposed to heavy industry. You have read this chapter and see the opportunity to expand employment in the market research service sector of your nation. Lay out a five-year plan whose end result would increase the number of products tested first in your nation. Comment specifically on (a) needed infrastructure; (b) changes in competition and other legislation; and (c) total employment that would result.

11. *Societal Rational Descriptive Global.* In the library find back issues of magazines (that carry advertisements) from as many nations as possible. Think of a new item that was introduced commercially during the period for which you have back copies of the magazines. Rank the nations by the date of the first advertisement of the item. Does your sequence correspond to the sequence of Vernon and Wells described in the chapter?

12. *Societal Rational Descriptive Global.* Review the criteria for a nation to be ranked first and a nation to be last for the launch of a product. What could a government of a low-ranked nation do to be ranked higher, assuming it desired this?

13. *Societal Emotional Normative Global.* When a new pharmaceutical has been developed it is tested for harmful effects on animals. Assuming no negative results on first-tested animals it is then tested on chimpanzees, whose physiology is similar but not identical to humans. Then human subjects must be tested and monitored for years. What are the different bases for conceptualizing the problem of which nationality should be the experimental subjects for mankind?

14. *Societal Emotional Normative National.* The problem with being guinea pig for new manufactured products is that they frequently are designed for another culture, they don't work as promised, and

spare parts are frequently unavailable unless the design sells well. Draft legislation to compensate your citizens.

15. *Societal Emotional Descriptive Global.* You are a theoretician for a particular kind of "ism" (for example, communism or capitalism) with global aspirations. How does your problem differ — or does it — from the one described in this chapter?

16. *Societal Emotional Descriptive Subsidiary.* List the qualities needed for a nation to be first to receive a new product. Launching new products brings to the nation the products themselves (with their consequences) and the scouting and pressure of determined executives. Will the long-run effect of these be a slight enhancement or a slight diminution of the qualities that made that nation first?

Bibliography to Chapter 8

Ayal, Igal, "Simple Models for Monitoring New Product Performance," *Decision Sciences*, Vol. 6, No. 2 (1975), pp. 221-236.

Boston Consulting Group, *Perspective on Experience* (Boston, Boston Consulting Group, 1970).

Charnes, Abraham, William W. Cooper, James K. DeVoe, and David B. Learner,"DEMON Mark II: An Extremal Equation Approach to New Product Marketing," *Management Science*, Vol. 14, No. 9 (1968), pp. 513-524.

Cyert, Richard M., Morris H. DeGroot and Charles A. Holt, "Sequential Investment Decisions With Bayesian Learning," *Management Science*, Vol. 24, No. 7 (1978) pp. 712-718.

De Groot, Morris H., *Optimal Statistical Decisions* (New York: McGraw-Hill, 1970).

Dillon, William R., Roger Calantone, and Worthing Parker, "The New Product Problem: An Approach for Investigating Product Failures," *Management Science*, Vol. 25, No. 12 (1979), pp. 1184-1196.

Ehrenberg, A.S.C. and G.J. Goodhardt, "A Comparison of American and British Repeat Buying Habits," *Journal of Marketing Research*, Vol. 5 (February 1968), pp. 29-33.

Green, Paul E. and Donald S. Tull, *Research for Marketing Decisions* (Englewood Cliffs, NJ: Prentice-Hall, 1978).

Heeler, Roger M. and Thomas P. Hustad, "Problems in Predicting New Product Growth For Consumer Durables," *Management Science*, Vol. 26, No. 10 (1980), pp. 1007-1020.

"How Kodak Clicked Worldwide on the Marketing Plan of its Famous Instamatic," *Business Abroad*, Vol. 31, No. 11, June 12, 1967, pp. 31-34.

Keegan, Warren, "Multinational Marketing: The Headquarters Role," *Columbia Journal of World Business*, Vol. 6, No. 1 (1971), pp. 1-6.

Kemp, Norman, "Japan's Amicable Alliance," *Datamation*, Vol. 26, No. 2, September 1980, pp. 74-82.

Martin, Warren S. and Al Barcus, "A Multiattribute Model for Evaluating Industrial Customer's Potential," *Interfaces*, Vol. 10, No. 3 (1980), pp. 40-44.

McConnell, J. Douglas, *Behavioral Factors in World Consumer Markets* (Palo Alto, CA: Long Range Planning Service, Stanford Research Institute, 1970).

Moyer, Reed, "International Market Analysis," *Journal of Marketing Research*, Vol. 5 (November 1968), pp. 353-360.

Raiffa, Howard and Robert Schlaifer, *Applied Statistical Decision Theory* (Cambridge: Harvard University Press, 1961).

Robertson, Thomas S., D.J. Dalrymple, and M.Y. Yoshino, "Cultural Compatibility in New Product Adaptation," *Journal of Marketing*, Vol. 34, No. 1, January 1970, pp. 70-75.

Sethi, S. Prakash, "Comparative Cluster Analysis for World Markets," *Journal of Marketing Research*, Vol. 8 (August 1971), pp. 348-354.

Sommers, Montrose and Jerome Kernan, "Why Products Flourish Here, Fizzle There," *Columbia Journal of World Business*, Vol. 2, No. 2, March-April 1967, pp. 89-97.

Staelin, Richard and Ronald E. Turner, "Errors in Judgemental Sales Forecasts: Theory and Results," *Journal of Marketing Research*, Vol. 10 (February 1973), pp. 10-16.

Terpstra, Vernon, *International Marketing* (New York: Holt, Rinehart and Winston, 1972).

Urban, Glen L. and John R. Hauser, *Design and Marketing of New Products*, (Englewood Cliffs, NJ, 1980).

Wells, Louis T., Jr., "A Product Life Cycle for International Trade," *Journal of Marketing*, Vol. 32 (July 1968), pp. 1-6.

CHAPTER NINE

Pricing

Introductory Note to the Case

Tyler Abrasives Inc.

This case is reminiscent of the First National City Bank case (Chapter 1) as it describes polycentric Tyler trying to do business with a multinational customer whose executives are irritated by Tyler's disarray. The case can be analyzed at a strategic and an operating level.

Genag is a half-million-dollar account that Tyler could sacrifice if inimical to its fundamental strategy. Yet Tyler seems to be starting to change its corporate strategy without realizing it. In its old form, Tyler was organized to take advantage of local situations. If Tyler's vision of its future in abrasives is to seek unique niches, then its present organization is appropriate, and its executives should resist and undo the ponderous coordination that the Genag deal foretells.

On the other hand, the Tyler executives may view the future of grinding as increasingly standardized for the following reasons:

1. There is a shakeout in the number of grinding machine manufacturers, and each is becoming multinational.
2. Metallurgical specifications are becoming more standard as concordances are being developed.
3. Many of the grinding machines are being sold to companies that hope to become subcontractors to multinational manufacturers and thus need to standardize.

If this is their vision of the future, then Tyler executives will have to reorganize the entire company, centralize product development, and bring coherence to distribution. Their strategic reorganization would necessitate the process of centralization we explored with Ford Motor Co. Ltd. of Chapter 3; Genag would be merely an experiment or pilot study.

Tyler Abrasives Inc.

"Now, Mr. Spencer, what we want to know is why you charge us one price for a grinding wheel in France, another price for the same wheel in Argentina, and a third price, which is almost two and one half times higher than the French price, for the same product in Australia? As you probably know, we have operations in Australia, Canada, Central and South America, and certain European countries, and we find that your prices vary in each country. Why can't we settle on one base price, let's say the prices current in France, for all these countries? Surely it would make things a lot easier in your organization and it would certainly be an advantage to us." The speaker was Mr. G. F. Middleton, president of General Agricultural Equipment Company, Inc. (Genag), who together with Mr. F.J. Horne, Jr., corporate vice president in charge of Genag's overseas operations, was receiving a visit from Mr. Robert Spencer, vice president and general manager, Grinding Wheel Division of Tyler Abrasives, Inc., of Cleveland, Ohio.

"We scheduled that meeting for July 31, 1981, and as soon as I walked in they nailed me to the wall on prices in the international market," Spencer recounted later to the case writer.

"We had been in regular contact with Genag over the previous 10 years. Our local salesman called weekly and occasionally management people also visited Genag. I expected to make a courtesy call to discuss their business, our standing as a supplier, and so on, so I checked through *Standard & Poors*, Genag's balance sheet, field reports, and current outstanding orders before going to see them."

During and after his return from the meeting with Genag's management, Spencer gave much thought to the problems that had been raised by Tyler's customer. The price variations he had been given were in some cases too large to be passed off as due to differences in local operating, transportation, and distribution costs. Additionally, since he was, at that time, general manager of Tyler's U.S. Grinding Wheel Division (GWD), he knew little of Tyler's current worldwide pricing procedures and could do no more than promise that the matter would receive immediate attention when he got back to Cleveland. A few days after the meeting, Spencer talked to Mr. Ed Pacifico, vice president of marketing for Tyler's International Division, about the questions raised at the meeting and asked for some information to shape a reply to satisfy Genag's misgivings.

In the following weeks, Tyler's management grappled with the problem to determine what the company's international pricing policy should be with respect to Genag and other multinational customers. By the fall, a tentative proposal had been worked out by Tyler's marketing staff. In October 1981, Spencer, together with Mr. John Stinson, group vice president of Tyler's International Division, was trying to decide whether to approve the proposal so that it could be submitted to Genag.

Background of Genag

Although slightly larger financially than Tyler, the sales of Genag were more concentrated both geographically and by product.

Genag was one of a number of full-line farm equipment manufacturers in the world. Although the company marketed and/or produced farm equipment throughout the world, most of its production, sales, and profits were derived from the United States and Canada, although the contribution from foreign sales had been growing recently, from 8 percent in 1976 to 35 percent in 1980.

In addition to its U.S. operations, Genag owned and operated plants in Australia, Argentina, Canada, France, Germany, Mexico, and South Africa.

A highly centralized organization itself, Genag believed there were many benefits to this form of organization on a worldwide basis and often extolled the merits of this approach.

In the late 1960s and early 1970s, Tyler enjoyed the major share of Genag's grinding wheel business, having an estimated 40 to 50 percent share. By 1980, Tyler's share was down to about 20 percent. The factors that affected this decline included a realization by Genag that it was too heavily committed to one supplier. Also during this time, Genag, while reequipping some production facilities, developed a relationship with one of the industry's major machinery suppliers. This company also manufactured and distributed its own line of centerless and horizontal grinding machines, as well as producing and selling grinding wheels. Exhibit 9.1 provides a breakdown of Tyler's worldwide sales to Genag.

In 1981, Tyler Inc. was one of the largest manufacturers of abrasives, posting sales of $243 million with after-tax profits of $8 million.

Starting with production of grinding wheels (bonded abrasives) in 1905, the company developed its facilities so that by 1981 it employed almost 10,000 people with 10 divisions operating in the United States and international activities in 21 countries outside the United States. The company was successful in its plans to diversify into products that complemented abrasives.

Abrasives had a variety of users in numerous markets. Very few manufactured products existed that had not been touched, either directly or indirectly, by abrasives. In 1981, abrasives accounted for $179 million or 73 percent of the total sales of Tyler Inc.

Abrasives were basically used in one of three forms: coated, bonded, and loose abrasive materials. Each had its own specific characteristics designed to meet the type and quality of finish required and the nature of the surface or product to be finished.

Bonded abrasives (mainly grinding wheels) were Tyler's major abrasive product line with total sales of $96 million in 1981, $56 million in the United States and $40 million outside the United States. Tyler produced over 200,000 different sizes of grinding wheels ranging from over 5 feet in diameter to 0.050 inch.

Coated abrasives were the second largest of Tyler's abrasives product categories with worldwide sales in 1981 amounting to $58 million.

Abrasive materials, or loose abrasives, accounted for $21 million of Tyler's total sales in 1981.

Tyler's International Operations

In the past, the company had always considered it a strategic strength to have its plants located near its customers' operations. This provided speedy access to the complete range of Tyler products, either through local manufacturing or by direct export from Tyler International Inc. (TII), a subsidiary

EXHIBIT 9.1
Tyler Abrasives Inc.

Actual and Potential Sales to Genag ($000)

UNITED STATES

Actual sales to Genag	1977	1978	1979	1980	1981
Vitrified	$228	$200	$258	$212	$190
Organic	154	144	180	115	102
Diamond	103	89	171	171	128
Total	$485	$433	$609	$499	$420
Total potential sales to Genag	$1,680	$1,800	$2,150	$2,500	$2,550
Actual as percentage of potential	29%	24%	28%	20%	17%

FOREIGN

Actual sales to Genag	1977	1978	1979	1980	1981
Canada	$39	$ 67	$ 73	$ 35	$ 4
Germany	n.a.	67	74	66	61
France	22	35	47	51	57
South Africa	—	—	1	1	2
Argentina	—	—	—	—	12
Australia	19	29	23	29	25
Total	$80	$198	$218	$182	$161

Potential sales to Genag	1977	1978	1979	1980	1981
Canada	$84	$112	$154	$162	$105
Germany	n.a.	n.a.	305	325	350
France	48	77	69	105	119
South Africa	n.a.	n.a.	n.a.	n.a.	20
Argentina	n.a.	n.a.	n.a.	n.a.	20
Australia	28	37	32	39	35
Total	n.a.	n.a.	$562	$633	$673

that also provided technical and managerial assistance and advice to foreign plants. Tyler management recognized that this strategy could lead to certain diseconomies in the manufacture and supply of abrasives. For instance, Tyler had not pursued a policy of product uniformity, which meant some lack of interchangeability of products between foreign plants. In some cases the basic raw materials differed from plant to plant according to availability and the manner in which "abrasive technology" had developed in each country. Differences in production processes and the varying age of foreign plants (e.g., the French plant dated from the 1930s while plants in Argentina and South Africa dated from 1975 and 1976) led to differing degrees of manufacturing independence and some variations in operating styles and costs.

Tyler wished to retain its philosophy of decentralized authority and responsibility but also wanted to get the benefits that a unified policy or approach might provide in certain opportunity areas. Management stated that the most important aspect in satisfying any given market was the ability to provide an overseas manufacturing and marketing capability having a competitive advantage in terms of manufacturing process, technology, and cost. Tyler's management felt that as time went on, changes in the world environment might in the future necessitate a move toward greater world integration in their international organization.

Tyler in 1980 had operations at 41 different locations in 21 countries around the world. International sales accounted for 40 percent of total sales in 1981.

The Second Meeting with Genag

During the weeks after Spencer's first meeting with Genag management, Spencer and Pacifico worked closely together building a complete picture of Tyler's worldwide trade with Genag. Figures available for the U.S. in late June 1981 showed potential sales of $2,500,000, 1980 sales of $499,000, and a 20 percent share of the market. In addition, the Market Research Department estimated that two other competitors had a similar share of Genag's bonded abrasives business and that the remaining 40 percent was divided between four other suppliers.

The figures for the international market took a little more time to collate as the information had to be obtained from Tyler's subsidiaries in each appropriate country. However, by

August 1981 the pattern for the position outside the United States could be estimated as follows:

Country	1981 Potential Sales ($)	1981 Actual Sales ($)	Full Cost Profitability Before Tax (%)	Expected Annual Growth (%)
Total	675,000+	161,000	—	5
Canada	105,000	4,000	15	5
Germany	350,000	61,000	7	5-7
France	119,000	57,000	5	5-7
Argentina	20,000	12,000	2	10
Australia	35,000	25,000	12	3-5

From the information that came back from the subsidiaries it was also found that most of the international business was conducted directly between Genag's and Tyler's local plants. The exception was Australia where Genag's orders came through a local distributor. Only Genag's Canadian plant had any dealings with Tyler's Grinding Wheel Division at Cleveland. In addition, management was able to compile the cost/price information shown in Exhibit 9.2.

EXHIBIT 9.2
Tyler Abrasives Inc.

Relative Cost/Price Position

Index (per unit price sold direct to Genag)		United States	France	Germany	Australia
Price indices					
Vitrified bore wheels					
$1\frac{1}{8} \times \frac{3}{4} \times \frac{3}{8}$ Qty. 25		100	79	90	n.a.
19A70-N6VBE Qty. 150		100	76	105	104
$2 \times 1 \times \frac{5}{8}$ Qty. 25		100	76	101	n.a.
19A70-N6VBD Qty. 150		100	65	115	113
Vitrified centerless wheels					
$20 \times 6 \times 12$ Qty. 1		100	43	61	49
A80-06V Qty. 10		100	48	61	57
Cost indices					
Alundum grain, landed cost/wheel		100	60	77	80
Direct labor cost per wheel Spec	1A	100	54	258	269
	1B	100	106	198	190
	2	100	47	294	192

On September 1, 1981, Spencer returned to Genag's offices together with Pacifico and Mr. C.W. Johnson, sales vice president of the Grinding Wheel Division. The proceedings were opened by Pacifico attempting to explain that the price differentials Genag complained of at the first meeting were mainly a function of differing manufacturing costs from country to country and Tyler's decentralized operating philosophy. Mr. Gavin, Genag's purchasing director, replied "If your costs do indicate such wide variances, then we suspect the validity of your costs or of your method of computing them. Your explanation of the revised bid for our Canadian business is not really satisfactory. We feel that as you were able to drop your prices on the second bid, you must have been overcharging us previously." The reference to Canada pertained to a recent situation in which the U.S. Grinding Wheel Division had resubmitted a lower bid on a particular grinding wheel order in an effort to arrest eroding Canadian sales to Genag.

Gavin went on to point out that service on nonstandard items through the Australian local distributor was very poor and that there was a lack of liaison on technical and R&D service. He further said that no reply had been received to a recent letter of his querying price increases. In reply to a suggestion that Tyler and Genag establish worldwide prices based on increased volume order quantities, Genag felt there was little point in discussing worldwide prices based on increased volume when current conditions were so bad and Tyler obviously considered Genag an "unimportant customer." Genag's position, stated by President Middleton, was:

> We should not have to tell you what your supply problems are or what kind of proposals you should make. This is your job as a supplier. You must do a better and more consistent job of pricing your products and you must also improve your standing in terms of service and interest before we can discuss any possibility of giving you an increased share of our business.

The session concluded with a promise by Spencer to arrange a further meeting before November 1, 1981.

Commenting later on the session, Johnson said he really wasn't sure what Genag's objectives were. He went on to suggest that industrial customers often were interested in obtaining better prices from one supplier in order to have a lever for gaining selective price concessions from other suppliers. This was especially true, he said, in industries such as abrasives where particular companies were viewed as price leaders.

Ed Pacifico, marketing vice president for Tyler's International Division, believed the issue involved more than simple pricing concessions:

> Genag not only seemed to want improved prices, but closer multinational coordination on R&D and technical problems as well. Mr. Horne kept stressing that some of our multinational competitors are already beginning to offer such coordination. He suggested that a company such as ours can't really be multinational and still afford to have decentralized decision making on the major points of product and marketing policy. In my opinion, however, the critical issue is how *far* to centralize and what parts of the operation to centralize for maximum flexibility.

The Selling Process

Tyler Inc. distributed its products in the United States both direct from its plant at Cleveland and through some 300 industrial distributors in major cities through the country. The company considered its distributors a major strength in its marketing effort.

Robert Spencer, general manager of the Grinding Wheel Division, thought that price, friendship, and availability were particularly important in selling Tyler's products in the United States. He said:

> Service and quality can be negative factors, but it's difficult to make them positive factors. We use an analogy of the water barrel. Service and quality problems represent leaks in the barrel that can cause you to lose business. When you repair them you stop the leaks but you aren't raising the water level.

Spencer also explained what he meant by friendship in selling Tyler products:

> You see there are still a lot of customers where the buying choice is technologically oriented. Over the years, our salesmen have built a strong bond with the people in manufacturing in their companies. It's more than good customer relations and it's stronger than is needed for technical liaison, it's friendship — these people really are good friends.

On advertising, he felt that since abrasives were in the mature phase of their product life cycle, it was only necessary to advertise new products as they came along.

On pricing, management estimated that only a few companies sold at a higher price than Tyler; most competitors were about the same or very slightly lower with just one or two companies as much as 10 to 15 percent lower. What Tyler did on pricing therefore had a strong effect not only on the company's own cash flow position but also on that of its competitors who would be forced to match any price concessions. This was an important strategic consideration for Tyler's management.

Sales Overseas

John Stinson, group vice president of the International Division, felt that it was necessary for a multinational company to recognize the sensitivity of operating in an international climate. Too many multinationals, he said, knew too little about their subsidiaries or the markets in which they operated; Tyler intended to make sure they did not fall into that category.

> We have a big job ahead of us to establish a structure which will allow for the monitoring of price, quality, and service. The logic of centralizing is overwhelming but rushing headlong into it leads to trouble. We must convince our own managers. There are still strong nationalistic feelings in Europe and you can't send a German salesman into France.

Stinson felt that this would break down if Tyler confronted its manufacturing costs in each nation, but this move would take time to accomplish. Pacifico agreed with Stinson's comments and added:

> I've been abroad recently and begun to realize the depth of emotions in this area. Originally the subsidiaries were completely autonomous. Consequently, the more we try to achieve international coordination the more they begin to kick about what they consider "crazy American ideas." When a buyer in a foreign country talks to one of our salesmen they both talk about "U.S. Imperialism." We have to realize that the French and Germans still look on themselves as French and German companies. However, we can get them to see that it's the customer who calls the shots. It's all a question of good communications.

Further Developments with Genag

By early October 1981, Johnson and his assistant, Mr. U.J. Adler, together with Mr. P.R. Schafer, manager of market services in the International Division, had prepared a plan which they suggested should be presented to Genag management and, if accepted by Genag, should also be offered to other farm equipment industry customers. Basically, the plan proposed to establish the U.S. prices of November 1, 1979, as the ceiling price for a given minimum quantity of a given size and specification of grinding wheel for all Genag's foreign plants. The minimum price would apply particularly to large-volume items that could be made in economic lot sizes. If Genag were able to increase its orders to Tyler, it might then be able to obtain a further price reduction. Where local prices were already lower than those in the United States, local price would operate. The plan further proposed that a worldwide agreement be negotiated for Tyler Abrasives to supply grinding wheels to all Genag plants throughout the world. The effect of those proposals on Tyler's sales revenue from Genag's overseas plants is shown in Exhibit 9.3 together with a price index for prices in each country before and after the proposal. In addition to Genag, it was estimated that the decrease in revenue from Genag's rival might amount to approximately $10,500, assuming, as was expected, that this customer negotiated for the same conditions as Genag. No calculations were available for the effect on revenue from other farm equipment industry customers but this was expected to be minimal.

The three Tyler executives were also concerned about the validity of the cost information used to establish the effect of their proposals on revenue. Management had estimated a typical breakdown of U.S. bonded abrasive prices as follows:

Selling price	100%	
Total cost	90%	
Selling and administration	30%	
Manufacturing cost	60%	
Direct labor		30%
Direct material		20%
Other factory costs		10%

However, the three executives knew that there was some variation in cost over differing sizes of grinding wheels and that the average quantity ordered could affect costs. They also knew that although the industry was currently a one-shift industry running at 40 percent to capacity, costs would only be marginally affected if the industry moved to a three-shift system. Finally, they knew that costs for grinding wheels manufactured overseas would exhibit characteristics

EXHIBIT 9.3

Tyler Abrasives Inc.

Financial Effect of Revised Farm Equipment Industry Prices on Sales to Genag

Sales Income (Fiscal 1981; $000)

	Before Revision				After Revision[a]				Gain/(Loss)
	Up to 2 in. Diameter	2-14 in. Diameter	Over 14 in. Diameter	Total	Up to 2 in. Diameter	2-14 in. Diameter	Over 14 in. Diameter	Total	
Germany	12	28	21	61	6	28	21	55	(6)
Canada	–	–	–	0	–	–	–	0	0
France	20	15	22	57	20	15	22	57	–
Australia	17	3	5	25	9	3	5	17	(8)
Argentina	10	–	2	12	10	–	2	12	–
Total	59	46	50	155	45	46	50	141	(14)

Comparative Price Indices (United States = 100)

	Before Revision			After Revision		
	Up to 2 in. Diameter	2-14 in. Diameter	Over 14 in. Diameter	Up to 2 in. Diameter	2-14 in. Diameter	Over 14 in. Diameter
Germany	190	55	55	100	55	55
Canada	100	90	90	100	90	90
France	60	60	60	60	60	60
Australia	190	70	60	100	70	60
Argentina	60	75	75	60	75	75
Ratio of Highest/Lowest[b]	3.2/1	1.8/1	1.8/1	1.7/1	1.8/1	1.8/1

[a]These estimates assume no change in the unit volume of business with Genag.
[b]This ratio is the world price spread from highest Tyler price to lowest Tyler price for any given size and specification of grinding wheel.

EXHIBIT 9.4
Tyler Abrasives Inc.

Indices of Popular Genag Prices

Product	United States	Canada	Argentina	Germany	France	Australia
No. 1	100	118	197	74	109	117
No. 2	100	108	197	140	107	92
No. 3	100	123	n.a.	27	115	95
No. 4	100	156	n.a.	26	95	156
No. 5	100	120	n.a.	66	102	44
No. 6	100	119	n.a.	70	95	111
No. 7	100	120	n.a.	110	108	113
No. 8	100	120	n.a.	66	108	91
No. 9	100	111	n.a.	86	107	110
No. 10	100	109	n.a.	72	111	111

somewhat different from those for wheels manufactured in the United States.

The comparison of Genag's worldwide prices for certain farm equipment and attachments that was also prepared is seen in Exhibit 9.4.

Summary

With the foregoing information in hand, Spencer and Stinson were trying to decide whether to approve the plan proposed by their staff or, if not, what alternative policy to adopt.

In reaching a decision, Spencer and Stinson felt they ought to consider the potential impact on Tyler's relationships with other multinational customers. If a worldwide price were offered to Genag, they believed that once the word got around Tyler would have little choice but to offer similar terms to other customers that bought from Tyler in several different countries and that individually accounted for at least $400,000 in annual sales. There were approximately 50 customers, collectively accounting for about $25 million in sales that fell in this category. Although Spencer and Stinson had no way of knowing the exact sales breakdown of these companies by country and product category, they believed that the overall sales configuration might be fairly similar to the pattern found at Genag.

One factor that complicated the information-gathering and decision-making process in this situation was Tyler's current organizational structure. Becuase Tyler's international operations were contained in a separate division and because foreign subsidiaries had traditionally been run on a relatively decentralized basis, it was difficult to coordinate internally any analysis on a worldwide basis.

Moreover, Spencer was aware that not all subsidiary managers would be enthusiastic about the idea of quoting worldwide prices to Genag. In fact several managers had already expressed concern. For example, the manager of Genag's Australian distributor had indicated that he was against the proposal inasmuch as Australia "runs a strong operation and already has 70 percent of Genag's local business despite relatively high prices. Consequently, any move toward worldwide prices would probably only serve to reduce the profitability of the Australian distributor operation."

The manager of the French subsidiary on the other hand was against any worldwide move that would tend to increase French prices since he felt Tyler's present low level of prices in France was absolutely necessary to maintain market share in a highly competitive market. Finally, the manager of the German subsidiary said he could understand the reason for a worldwide pricing agreement insofar as it applied to Genag, but he was very concerned about the possible impact should the agreement become public knowledge within the industry. Consequently, he had written to headquarters as follows: "We feel that it is of the utmost importance that knowledge of any agreement be regarded as a highly confidential matter and restricted to the smallest number of people within Tyler and Genag. I would personally appreciate it if you would issue very strong instructions to this effect."

Questions

1. Would you describe the Tyler organization as polycentric, ethnocentric, or geocentric? Explain.
2. Would you describe the Genag organization as polycentric, ethnocentric, or geocentric? Explain.
3. Do you think that Tyler is currently setting prices and sales efforts optimally?
4. For small changes in the quantity to be manufactured, would you expect the marginal cost to be altered substantially?
5. Elasticity of demand is defined as the percentage change

of quantity demanded per percentage change of price. What is your estimate of demand elasticities in Germany, France, and Australia?

6. Genag buys only a few of the many products produced by Tyler. If the price of the items purchased by Genag is changed, sales of neighboring products would be affected as customers switched to or from the changed prices. How could Tyler predict the switch quantity?

7. How much money should the Tyler management be willing to invest to study the rationalized pricing scheme so as to intelligently respond to Genag's initiative?

Introduction

This chapter is addressed directly to corporations dominant enough to be the price setters for certain products. The price takers who exist under the price umbrella of the dominant competitor should clearly understand those forces that hold up the umbrella so they can realistically assess the risks of their environment.

In this chapter, we investigate pricing considerations from the viewpoints of oligopolistic competition, legal constraints in various nations that affect sales price, and the relationship between administrative coherence and the taking advantage of market opportunities. We are not concerned with transfer prices, for they may be adjusted to maneuver liquid assets as described in Chapter 3. Nor are we concerned with raw material commodity prices, though some of the concepts from Chapter 2 may be useful guides.

Most of today's worldwide manufacturers were once domestic companies, vying with their home competitors for a share of a market that seemed too small. When one of the competitors expanded abroad, it changed the basis for competition. As was described in Chapter 1, the remaining competitors had to choose between specializing in narrow market niches or also expanding abroad. Knickerbocker (1973) has shown that a powerful motivation to become multinational is competition — that is, the competitors have become multinational.

Oligopoly theorists would say that market share is valuable. But the share of which market? Mason (1969) presents a case study of an abrasive manufacturer trying to decide whether abrasives were becoming a commodity (in which case its strategy should be to go multinational so as to increase its share of the worldwide market) or whether abrasives were becoming individually tailored for particular applications (in which case its strategy should be to stress R&D and upgrade its sales force by hiring technical specialists who would be able to translate peculiar cutting problems into particular chemical compositions). Either strategy can be viable; both can coexist. Multinational corporations are those that have adopted the former: there are benefits to standardizing their product around the world. In the case you have just read Genag certainly adopted that strategy and is attempting to force it onto its suppliers such as Tyler.

In most nations one sees multinational corporations in competition with local businesses. The locals do not wither away (unless they foolhardily pit themselves in head-on competition with the multinationals). Rather, the two groups compete on different bases, with the local firms specializing in niches that require individually tailored responses to the market so that the multinationals cannot compete. Expressed differently, each may strive to maximize market share, but they are really working within different markets.

Experience curves portray the importance of market share. The manufacturing and marketing cost of an item, adjusted for inflation, decreases 15 to 25 percent with every doubling of cumulative production experience. For a multinational corporation the relevant market is the entire world; market share is the share of the world market. This means that cost-saving ideas in production, distribution, and marketing should be quickly shared worldwide within the corporation if unit costs are to be reduced by the target 15 to 25 percent per doubling of cumulative experience. Accounting controls must be targeted to achieve this. Manufacturers move down the experience curve at a rate proportional to their market share — the one with the largest market share moves down faster and hence has lower costs. In fact, when the price leader sets an umbrella price, its height determines just which of the marginal firms will cover their costs and hence survive. In Britain, the price leader in tractors set a low umbrella price. According to Schwartzman (1969, p. 131), "Harry Ferguson, like Henry Ford, apparently sought a large volume of sales by means of low prices, and British tractor prices consequently were low. Prices in other countries were fixed at higher levels. Low prices discouraged entry in Britain; high prices elsewhere encouraged entry. The small scale of entrants led to high costs, which discouraged them from reducing prices. Collusion may also have been an element."

Umbrella Pricing

The price leader sets a price umbrella for the industry. Should it hold this umbrella price high enough to let the marginal competitor survive? In the U.S. automobile industry, Chrysler is the marginal competitor. In addition to obvious antitrust reasons, General Motors may perceive an economic rationale for not pricing Chrysler out of existence. In contrast, Texas Instruments chose to reduce prices of digital watches, steadily squeezing out marginal competitors until there were only three effective companies left in the business. Texas Instruments may also perceive an economic rationale. How many competitors does a market leader prefer? The price leader, Firm 1, knows that its market share will decrease with an increasing number of competitors in the industry (Ijiri and Simon, 1977). By umbrella pricing, the leader influences this number.

To develop an economic (not antitrust) rationale for umbrella pricing we will make two assumptions. First, if the price umbrella is lowered below the unit cost of the marginal producer, he will quit and the remaining rivals will grab his customers in proportion to their preexisting market shares. Second, because of the experience curve effect, the inflation-adjusted unit cost experienced by a firm decreases over time (and decreases faster with a larger market share). Learning by doing and economies of

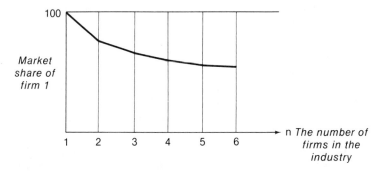

EXHIBIT 9.5

Market share of Firm 1 decreases with number of firms in the industry.

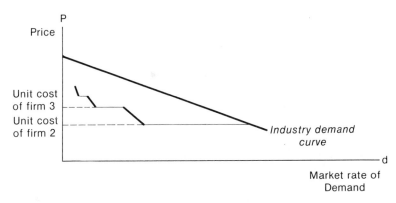

EXHIBIT 9.6

Demand curve seen by Firm 1 depends on its market share of the industry demand.

scale mean that tightly managed larger firms can usually produce at a lower unit cost than their smaller rivals.

Industry demand increases when the umbrella price is lowered. Because the marginal competitors will drop out if the price is set below their unit costs, an insight into these unit costs allows the lead firm to calculate how much its market share would increase with a given decrease in price. Thus it may calculate its demand curve. The managers of Firm 1 can analyze each segment of this demand curve and, knowing their own unit cost c_1, they can calculate a price that maximizes Firm 1's profit. (Each sloped segment of the Exhibit 9.6 demand curve of Firm 1 should be analyzed separately.) To draw Exhibit 9.6, Firm 1 requires excellent knowledge of the cost structures of its rivals. In corporate practice, the leader gathers extensive intelligence about the financial health of marginal firms, whereas the marginals focus their intelligence gathering on keeping up with the leader's new product development.

As a new product emerges there is a "shake-out" as rivals scramble to improve their technology and compete for the market. The dynamics of this process is poorly understood and thus unpredictable, but eventually one firm will emerge as the price leader. Once leadership is established, the interesting question is whether the price leader tends, through time, to want fewer or more competitors. Will the leader continuously lower the (inflation-adjusted) price umbrella to squeeze out the marginal producer, or will it tend not to decrease the price umbrella quite as fast as the marginal producer cuts costs? It can be shown that it is in the leader's economic self-interest to *gradually* allow the entrance of a few more rivals.

Each national market is growing at a different rate. In a stagnant market for this product, competitors will guard their market shares with vigilance. Nevertheless, the multinational, accumulating experience in faster growing markets, can stream ideas to its subsidiary in the stagnant nation and cut the subsidiary's costs correspondingly faster than can domestic competitors.

Constraints on Price Policy

Well-managed costs not only yield better current profits but allow the price leader flexibility in coping with rivals, both potential and existing. The way to deal with rivals differs among national markets. It depends on a corporation's rank in this industry, the number of competitors, and the legal, commercial, and social means in which existing competitors vie with one another. The government and other stakeholders in each nation set many constraints on pricing policy.

In the United States, the Justice Department is especially watchful for monopoly power. The Aluminum Company of America was cited in a 1945 Supreme Court decision that is one of the landmarks in U.S. antitrust law. Alcoa sold aluminum ingots as well as sheet aluminum, but it set its prices for ingots — of which it was by far the largest supplier — high enough so that other firms could barely afford to buy the ingots, convert them into sheet, and compete with Alcoa in the sheet metal market. This "Price Squeeze" was held to be an "unlawful exercise of Alcoa's power." In some other nations it is common practice.

Although U.S. law is by far the most restrictive in the world, other nations do have similar provisions. In West Germany, retail price maintenance was forbidden as of January 1, 1974, and a ban on concerted practices is left open to wide interpretation by the courts, including restrictions on parallel pricing. Previously, in 1972, Germany's Federal Cartel Office had fined nine synthetic fiber companies more than $15 million for domestic and export price fixing, among other charges.

The European Economic Community has also been strengthening its antitrust powers. Article 85(1) of the Rome Treaty bans "concerted practices," and Article 86 prohibits "the direct or indirect imposition of any inequitable purchase or selling prices" (Bellamy and Morris, 1978) and attempts to prevent "abuse by one or more undertakings of a dominant position within the common market." For example, in 1976 United Brands was charged with "systematically setting prices at the highest possible level, resulting in wide price differences" for fruit among member states. This price discrimination was possible because United Brands had prohibited its distributors and ripeners in Belgium, Luxembourg, Denmark, West Germany, the Republic of Ireland, and the Netherlands from reselling green bananas. The Commission's concern is also illustrated by its 1972 $108,000 fine imposed on Pittsburgh Corning Europe SA (PCE), the Belgian-based subsidiary of a U.S. joint venture between PPG Industries and Corning Glass Works Co. PCE's pricing policy gave discriminatory discounts to Dutch and Belgian customers who limited use of the products to their own nations. Their purpose was to shield PCE's German marketing subsidiary, whose prices were up to 40 percent higher and which was threatened by parallel imports from the Netherlands and Belgium. On the other hand, the commission ruled that a market-sharing agreement between Christiani and Nielsen — a Danish civil engineering firm — and its wholly owned subsidiary in the Netherlands was legal because a company could not compete against itself.

Governments have to be careful in effecting remedies for antitrust violations. The United Kingdom's Monopolies Commission ruled that Kodak had "acted against the public interest" and forced Kodak to reduce its prices. As a result, Kodak's chief competitor was driven out of the British market exactly as just analysed in "Umbrella Pricing".

Antitrust laws are just one constraint on pricing. The effects of price changes on customer relations must also be considered. Even in inflationary times a manufacturer of industrial goods must not change prices as frequently as a retailer might. Such a company's customers, manufacturers too, have to plan their capital expenditures *considerably* far in advance so as to get approval of each of several layers of management. When the supplier raises the price of equipment, the echelons of executives supporting the purchase are embarrassed by the need to prepare supplemental capital appropriation requests. If such changes occur too frequently, a buyer will probably decide that the prices are too uncertain and will turn to a supplier willing to quote stable prices.

Any price changes incur a *fixed* cost. All salesmen and other persons who deal with sales figures must be informed of any price change as rapidly as possible. The cost of this worldwide education skyrockets with frequent changes, not only because they have to keep memorizing new figures but also because the assurance of a salesman is undermined if he cannot remember the latest price.

Data Required for Multinational Pricing

Marginal Cost

Let us develop pricing theory for one nation. For each item in the line, the most likely price and marketing budget is chosen and with these the life cycle curve is estimated for each of the products. The areas under these curves represent the expected total sales. After modeling the production process, we can approximate the marginal cost of the product.

In this chapter, the first step is to calculate c, the landed direct cost of each item in each nation (recall Chapters 6 and 7). This vector of costs is the only source of interconnectedness in the polycentric pricing scheme. Then for each nation separately, calculate optimal price adjustments for items in the line following the steps of Appendix 1. The base case profitability equals the revenue minus production and marketing costs. The intent is to adjust the prices and marketing budgets to increase profitability. To do this, we must consider price elasticities of demand among the products as well as their responses to the marketing expenses.

Effect of Price on Sales

The price leader has an estimate of industry demand as a function of industry price, which becomes less elastic with product maturity. By careful competitive analysis the leader estimates the costs of each marginal producer and the percentage market share he would get if a marginal producer was forced out. In each national market we need an analysis of these price effects, summarized as linear demand curves and cross-elasticities between items. (See Appendix 1.) Statistical methodologies for estimating sales elasticities of price and advertising, mostly developed in the 1970s, are surveyed by Comanor and Wilson (1979).

Effect of Marketing on Sales

Marketing consumer goods calls mostly for advertising. Marketing industrial goods, on the other hand, calls mostly for personal sales representatives and sales engineers. Within reason, a particular increase in sales can be achieved by either a price cut or a marketing increase. Governments (and competitors' salesmen) monitor prices because they are simple to monitor. Marketing expenditures are intricately detailed (whether advertisements or salesmen) and therefore are messy to monitor. When a multinational corporation constrains its pricing, it can compensate with marketing. Marketing budgets will differ between nations, and the relative emphasis on different items also should differ, to compete with partial line rivals.

Throughout this chapter we will assume that the product has already

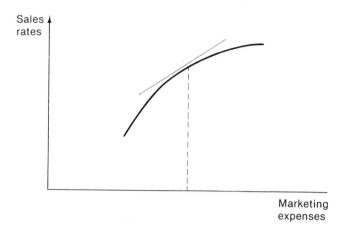

EXHIBIT 9.7
Demand responses to marketing budget.

been launched and has a budget for sustained advertising. Usually such budgets are sufficiently large to be in the region of decreasing marginal effectiveness seen in Exhibit 9.7. An estimate of the shape is required for Appendix 1.

Three Pricing Schemes

Multinational price leaders generally use one of three worldwide pricing schemes. Polycentric pricing gives pricing autonomy to each national subsidiary, so there is no systematic relationship among national prices. Following a geocentric scheme, prices of the items are set in a benchmark nation and the prices in any other nation are a national percentage mark-up of, or weighting factor times, the benchmark prices. For example, if the United States is the benchmark, then prices in India might be 80 percent of U.S. prices and those in Saudi Arabia might be 115 percent of U.S. prices for all items in the line. The ethnocentric practice is to constrain all national prices of an item to be identical (perhaps with a fixed increment for freight plus import duties from the "home" factory).

The more a price is "tailored" to a particular market, the greater profits can be expected. Hence we can assume that the greater the constraints placed on a subsidiary or foreign branch, the lower will be the profits contributed by its markets. Thus the model profits are ranked: $\pi_p > \pi_g > \pi_e$ where model profit π means worldwide revenue minus total variable cost of global production, and the subscripts refer to polycentric, geocentric, and ethnocentric pricing schemes.

Unfortunately, the administrative costs are similarly ranked. Suppose the corporation currently enforces an ethnocentric price standardization around the world (perhaps because it supplies other multinationals whose centralized purchasing departments flag discrepancies in national prices just as Genag's did) and it is considering the adoption of geocentric national weighting factors.

The administrative cost will rise, but by how much? The market analysis staff must ensure that the added administrative cost would be less than the added profit ($\pi_g - \pi_e$) before the geocentric scheme is adopted.

The remainder of this chapter demonstrates how to calculate the three model profits. The mathematical formulations are found in the appendices. We will use linear approximations to demand curves and marketing response surfaces, so that profit will be quadratic in terms of prices and marketing budgets. In this way, we can more easily calculate optimal prices and marketing budgets. Our input data are subjective, so there is little justification for more elaborate computational schemes. On the other hand, the computational ease of this method makes sensitivity analysis feasible. We will follow industrial practice by setting a base case and then making incremental adjustments to maximize the added profit.

Polycentric Pricing Scheme

In a polycentric organization, prices and marketing budgets in each nation are set optimally with no constraint that prices be coordinated. Thus the price of one product may vary widely between different countries. In his study for the Canadian Royal Commission on Farm Machinery, David Schwartzman (1969, p. 132) showed national price differences between items of each manufacturer. The lack of relationship between the national price data can be seen vividly when the prices are plotted in Exhibit 9.8. These are net wholesale prices, set by the manufacturer.

There are limits to the price discrimination a multinational can effectuate. Tractor manufacturers sell through dealers. It would appear that a Canadian dealer could profit by buying from dealers in Britain. However, the British dealers were prohibited from reselling new tractors for export under the threat of terminating the franchise and/or canceling the dealers' quantity discounts. In 1969, according to Schwartzman (1969, p. 143), manufacturers were investigating and rejecting dealer orders that were unusually large or called for specifications unusual in Britain. Although the export prohibitions had dubious legal validity, "understandably no individual dealer was willing to risk offending his supplier by testing his contract in court." The company's enforcement procedures were adequate even though legally uncertain.

Canada imposes no import duty on agricultural equipment imports, so the only economic constraint would be the freight cost of shipping tractors. From Britain to Canada in 1969, this was estimated by Schwartzman

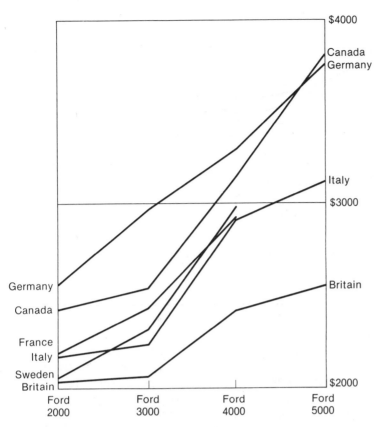

EXHIBIT 9.8
*Wholesale prices for Ford tractors with eight-speed transmissions,
1966–1967.*

to be only $110 for each Ford 2000 or 3000, and $144 for each Ford
4000 or 5000 (because Britain at that time was not a member of the EEC,
the cost of shipping a Ford 2000 across the channel to France would have
been $421).

Arbitrage opportunities like this sour dealer relations and invite government attention. An analyst should be able to calculate the reduction in
model profits that would result from raising British and lowering Canadian
prices to eliminate the arbitrage "opportunity."

By raising the British price, Ford would forgo the profits shown by the
lower left to upper right curve in Exhibit 9.9. By lowering its Canadian
price, Ford would forgo profits shown by the lower right to upper left
curve. The temptation to arbitrage could be eliminated by raising the
British price and lowering the Canadian price so that the adjustments
eliminate the price gap. The combination giving the lowest *total* forgone
profits is at the minimum of the line called "sum of costs."

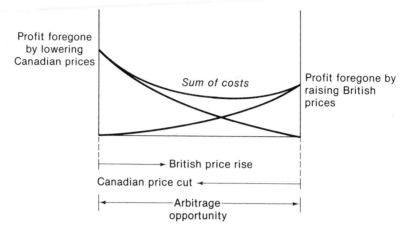

EXHIBIT 9.9
Model of profits forgone if arbitrage is eliminated.

Geocentric Pricing Scheme

"Firms can and do . . . make proper use of markup pricing by first employing economic analysis to formulate pricing policy and then translating the results of their analysis into appropriate markup formulas . . . . The pricing formulas can be tailored for individual markets by adjusting the markup percentages. . . . Large markups can be assigned to markets with high demand and small markups to markets with small demand" (Kolde, 1968, p. 395).

One nation is designated as the base, and benchmark prices are established (Appendix 2). Prices for the line in any other nation are these benchmark prices multiplied by a markup weight, the scalar w. This weight is an across-the-board markup or markdown on prices of all items in the line (in the United States, too, prices west of the Rockies are sometimes 15 percent higher on all items in a line).

This geocentric pricing scheme allows flexibility in dealing with foreign economic changes such as inflation and exchange rates. The different rates of inflation can be compensated for by adjusting each nation's weight $W_n^o + \Delta W_n$. If Saudi prices are 120 percent of U.S. prices, perhaps they should be adjusted to 130 percent to account for Saudi's recent high inflation rate. The fluctuations in exchange rates discussed in Chapter 2 can be handled similarly.

This model also allows flexible accommodation to *full line* competitors although it is less flexible in responding to a local competitor entrenched in only *part* of the product line. For example, IBM markets a full line of computers worldwide. The Amdahl Corporation produces only large computers and sells mostly in the United States, Germany, and Japan. IBM considered reducing worldwide prices of its largest computers to compete with Amdahl, but this would have underpriced its line in the rest of the world. Instead, IBM increased U.S. marketing support for its large computers. As another example, in Britain, IBM faced intense competition in its medium-sized computers but less competition in its low end and high end. IBM preserved interval pricing coherence by using competition techniques other than pricing, detailed marketing support in this case, for its medium-sized machines.

In some nations goods are purchased by a government agency. For example, a national health scheme purchases pharmaceuticals for its citizens. The purchasing committee will usually check prices in the nation of the multinational headquarters and negotiate for parity. It may be more profitable to raise home country prices than to lower prices abroad, as can be determined by the model of Appendix 2.

Geocentric pricing may be preferable to polycentric pricing because it reduces administrative costs and confusion. But if the difference in model profits is excessive, perhaps an intermediate formulation would be better. The computer examples suggest dealing separately with small, medium, and large computers. But there are cross-elasticities of demand and marketing spillovers in the data input. It would be possible to accommodate three sets of national weighting factors, all to be determined optimally. The predetermined model profit gives a measure of incentive to tolerate the resulting administrative problems.

Ethnocentric Pricing Scheme

The ethnocentric pricing scheme has been criticized by Robinson (1978, p. 94):

> The standard worldwide base price is most likely to be looked upon by management as full-cost pricing, including an allowance for manufacturing overhead, general overhead, and selling expenses. Often ignored are (1) the necessarily arbitrary nature of these cost allocations, (2) differences in costs from market to market (in labor, capital, materials, and management in the case of overseas manufacture; in shipping, crating, insurance, tariffs, taxes, internal transport, distribution, and promotion in the case of exporting), (3) possibly lower marginal cost of goods moving into foreign markets (particularly in reference to domestically oriented research and development), (4) differences in competitive position within the foreign markets, (5) differing degrees of optimum penetration for different foreign markets, (6) price controls enforced by a government or by a dominant supplier.

However, a domestic corporation that does a small amount of exporting will usually price abroad at the home price plus freight and duty. This is the easiest way to price and the most sensible as long as the number of exports remains small. This pricing scheme may also be necessary for expensive, compact products that have unequivocal specifications and are sold to multinational customers, whether corporations, trading companies, or individuals. It may be a necessary pricing scheme if the product becomes embroiled in issues of equity.

Ethnocentric pricing helps avoid some of the problems associated with differential pricing. For example, an international computer company might sell to an international oil company. The latter may accept higher prices in Bahrein, reflecting the higher cost of doing business there, but will object if prices are disproportionately higher on some items than on others. (The company will hardly be mollified by a lecture on the economics of a discriminating monopoly.)

For another example, a large U.S. steel corporation sustained its entry in the European market by absorbing freight and duty on its export shipments. One customer was the German subsidiary of a U.S. auto manufacturer. The Detroit plant of the automaker demanded the same treatment from the steel company. The firm abandoned the European market.

A further problem with polycentric pricing is the cost of oversight. An electronics firm, for example, might sell 10,000 products in 75 nations (the model analysis would not be done on so large a problem). If headquarters is to maintain any degree of control, keeping price books becomes a huge data processing job as national subsidiaries experience varying degrees of inflation. Some system is needed to preserve control and to give guidelines for evaluating subsidiary performance.

In nation n, the initial vector of prices is p_n^0. In nation m, the initial prices *may* be different, say p_m^0. The difference in the prices $(p_n - p_m)$ is, however, fixed and predetermined (such as freight plus import duty). This difference in prices could be set equal to zero. When the line of prices is changed by Δp in one nation, the Δp change in prices has to be made in all other markets. Appendix 3 shows how to calculate the Δp optimal for global profitability. With an ethnocentric corporation, the natural temptation is to optimize the home prices using home data; these home prices then become the export prices. Sometimes a higher or lower export price would be preferable. Appendix 3 raises or lowers the home price because of price considerations in all the markets. It is therefore susceptible to the accusation that "the tail is wagging the dog." This will hardly occur if the foreign markets are tiny. If it does occur, and is significant, it may be better to convert to the geocentric pricing scheme. Nevertheless, as Kolde (1968, p. 403) wrote:

> The conversion from rigid full-cost export pricing [ethnocentric] to demand based pricing [geocentric] has been generally much slower than can be justified in the light of prevailing market conditions. Too many executives are (self) righteously resisting any changes in their unilateral "right" to prescribe the price for all their markets .... They have, literally, priced themselves out of the market, not because the market price was too low, but because their pricing policies and strategies were based on the wrong premise.

The Three Pricing Schemes Discussed

All three pricing schemes require identical input information—derived from judgment, competitive insight, test marketing, and regression analysis on similar products. Regardless of the input data precision, the three schemes are ranked in order of their model profits, $\pi_p > \pi_g > \pi_e$. The polycentric scheme has the fewest constraints. It may be that its optimal prices will fall into line so that there is a constant percentage markup for all goods in each nation, but this is unlikely. Imposing the geocentric constraint of a constant percentage markup for goods sold in each nation will reduce model profits, hence $\pi_p > \pi_g$. Similarly, with geocentric pricing all nations might have identical percentage markups over cost, but this too is unlikely. Imposing this ethnocentric constraint will reduce model profits. Hence $\pi_g > \pi_e$. Reflecting on the differences between the profitabilities $(\pi_p - \pi_g)$ and $(\pi_g - \pi_e)$ may help corporate executives select a better pricing scheme.

Collecting data for a multinational marketing model is very expensive. The first runs should incorporate data for only part of the product line, and only some of the nations; even so, the available data generally are subjective modifications of Comanor and Wilson (1979) statistical estimates.

Once the model has run, it can be used to "bootstrap" its way toward better data by means of sensitivity analysis. One input coefficient is considered, say a price elasticity between items i and j (that is, P_{ij}). Being unsure of the number P_{ij} we vary it and determine the change in profit. Ideally, while an analyst is estimating P_{ij}, he should also guess at the percentage change in P_{ij} that might come from another, say, \$250 further investigation. Then the computer can do a sensitivity analysis over this coefficient range, so as to rank all the input coefficients as to the cost-benefit trade-off of further investigation. This should be repeated after each round of investigation, because the new coefficients alter the slope and position of the sensitivity lines, and the work of investigation alters the analyst's cost estimates.

Behavioral Aspects

Once a pricing scheme has been chosen, each national subsidiary should set its own marketing budget. These will probably be set subjectively, if only because of the complexity of advertising carryover from one period to the next. For purposes of headquarters control, marketing goodwill is a crucial (though difficult to measure) gauge of managerial performance.

In the administration of polycentric pricing, headquarters has no direct involvement, except for setting the landed cost c. To administer geocentric pricing, headquarters must set the base prices but can leave the subsidiaries to decide on their markup weights and marketing budgets. With ethnocentric pricing headquarters issues detailed prices to each national subsidiary.

305

When measuring costs of a particular scheme the emotional commitments of headquarters executives as well as customer and competitor relations must be considered. The tenacity with which some headquarters executives cling to ethnocentric pricing deserves thought. A headquarters executive, setting prices worldwide, has a firm sense of his direct authority. He will enjoy the responsiveness of subsidiaries, for they know that if they retaliate with passive resistance, he will lose confidence in their managerial capabilities. Any sloppiness by the subsidiaries will validate xenophobia in the executive's perceptions, and lock the subsidiaries tighter into an ethnocentric pricing policy. Furthermore, headquarters marketing executives have usually come up from field sales management. Strategic planning may be psychologically painful to these aggressive line executives not only because of its vexing nature but also because it lacks immediate feedback. Line executives are eager to stay abreast of current market events, and ethnocentric pricing offers legitimacy by keeping them involved in detailed subsidiary operations. If these men have spent their lives involved in operations, it is not surprising that they are reluctant to relinquish such involvement merely because they have been promoted to headquarters. These emotional considerations are real; how expensive they are to the corporation can be gauged by comparing model profits.

Input from Other Chapters

This model is interconnected with the others in this text. In this exposition, it has been assumed that profit is equally attractive, regardless of where it is generated. Chapter 3 provides weighting coefficients for profit (the dual variable at each year–nation node) with which to weigh each element of $\Delta\pi$. Chapter 6 devoted much attention to the dual variables in the transportation problems, both the duals at each factory and those at each market. In this chapter the cost c for item i in market m is a time-weighted average of v^t_{im} from Chapter 6. These will be the same as the transfer prices from Chapter 3, *unless* that analysis raised the reported prices.

Chapter 7 may also have to be iterated with this chapter. If the product is manufactured in a few huge plants, each new plant will significantly vary the landed costs c, and a change in pricing should be evaluated. Conversely, the quantity sold determined by this chapter provides market demands for plant location studies.

Appendix 1. A Mathematical Formulation of the Pricing Model

Necessary Input

I: the number of items sold $i = 1, \ldots, I$
Vector p^o: the list of initial prices

Vector m^o: the list of initial marketing budgets

Vector d^o: a list of expected total sales derived from the area under the life cycle curve for each of the products

Vector c: a list of the marginal costs (each element of the vector is an item)

Matrix P: matrix of price cross-elasticities

Matrix M: matrix of responses to marketing budgets

Vector q: an estimate of the decreasing marginal effectiveness of the marketing expenditures.

$$\text{base case profit} = \text{revenue} - \text{production cost} - \text{marketing cost}$$

$$\pi^o = p^{o\prime}d^o - c(d^o) - 1'(m)$$

where demand $d^o = f(p^o, m^o)$, $1' = [1,1,1, \ldots, 1]$, and the superscript prime means transpose.

Incremental adjustments can now be made to the vector of prices and marketing budgets so that these become $p = p^o + \Delta p$ and $m = m^o + \Delta m$, respectively. The intent is to optimize Δp and Δm.

After adjustments Δp and Δm the profitability becomes

$$\pi = (p^o + \Delta p)(d^o + \Delta d) - 1'(m^o + \Delta m) - c(d^o + \Delta d)$$

where $d^o + \Delta d = f(p^o + \Delta p, m^o + \Delta m)$.

The influence of price or sales is summarized as linear demand curves and cross-elasticity effects in the $I \times I$ matrix P in Exhibit 9.10 so that

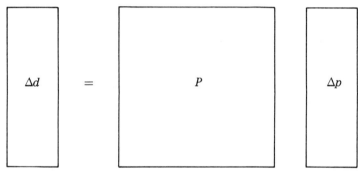

EXHIBIT 9.10

The demand response to the marketing budget is represented mathematically by a quadratic approximation, Exhibit 9.11:

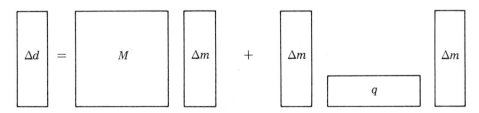

EXHIBIT 9.11

where q is an estimate of the decreasing marginal effectiveness of the marketing expenditures portrayed in Exhibit 9.7.

Optimization

The vectors of changes Δp and Δm will cause a change in daily profits $\Delta \pi$.

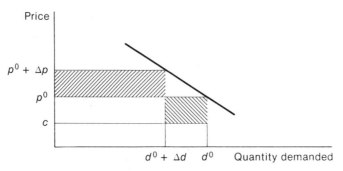

(where Δd is a negative quantity)

EXHIBIT 9.12
Change in profits excluding marketing.

Thus

$$\Delta \pi = \Delta p'(d^\circ + \Delta d) + (p^\circ - c)'\Delta d - 1'\Delta m$$

Substitute in the expression $\Delta d = P\,\Delta d + M\,\Delta m + \Delta m'q\,\Delta m$ so that

$$\Delta \pi = \Delta p'(d^\circ + P\,\Delta p + M\,\Delta m + \Delta m'q\,\Delta m)$$
$$+ (p^\circ - c)'(P\,\Delta p + M\,\Delta m + \Delta m'q\,\Delta m)$$
$$- 1'\,\Delta m$$

Some of these terms are linear (such as $\Delta p\,d^\circ$), others are quadratic (such as $\Delta p'P\Delta p$) and a few such as $\Delta p'\Delta m'q\,\Delta m$ are so small we discard them. Let us separate the terms of $\Delta \pi$ into two groups so that, Exhibit 9.13:

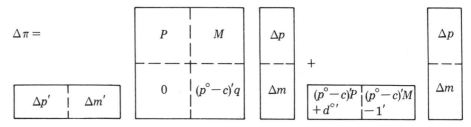

EXHIBIT 9.13

This is a lot to keep writing, so rename variables and matrices as

$$\Delta \pi = x'Gx + h'x$$

Profit has a maximum because of the decreasing marginal effectiveness of advertising. To maximize the increment of profit, set the derivative equal to zero then compute the value of $x = x^*$ at which the maximum occurs.

$$x^* = -[G + G']^{-1}h$$

On resubstituting for x, G, and h we get the computational scheme of Exhibit 9.14:

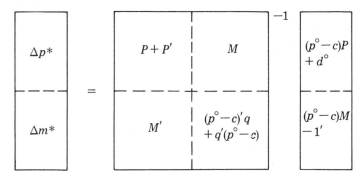

EXHIBIT 9.14

The superscript -1 means calculate the inverse of the matrix, for which there are standard computer programs. (A sophisticated analyst could reduce computation time by finding the inverse by parts since the off-diagonal matrices [M and M'] are almost identical.)

Appendix 2. Mathematical Formulation of Geocentric Pricing Scheme

In nation n the starting price is $p_n^o = [w_n^o]p^o$. Adjustments Δp are made to the base prices p^o, and Δw to the weights w^o. The vector of prices thereby becomes $p_n^o + \Delta p_n = [w_n^o + \Delta w_n](p + \Delta p)$. Thus

$$\Delta p_n = w_n^o \Delta p + \Delta w_n p^o + \Delta w_n \Delta p$$

In this scheme nation 1 is the base, so $w_1^o = 1$ and $\Delta w_1 = 0$. In nation n, $\Delta d_n = P_n \Delta p_n + M_n \Delta m_n - \Delta m_n' q_n \Delta m_n$. Because of the interdependencies between prices we must maximize the sum of profits simultaneously. Thus for all N nations together

$$\sum_{n=1}^{N} \Delta \pi = \sum_{n=1}^{N} \Delta p_n (d_n^o + \Delta d_n) + \sum_{n=1}^{N} (p_n^o - c)' \Delta d_n - \sum_{n=1}^{N} 1' \Delta m_n$$

$$= \sum_{n=1}^{N} (w_n^o \Delta p + \Delta w_n p^o + \Delta w_n \Delta p)[d_n^o + P_n(w_n^o \Delta p + \Delta w_n p^o + \Delta w_n \Delta p)$$

$$+ M_n \Delta m_n - \Delta m_n' q_n \Delta m_n] + \sum_{n=1}^{N} (w_n^o p^o - c_n)'[P_n(w_n^o \Delta p + \Delta w_n p^o$$

$$+ \Delta w_n \Delta p) + M_n \Delta m_n - \Delta m_n' q_n \Delta m_n] - \sum_{n=1}^{N} 1' \Delta m_n$$

As in Appendix 1 we will collect terms to create $\Delta \pi = x'Gx + hx$, discarding the few terms that are higher multiples of various Δ. If there are two nations, $x' = [\Delta p, \Delta w, \Delta m^1, \Delta m^2]'$ a vector of length $I + (n-1) + I + I$. The profit maximizing adjustment is

$$(\Delta p^*, \Delta w^*, \Delta m_1^*, \Delta m_2^*)' = -[G + G']^{-1} h$$

This $[G + G']$ matrix is large but efficient computer programs can calculate the inverse of such a matrix quite cheaply.

In some markets government purchasing agents check prices in the headquarter's nation. It becomes necessary to constrain these weighting factors to be less than or equal to one.

Maximize $x'Gx + h'x$

Subject to $w_g \leqslant 1$

This program will calculate the change in worldwide profits if the headquarters prices are raised and the monitoring nations' weighting factors are lowered to equal one.

Appendix 3. Mathematical Formulation of Ethnocentric Pricing Scheme

We follow the same mathematical development as in the earlier schemes. That is, we analyze a base case with vectors of prices $p_1^o \ldots p_N^o$ and marketing budgets $m_1^o \ldots m_N^o$. Then we optimize profits by altering prices and marketing budgets. Because price adjustments in all nations are to be identical, the control vector is

$$x' = [\Delta p, \Delta m_1, \ldots, \Delta m_N]$$

Change in profits:

$$\Delta \pi = \sum_{n=1}^{N} (p_n^o - c_n)\Delta d_n + \Delta p \sum_{n=1}^{N} (d_n^o + \Delta d_n) - \sum_{n=1}^{N} 1' \Delta m_n$$

$$= \sum_{n=1}^{N} (p_n^o - c_n)(P_n \Delta p + M_n \Delta m_n + \Delta m_n' q_n \Delta m_n) + \Delta p \sum_{n=1}^{N} (d_n^o + P_n \Delta p$$

$$+ M_n \Delta m_n + \Delta m_n' q_n \Delta m_n) - \sum_{n=1}^{N} 1' \Delta m_n$$

As before, we collect the terms into an expression for the change in profit $\Delta \pi = x'Gx + h'x$, the maximum of which occurs at $[\Delta p^*, \Delta m_1^*, \ldots, \Delta m_N^*] = -[G + G']^{-1} h$.

$$G = \begin{bmatrix}
\displaystyle\sum_{n=1}^{2} (w_n^o)^2 P_n & \displaystyle\sum_{n=1}^{2} w_n^o p^o P_n & w_1^o M_1 & w_2^o M_2 \\[2ex]
\text{where } w_o^1 = 1 & & & \\[3ex]
\displaystyle\sum_{n=1}^{2} p^o w_n^o P_n + \sum_{n=1}^{2} q_n^o + \sum_{n=1}^{2} (w_n^o p^o - c_n) P_n & \displaystyle\sum_{n=1}^{2} p^o p_n p^o & P^o M_1 & P^o M_2 \\[3ex]
0 & 0 & -(w_1^o p^o - c_1) q_1 & \begin{array}{c} 0 \\ \text{if no advertising} \\ \text{spill over} \end{array} \\[3ex]
0 & 0 & 0 & -(w_2^o p^o - c_2) q_2
\end{bmatrix}$$

$$h = \begin{bmatrix}
\displaystyle\sum_{n=1}^{2} w_n^o (w_n^o p^o - c_n) P_n + \sum_{n=1}^{2} w_n^o d_n^o \\[3ex]
\displaystyle\sum_{n=1}^{2} P^o (w_n^o p^o - c_n) P_n + \sum_{n=1}^{2} P^o d_n^o \\[3ex]
(w_1^o p^o - c_1) M_1 - 1 \\[2ex]
(w_2^o p^o - c_2) M_2 - 1
\end{bmatrix}$$

EXHIBIT 9.15

Arrangement of input data for geocentric pricing scheme (illustrated for two nations).

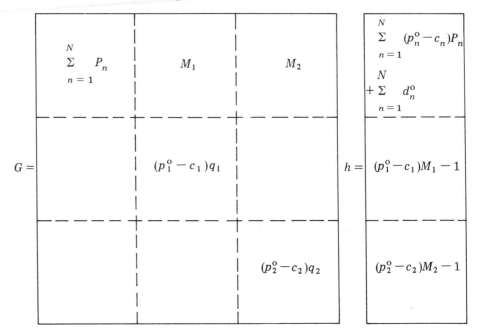

EXHIBIT 9.16
Arrangement of input data for ethnocentric pricing scheme 3.

Questions from Other Viewpoints

1. *Corporate Rational Normative Global.* You just covered this viewpoint in the chapter.
2. *Corporate Rational Normative Subsidiary.* Instead of having the calculation of Appendix 2 or Appendix 3 done centrally, devise an iterative scheme to arrive at the same results by means of bids and side payments.
3. *Corporate Rational Descriptive Global.* In any marketing textbook there is a concept called a "product life cycle," with four phases: introduction, growth, maturity, and decline. What pricing considerations are most important at each phase? During which phases would the model presented here most usefully exceed the data-gathering costs?
4. *Corporate Rational Descriptive Subsidiary.* Describe the standard marketing research methods used to estimate the cross (and direct) elasticities of price and marketing.
5. *Corporate Emotional Normative Global.* As actual sales data come in, actual sales will rarely be what you predicted. How do you disentangle explanations to analyze whether prices should be changed?
6. *Corporate Emotional Normative Subsidiary.* In an ethnocentric

corporation, what can be done to create the impression in subsidiaries that nothing can be done to alter prices? In a geocentric corporation, as inflation rates vary, how can one manage to get energetic input into the decision about the scale factor without opening up discussion about base prices?

7. *Corporate Emotional Descriptive Global.* When each nation sets its own prices there are certain problems that have been mentioned in the chapter. But putting a geocentric or ethnocentric straitjacket on prices seems like an expensive and artificial way to resolve conflicts between individual national product managers. What other means of conflict resolution could headquarters support?

8. *Corporate Emotional Descriptive Subsidiary.* Make up an incident in which the geocentric pricing scheme allows a competitor to out-maneuver your subsidiary. Imagine that you are a subsidiary salesman. Write a one-page "Lost Sale Report."

9. *Societal Rational Normative Global.* A pharmaceutical product usually has a very high fixed (sunk) cost of research, development, and testing, but a comparatively low marginal cost of manufacture. At present corporations charge different prices in different nations. Assuming you want to keep competition in the research and development of pharmaceuticals devise different schemes for rewarding R&D success and for pricing the products.

10. *Societal Rational Normative National.* Your nation is instituting price controls to slow inflation. Among the vociferous opponents are the foreign multinationals. The Minister of Finance has asked you to prepare a prototype or sample letter of response to be sent out over his signature, with appropriate phrases tailored to each company. Draft such a one-page single-spaced letter. Indicate which sentences should be individually tailored. On a separate sheet write substitute paragraphs which may be necessary, keying each clearly to a specific class of company objection.

11. *Societal Rational Descriptive Global.* Which major national markets operate under price controls? Group the nations by the manner in which price controls appear to be administered.

12. *Societal Rational Descriptive Global.* Based on the pricing models in the Appendices, list government actions that would result in lower prices within a nation.

13. *Societal Emotional Normative Global.* Issues of equity arouse powerful emotions. Is it fair that citizens of a poor nation should be charged as much for an item as citizens of a rich nation? Write a strong emotional pitch for the following scheme. Price in any nation should equal marginal cost plus a markup to cover overhead. Overhead should be assigned to national prices in proportion to national disposal personal income.

14. *Societal Emotional Normative National.* Price controls not only contain inflation and prevent exploitation by rapacious multination-

als, they also are an affirmation of national identity that can thwart the monolithic multinational. These three ideas can be sequenced in several ways. For which national stakeholder (see Chapter 4) would each sequence get the greatest response?

15. *Societal Emotional Descriptive Global.* Please review the tractor pricing data. What configuration of data would excite the antitrust interest of (a) the United States, (b) Canada, (c) the EEC Commission in Brussels?

16. *Societal Emotional Descriptive National.* A particular nation has administered price controls for five years. Now prices are to be decontrolled. Identify each affected party and predict their actions from now to decontrol day and in the months immediately following decontrol.

Bibliography to Chapter 9

Bellamy, Christopher W., Graham D. Child, and Anthony L. Morris, *Common Market Law of Competition* 2 ed. (London: Sweet & Maxwell, 1978).

Boston Consulting Group, *Perspectives on Experience* (Boston: Boston Consulting Group, 1970).

Cleland, David and William King, "Competitive Business Intelligence Systems," *Business Horizons*, Vol. 18 (December 1975), pp. 19-28.

Daniels, John D., Ernest Ogram, and Lee Radebaugh, *International Business: Environments and Operations*, 2 ed. (Reading, MA: Addison-Wesley, 1979), Chapter 19.

"Flexible Pricing: Industry's New Strategy to Hold Market Share Changes the Rules for Economic Decision Making," *Business Week*, Vol. 25, December 12, 1977, pp. 78-88.

Ijiri, Yuji and Herbert Simon, *Skew Distributions and the Sizes of Business Firms*, (Amsterdam: North Holland Publishing, 1977).

Knickerbocker, Frederick T., *Oligopolistic Reaction and Multinational Enterprise*, (Boston: Division of Research, Harvard Business School, 1973).

Kolde, Endel J., *International Business Enterprise* (Englewood Cliffs, NJ: Prentice-Hall, 1968), Chapter 26.

Kotler, Philip, *Marketing Decision Making—A Model Building Approach* (Toronto: Holt, Rinehart and Winston, 1971).

Mason, Richard O., "A Dialectical Approach to Strategic Planning," *Management Science*, Vol. 15, No. 8 (1969), pp. 403-414.

Mesak, Hani I. and Richard C. Clelland, "A Competitive Pricing Model," *Management Science*, Vol. 25, No. 11 (1979), pp. 1057-1068.

Monroe, Kent B. and Albert J. DellaBita, "Models for Pricing Decisions," *Journal of Marketing Research*, Vol. 15, No. 3 (1978), pp. 413-428.

Robinson, Richard O., *International Business Management*, 2 ed. (New York: Holt, Rinehart and Winston, 1978).

Schwartzman, Harry, *Special Report on Prices of Tractors and Combines in Canada and Other Countries*, Royal Commission on Farm Machinery (Ottawa: Queen's Printer, 1969).

CHAPTER TEN

Product Design

Introductory Note to the Case

Black and Decker (Canada) Inc.

The idea of this case is simple. A product is designed in subassemblies. Some subassemblies will be common to the world so that economies of scale can be achieved. Others will be tailored to national needs to satisfy technical and marketing considerations.

Black and Decker follows the belief that the long-run demand curve is elastic, so if the price of a product is reduced (by taking a smaller profit margin, or by increased productivity, or both) sufficiently more of the product can be sold to result in an overall increase in profits despite the smaller margin. This in turn allows economies of scale to be realized from volume production. B & D Canada's vice-president of Intercompany Business and New Business Development, Ralph Butt, describes this as "banking profits, not percentages." The adoption of this aggressive pricing strategy by B & D in the mid-1960s (coinciding with rapid growth in the do-it-yourself market) resulted in greater sales, increased market share, and higher profits.

Although B & D knows that lowering the price of its products can expand the size of the market, the company is also aware that the price–volume profit relationship has a relevant range in any year. In the long run B & D assumes that 85 percent saturation is the most it can achieve — that is, 15 percent of householders would not want their products even if B & D were to give them away. Well before the 85 percent level, there is a point at which additional reductions in price will not increase profits. Also, there are limits to productivity increases that must be anticipated. Therefore determining the price trajectory which maximizes the present value of profitability over the product's life cycle is by no means an easy task.

To avoid dependence on the economy of a single nation, B & D's marketing strategy is global. Expansions abroad in less-developed countries mean that global sales will continue to grow. Management considers a dominant market share of prime importance, so as a long-term strategic move it expands into new markets in which no competitor has become strongly established.

A very important aspect of its global marketing strategy is B & D's firm belief in decentralization and subsidiary autonomy. Each local company knows its market best and is therefore given the authority to develop the opportunities within its particular market. B & D Canada, faced with the challenge of growing in a rather saturated market, of which it already holds a substantial share, realizes that the solution lies in new products and in expanding exports to other B & D subsidiaries. B & D Canada exports 50 percent of its production. This places it in the paradoxical position of wanting more export business but at the same time trying to avoid overdependence on any single customer — in this case the U.S.A. Because it has no control over other subsidiaries' marketing services, B & D Canada in effect becomes their hostage.

B & D firmly believes in the experience curve; that with each doubling of cumulative experience it can reduce the cost of a unit by almost 30 percent (after adjusting for inflation). Cost accounting, manufacturing planning, and managerial evaluation are used together to sustain this goal. A corporate movement to rationalize selective products into certain plants around the world began in 1966 and two years later led to B & D Canada's being awarded the global product mandate for orbital sanders. As was explained in Chapter 1 there is no reason why the management of every product has to be in the headquarter's nation. Canadian management convinced corporate headquarters that not only would savings be realized from economies of scale and accumulated experience, but the cost of sander subassemblies common to other products (drill, jig-saws, and hedge trimmers) would be lower, providing an opportunity to reduce prices and expand the domestic market. Also in the Canadian subsidiary's favor was its proximity to the large American market, the demonstrated quality of the Canadian plant output, and the country's status as a respected and stable nation.

Having a global mandate for a product, in this case sanders, means taking the responsibility to keep up to date on every technical/legal change in the world that might relate to sanders. B & D Canada had technical aspects well in hand. Study Exhibits 10.2–10.5 to understand how they were able to reduce the number of models that they envisioned would be needed to meet the international demand.

B & D Canada executives wondered whether more market research could have been incorporated into the sequence of decisions to reduce model numbers, when the research might have been scheduled, and, specifically, which results would have been helpful to the Workwheel design team.

Black and Decker (Canada) Inc.

The Birth of the Workwheel

On January 7, 1977, Colin Overy, a project engineer with Black and Decker Canada, was sitting in the Alpine Inn restaurant in Media, Pennsylvania. He was in the Philadelphia area conducting market research on a completely different B & D product and had just paid a visit to a local hardware store. There, he had seen a competitor's product designed to make the sanding of curved objects easier. The Industrial Sand-O-Flex flap wheel was to be used on a small electric drill, a tool Overy felt lacked the power and was too fast to drive the accessory adequately.

He remembered a few months earlier when he and two colleagues from B & D Canada had visited three furniture manufacturing companies in Southern Ontario to see how professionals sanded wooden shapes such as chair arms. They had been shown a large pedestal on which was mounted a powered flapwheel (about 40 centimeters in diameter) some-

This case was written by Detlev Hoch and Janet Hendry under the supervision of Professor David Rutenberg of Queen's University, Kingston, and with financial support from the National Sciences and Engineering Research Council of Canada. "Workwheel" is a Black and Decker registered trademark.

what resembling the paddlewheel of a boat where each paddle is a flap of sandpaper supported by brushes.

As manufacturers of power tools for the consumer, B & D Canada was aware that rising labor costs and increased leisure time were largely responsible for growing interest in their products. Furniture refinishing was a firmly established hobby. Thousands of do-it-yourselfers were tediously stripping and sanding antiques by hand, since no power tool readily available to the public had yet been developed to make the job less laborious. Overy decided that the need would best be met by a hand tool rather than one on a fixed base and proceeded to sketch a first draft of what would later become the Workwheel power stripper and sander.

On that day, many questions remained to be formulated, let alone answered. Aside from financial and marketing considerations, technical problems (such as how power from a high-speed motor would be transmitted to a low-speed flap wheel) had to be solved. No one could foresee the multiple applications of the Workwheel. Nevertheless, the Workwheel had been born.

Standards Requirements

Black and Decker Canada, wholly owned subsidiary of the Black and Decker Manufacturing Company of Towson, Maryland, exports approximately 50 percent of its production to B & D marketing subsidiaries in 45 countries. To do so, it designs products to meet a great many differing national standards which constitute effective nontariff barriers to trade. As will be explained, not all importing nations have the same electric current or receptacle configuration; thus a single design is impossible from a technical as well as a legal standpoint.

Regulations

Although many sets of standards exist, some nations have regulations common to others' (as is frequently the case with countries and their former colonies). Recognizing that commonality is mutually beneficial, international consultations have been taking place almost from the beginning of the century. The International Electrotechnical Commission (IEC) was established early in the century for the purpose of developing world standards. In the early 1930s, the CEE, a Commission on Rules for the Approval of Electrical Equipment, was formed with the objective of harmonizing European standards. With the formation of the European Common Market, CEE's work continued with renewed impetus. Progress toward the adoption of common standards is slow, however, and meanwhile, a manufacturer wishing to export is left with the task of satisfying existing requirements while keeping costs sufficiently low to remain competitive.

Radiosuppression is an issue which illustrates how a manufacturer handles these requirements. The operation of most electric power tools creates electromagnetic interference, which disrupts radio and television reception. As cosmic rays are a pervasive source of interference, the North American solution has been to partially shield televisions; therefore, suppression of power tools is not legally required in the United States and Canada. Other countries demand a specific level of suppression, often with different standards for the radio band (0.15–30 megahertz) and the television band (30–300 megahertz). The suppression parts require space, which must be designed into the housing of the power tool. Black and Decker could manufacture two different housings: a bulky version with space for suppression parts, and a trim version, attractive to consumers who cite compactness as a desirable product attribute. However, there are substantial economies of scale in manufacturing a single housing. At the expected production volume for Workwheel, economies of scale dominated, so B & D decided to manufacture only the bulky housing design, though they naturally omit suppression parts from tools to be sold in North America.

Besides radiosuppression, other features of power tools are regulated. Detachable power cords may or may not be permitted. Push-in terminals may or may not be allowed in place of screw terminals. The type of switch may be prescribed. Minimum clearances may be set for the distance between open contacts (e.g., 3 millimeters is required in Germany) as well as minimum creepage distances (that between a live part and accessible metal measured over a surface, 8 millimeters in Germany).

Differing standards present problems, not only by virtue of the fact that they exist, but also because the same characteristics can be measured in different ways and because standards frequently are changed. The Japanese measure electromagnetic interference in a manner uniquely theirs — with a highly sophisticated piece of equipment costing $50,000. Black and Decker Canada has not purchased this equipment, reasoning that Japan will "soon" adopt the international standard measuring practice.

The additional cost of meeting a nation's standards must be weighted against the profit expected from its market. In the past, German regulatory authorities have allowed plastic housings to be made of ABS, a universally accepted plastic. Now it appears that ABS fails to satisfy CEE standard 20, which describes the permissible deformation a plastic may sustain at high temperature. The test involves heating the part to 85°C above its normal operating temperature and subjecting it to a specified pressure for a stated period using a 4-millimeter ball bearing. (The resulting impression must be less than 2 millimeters in diameter.) Alternative housing materials would be nylon-reinforced glass fiber or a polycarbonate resin such as General Electric's Lexan, both of which are more expensive and have other undesirable characteristics. The additional cost incurred from retooling for nylon or Lexan would have to be carefully weighted against the expected loss in profit from withdrawing from the German market.

Differences in standards often constitute a less formidable problem for product design than does determining precisely what the standards are. Most nations have special Test Boards that carry out prescribed procedures to determine whether a potential import meets its requirements. Usually a Test Board publishes its procedures so methodically that an engineer abroad not only can replicate their measurements but can actually determine a minimum cost design that can be reliably predicted to just satisfy the national standards. In other nations the procedures are so vaguely described that the design engineer crafts in the dark.

In the past, the Japanese Test Board has released so little information about its test results that B & D often had trouble inferring why its product had passed. In 1979, the first unofficial English translation of Japanese standards was published. If a product meets these standards, the manufacturer is allowed to mark it with a "T-Mark." But after paying the $400 price tag, B & D Canada concluded that the book was decidedly inadequate. Power tool approval is described in two pages of generalities — compared to 100 pages in the equivalent U.S. publication. That testing methods are not described presents a real problem for a manufacturer; for example, there are innumerable ways to measure the temperature of a power tool. Moreover, not only are Canadian manufacturers aiming at a target they cannot see clearly, but the target moves. Japanese product approval is granted for five years only. Japanese standards appear to be moving but specifically which ones and by how much are often extremely difficult for a B & D Canada engineer to determine.

Technical Considerations

The voltage and frequency of power supply is not the same everywhere. Hence electric motors require different winding patterns, different commutators, and so on. The standard in most nations is 220 volts/50 cycles; some use 220 volts/60 cycles; Canada and the United States use 115 volts/60 cycles. Japan is the only country using 100 volts/60 cycles.

Receptacle configuration differs from country to country. The four common configurations are shown in Exhibit 10.1.

Within some nations, different regions use different receptacle configurations. In Britain it is not uncommon to find variations within one house. Black and Decker U.K. responds to this by selling power tools to the British retailer without a plug. It is then the retailer's responsibility to attach the plug of the customer's choice.

The manufacturer of power tools for export faces a challenging task: manufacturing a product which meets the technical and legal requirements of the importing country while satisfying consumer preferences and, at the same time, standardizing components to realize economies of scale from long production runs. To achieve these economies of scale

Africa, Great Britain, Ireland, Hong Kong	
Europe—East & West, Great Britain, (shavers), Middle East, Parts of Africa, Asia & South America	
Australia, New Zealand, Argentina, Mainland China, Fiji	
Chile, Peru, Tahiti Philippines	

EXHIBIT 10.1
The shapes of plugs.

EXHIBIT 10.2

First Draft of Model Numbers Based on Technical and Legal Requirements of Each National Market

Model Number	Country	Test board submittal required?	Local voltage	Cable: material, color, length (in meters)	Strain relief	Legally specified plug	Switch	Suppression required?	Color Preferred
-00	U.S.A.	UL	120		Detach		Push-in	No	Orange
-01	Holland	No	220	PVC, 0.75 mm², Blue/Brown, 2M	Separate with cord clamp	CEE 7XVII 8mm	Push-in	No	Blue
-26	Holland-Special								
-02	Argentina, Greece, Iran, Israel, SE Asia, Portugal	No	220/220/240 240	PVC, 18-2 SJT, Blue/Brown, 2M	Separate with cord clamp	No plug	Push-in	No	Blue
-03	Japan	T-Mark	100	PVC, 0.75 mm², Black/White, 2M	Separate with cord clamp	T-Mark	Push-in	Yes	Orange
-04	Canada	CSA	120		Detach		Push-in	No	Orange
-05	France Spain	No	220	PVC, 0.75 mm², Blue/Brown, 2M	Separate with cord clamp	CEE 7XVI Version 1	Push-in	No	Blue
-06	Australia	Yes	240	PVC, 23/.0076, Blue/Brown, 2M	Separate with cord clamp	SAA C112	Screw terminal	No	Orange
-07	U.K.	Yes—check with B&D, U.K.	220/240	PVC, 18-25 SJT, Blue/Brown, 2M	Separate with cord clamp	No plug	Push-in	Yes	Blue
-08	Italy	Yes	220	PVC, 0.75 mm², Blue/Brown, 2M	Separate with cord clamp	CEE 7VXI IMQ App'd	Screw terminal	No	Blue
-09	Brazil	No	120	PVC, 0.75 mm², Blue/Brown, 2M	Non detach	CEE 7XVI Version 1	Push-in	No	Orange
-10	New Zealand, South Africa	Yes	220	PVC, 23/.0076, Blue/Brown, 2M	Separate with cord clamp	SAA C112	Push-in	Yes	Blue
-11	Norway, Denmark, Sweden, Finland,	Yes	220/230	Rubber 1.0 mm², Blue/Brown, 2M	Separate with cord clamp	CEE 7XVII	Screw terminal	Yes	Blue
-12	Switzerland	Yes	220	PVC, 0.75 mm², Blue/Brown, 2M	Separate with cord clamp	CEE 7XVI Version 2	Screw terminal	Yes	Blue
-13	Austria, Belgium, Germany	Yes / No	220	PVC, 1.0 mm², Blue/Brown, 2M	Separate with cord clamp	CEE 7XVII	Screw terminal	Yes	Blue
-05	Brazil	No	220	PVC, 0.75 mm², Blue/Brown, 2M	Separate with cord clamp	CEE 7XVI Version 1	Push-in	No	Orange

EXHIBIT 10.3
Black and Decker (Canada) Inc.

Model Numbers Proposed on March 23, 1979

-00	United States (120 V)
-01	Belgium, Holland (220/240 V unsuppressed)
-02	Argentina, Greece, Iran, Israel, Southeast Asia, Portugal (220/240 V)
-03	Japan (100 V)
-04	Canada (120 V, bilingual packaging)
-05	France, Spain
-06	Australia
-07	United Kingdom (220/240 V suppressed)
-08	Italy
-09	Brazil (120 V)
-10	New Zealand, South Africa (220/240 V suppressed)
-11	Scandinavia (220/240 V suppressed)
-12	Switzerland (220/240 V suppressed)
-13	Austria, Germany, Belgium (220/240 V suppressed)
-14	Brazil (220 V)

Construction features have been optimized for each country with regard to test board approval in order to minimize cost.

B & D supplies models with features in excess of those legally required unless the market forecast is sufficiently large to justify another model.

This is often the case with Israel, which has no radio-suppression standard but the same power characteristics as the United Kingdom, which does require suppression. Black and Decker's Israeli sales are too small to justify a separate model, so Israel receives a radiosuppressed product. (Compare Exhibit 10.3 with Exhibit 10.4.)

The Product Development Cycle

The development of a product from an idea to an established international success involves the cooperation and coordination of many individuals and functional areas, and it involves risk. Luck plays a part, as do intuition, technical know-how, and experience. Although a considerable number of new product ideas originate from outside Black and Decker Canada, their Product Development Group is the source of most product extensions. For example, the Workwheel is in the sander family within Black and Decker, and B & D Canada has the global product mandate for orbital sanders.

EXHIBIT 10.4
Black and Decker (Canada) Inc.

Workwheel Model Reduction of March 29, 1979[a]

Recommended Model[b] number	Country	Concessions	Cost penalty of concession ($/unit)	Annual sales forecast
-00	United States			65,000
-03	Japan			?
-04	Canada			50,000
-05	France	Capacitor, screw terminal	.80	7,000
	Spain	Capacitor, screw terminal	.80	?
	Brazil (220)	Capacitor, screw terminal	.80	2,500
	Switzerland			?
-06	Australia	Capacitor, blue unit	.45	?
	New Zealand	Screw terminal	.35	?
	South Africa	Screw terminal	.35	500
-07	United Kingdom			30,000
	Argentina	Capacitor		
	Greece, Iran	Capacitor	.45	1,000
	Israel, etc.	Capacitor		
-08	Italy			5,000
-09	Brazil (120)			?
-11	Norway			
	Denmark			6,500
	Sweden			
	Finland			
-13	Belgium	Screw terminal	.35	1,000
	Holland	Capacitor, screw terminal	.80	4,000
	Austria			1,000
	Germany			10,000

[a]Minimum number of variations possible while maintaining appropriate cord set and plug for each country.
[b]10 units instead of 15. If Scandinavian countries accept vinyl cord sets they will be grouped in with -13, resulting in 9 models.

It was for this reason that Colin Overy had little difficulty convincing his boss, Jack Beckering, to commit an initial $1,000 to further develop his idea.

New product development within B & D Canada takes place in an informal but not unstructured environment. The potential for omitting a crucial step is too great for development to proceed without a plan, and a 560-item checklist is followed. In the case of the Workwheel, bimonthly meetings were held of the Product Management Advisory Committee, consisting of the president and representatives from Marketing, Manufacturing, Product Development, Quality Control, and Engineering. Product costing and ROI calculations were performed on a continual basis and weighted decisions were made in light of these figures. Although they overlap, five main steps in the development of the Workwheel may be distinguished:

|1977 | 1978 | 1979|

1. Concept study
2. Design and building of prototypes
3. Testing
4. Redesign for manufacturing and engineering release
5. Production tool-up

The Concept Study

The concept study, which extended over a period of approximately a year and a half, was completed just before the engineering release. Three almost parallel concept studies were required for the Workwheel.

The first began with some detailed illustrations and product descriptions which were used for patent disclosure. Urethane foam models were constructed to help decide the location of the motor and shape of the handle. Next, colored foam models were produced so that the designers could evaluate alternative configurations with an eye to aesthetics. Finally, a technician meticulously carved a wooden model which, when painted and fitted with a flapwheel, appeared indistinguishable from the anticipated final Workwheel. Ten envisioned uses for the Workwheel were simulated using the wooden model fitted with appropriate accessories. A large colored photograph of each use was prepared for focused group interviews, part of the market research program.

The second parallel study was to build a crude working model of a flapwheel, belt driven by a motor. In appearance, this working model was not very elegant for it was constructed from off-the-shelf items and a simple welded frame, but it allowed engineers to try using the Workwheel and to improve its operating design. They measured actual belt loads in a working Workwheel for the third parallel study.

The purpose of the third study was to improve mechanical design and development. Both the transmission system and motor size had to be selected. No one had ever used a very small belt to transmit as large a power load as was necessary, so an extensive program of belt transmission development and testing, lasting nine months, was carried out. When it was finished, the appropriate belt width, pulley diameter, and transmission speed had been determined. For example, Colin Overy knew that twin belts would do the job but twin belts are relatively bulky and expensive. After much testing, both Goodyear and Uniroyal rubber companies were able to design a single belt that worked.

Black and Decker is a multinational corporation; therefore, from the very beginning, a new product is designed with international markets in mind. Additional design criteria include maintainability, reliability, safety, economy, ease of operation, aesthetics, and modularity of subassemblies. Testing, carried on throughout product development, has two objectives: improvement and justification. Equipment is used to measure electromagnetic interference, noise, vibration, and resonance. Performance is evaluated under both normal and extreme conditions. The results provide project engineers with information necessary to ensure that components fit exactly and operate within tolerance limits.

Product improvement may result from the suggestions of the marketing, manufacturing, and quality control departments as well as from within the development group itself. Technical knowledge enables B & D to build a better product. Experience makes the designers aware of every feature a consumer could want. But the product could easily become too expensive to market successfully. Judgment is a critical element in issues such as how long a product should last. Black and Decker Canada designed the Workwheel to pass a 150-hour accelerated life test with no cooldown period. The challenge is to achieve the right balance of features, quality, and cost.

It was a low-risk venture for Jack Beckering to commit funds for the construction of wooden prototypes, a working model, and belt drive for the Workwheel, because of the size of the budget involved. The next stage, however, was different. Approximately $200,000 was needed to design and build the 100 working prototypes needed for broad-range market survey and test purposes. The actual bill for product development rose to $300,000 by the time the Engineering Release was completed in July 1978.

Since the ABS plastic housing and handle accounted for $50,000 of this sum, it is little wonder that B & D viewed with concern the German pressure to reengineer the housing material. In addition to the development costs, it was estimated that retooling for Lexan or nylon would cost $40,000. The annual profits from sales of Workwheel in Germany were expected to be only $30,000.

Intercompany Business

Black and Decker Canada starts to design "internationality" into its products as soon as the concept proves itself. Sales in each nation are handled by the B & D subsidiary located there, which is under no obligation to accept the product. Hence it was essential that B & D Canada convince sister subsidiaries to buy Workwheel. Black and Decker has standard procedures for the intercompany introduction of new products such as Workwheel.

The international sales pitch began with product demonstrations held at regional meetings, using working prototypes approximating the requirements of the importing country. A brochure was distributed with photographs and information regarding the date of market introduction, estimated intercompany price, minimum volume requirements (economic order quantities), shipping container volume, product and accessory descriptions, as well as a request for feedback regarding special requirements and sales forecasts. Final production tooling and capacity had not been established at this stage, so design adjustments could still be made. If importing countries had underestimated forecasts, no product would be available and they would have lost sales.

The next step was for each importing country to test a sample Workwheel from a marketing as well as an engineering standpoint. It was for this reason that 100 working prototypes had to be constructed. Although this appears expensive initially, B & D believes it pays off in the long run. The more accurate the marketing information, and the more complete the standards requirements, the better able B & D Canada will be to meet and take advantage of each sales opportunity. Standards requirements were reported on an exception basis only, as they had already been detailed in feedback to the product demonstration. The importing country's marketing division prepared to issue a Product Development Request to commit their intentions.

Although working prototypes of the new product had been tested in the importing country's B & D laboratory, the product had yet to obtain that country's test board approval. Prototypes do not suffice; samples from production tooling, incorporating all details of final production, must be used. A translated Owner's Manual is usually required. The number of samples needed for testing varies from country to country as does the time required for approval to be granted— anywhere from three months to one year. Black and Decker expedited the process by designating the responsibility for handling the approval to one individual in the importing country's B & D subsidiary.

Final product samples were also required for the importer's marketing purposes and again, following common practice, a marketing contact person was designated for the product. Canada, as the exporting country, launched the product on its domestic market six months before exports began so that advertising and merchandising material could be developed and tested. Although lower overall advertising costs could result from a cooperative effort between countries, such cooperation is by no means required, a fact which B & D Canada had cause to regret. Exports of Workwheel to the United States were begun in January 1980, and because of the 1980 recession B & D U.S. allocated only a limited budget for advertising. As a result, few retailers decided to stock it, so Workwheel did not sell well. The only recourse for B & D Canada was to encourage sales in Canada and hope that the results would be successful enough that the Americans would relaunch the product with greater enthusiasm.

Within B & D it is considered the responsibility of the importing country to prepare the necessary artwork and wording in their language for instruction manuals and accessory information. In Europe literature and guarantee cards are inserted at national warehouses through a "postal slot" in the specially designed carton. For other nations the carton has to be uniquely printed for each nation, which results in higher overall inventories.

Overseas shipment is an additional consideration in the design of export packaging. Air freight is prohibitive and ocean shipments to Europe, Japan, and Australia can take up to six weeks, during which the merchandise (even though packed in containers) can be exposed to harsh climate and rough handling. Good unit carton design and pallet shrink-wrapping prevent much shipping damage.

Armed with product information, price, scheduled introduction time, and production rates, each interested importing subsidiary issued an official Sales Inventory Report. The subsidiary's forecast for the next six months is considered to be a firm order. Nine-month forecasts can be changed, and a twelve-month forecast is updated on a quarterly basis.

When customers require maintenance on their purchase, they bring the tool back to B & D in their nation. There the service department is instructed not only to repair the problem but also to report in detail to B & D Canada so that the product might be redesigned, and so that service parts can be inventoried.

To the Workwheel engineers it is clear that quality control is even more important in products for export than it is for the domestic market. Recalling for repair a product that is 6,000 miles away would be very expensive. Each marketing subsidiary has to stock spare parts, so a good audit system on export products and careful study of spare parts usage rates were deemed to be essential.

By late 1980 it was becoming apparent that Workwheel sales were substantially above forecast in Canada, but that it had not succeeded in the U.S.A. Part of the failure could be attributed to the recession, but the question was also raised as to whether anything could be learned from and improved upon in the decision-making process. Sales and market information are presented in Exhibits 10.6 and 10.7.

EXHIBIT 10.5
Black and Decker (Canada) Inc.

Model Numbers Available April 30, 1980[a]

-00	U.S.A.
-03	Japan
-04	Canada, Brazil (120 V, bilingual packaging)
-05	France, Spain, Brazil (240 V)
-06	Australia, New Zealand, South Africa (220/240 V suppressed)
-07	U.K. (220/240 V suppressed)
-08	Italy
-12	Switzerland (220/240 V suppressed)
-13	Austria, Germany, Belgium, Holland, Scandinavia (220/240 V suppressed)

[a]Available mid- to late 1981, subject to test board approval (where applicable).

EXHIBIT 10.6
Black and Decker (Canada) Inc.

Actual Sales Information as of March, 1981

Canada	Workwheel launched in June 1979. Sales in 1980 were 55% above the forecast of 50,000 units/yr (Exhibit 10.3) and still rising
United States	Workwheel was launched in January 1980. Sales in 1980 were substantially below the forecast of 65,000 units/yr.

Possible explanation of such low sales:
"Not invented here" syndrome
Workwheel was lost amongst the numerous other new B & D products launched in U.S. at that time
Many retailers (facing 20 percent prime interest) refused to start stocking

United Kingdom, France, Germany, Italy	Workwheel was launched, in this sequence, during the spring of 1981.

EXHIBIT 10.7
Black and Decker (Canada) Inc.

Marketing Questionnaire Results

In December 1980, 18 months after the launch of Workwheel in Canada, users were mailed a questionnaire. Results included:

83% of those answering stated that they were either "satisfied" or "very satisfied" with their Workwheel.

87% would recommend it to a friend.

Television appears very influential in the purchase decision, with 64% stating that T.V. was how they learned about the Workwheel.

Workwheel owners tend to own many other tools:
44% own Radial or Table saw
62% own Workmate bench
78% own a Sander.

Type of store where Workwheel was purchased:
39% Canadian Tire (a Canada wide discount chain that began as an automotive supply house, and has since expanded.)
26% Department Stores
15% Hardware Stores
11% Building Supply
9% Other

Introduction

The scope of this book is limited to tactical planning, so we will take the corporate product strategy as given. In General Electric the strategic business units include jet engines, nuclear reactors, light bulbs, small appliances, and about 100 others. This chapter is limited to analyzing the depth of any one product line of one business unit. Kotler (1967, p. 298) calls this the product mix problem. "The company's current product mix is said to be optimal if no adjustment would enhance the company's chances of achieving its objectives. If the company's objective is primarily profit maximization, then the product mix is optimal if profits could not be improved by deleting, modifying, or adding products." For example, the decision problem for this chapter is how many different toasters to sell and how to design each.

A polycentric attitude to product design is that it is most profitable to understand the subtle intricacies of the consumer purchase decision in each nation and to design products to satisfy the consumers' specific preferences. Hence no standardization should be imposed. An ethnocentric attitude about product design follows from a belief that people of all nations basically want a serviceable and inexpensive product; this can best be achieved by standardizing design worldwide and optimizing production to achieve the lowest cost worldwide manufacturing network. This chapter proposes that it is possible to reconcile these two views. In a geocentric corporation, the product is designed in modules, most of which are standard worldwide in order to cut costs, but some of which are tailored to particular desires. The optimal balance depends on both the national markets and the particular product. Let us begin with the polycentric view that national differences do affect sales.

Polycentric View of Product Design

Why did the tea bag, a popular product in America, meet with little success when first introduced in England? Most English housewives believe that good tea is made in a pot, not in a cup. Had the product designer been aware of this cultural difference, he would have designed a four-spoon teabag, without a string, intended for an English teapot. In England, a piece of cake must be strong enough to be held in one hand or to rest on the side of a saucer. A light fancy cake lacks structural integrity. Hence rather than attempting to sell the English a mix for a light fancy cake, the astute marketer would design a mix for a cake with body.

These stereotyped examples illustrate cultural and social factors that might affect a new product's success in England. Scotland is slightly different; Thailand is very different. Unless the product designer is a sensitive person who has experienced a rich multinational life, his own intuition will not provide sufficient input for a design strategy. He will have to plod consciously through many factors which he would have handled intuitively in his home nation. Isn't this too much to ask of one central design team? Shouldn't each nation design its own products?

Climate is a factor that should be considered when designing some products. For example, an automobile in Singapore or Hong Kong must have protection from tropical humidity, whereas a car in Australia or South Africa would require dustproofing. Both features are required in Ghana, where the climate ranges from desert heat to rain forest humidity.

Where there are considerable differences in economic well-being and standards of living, consumers have different needs and different means of satisfying these needs. Motor scooters in Thailand satisfy a need for reliable, affordable transportation; in America, they satisfy a desire for fun and pleasure. To a polycentric corporation this implies two different scooters. A geocentric designer would want to start out designing a basic motor scooter body, with options to be added, depending on the target market: for the American model, flashy chrome, white-walled tires, and an electric start, for the Thai market, a kick start and no frills. These tangible geographic and economic factors are easy to visualize and to consider when designing a product.

Cultural factors are more subtle. They include the values and attitudes of a society and thus, in part, they determine behavior. The preferred cycles of a washing machine vary with culture. In the United States several rinses are desired. The English require a heater capable of boiling the load at the end of the wash cycle. In France and Italy several wash cycle options are called for since the number of options has become a measure of the quality of the machine.

Tradition is another cultural variable that affects a consumer's needs and wants. Even within one nation, a more industrial segment of culture may value novelty, while the less industrial segment may cherish consistency. In Australia, the traditional sign of a good homemaker is the ability to bake a sponge cake from scratch. No seller of sponge cake mixes has yet succeeded in Australia. The norms of tradition prevent the product's acceptance by the consumer.

Consumer tastes vary. The Nestle Corporation has chosen to make over 40 varieties of instant coffee to satisfy international tastes. Heinz ketchup is manufactured to a different recipe in each nation.

Attitudes concerning nationality are important to product design. In some market segments of some countries, the label "Made in U.S.A." or "Made in Switzerland" symbolizes a way of life to which the consumer aspires, and therefore its presence will aid the sales of the particular product. Usually, however, these attitudes prevent a foreign product's successful introduction in a country no matter how excellent the design. Most tourists shopping for souvenirs prefer those made locally rather than a superior product made in Japan.

Government pressure for local manufacturing is felt in those industries whose principal customer is the government or a quasi-government agency. Governments use moral suasion or the threat of tariffs to encourage local production. Having succumbed to this pressure some companies may feel that they should also tailor the product design to local requirements. A polycentric design policy results.

Ethnocentric View of Product Design

Managers who believe that all customers are basically alike also seem to believe that the long-run demand curve for their product is elastic. "If only the price were lower, all those poor people out there could afford our product. The corporation requires its return on investment so we can cut our price only if we cut our costs. Let's standardize."

An ethnocentric market researcher emphasizes that market research panelists must be *informed*. Consumers become informed only through years of trying different products. Therefore, it follows that consumer panel tests performed in advanced nations are more reliable predictors of the purchase behavior of a less developed nation than are consumer panel tests performed in that nation, particularly when the product is unfamiliar to the people of the less developed nation. Hence for some products an ethnocentric U.S. corporation would use the United States as a test market for the world.

There are substantial managerial advantages to worldwide product standardization. As has been mentioned in earlier chapters, there would be savings of time and money since marketing and administrative tasks would be simplified. Economies of scale would be realized through standardized production and tooling equipment and standardized maintenance and repairs. Standardization would allow a redirection of flows of goods between countries such that if there was excess demand in one market, it could be met using the excess capacity in distant plants. This also implies that safety stocks could be reduced. Furthermore, if strikes, fire, or other crises prevented production in one plant, its market could be satisfied by other plants. A reliability analysis of the worldwide factory network is meaningful only if there is design standardization. In Chapter 3 we saw that it is sometimes desirable to alter transfer prices — how much easier to do if there is a rich flow of subassemblies and finished products.

However, there are physical limits to standardization, such as differences in electric voltages or test standards as described in the Black and Decker case. Physical measurements also limit standardization.

Consider the problem of turning steel on a lathe. The lathe can be set to turn to a constant diameter, but only to a certain number of fixed settings. On U.S. lathes, these fixed settings are in inches. On metric lathes used in other countries these fixed settings are in millimeters. To overcome this limit to the export of standardized products, approximate equivalent measures must be used depending on the tolerance and sensitivity of the product. For example, 2¾ inches = 7 centimeters (just over 6.985 centimeters, actually). This search for feasible equivalence typifies geocentric thinking.

Geocentric View of Product Design

The idea of a product may seem intuitively obvious until one analyzes the consumer's motivation to buy. Kotler (1967, p. 288) illustrates the difference with the example of a camera.

> Viewed physically, it is an air filled assembly of metal or plastic parts surrounding a lens. It may come with a case, accessories, and instruction, all packaged in an attractive box bearing a bright brand trade mark. . . . The buyer sees the camera as a means of satisfying certain needs and desires. The camera promises him pleasure, nostalgia, a form of immortality. It may be a means of expressing artistic or craftmanship instincts. It can be a symbol of status and means of relating to other people.

In each market segment of each nation people have different motivations to buy. The challenge to a multinational marketing manager is to capitalize on, and to cater to, different motivations but, at the same time, to keep the manufacturing costs down by producing as much as possible: "an air filled assembly of metal or plastic surrounding a lens."

In Geneva, Switzerland, many cultures coexist and the optimum cycles of a washing machine vary with each culture. To satisfy the varied requirements in Geneva, a geocentric washing machine is sold. The six control variables (fill cold, fill hot, electric heat, agitate, drain, spin) are sequenced and controlled by a clock moved template. When a customer buys a washing machine, the salesman's job includes helping her select the appropriate control templates from a wide selection. Thus a geocentric manager tries to find that point between the marketing and manufacturing extremes of sales maximization and cost minimization which will maximize profits. Certain subassemblies or modules of a product can be standard worldwide, others can be designed for groups of markets having similar behavioral and environmental characteristics, and yet other subassemblies or modules can be tailored to particular segments. When assembled, the product satisfies specific consumer needs, while simultaneously realizing the many benefits of standardization.

The principle of modular design is ancient. Drucker (1974, p. 208) notes:

> The enormous number of Japanese Buddhist temples built between AD 700 and 1600 were built by flexible mass production methods. Each of the temples looks

quite different. And yet each is put together out of essentially standardized parts, such as beams standardized as to width and length; standardized roofing and roof tiles; standardized intervals between the various levels of a pagoda, and so on. The individually distinctive features such as the doors, iron grills, or the ornamentation of the tiles on the roof's edge, were added only at the very end, thus creating brilliant diversity based, however, on true mass production, that is, on standardized parts assembled according to prearranged patterns.

Module Market Research

A multinational corporation may be dealing with as many as 50 nations, the larger of which are subdivided, to yield a total of perhaps 100 market segments. Each segment should be researched separately. Care must be taken to avoid problems of translations and to avoid erroneous conclusions due to different national perceptions of the research questions being posed. This market research is focused on designing the most suitable modules for many regions.

Step 1 (at headquarters). Decide N, the maximum number of items a marketing region should be allowed to sell.

Step 2 (by the regional marketing managers). Given the chance to position N items, decide how you would design each of them. Introspection, unstructured group interviews, and an analysis of complaints are called for. Step 2 identifies attributes desired in each region.

Step 3 (at headquarters). Cluster the regional designs into like groups. A particular design may be wanted in many nations leading to a lower cost of production. Create one design typical of each group, and estimate a lower and upper bound on its unit cost.

Step 4 (in each region). Assemble a small sample of potential customers as a panel. Each individual on the panel is asked to order, in terms of preference, a series of cards. Each card should illustrate a product sample, including products of competitors and designs emerging from Step 3. These data are analyzed in terms of rational/physical and irrational/emotional preferences that would affect purchasing behavior. The regional marketing manager should also interview in depth a few panelists, so that his report to headquarters will clearly articulate the attributes perceived as important. He must also estimate the sales forecast of each of the designs from Step 3.

Step 5 (at headquarters). Aggregate the sales estimates for each design from Step 4 and estimate costs for this volume of sales. Again consider consolidating the designs that seem similar to achieve economies of scale, and estimate the new unit costs for each of the consolidated sales volumes (see Exhibit 10.8).

Step 6 (in each region). The consolidated design incorporates design compromises which reduce the product's utility to consumers of each nation. Conduct market research on the attributes each region views as compromised to determine how much the price would have to be lowered to maintain sales volume.

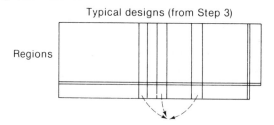

Typical designs (from Step 3)

Regions

EXHIBIT 10.8
Consolidating typical designs for modular design determination.

Step 7 (at headquarters). Consolidation provides cost savings (Step 5) and disutility, which necessitates lower prices (Step 6). These are the data required to determine the product mix — the number of different models and the design attributes of each. (For computer models see Rutenberg and Shaftel, 1971.) Some items will be standardized worldwide, so their design should be refined and then frozen. That having been done, the design of the other subassemblies can proceed in those regions where they will be used and produced.

Step 8 (in each region). Convene a representative panel (larger than Step 4 but smaller than Step 6) and conduct tests of the items and their substitutes so as to evaluate advertising themes; perform a final check on the product attributes. If the variances about the sales estimates remain excessively large, consider staging the launches (Chapter 8). Note that staging would imply rerunning the design program on the restricted demand, which would tend to reduce the number of items marketed, temporarily at least.

The regional managers, aided by market research, have unique knowledge about the desires of their customers, but their only cost estimate is that of local manufacture. A consolidation of designs is prudent only if it results in a lower unit cost. There is an exchange of information between headquarters and the marketing regions because market research is so expensive that it must be focused. The narrower the focus, the less expensive it becomes, but the greater the chances are of misdefining the problem and choosing an inappropriate mix.

One aspect of the product mix problem is the choice of a series of standard sizes. Logarithmic series are used in a systematic and elegant way in the Deutsche Industrie Normen, the famous German DIN standard sizes (Kienzle, 1950). Bongers (1980) describes how DIN and other standards have evolved, and focuses on the economic rationale for standardization. In this chapter the decision on the series of sizes is viewed as an economic reconciliation between economies of scale and the disutility of not providing the customer with his ideal product.

Demands for products are forecast to grow through time and therefore only a few models will be built for product introduction. However, these early models should be designed with an eye to satisfying both present and future needs. Mathematically the problem is analagous to that of plant location; a tentative product is analagous to a tentative plant site, and customer disutility is analagous to transportation cost. Thus the computer models of Chapter 7 can be used for product design.

Module Production Costs

The product is to be designed in modules or subassemblies. A product may have as few as three or four levels — parts preparation, component subassemblies, major subassemblies, and final assembly. More complicated products have more levels. At each level the economies of scale must be analyzed. For example, if complex production methods are used for parts preparation, it would be most economical to produce them centrally and export them to the various plants, thus taking advantage of economies of scale. On the other hand, component subassembly may show few economies of scale; it would be economical to position many such assembly plants around the globe because the transportation costs of components is lower than of finished products. Chapter 7 suggested that a company should evaluate and probably discard innumerable possible plant sites. The focus of this chapter is on using the existing (and seriously contemplated) factories to decide how these facilities affect subassembly design.

Data collection begins with a survey of all plants, to estimate their standard capacities for each of the assembly levels. Many plants will lack the equipment needed for certain levels of production (such as heavy castings) and thus have zero capacity at that level. Other plants may have some flexibility to substitute between levels of production.

As more items are manufactured in a plant, worker and manager confusion increases and the effective capacity of a plant drops. Corporations manufacturing thousands of items use computer controls with items, pallets, and floor locations, each uniquely indexed. The lost capacity arises from an increased number of inventories of work in process, which take up valuable floor space. It also arises from a loss of production time as machines are retooled between items, and from an increased chance of errors and spoilage. Tolerance for the confusion of variety appears to vary by nation, hence we need a separate Exhibit 10.9 for each department in each nation.

From Chapter 6 and from the concepts of reliability introducing Chapter 7, it is clear that a global manufacturing manager can risk holding less inventory if he has several sources of supply for a particular subassembly, as depicted in Exhibit 10.10. While achieving a stated level of assurance of supply a corporation can cut its total safety stock of this item as more of its plants produce an item. Additional inventory savings may also be expected from reduced inventory in transit. A more sophisticated analysis to determine actual inventory safety stocks should consider the capacities

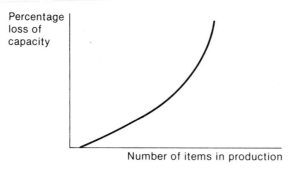

EXHIBIT 10.9
Tolerance for the confusion of variety.

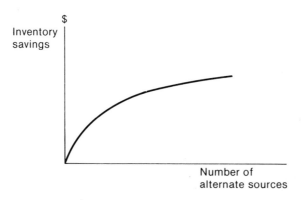

EXHIBIT 10.10
Inventory savings.

of the plants, their excess capabilities, probabilities of supply interruption, the location of inventories, and the lead time to activate potential sub-contractors as was covered in Chapter 6.

Designing to Avoid Tariffs

Chapter 5 presented the rudimentary structure of 120 national tariff classification schemes, in particular the Brussels Tariff Nomenclature (BTN). As the Black and Decker case showed, there is also a structure for nontariff barriers to trade such as national safety and health standards. For each importing nation study the tariff code. For each design, find the relevent BTN six-digit descriptions of the product and each of its components. Think creatively of alternate ways to describe each item to identify material or dimension constraints that might alter the item's tariff classification. Calculate tariff costs before and after redesigning.

Conclusions

If products are designed for the home nation, and then adapted for export, the adaptation itself may be expensive and customers abroad will perceive a disutility. This disutility of a product which is far from the customers' ideal point, presents a ready-made market for a competitor who is sensitive to local desires.

The geocentric theme of this chapter is that a product can be designed in modules, some standard to achieve economies of scale, and others tailored to local desires to reduce customer disutility. The concept of modular design is commonplace, but extending it to multinational marketing requires many years of diligent work.

The case study of Black and Decker Canada's Workwheel describes engineers surmounting diverse technical standards and market preferences. During the 1980s and 1990s a great deal of work will have to be done developing market research procedures that will yield comparable information from peoples of many nationalities, and then learning how to present the information in a form that design engineers can use.

Appendix. Two Market Research Techniques

If we alter a design to standardize a module worldwide, will the customer be perturbed? It depends on the customer's perception of the product. Market research is used to measure customers' perceptions. Two excellent books are Green and Tull's *Research for Marketing Decisions* (1978) and Urban and Hauser's *Design and Marketing of New Products* (1980).

A worldwide marketing research program can be an unwieldy undertaking unless managed with a tight focus. For product design the data needed are the trade-offs between price and several design features and the disutility of not providing a product at the customer's ideal point.

The first market research technique, conjoint analysis, focuses on this trade-off by asking people to rank their preferences. For example, in conducting research about automobiles, ask a person to make a trade-off between two attributes, say speed versus price (see Exhibit 10.11).

By filling in a table a respondent merely has to say that he prefers a 100-mile per hour car that costs $8,500 (his rank 2) to a 130-mile per hour car that costs $14,000 (his rank 3). From this ranking a computer program can calculate the respondent's utility for speed. The computer calculates indifference contours all of the same mathematical shape and noncrossing (Exhibit 10.12.)

A product has many possible attributes, and each becomes a dimension in the space that characterizes the product, over which the respondent has to state preferences. Beyond four dimensions, respondents often become fatigued, which reduces the quality of their responses.

Rather than trying to visualize indifference curves in four dimensions it is more convenient to assign utility levels to each indifference curve. Cross checks within the data give robustness to the conclusions. For example, the trade-offs among price,

Miles per hour

$8500	1	2	5
$14000	3	4	6
$19 500	7	8	9

EXHIBIT 10.11
Input the rankings.

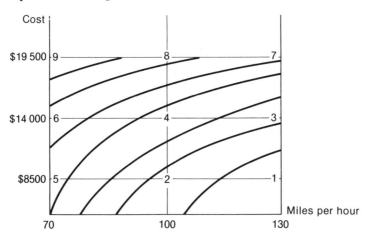

EXHIBIT 10.12
Indifference curves through the rankings.

fuel economy, and speed give additional support to the Exhibit 10.12 price versus speed trade-off.

This analysis has to be repeated for each individual respondent, from the sample of respondents chosen to represent the society. Usually there are competing products already on the market, each with its own characteristics. We have to assume that each respondent will select the product that maximizes his utility. For each of the possible designs, we can count the number of respondents who prefer that design. Our designs differ in cost, so we should produce the one that would maximize our profits.

The second market research technique, nonmetric scaling, can measure products with emotive attributes. The method of conjoint measurement presupposes the product attributes were concrete enough to be described (100 miles per hour, six seats, etc.) or that a sample could be displayed (the color of lemon chartreuse). With nonmetric scaling, the attributes of different brands of beer could be as disparate as taste and social acceptance. (Urban and Hauser, 1980). For example, "Dow" had a strong taste and an old fashioned image, "Labatt" had an intermediate taste and was modern and young, while "Molson" was very strong in taste and evoked an image of average sociability. In Chapter 4 we used nonmetric scaling without even naming dimensions.

For nonmetric scaling there must be at least nine items if the results are to have statistical significance, but rarely should there be more than 15 items if the panelist is to remain alert. Fifteen items means 105 pairs of items. Each pair of products is portrayed on a separate card. The panelists sequence these pairs, ranging from the pair most similar to the pair least similar. As before, a separate map is made for each respondent. The challenge then is to design a product and an advertising campaign such that the product is perceived to have preferred attributes of a particular product space. The several design attempts can be verified only by repeated panel testing.

Products have both physical and emotional appeals. So it seems wise to use both conjoint measurement and nonmetric scaling, their strengths and weaknesses being complementary. Conjoint measurement is easier to administer and less expensive than nonmetric scaling. It can easily handle noncontinuous characteristics such as two, four, or six car seats, and it can handle a large number of attributes, limited only by the respondents' becoming tired. Nonmetric scaling begins with preferences between product pairs, and it is the computer program that calculates the attributes (which still remain to be named). It can depict an ambiance and guide the way to attributes never thought of before (but only two or three). Finally, nonmetric scaling is less dependent on language and the authenticity of translation because it could use physical objects or pictures.

Questions from Other Viewpoints

1. *Corporate Rational Normative Global.* You just covered this viewpoint in the chapter.
2. *Corporate Rational Normative Subsidiary.* Suppose that the initial product design configuration was made by sampling 10 different national subsidiaries. Your subsidiary was not included. Given that headquarters has established a tentative design, what information do you and other subsidiaries have to submit to achieve a global optimum?
3. *Corporate Rational Descriptive Global.* Consider a simple electric typewriter. The proposal of this chapter is the processing of information pertinent to a typewriter designer. Systematically prepare an estimate of how many variables would have to be collected to achieve this goal. Give a numerical estimate.
4. *Corporate Rational Descriptive Subsidiary.* A most necessary input to product design decisions is the market research done by each subsidiary. Which techniques would be most accurate in an illiterate market where no similar products have yet to be marketed? (Remember that illiterate people may be very intelligent.)
5. *Corporate Emotional Normative Global.* Why is it important to keep one common logo, one consistent set of trademarks, one design *style* that represents the corporation worldwide?
6. *Corporate Emotional Normative Subsidiary.* Even though headquarters executives make speeches worldwide about how geocentric they are, to you in your subsidiary they seem thoroughly ethnocentric. A headquarters design team will be visiting you soon for two days. What can you do to make them very aware of the design peculiarities of your nation? Prepare a specific agenda for their visit.

7. *Corporate Emotional Descriptive Global.* The chapter has implicitly described a product designer as being rather mechanical. Describe the kinds of characteristics needed to appreciate the variety of impressions around the world of the use of one product. Describe the travel and continuous practice a designer must sustain.

8. *Corporate Emotional Descriptive Subsidiary.* Give some examples of foreign products in your nation whose designs are inappropriate. Be very specific as to what should be learned from each.

9. *Societal Rational Normative Global.* Select two major religions that span many nations. Compare and contrast how they adapt to local myths and images while simultaneously having an international integrity, a brotherhood of all believers.

10. *Societal Rational Normative National.* You work in the Ministry of Culture of a nation with a long and rich heritage of artistic handicrafts, such that patterns of symbols, textures, and form are all identifiable with your nation. The bland, cheap, standardized designs of the multinationals, homogenized to the lowest common denominator of global mediocrity, are slowly undercutting the livelihood of your artists, guardians of your cultural heritage. Your Minister has complained to the Minister of Industry, an economist by training, who told your Minister about cost/benefit analysis. Your Minister feels badly outgunned by the language of Industry, but also deeply feels his conviction. Please prepare a one-page outline that your Minister can use to undercut the Minister of Industry.

11. *Societal Rational Descriptive Global.* Almost every nation has government regulations about the environment that affect product design concerning, for example, noise, pollution, and safety. These regulations change frequently, both by statute and interpretation, and monitoring the laws requires systematic organization. Describe other monitoring organizations that face similar challenges. Clarify how their organization may provide templates for corporations attempting to keep up to date with developments in product design legislation.

12. *Societal Rational Descriptive National.* Describe examples of differences in the extent of coverage allowed by patent law in two or more nations.

13. *Societal Emotional Normative Global.* One virtue of ethnocentric design is that it is blatantly foreign. This contrasts with modular design, which is really a subversion of national taste, convincing a nation to adopt a product that has been adapted to its tastes in an artificial way. It could be seen as a pernicious form of neocolonialism. Prepare a one-page manifesto expounding on the idea that all products be labeled "Design conceived by Americans" (or Germans, or whomever).

14. *Societal Emotional Normative National.* The artistic soul of your nation cries out for articulation. Yet your poets, artists, musicians,

and dancers can no longer live on their talent. Meanwhile cheap, bland designs encroach upon your citizens' sensibilities. As Minister of Culture, a poet by training, what can you do?

15. *Societal Emotional Descriptive Global.* Is it possible for people to feel the disorientation of withdrawal symptoms if a product that they were long familiar with is suddenly no longer available (declared obsolete, and replaced by a new, improved version)? For which kinds of societies might this be a problem?

16. *Societal Emotional Descriptive National.* You work for a market research and public opinion polling organization that combines imaginative flair with statistical rigor. A major charitable foundation has decided, for reasons known best to themselves, to fund a "census" every 10 years for the next 100 years to measure the aesthetic sense of the people. Your boss, knowing your powers of imagination, has turned this possible client over to you to evaluate whether your organization could contribute information about likely movements in aesthetic values during the next 100 years. Prepare two pages of conceivable ideas about: (a) Questions to put directly to an individual; (b) Indirect and unobtrusive measures of aesthetics.

Bibliography to Chapter 10

Bongers, C., *Standardization* (Boston/The Hague: Martinus Nijhoff, 1980).

Claycamp, Henry J. and William F. Massey, "A Theory of Market Segmentation," *Marketing Research*, Vol. 5 (1968), pp. 388-394.

Drucker, Peter, *Management* (New York: Harper and Row, 1974).

Green, Paul E. and Donald S. Tull, *Research for Marketing Decisions* (Englewood Cliffs, NJ: Prentice-Hall, 1978).

Keegan, Warren J., "Multinational Product Planning: Strategic Alternatives," *Journal of Marketing*, Vol. 33 (1969), pp. 58-62.

Kienzle, Otto, *Normungzahlen* (Berlin: Springerverlag, 1950).

Kolde, Endel J., *International Business Enterprise* (Englewood Cliffs, NJ: Prentice-Hall, 1968), pp. 317-321.

Kotler, Philip, *Marketing Management* (Englewood Cliffs, NJ: Prentice-Hall, 1967).

Rutenberg, David P. and Timothy Shaftel, "Product Design: Subassemblies for Multiple Markets," *Management Science*, Vol. 18, No. 4 (1971), pp. 220-231.

Sadowski, Wieslaw, "A Few Remarks on the Assortment Problem," *Management Science*, Vol. 6 (1959), pp. 13-24.

Starr, Martin K., "Modular Production — A New Concept," *Harvard Business Review*, Vol. 43, No. 6, November-December 1965, pp. 131-142.

Wolfson, M.L., "Selecting the Best Lengths to Stock," *Operations Research*, Vol. 13, No. 2 (1965), pp. 570-585.

Urban, Glen L. and John R. Hauser, *Design and Marketing of New Products* (Englewood Cliffs, NJ: Prentice-Hall, 1980).

To a multinational corporation only markets are anchored to nations. Factories, sources of capital, and executives can move, but they move in relation to the markets of the nations. This is the familiar marketing concept, extended on a global scale.

National markets are more than anchors in a floating world. Each market constitutes a real asset. Although this asset does not appear on a corporate balance sheet, the corporate name with both consumers and distribution channels is an asset to be invested in, maintained, and cared for. This is the basis for polycentric thinking, for the surest way to deflate the intangible asset of a name is to impose foreign standards in marketing. It is safest to let each nation market in its own way.

Nevertheless, there is a chance to increase expected profit — though at some risk, however slight — by headquarters coordinating *some* marketing decisions. The decisions of marketing managers are traditionally summarized as price, promotion, product, and place.

"Place" was the central theme of Chapter 8, "New Product Launch." In a multinational corporation it makes sense to think carefully about where in the world to begin launching a new product. The advantage to being multinational derives from the fact that the early markets (where the product was first launched) can be viewed as massive sources of market research information, of quite a different nature, and a useful complement to consumer panel tests.

"Price" is covered in Chapter 9, "Pricing." In inflationary times it is particularly difficult to set incentive schemes so that salesmen, those closest to the customer, have an incentive to increase prices fast enough. Because inflation rates differ in different nations, it is difficult to sustain pricing harmony on a global basis. Customers with international intelligence will want to buy where the product is cheapest, and ship it themselves. This possibility pressures the multinational to keep some harmony in its prices for an item. As a rule of thumb, a competitor with a large market share finds it more profitable to pursue a new market segment with a specific marketing campaign rather than an across the board price cut. In general, multinationals have large market shares, and so tend to be careful about adjusting price.

"Product" is covered in Chapter 10, "Product Design." A product has both physical and psychological attributes. In a multinational corporation a substantial cost reduction can be achieved if much of the product design can be standardized. The psychological attributes of the product, specific to a particular nation, can best be accommodated by tailoring the advertising of the product and some few physical attributes.

"Promotion" used to be centralized in some multinational corporations.

The high fixed cost of developing advertising compaigns could then be spread over wider markets. During the 1970s the disadvantages of common promotion became apparent as the significance of nationalism became apparent. During the 1980s common promotion is used for only a few products.

PART FOUR

Multinational Executive Development

CHAPTER ELEVEN

International Executive Development

Introductory Note to the Case

The Road to Hell . . .

A government foreign service officer, after reading this case, commented that it was simplistic and that no experienced diplomat would ever commit a series of blunders such as John Baker's. Young diplomats occasionally do silly things, and are removed from the foreign service if they fail to learn how to undo minor errors. "Of course," he continued, "international businessmen can't afford such luxury of selection, supervision and coaching."

Most students find this case a release from the analysis of the earlier chapters. All readers use the case as a mirror in which they see aspects of themselves in both John Baker and Matt Rennalls. Each of us is a little ethnocentric.

One sad part of the case is Baker, who seems to have learned so little from his opportunities in the Far East, several countries of Africa, and Germany, a string of assignments far richer than most people have the opportunity to experience.

Clearly, although foreign assignments are necessary they are not sufficient to becoming a competent international executive. For this reason the text of the chapter deals both with the quantitative and the qualitative aspects of executive development.

The Road to Hell . . .

John Baker, chief engineer of the Caribbean Bauxite Company of Barracania in the West Indies, was making his final preparations to leave the island. His promotion to production manager of Keso Mining Corporation near Winnipeg — one of Continental Ore's fast-expanding Canadian enterprises — had been announced a month earlier and now everything had been tidied up except the last vital interview with his successor — an able young Barracanian, Matthew Rennalls. It was vital that this interview be a success and that Rennalls should leave the office uplifted and encouraged to face the challenge of his new job. A touch on the bell would have brought Rennalls walking into the room but Baker delayed a moment and gazed thoughtfully through the window considering just exactly what he was going to say and, more particularly, how he was going to say it.

John Baker, an English expatriate, was 45 years old and had served his 23 years with Continental Ore in many different places: the Far East; several countries of Africa; Europe; and, for the last two years, in the West Indies. He hadn't cared much for his previous assignment in Hamburg and was delighted when the West Indian appointment came through. Climate was not the only attraction. Baker had always preferred working overseas (in what were termed the developing countries) because he felt he had an innate knack — better than most other expatriates working for Continental Ore — of knowing just how to get on with regional staff. Twenty-four hours in Barracania, however, made him realize that he would need all of this "innate knack" if he was to deal effectively with the problems in this field that now awaited him.

At his first interview with Hutchins, the production manager, the whole problem of Rennalls and his future was discussed. There and then it was made quite clear to Baker that one of his most important tasks would be the "grooming" of Rennalls as his successor. Hutchins had pointed out that not only was Rennalls one of the brightest Barracanian prospects on the staff of Caribbean Bauxite — at London University he had taken first-class honors in the B.Sc. Engineering Degree — but, being the son of the Minister of Finance and Economic Planning, he also had no small political pull.

This case was prepared by Mr. Gareth Evans and is reproduced with his permission.

350

The company had been particularly pleased when Rennalls decided to work for them rather than for the government in which his father had such a prominent post. They ascribed his action to the effect of their vigorous and liberal regionalization program which, since World War II, had produced 18 Barracanians at mid-management level and given Caribbean Bauxite a good lead in this respect over all other international concerns operating in Barracania. The success of this timely regionalization policy has led to excellent relations with the government—a relationship which had been given an added importance when Barracania, three years later, became independent, an occasion that encouraged a critical and challenging attitude toward the role foreign interests would have to play in the new Barracania. Hutchins therefore had little difficulty in convincing Baker that the successful career development of Rennalls was of the first importance.

The interview with Hutchins had been held two years earlier, and Baker, leaning back in his office chair, reviewed just how successful he had been in the "grooming" of Rennalls. Which aspects of Rennalls' character had helped and which had hindered? The first item to go on the credit side would, without question, be the ability of Rennalls to master the technical aspects of his job. From the start he had shown keenness and enthusiasm and had often impressed Baker with his ability in tackling new assignments and the constructive comments he invariably made in departmental discussions. He was popular with all ranks of Barracanian staff and had an ease of manner which stood him in good stead when dealing with his expatriate seniors. These were all assets, but what about the debit side?

First and foremost, there was his racial consciousness. His four years at London University had accentuated this feeling and made him sensitive to any sign of condescension on the part of expatriates. It may have been to give expression to this sentiment that, as soon as he returned home from London, he threw himself into politics on behalf of the United Action Party, which was later to win the preindependence elections and provide the country with its first Prime Minister.

The ambitions of Rennalls—and he certainly was ambitious—did not, however, lie in politics for, staunch nationalist as he was, he saw that he could serve himself and his country best by putting his engineering talent to the best use possible, for was not bauxite responsible for nearly half the value of Barracania's export trade? On this account, Hutchins found that he had an unexpectedly easy task in persuading Rennalls to give up his political work before entering the production department as an assistant engineer.

It was, Baker knew, Rennalls' well-repressed sense of race consciousness that had prevented their relationship from being as close as it should have been. On the surface, nothing could have seemed more agreeable. Formality between the two men was at a minimum; Baker was delighted to find that his assistant shared his own peculiar "shaggy dog" sense of humor so that jokes were continually being exchanged; they entertained each other at their houses and often played tennis together — and yet the barrier remained invisible, indefinable, but ever present. The existence of this "screen" between them was a constant source of frustration to Baker since it indicated a weakness he was loath to accept. If successful with all other nationalities, why not with Rennalls?

But at least he had managed to "break through" to Rennalls more successfully than any other expatriate. In fact, it was the young Barracanian's attitude — sometimes overbearing, sometimes cynical — toward other company expatriates that had been one of the subjects Baker had raised last year when he discussed Rennalls' staff report with him. He knew, too, that he would have to raise the same subject again in the forthcoming interview because Jackson, the senior draftsman, had complained only yesterday about the rudeness of Rennalls. With this thought in mind, Baker leaned forward and spoke into the intercom. "Would you come in Matt, please? I'd like a word with you," and later, "Do sit down," proffering the box, "Have a cigarette." He paused while he held out his lighter and then went on.

"As you know, Matt, I'll be off to Canada in a few days' time, and before I go, I thought it would be useful if we could have a final chat together. It is indeed with some deference that I suggest I can be of help. You will shortly be sitting in this chair doing the job I am now doing, but I, on the other hand, am 10 years older, so perhaps you can accept the idea that I may be able to give you the benefit of my longer experience."

Baker saw Rennalls stiffen slightly in his chair as he made this point so added in explanation, "You and I have attended enough company courses to remember those repeated requests by the personnel manager to tell people how they are getting on as often as the convenient moment arises and not just the automatic 'once a year' when, by regulation, staff reports have to be discussed."

Rennalls nodded his agreement so Baker went on. "I shall

always remember the last job performance discussion I had with my previous boss back in Germany. He used what he called the "plus and minus" technique. His firm belief was that when a senior, by discussion, seeks to improve the work performance of his staff, his prime objective should be to make sure that the latter leaves the interview encouraged and inspired to improve. Any criticism must, therefore, be constructive and helpful. He said that one very good way to encourage a man—and I fully agree with him—is to tell him about his good points—the plus factors—as well as his weak ones—the minus factors—so I thought, Matt, it would be a good idea to run our discussion along these lines."

Rennalls offered no comment, so Baker continued. "Let me say, therefore, right away, that, as far as your own work performance is concerned, the plus far outweighs the minus. I have, for instance, been most impressed with the way you have adapted your considerable theoretical knowledge to master the practical techniques of your job—that ingenious method you used to get air down to the fifth-shaft level is a sufficient case in point—and at departmental meetings I have invariably found your comments well taken and helpful. In fact, you will be interested to know that only last week I reported to Mr. Hutchins that, from the technical point of view, he could not wish for a more able man to succeed to the position of chief engineer."

"That's very good indeed of you, John." cut in Rennalls with a smile of thanks, "My only worry now is how to live up to such a high recommendation."

"Of that I am quite sure," returned Baker, "especially if you can overcome the minus factor which I would like now to discuss with you. It is one which I have talked about before so I'll come straight to the point. I have noticed that you are more friendly and get on better with your fellow Barracanians than you do with Europeans. In point of fact, I had a complaint only yesterday from Mr. Jackson, who said you had been rude to him—and not for the first time either.

"There is, Matt, I am sure, no need to tell you how necessary it will be for you to get on well with expatriates because until the company has trained sufficient men of your calibre, Europeans are bound to occupy senior positions here in Barracania. All this is vital to your future interests, so can I help you in any way?"

While Baker was speaking on this theme, Rennalls had sat tensed in his chair and it was some seconds before he replied. "It is quite extraordinary, isn't it, how one can convey an impression to others so at variance with what one intends? I can only assure you once again that my disputes with Jackson — and you may remember also Godson — have had nothing at all to do with the color of their skins. I promise you that if a Barracanian had behaved in an equally peremptory manner I would have reacted in precisely the same way. And again, if I may say it within these four walls, I am sure I am not the only one who has found Jackson and Godson difficult. I could mention the names of several expatriates who have felt the same. However, I am really sorry to have created this impression of not being able to get on with Europeans — it is an entirely false one — and I quite realize that I must do all I can to correct it as quickly as possible. On your last point, regarding Europeans holding senior positions in the company for some time to come, I quite accept the situation. I know that Caribbean Bauxite — as they have been doing for many years now — will promote Barracanians as soon as their experience warrants it. And, finally, I would like to assure you, John — and my father thinks the same too — that I am very happy in my work here and hope to stay with the company for many years to come."

Rennalls had spoken earnestly and, although not convinced by what he had heard, Baker did not think he could pursue the matter further except to say, "All right, Matt, my impression *may* be wrong, but I would like to remind you about the truth of that old saying, 'What is important is not what is true but what is believed.' Let it rest at that."

But suddenly Baker knew that he didn't want to "let it rest at that." He was disappointed once again at not being able to "break through" to Rennalls and having yet again to listen to his bland denial that there was any racial prejudice in his makeup. Baker, who had intended ending the interview at this point, decided to try another tack.

"To return for a moment to the 'plus and minus technique' I was telling you about just now, there is another plus factor I forgot to mention. I would like to congratulate you not only on the calibre of your work but also on the ability you have shown in overcoming a challenge which I, as a European, have never had to meet.

"Continental Ore is, as you know, a typical commercial enterprise — admittedly a big one — which is a product of the economic and social environment of the United States and Western Europe. My ancestors have all been brought up in this environment for the past 200 or 300 years and I have, therefore, been able to live in a world in which commerce (as we know it today) has been part and parcel of my being. It has not been something revolutionary and new which has suddenly entered my life. In your case," went on Baker, "the situation is different because you and your forebears have only had some 50 or 60 years' experience of this commercial environment. You have had to face the challenge of bridging the gap between 50 and 300 years. Again, Matt, let me con-gratulate you — and people like you — on having so success-fully overcome this particular hurdle. It is for this very reason that I think the outlook for Barracania — and particularly Caribbean Bauxite — is so bright."

Rennalls had listened intently and when Baker finished, replied, "Well, once again, John, I have to thank you for what you have said, and, for my part, I can only say that it is gratifying to know that my own personal effort has been so much appreciated. I hope that more people will soon come to think as you do."

There was a pause and, for a moment, Baker thought hopefully that he was about to achieve his long-awaited "breakthrough," but Rennalls merely smiled back. The barrier remained unbreached. There remained some five minutes' cheerful conversation about the contrast between the Caribbean and Canadian climate and whether the West Indies cricket team had any hope of beating England in the Fifth Test March before Baker drew the interview to a close. Although he was as far as ever from knowing the real Rennalls, he was nevertheless glad that the interview had run along in this friendly manner and, particularly, that it had ended on such a cheerful note.

This feeling, however, lasted only until the following morn-ing. Baker had some farewells to make, so he arrived at the office considerably later than usual. He had no sooner sat down at his desk than his secretary walked into the room with a worried frown on her face. Her words came fast. "When I arrived this morning I found Mr. Rennalls already waiting at my door. He seemed very angry and told me in quite a peremptory manner that he had a vital letter to dic-tate which must be sent off without any delay. He was so worked up that he couldn't keep still and kept pacing the room, which is most unlike him. He wouldn't even wait to read what he had dictated. Just signed the page where he thought the letter would end. It has been distributed and your copy is in your in-basket."

Puzzled and feeling vaguely uneasy, Baker opened the "Confidential" envelope and read the following letter:

14 August 19xx
From: Assistant Engineer
To: The Chief Engineer, Caribbean Bauxite Limited
Assessment of Interview Between Messrs. Baker and Rennalls

It has always been my practice to respect the advice given me by seniors, so after our interview, I decided to give careful thought once again to its main points and so make sure that I had understood all that had been said. As I promised you at the time, I had every intention of putting your advice to the best effect.

It was not, therefore, until I had sat down quietly in my home yesterday evening to consider the interview objectively that its main purport became clear. Only then did the full enormity of what you said dawn on me. The more I thought about it, the more convinced I was that I had hit upon the real truth — and the more furious I became. With a facility in the English language which I — a poor Barracanian — cannot hope to match, you had the audacity to insult me (and through me every Barracanian worth his salt) by claiming that our knowledge of modern living is only a paltry 50 years old whilst yours goes back 200–300 years. As if your materialistic commercial environment could possibly be compared with the spiritual values of our culture. I'll have you know that if much of what I saw in London is representative of your most boasted culture, I hope fervently that it will never come to Barracania. By what right do you have the effrontery to condescend to us? At heart, all you Europeans think us barbarians, or, as you say amongst yourselves, we are "just down from the trees."

Far into the night I discussed this matter with my father, and he is as disgusted as I. He agrees with me that any company whose senior staff think as you do is no place for any Barracanian proud of his culture and race — so much for all the company "clap-trap" and specious propaganda about regionalization and Barracania for the Barracanians.

I feel ashamed and betrayed. Please accept this letter as my resignation which I wish to become effective immediately.

c.c. Production Manager
      Managing Director

Questions

1. Evaluate John Baker with respect to each of IBM's six psychological dimensions of a good international executive as outlined in this chapter.
2. Which of Erikson's eight stages of man's development best describes the behavior of Matthew Rennalls? Of John Baker?

3. Cross-cultural work attracts some individuals who want a change from a blocked career. Others are discontented with their own society. Still others are overly idealistic. What is John Baker's motivation for cross-cultural work?

4. Given Rennall's sense of racial consciousness, what might have motivated his decision to work for the foreign-owned Continental Ore Company rather than for the Barracanian government or the United Action Party?

5. Many U.S. corporations still fear that their Japanese managers are more loyal to Japan than they are to their corporation. Is there any evidence that Continental Ore need be concerned with divided loyalties in Barracania?

6. Drawing from your knowledge of management psychology evaluate the pluses and minuses of John Baker's "plus and minus" technique.

7. You are Baker's boss; Baker's salary is substantial. Identify the executive positions in Continental Ore where he can function and contribute more than his salary costs. (Are these positions more valuable as steppingstone training experience for the training of other upcoming managers?) Baker has 20 years to retirement. If you fail to forsee an adequate set of jobs to offer him, prepare notes to help you during your interview with Baker when you fire him.

8. John Baker has applied for a job with Brunswick Mining and Smelting Company. As part of a letter of recommendation for him draft one paragraph evaluating his "innate knack" and another explaining the Barracanian incident.

9. Given the task that faced John Baker when he came to Barracania and given your reconstruction of his personality when he joined Continental Ore at age 22, what sequence of jobs in Continental might have better prepared him?

Introduction

As has been shown in Chapters 2 to 10, the functional activities of finance, production, and marketing require agenda to mesh them smoothly into a global network. For a matrix organization, the geocentric archetype of this book, the agendas become particularly complex. Yet, as pointed out in Chapter 1, the intricate coordination of a geocentric organization depends on effective and capable international executives. The personal contacts necessary to make a matrix organization work take years to nurture. Therefore, the corporation must develop international executives adequate for its overall long-term objectives.

Newly recruited employees rarely move directly into the grooming process because the risk of their leaving the company is too great. If systematic development begins at age 25, with the hope of producing a capable international executive at age 55, the process of development can be only 30 years in duration. If assignments average three years in duration, there is room for only 10 major assignments in the grooming of an international executive. In this chapter, the series of assignments an individual uses will be likened to steppingstones across a river.

This chapter sketches the future management needs of the corporation and *describes* a model for an executive development program. The chapter begins with a consideration of how the future management needs of the corporation are projected and continues with a discussion of program development — the selection and assignment of chosen individuals to the steppingstones of their careers. Compensation and assessment of performance are also discussed.

Future Management Needs

The future management needs of the corporation must be forecast quantitatively and qualitatively. Considering the heavy investment in human capital, it is better that a forecast of need be approximately right rather than precisely wrong.

Quantitative Forecast

Few corporations, particularly young multinationals, have conceptualized their need for executives 30 years hence. Actually, most personnel managers are more aware of their pension fund liabilities in 2010 than they are of their need for executives then. To implement a program of executive development, the initial step is to forecast the needs.

From the corporate planning group of your corporation or the corporation you are considering, get an estimate of the rate of growth of the corporation as a constant percentage over the next 30 years. Because productivity can be forecast to increase, let g be the growth in sales minus productivity growth.

To calculate future management needs assume, for simplification, that the organization will remain hierarchical in structure, with one chief executive officer and a constant span of control. His span of control is c, and each of these people in turn controls c people in the level below, and so on. From the top to the bottom, each level is ranked 1, 2, 3, . . . , where $n + 1$ is the bottom level ($n + 1$ levels are used for simplicity in calculations).

Since there is 1 person in level 1 and c people in level 2, at the bottom level $n + 1$ there should be c^n workers. Call this number of workers $W = c^n$. The growth factor g is applied to these W workers. The need for future managers for all the levels above can be calculated.

g = growth rate (for example, 5 percent growth is written as $g = 1.05$).

n_0 = number of levels within the organization now at time $t = 0$.

W_0 = number of bottom level workers now at time $t = 0$.

Spans of control of various groups differ within the organization. Now at time $t = 0$, the *average* span of control c can be calculated because

$$\log c = \frac{\log W_0}{n_0}$$

Thus to find the span of control

$$c = \text{antilog} \ \frac{\log W_0}{n_0}$$

Positions in each of the original levels of the organization will grow. Because this is compound interest, the number of years to double size, multiplied by the growth rate, will equal 70. For example, if the number of workers is forecast to grow at 5 percent per year, the number of positions in each existing management level will double every 14 years ($70/5 = 14$).

Thus in addition to the expansion of existing positions, new levels will have to be created: As the organization grows, the number of levels will have to increase. The manager of key personnel has the immediate task of forecasting steppingstones over the next year as well as the long-run task of envisioning steppingstones 10, 20, and 30 years hence. In the long run, newly created layers of the organization will increase the rate of growth of executive positions. The number of levels in the organization at time t can be projected using the forecast number of workers ($W_t = g^t W_0$).

At time t, the number of levels becomes

$$n(t) = \frac{t \log g}{\log c} + n(0)$$

or

$$\frac{\text{number of}}{\text{levels}} = \frac{\text{number of}}{\text{years}} \times \frac{\log (\text{growth rate})}{\log (\text{span of control})} + \frac{\text{original number}}{\text{of levels}}$$

At the present ($t = 0$), there are W_0 bottom-level employees $[W_0 = c^n(0)]$. The number of managers needed for the organization is the sum of a geometric series approximated as follows:
Current number of managers:

$$M_0 = \frac{[c^n(0) - 1]}{(c-1)} = \frac{\text{original number of bottom level workers}}{\text{span of control} - 1}$$

So at time t, the number of managers will be

$$M_t = \frac{[c^n(t) - 1]}{(c-1)} = \frac{\text{forecast number of bottom level worker}}{\text{span of control} - 1}$$

The new positions evolved would be the difference of this value and the value at time 0.

$$M_t - M_0 = \text{new positions over the time period 0 to } t.$$

$$\frac{[c^n(t) - c^n(0)]}{(c-1)} = \frac{\text{forecast number of bottom-level workers}}{\text{span of control} - 1} - \frac{\text{original number of bottom-level workers}}{}$$

The manager of key personnel originally had M_0 steppingstones on which to place aspiring executives for their individual career development. As the organization grows, the number of steppingstone positions also grows. The foregoing calculation of M_t shows the placement challenge the manager of key personnel can anticipate.

The manager of key personnel also has data on turnover and topping-out, although frequently they are buried in old personnel records. Suppose that for 2010 the corporation is forecast to need 50 executives at the vice-presidential level and above. How many individuals born after 1950, who now seem capable of ultimately working at that level, should it now be guiding upward? Some will withdraw for medical reasons, others will decide that it's not worth the effort, and others will be judged not capable. On the other hand, a few will have been overlooked and will appear from within the corporation, and a few positions will exist into which capable outsiders can be recruited and still have time to master the corporation. The manager of key personnel needs to forecast flows on these five tributaries to his mainstream goal of developing 50 vice presidents. A variety of analytic techniques have been used—from guesses to Markov chains (Vroom and MacCrimmon, 1968) which transform masses of data into the five tributaries.

After the number of positions has been forecast and the turnover estimated, the next step is to census the corporation's available cadre of potential executives of each age group. Most corporations have peculiar voids in the demographic age distributions of their managers, often quite different in each major national subsidiary. This data analysis can be performed quietly from existing personnel records.

The manager of key personnel can thereby assess the severity of the corporation's problem, and can forecast years of particular strain. This information may be valuable feedback to the corporate planning group, which provided the original growth forecasts g.

Certain age cohorts of future executives have been identified as being in short supply. One remedy is to hire outsiders now and acculturate them. The second remedy is to search harder for people of the right age within the corporation who could conceivably function as executives. The third remedy is to work systematically to reduce the turnover of this cohort. Once current executives agree that these steps are necessary, one can justify thinking explicitly about investing in human capital, articulating the attributes of executives and jobs, and ascertaining how particular positions help people develop.

Qualitative Forecast

The qualities that a good international executive might need in 2010 must be forecast for this corporation. In general, he or she must possess certain levels of interpersonal skills, technical or functional skills, and personal skills. Acquiring these skills depends on the individual's own initiative in becoming involved in necessary experiences and in developing appropriate attitudes and aptitudes. The corporation can remove impediments from the individual's growth path and provide the appropriate opportunities or steppingstones. Even this corporate work requires incredibly hard thinking because of the number of executive candidates. Nevertheless, the essential work has to be done within the individual's mind.

The technical and functional skills come from experience. The precise qualities vary by corporation, so let me create an example of an experienced cosmopolitan executive for the year 2010. She or he must have managed at least four different types of product (one competitively dominant and one competitively weak each in a high-growth industry and in a stagnant industry). She or he must have assimilated the pressures of different managerial positions (line manager, project integrator, and staff analyst) and experienced different types of business relationship (mergers, joint ventures, divestments). She or he must be competent in accounting and treasury operations, manufacturing and labor relations, marketing and negotiating. She or he must have lived in at least five nations: exposure to different types of national behavior, each affected by economic wealth, political sympathies, and cultural attitudes, is invaluable. Attitudes in a communist country differ greatly from those of capitalist and from religiously dominated countries, and a cosmopolitan executive should have experienced each. An individual with this portfolio of experiences by the year 2010 would probably be useful to most multi-national corporations, though each will have its unique requirements in addition.

As was mentioned earlier, this variety of experience has to be fitted into 10 steppingstone positions. The corporation needs executives who have not only lived in these different environments but have internalized and integrated this variety of experience to enable them to adapt to any new and unfamiliar environment. In the face of long-run uncertainty, executive adaptability assures the corporation's survival; the executive may not be perfect but at least he or she can cope. The executive's attitude determines the extent to which he or she integrates experience into his or her personality. Attitude is dependent on many factors, of which family and cultural background are primary. Sometimes a person who superficially appears to have the multinational attitude may be a completely inappropriate nomad:

> The person who runs away from his family of origin is as emotionally dependent as the one who never leaves home. They both need emotional closeness, but they are allergic to it. The one who runs away geographically is more inclined to impulsive behavior. He tends to see the problem as being in the parents and running away as being a method of gaining independence from the parents. The more intensive the cutoff, the more he is vulnerable to duplicating the pattern with the parents with the first available other person. He can get into an impulsive marriage. When problems develop in the marriage, he tends also to run away from those. Exaggerated versions . . . occur in relationship nomads, vagabonds, and hermits who either have superficial relationships or give up and live alone. (Bowen, 1978, pp. 382–383)

Most psychological theory claims that a person's ambitions and motivations stem from background pressures. With each foreign assignment, both the executive and the executive's family must adjust to the culture shock of an alien environment. The executive can become conscious of how cultural biases affect actions. In the case that opened this chapter, for example, John Baker had the attitude that Barracaneans were inferior. With the inevitability of a Greek tragedy, his attitude led to the loss of two able executives at a crucial time. Tolerance for the ambiguity of multiple viewpoints is a necessary asset of international executives; it is even better if executives desire and enjoy multiple viewpoints. Motivation and initiative are vital to the success of their work and self-development. An individual must *want* to become an international manager to relish the rigors of the development process. To this end, individuals should be consulted in a straightforward manner concerning decisions about their future career. They need counseling while setting achievable goals.

Aptitude is closely linked to attitude. Nobody should plunge into the 30-year development process without feeling sure that he or she has the necessary aptitude. Objectivity requires independence of thought, which is not possible without a certain level of intelligence. Sensitivity to emotional and physical changes is crucial to interpersonal contact. One must possess empathy to work with people of another culture. Decisiveness may also be thought of as an aptitude. Managers must be able to initiate and implement plans. They must be able to make intelligent guesses and be willing to change a course of action should the need arise. In essence, managers need the prowess to manage a changing environment.

The preceding description of an international manager stresses the need for a multiskilled individual who is not only technically competent but also possesses self-descipline through self-knowledge. Self-knowledge accompanied by self-discipline permits executives to retain a sense of integrity in the face of a totally foreign environment, allowing them to gain understanding from the tensions of their position rather than feeling so vulnerable that they need to shut tensions out.

In addition to personal skills, a cosmopolitan executive must have well-honed interpersonal skills. He or she must possess the ability to communicate: powers of suasion are vital for a manager, especially when there is cultural and organizational conflict. The executive must have the sensitivity to realize the underlying motives of human reactions.

An IBM World Trade study summarized these necessary qualities:

1. Self-confidence to manage change.
2. Organization to think clearly.
3. Activity or energy level.
4. Influence or persuasion.
5. Communication abilities.
6. Interpersonal sensitivity, ability to develop the confidence of subordinates while exercising authority.

This section has sketched the qualities of an international executive for the year 2010. With this goal in mind, the series of 10 steppingstones can now be designed. The challenge lies in the number of executive candidates to be considered simultaneously.

Program Development

In the headquarters of a corporation there is usually a manager of key personnel, not with line power to decide promotions but with the staff assignment of keeping files on executive candidates. The task of the manager of key personnel is to monitor all stages of growth of each executive candidate toward a level within the organization where the candidate's potential is fully realized.

For every executive, the manager of key personnel usually keeps a replacement list of qualified individuals who could fill each position if the occupant were to vacate it by death, transfer, or quitting (Lee, 1977). Replacement tables are necessary but not sufficient. Because a position changes a person, the corporation may gain if a position is given to someone who needs the experience as a steppingstone to another position. Thus each possible assignment of individuals to jobs leads to quite different implications for the next round of jobs, and the round after that, and so on, for the next 30 years. In short, replacement tables tend to be myopic. They are an invaluable start but do not, in themselves, provide a structure within which to envision developing multinational managers for the decades to come.

A Personnel Department keeps an official file on each employee; files of executive candidates are usually kept in headquarters. In addition, the manager of key personnel usually keeps his own filing system, usually configured to aid *his* memory. His file often consists of a reverse replacement table, of where this executive could get promoted to and a subjective forecast of how high in the organization this executive might rise. Most managers of key personnel have good memories as to individual rates of development and growth needs (usually expressed as anecdotes). In the metaphor of steppingstones across a river, the manager of key personnel knows who else could hop onto each stone, and how far across the river each individual has the energy to reach *if* steppingstones are available.

If the assignment of executives to steppingstones is too bold, some will fall down on the job; nevertheless, such boldness increases the probability that others will reach the far shore. If the assignments are consistently too timid, the corporation will be liquidating its executive capital, improving short-term profitability at the expense of long run gain. In reality, most corporations pay sequential attention to the goals of current performance and long-term executive growth; such oscillations impair both.

A computer model can be developed as an aide to the manager of key personnel. Such computer models were developed for the U.S. Navy and have been used since the early 1970s (Niehaus, 1979). They provide a means to reduce the conflict between current executive performance and long-term executive development, by improving the matching of executives to positions, with the intention of using all positions as steppingstones to the future. Although the data input is difficult, the computer model itself is relatively simple (Charnes, Glover, and Klingman, 1971) and can be used to explore the trade-off between current performance and long-run development.

The information needed has to be arranged more systematically for computer data input than it has to be for human use. Thus it makes sense to begin with a pilot study of perhaps 10 high-potential executive candidates who could work through perhaps 60 positions.

A position usually has a job description. Analyze the 60 positions to develop a list of attributes (both skills and attitudes) necessary. For each position, summarize as a set of scores how much of each attribute is necessary. In other words, express each job description as a vector of requirements r_j. When thinking in terms of a replacement table, usually some candidates cannot yet meet all the required attributes of the position. Associated with the vector of requirements is another vector c_j of the annual cost to the corporation if the occupant falls one unit short of meeting the requirements. It is a measure of the corporate vulnerability to incompetence for this position.

Individual executive candidates have to be scored on the same attributes. For each of the 10 candidates, summarize their present state of readiness (skills and attitudes) in the vector s_i using the same list of attributes.

In the static world of a replacement table, we would match individuals to jobs in order to minimize the sum of total incompetence, where incompetence is the gap between the job requirement r and the individual's state of competence s. We should weight different forms of incompetence to reflect the corporate vulnerability to a gap in each attribute, using the cost vectors c_j.

A dynamic model is needed to depict the growth of an individual as he learns from experience. At the start of period t, individual i has attributes that are summarized by the vector s_{ai}^t. Work on job j will transform him to s_{ai}^{t+1}, a different result for each job. A particular job adds to some of his attributes and subtracts from others. A few moments of introspection will convince any reader that he will learn less from a job if he is grossly overqualified. Similarly, if he is grossly underqualified, he will find the job overwhelming and will not be able to cope, let alone master the experience and make it part of himself. An individual who is competent in *most* attributes required for the position will be able to proceed to remedy any weaknesses and master the job. This movement toward adequacy depends on the individual's starting state and on the job. For a dynamic model, the simplest approximation of this process is to use a transition matrix T^j which describes how the particular job j affects its incumbents. The individual's interaction with the job is depicted as a multiplication of the job transition matrix T^j and the individual's previous state:

$$s_{ai}^{t+1} = T^j\, s_{ai}^t$$

If the individual is strong at the start, he has reserve energy to focus on his weaknesses. If he is uniformly weak, however, he cannot develop as quickly. This is represented through a transition matrix.

A real job may involve 100 attributes, but let us work through an example problem of only three attributes. First we show how the transition matrix T works, and then we discuss patterns in the coefficients of T.

For some particular job suppose the transition matrix T were

$$T = \begin{array}{ccc} 0.9 & 0.3 & 0.5 \\ 0.2 & 0.8 & 0.5 \\ 0.3 & 0.4 & 1.1 \end{array}$$

Let us work through how this job would affect three different individuals A, B, and C. Each comes to the job with different attributes, and so would develop differently by working in the position.

The executive A has only one strong component in his starting attributes, which is weakened by the attempts to remedy the other weaknesses.

Individual A before job j s^t_{ai}		$T^j \, s^t_{ai}$		Individual A after job j s^{t+1}_{ai}
9		$8.1 + 0.3 + 0 = 8.4$		8.4
1	$\rightarrow$	$1.8 + 0.8 + 0 = 2.6$	$=$	2.6
0		$2.7 + 0.4 + 0 = 3.1$		3.1

The uniformly endowed executive B shows some improvement, but change is not very large because of the composition of this particular T matrix.

Individual B before job j				Individual B after job j
3		$2.7 + 1.2 + 1.0$		4.9
4	$\rightarrow$	$0.6 + 3.2 + 1.0$	$=$	4.8
2		$0.9 + 1.6 + 2.2$		4.7

Executive C shows the greatest improvement because he has more strong components and the job strengthens his one lagging attribute.

Individual C before job j				Individual C after job j
1		$0.9 + 2.1 + 4.0$		7.0
7	$\rightarrow$	$0.2 + 5.6 + 4.0$	$=$	9.8
8		$0.3 + 2.8 + 8.8$		11.9

The manager of key personnel has to create a T matrix to represent each job. If the job would leave any individual unchanged, the transition matrix would be an identity matrix (diagonal elements = 1; other elements = 0).

If the position would augment each attribute (say, 10 percent growth across the board) regardless of the individual's particular mix of attributes, the T matrix would again be diagonal (0 everywhere else) but this time the diagonal elements would be greater than 1 (1.1 for 10 percent growth).

The off-diagonal elements of T depict the effect of one attribute on the development of another. These effects need not be symmetrical; an executive's strength in one attribute can greatly facilitate development in another but need not be reciprocal to the same extent. In this case, the off-diagonal coefficients would not be symmetrical.

To develop a T matrix, the manager of key personnel should study the job by thinking about the people who have held the position. Focus on one attribute at a time, pick a particular level of outcome in that attribute, and consider which executives coming into the job could attain that outcome. This means building up the T matrix one *row* at a time, for each row of coefficients delineates the job's effect on one attribute of an executive.

Executive development programs at universities constitute just another job. They can be expected to help the executives develop some attributes. Nevertheless, if there is too great a gap between the individual's attributes on entering and the requirements of the program, the experience will not transform this individual because he or she will not be able to learn.

Several very experienced multinational corporations have programs called "deputization" or "secondment." When an executive is to be absent from his position for several weeks (for vacation, training, etc.) the temporary vacancy creates an opportunity for a promising manager to deputize for him.

The deputized manager, and his entire family, are moved to where the executive is. After a two-week overlap, the executive goes away, leaving the deputized manager in charge. Deputization provides a dress rehearsal to the manager, and broadens the experience and outlook of his entire family. Clearly the cost of applying for visas, travel, and living makes deputization expensive. The executive development benefit is obvious because the deputized manager has a powerful incentive to learn (ahead of time and in the nation) about the culture, geography, politics, language, and business practices of the nation. The corporation benefits because the deputized manager does not sit passively. He introduces new ideas and techniques, and has some time to implement the ideas. Furthermore, he evaluates his temporary subordinates with an impartial and unbiased eye, in the hope of uncovering hoarded talent. The familiarity with the operation allows him later to provide more pertinent judgment appropriate to the unique opportunities and problems of this nation.

Each person attempts to achieve a balance between work life and personal life. This balance will vary through one's lifetime. There may be a quick trajectory to reach the top, but most people have personal reasons for preferring a slightly longer route. To aid their decision, they would like to be able to forecast the lifetime career consequences of their personal decisions. These consequences may be insignificant or serious. In some corporations an aspiring executive is allowed to refuse *one* transfer; refusing a second transfer is deemed a statement that the individual wants no further promotion. What unnecessary nonsensical anxiety this causes! How much better if the aspiring executive could plot sequences of stepping-stones and in private see their likely outcome.

For example, professionals often marry professionals, so each has to consider a move's effect on a spouse's career. Many women executives wonder when and for how long they can take time to have and start raising children without imperiling their long-term career prospects.

Personal life may impose constraints on the executive aspirant's willingness to transfer. There are four major periods of family life:

1. Before children—no restrictions on transfers.
2. Preadolescent children—restricted by the need of the children for proper schooling, but family can still move frequently.
3. Adolescent to college age—it is best that the family home not be moved, but the executive is able to change functional responsibility or product line in the same city. During this period, he can still deputize or second in other nations to stay current.
4. All children college age or older—no restrictions on transfers, though the executive now has less desire to move.

A computer model of executive development can include these constraints on feasible steppingstones.

Compensation and Quitting

A cruel dilemma can rot the core of an executive development program. Suppose the corporation invests heavily in the development of a person. A competitor, not needing to invest in training, can afford to pay higher wages than could the original corporation. So the person quits, or stays and feels exploited. One remedy is to design the pension plan so that only those who stay until retirement receive a pension—commonly called the golden handcuffs. A second remedy is to nurture group loyalty so that an individual who merely considers an outside offer experiences acute dissonance. A third remedy is to design each executive candidate's career steps for *steady* growth in the combination of pay, power, and status to parallel that of likely job offers from other corporations.

The person's authority (power of position) should be on par with ability and perception of the importance of the job role. The composition of monetary and nonmonetary rewards in the compensation "package" must depend on an individual's perceptions and personal needs. These will change as the individual changes and grows. A well-managed system of compensation would be instrumental in the production of confident, loyal, and effective managers.

The familiar idea that a manager should be rewarded and promoted on the basis of performance in the current job does *not* make sense for the cadre of multinational managers. A corporation needs better predictors of success. If success in one's current job is necessary for promotion, then none but the boldest managers will stray from "normal lines of progression." Such normal lines of progression assure current productivity at the expense of long-run executive development. They also shield an individual from the sense of disorientation and incipient failure that comes from switching to unfamiliar work. Yet this disorientation is the essence of culture shock, the self-management of which a multinational manager must learn. Individuals differ in the amount of change they can master in one move. If the corporation would like multinational managers to nurture this ability in themselves then the *kind* of change should be tailored to the character and maturity of the individual. Furthermore, after a particularly large move, an individual will probably want to take the time to evolve a sense of mastery. So long as a manager's promotion depends on performance in the current job, he or she risks failure when crossing normal lines of progression. Who should bear that risk and what actions will be taken if the manager fails need to be made explicit by both the individual and corporation.

The familiar idea of equal pay for equal work does not make sense for the cadre of multinational managers. If perceived equity is a problem, the best solution is to pay the multinational manager the going local rate in local currency and pay a supplement into an individual trust fund in Switzerland or the Bahamas. The reason for this splitting is that some governments tax their citizens on the basis of worldwide income, while others do not. Furthermore, an individual who moves in the same job from a low- to a high-tax nation will take a cut in after-tax pay. In light of the problems of individual tax planning, it seems prudent to sever the direct connection between job and pay for the multinational managers and allow an individual the job sequence flexibility of sometimes moving down in job level.

Nevertheless, managers will sometimes consider quitting. The manager's cues will cause co-workers to start to disengage from bonds of friendship so the manager will start to feel lonely. His superior, concerned that he might not see it through to completion will be less likely to assign him large new projects, so the manager will feel a sudden plateau in his career. These unstable dynamics occur in all organizations. In a multinational corporation, this unstable dynamic is exaggerated because interpersonal cues of respect differ between cultures, and in a multinational an individual is typically receiving a babel of discordant cues from different nationalities of co-workers and supervisors. Where perceptions are fluctuating, it is especially important that there be stable growth in the underlying reality of the executive's position. Hence the importance of a steady sequence of steppingstones.

Evaluation

An individual's performance must be evaluated in both its technical and its psychological dimensions. Technical proficiency measured against sales, production, and accounting data is important, is fairly well understood, and can be fairly explicit. This explicitness tends to overshadow the more subjective aspects of the executive's psychological development. Yet the more senior the international executive, the more important is his personality. (Expressed another way, the more destructive are his frailties of personality.) Psychoanalyst Erik Erikson (1964) classified eight stages in the adult development. As condensed in Exhibit 11.1, they provide a basis for fathoming the current stage and a diagram for articulating the future development of an individual.

The attributes of an executive (and the attributes necessary for success in a position) include personality descriptions such as these eight stages of development. Occupying a position affects not only the executive's technical skill, but also his self-perceptions of his personality. If the distance between steppingstones is too great, the attributes that will diminish most will be those pertaining to his personality. Individuals find that regression of self is both painful and disconcerting unless they have robust self-knowledge and the counseling support of an insightful superior.

The concept of a multinational executive failing to perform a job needs to be clearly thought through. Inevitably, the environment will change in unforeseen ways from what had been envisioned for this position. Executive talent is insight into determining which changes are important to the global system, how to redeploy assets under control, and how to inform relevant parts of the global system that their interface agreements are undergoing change. An executive whose subsidiary has severe internal problems may foresee a need to have the subsidiary temporarily opt out of the global networks in manufacturing, marketing, or finance. On the other hand, such interface changes are very expensive to the corporation as a whole, and the executive has responsibility to redeploy assets to strive to maintain commitments. Usually this entails sacrificing the long run for current performance. Thus an executive has quite a choice of how to fail technically and how to manage the failure psychologically.

As tension mounts there is an increasing incidence of emotional issues between people; people tend to withdraw from the group or become silent, to form cliques or alliances between members, or talk or gossip about an absent member. The goal (of my management) is to listen to the incidence of these phenomena, rather than focusing on the content of what is said. My effort is always to avoid an unwitting

Depressed and morose about life, emphasizing failures; would change life or career if had another chance; fears getting older and death.	**8** *Despair vs. Integrity*	Happy and content with life, work, accomplishments; accepts responsibility for life; maximizes success.
Seems to be vegetating; does nothing more than routines of work and necessary daily activities; is preoccupied with self.	**7** *Stagnation vs. Generativity*	Plans for future with sustained application of skills and abilities; invests energy and ideas in exploring new ideas; senses continuity with future generations.
Lives relatively isolated from spouse, children; avoids intimate contact with others. Either absorbed in self or indiscriminately sociable, in a stereotyped manner.	**6** *Isolation vs. Intimacy*	Has close intimate relationship with spouse and friends. Enjoys sharing thoughts, spending time with them and expressing warm feelings for them.
Ill at ease and lacking conviction in roles; lost in groups and affiliations; may abruptly switch work, residence or marriage without meaning or purpose.	**5** *Role diffusion vs. Ego identity*	Is definite about self and enjoys role in work, family, and affiliations; has sense of belonging; feels continuity with past and present.
Is passive; leaves things undone; feels inadequate about ability to do things. Feels that his product is unsatisfactory.	**4** *Inferiority vs. Industry*	Likes to make things and carry them to completion; strives to master skills. Feels proud of his product.
Lets others initiate action; plays down success or accomplishment.	**3** *Guilt vs. Initiative*	Takes pleasure in planning and initiating action; plans ahead and designs own schedule.
Awkwardly selfconscious of own ideas. Stays within familiar ways; needs the approval of others and avoids asserting self against group.	**2** *Shame and doubt vs. Autonomy*	Confident to hold own opinions and to do what he or she feels is best. Owns his own attitudes.
Distrusts self and doubts the world. Believes that coworkers "get you into trouble". Uneasy about confiding in anyone.	**1** *Basic mistrust vs. Basic trust*	Confident in self and in the world. Trusts work associates. Feels optimistic about people's motives.

EXHIBIT 11.1

Erikson's eight stages of adult development.

focus on the content of the issues, and to focus on the process. One of the biggest hazards in the principle that says "be responsible for yourself and the emotional issue will resolve itself" has to do with the inner orientation of self. It is easy for a person in such a position to say the situation is his "fault" and to accept the "blame" without being responsible. There is a fine line between accepting the responsibility for the part self plays in a situation and accepting the "blame" for it. (Bowen, 1978, p. 464)

Geographically decentralized multinational corporations exist and run comfortably with few headquarters executives. Other multinationals are organized on the basis of global product divisions; they require more headquarters executives. Any serious attempts to synthesize both into a matrix organization will fail unless the corporation has enough experienced executives. The nine central chapters of this book identify complex maneuvers that promise profits if implemented well, they promise only snarled confusion if implemented poorly. The first necessary investment is in years of executive development.

Bibliography to Chapter 11

Argyris, Chris, *Management and Organizational Development* (New York: McGraw-Hill, 1971).

Bass, Bernard M. and James A. Vaughan, *Training in Industry: The Management of Learning* (Belmont, CA: Wadsworth, 1966).

Bowen, Murray, *Family Therapy in Clinical Practice* (New York: Jason Aronson, 1978).

Bryant, D. and Richard J. Niehaus, *Manpower Planning and Organization Design* (New York: Plenum, 1977).

Charnes, Abraham, Frederick Glover, and Darwin Klingman, "The Lower Bounded and Partial Upper Bounded Distribution Model," *Naval Research Logistics Quarterly*, Vol. 18, No. 2 (1971), pp. 277-281.

Daniels, John D., *International Mobility of People*. Essays in International Business No. 1, March 1980, The University of South Carolina.

Edstrom, Anders and Jay Galbraith, "Transfer of Managers as a Coordination and Control Strategy in Multinational Organizations," *Administrative Science Quarterly*, Vol. 22 (June 1977), pp. 248-263.

Erikson, Erik, *Childhood and Society* (New York: Norton, 1964).

Flory, Charles D. and the staff of Rohrer, Hibler and Replogle, *Managers for Tomorrow*, (New York: American Library, 1967).

Foa, Uriel G. and M.M. Chemers, "The Significance of Role Behavior Differentiation for Cross-Cultural Interaction Training," *International Journal of Psychology*, Vol. 2, No. 1 (1967), pp. 45-57.

Glidewell, John C., *Choice Points: Essays about the Emotional Problems of Living with People* (Cambridge, MIT Press, 1970).

Grinold, Richard C. and Kneale T. Marshall, *Manpower Planning Models* (New York: North-Holland, 1977).

Gullotta, Thomas P. and Kevin C. Donahue, "The Corporate Family: Theory and Treatment," *The Journal of Marital and Family Therapy*, Vol. 7, No. 2 (1981), pp. 151-158.

Harari, Ehud and Yoram Zeira, "Genuine Multinational Staffing Policy: Expectations and Realities," *Academy of Management Journal*, Vol. 20, No. 2 (1977).

Harrison, Roger and Richard Hopkins, "The Design of Cross Culture Training: An Alternative to the University Model," *Journal of Applied Behavioral Science*, Vol. 3, No. 4 (1967), pp. 431-460.

Kaufman, Herbert, *The Forest Ranger: A Study in Administrative Behavior* (Baltimore: Johns Hopkins Press, 1960).

Lee, Fred E., "Planning the Pecking Order for the Company Totem Pole," *Planning Review*, Vol. 5, No. 1 (1977), p. 14.

Levinson, Harry, *The Exceptional Executive: A Psychological Conception* (Cambridge, Harvard University Press, 1968).

Levinson, Harry, *The Great Jackass Fallacy* (Cambridge: Harvard University Press, 1973).

Niehaus, Richard J., *Computer-Assisted Human Resources Planning* (New York: Wiley-Interscience, 1979).

Roberts, Karlene H., "On Looking at an Elephant: An Evaluation of Cross Cultural Research Related to Organizations," *Psychological Bulletin*, Vol. 74, No. 5 (1970), pp. 327-350.

Sofer, Cyril, *Men in Mid Career: A Study of British Managers and Technical Specialists* (Cambridge: Cambridge University Press, 1970).

Vroom, Victor and Kenneth MacCrimmon, "Toward a Stochastic Model of Managerial Careers," *Administrative Science Quarterly*, March 1968.

Wilson, A. Thomas M., "Recruitment and Selection for Work in Foreign Cultures," *Human Relations*, Vol. 14, No. 1 (1965), pp. 3-21.

Wilson, Godfrey and Monica Wilson, *The Analysis of Social Change: Based on Observations in Central Africa* (Cambridge: Cambridge University Press, 1968).

Zaleznik, Abraham and Manfred F. R. Kets de Vries, *Power and the Corporate Mind* (Boston, Houghton Mifflin, 1975).

When you first work for a corporation you will probably work in one function, perhaps financial accounting, manufacturing, or sales. Nobody will encourage you to ponder how your tasks interconnect with other functions and the pressure of work will mean that any pondering will have to be done on your own time.

And then, like an aircraft pulling up above the cloud cover, you will suddenly find yourself expected to maintain liaison among the functions. Project management, however small the project, requires interconnected functions. This summary will therefore be more useful if it connects the functions.

We will first examine short-term decisions which pull together the first finance chapter (exchange risk), the first production chapter (logistics), and the first marketing chapter (product launch). After we have looked at this tier of short-term decisions we will turn to the tier of medium-term and finally the tier of long-term decisions. The three tiers can be visualized as layers of an elegant wedding cake. Before proceeding to inter-connect the nine central chapters you will find it helpful to review Chapter 1.

Short-Term Decisions

Short-term finance, marketing, and production plans have to be made with an eye to flexibility. For example, the corporation's ability to re-spond to exchange rate variation and its ability to stage the launch of a new product are critically dependent on logistics.

As exchange rates vary, so do the costs of manufacturing an identical item at each factory in the global production network. As explained in Chapter 2, it is unfair to penalize or reward a manager for variables over which he has no control — such as exchange rates. Rather, an effective evaluation should center on how adroitly the manager responds to the new exchange rates. The manager needs an immediate understanding of logistics costs and feasibility in order to reassign products to the new lower cost plants, lower cost in terms of the headquarter's *numeraire* currency.

Exchange rates vary for a reason and when they do the corporate mar-keting managers must often re-evaluate the value of the national market. In theory this is the discounted present value of the stream of net revenue. Like changes on a barometer, unanticipated changes in an exchange rate are a symptom of the need to assess implications.

The final short-term decision to be considered is new product launch. Confusion abounds during the launch of a new product. Chapter 8 recom-mended that the new product be launched in a sequence of nations. First launches provide test market data for the rest of the world, and the subsequent sequence can be adapted to whatever new information is revealed. The logistics implications are staggering. Firstly, the early markets are intended for market research so must never run dry of product even though the demand forecast was quite hazy. If sales exceed expectations there is a furious scramble for the product. Secondly, the sequence is adaptive. This means that nobody will know, for sure, which markets will be launched in the second phase until data from the first launch has been analyzed. One key input to the sequencing in a staged launch is whether to pre-empt competitors in each nation. The value of this depends on the value of greater market share, which depends on what the managers expect government policies will be. Thus the logistics problem is that a lot of inventory has to be accumulated and prepared for shipment to not-yet-known destinations by a not-yet-known deadline.

Connections Between Short- and Medium-Term Chapters

In an elegant wedding cake there are supports between each of the tiers; so it is in this book.

Medium-term decisions on maneuvering liquid assets require information on exchange rates. Exchange rates were analyzed in Chapter 2. Nobody knows how to forecast exchange rates *precisely*, and Chapter 3 merely requires that forecasts be consistent.

Production smoothing in a multinational corporation, a medium-term decision, allows markets to be switched among factories. Such switching redirects the streams of logistics, so to undertake multinational production smoothing the corporation must exhibit flexibility in its logistics.

Medium-term marketing decisions critically depend on the corporation's competitive position. A market leader has price flexibility; a smaller rival has to follow the prices of the leader. The launch of a new product (Chapter 8) determines the corporation's competitive position in each national market. If the corporation was first to launch a new product in the nation, it can likely maintain that lead after rivals launch their competitive products. The value of launching first (an input for Chapter 8) can be analyzed in terms of price flexibility by the models of Chapter 9.

Medium-Term Decisions

Maneuvering liquid assets, production smoothing, and pricing policies are a tier of connected medium-term decisions. A solution to each one can sharpen the solution to the other decisions.

Maneuvering liquid assets is an attempt to get needed liquidity to each subsidiary, mindful of taxes and interest to be paid. Because this problem was formulated as a linear program, the solution will produce dual variables which give the value of an increment more cash in each subsidiary. This is vital input to production smoothing.

In production smoothing each plant serves a cluster of markets. Markets at the interface between two plants are switched as economies dictate. This requires the comparison of the value of an increment more profit in one producing nation and less in another. The dual variables of maneuvering liquid assets provide these values for each year.

In Chapter 9 three pricing models were presented. In the polycentric case the objective is to maximize profitability with each nation considered separately. More profit is better than less regardless of the currency and in the polycentric case there is no need to make comparisons across nations. However, the geocentric and ethnocentric pricing schemes establish a tie among national markets; more profit in one nation will mean less in another. To compare the value of altered profit levels in the two nations the dual variables from maneuvering liquid assets are needed.

To calculate prices requires the marginal cost of items in the product line. As explained in Chapter 6, these marginal costs derive from analysis of production smoothing. Conversely, pricing and marketing calculations yield sales estimates—a necessary input to production smoothing.

The maneuvering liquid assets calculation requires as an input the cash requirement (or available outflow) for each year for each subsidiary. To estimate this data, the pricing and plant loading decisions must first be approximated. Furthermore, transfer prices can be adjusted only if items flow between two subsidiaries. Product flow is calculated in production smoothing; if the flow is zero, one consequence will be to close a route for maneuvering funds.

Note that just because decisions are interconnected does not mean that they have to be solved simultaneously. Prudent business practice is to work first on the worst problem, using managerial judgment about input data whose values can be firmed up later.

Connections Between Medium- and Long-Term Chapters

Stakeholders of a division in a nation may be affected either visibly or, sometimes, invisibly by some of the liquid asset maneuvers presented in Chapter 3. If a critical stakeholder has difficulty with one maneuver, it would certainly be prudent to evaluate the next cheapest maneuver. Decisions of some stakeholders are affected by financial statements, yet subsidiary financial statements are the artificial result of the maneuvers. Conversely, if stakeholder hostility means that the corporation should withdraw from a nation, one such method is systematically to liquidate the investment, maneuvering so as to withdraw funds and make the subsidiary appear unprofitable.

The plant location analysis, a long-term decision, requires both logistics and production smoothing analyses. The rough cut analysis of plant location ignores risk and makes direct use of Chapter 5 logistics. Once a few sites have been selected, the role each would play in the global production smoothing network can be evaluated.

Long-Term Decisions

The analysis of stake holders in each nation as part of multidivisional expansion, the decision to close down or open plants, and the design of one's products are strategic decisions on which all else depends.

The analysis of stakeholders articulates the risk facing the corporation's activities, and identifies the strategic alternatives necessary to contain that risk. One alternative might be to build a plant for one of the corporation's product divisions in that nation, keeping in mind that each plant opening or closing makes a political statement of long-run significance.

A plant opening can also be used as a competitive weapon in the battle for market share (Chapter 7), it can mollify stakeholders, and intimidate competitors. Political and competitive statements can be made in many combinations but most such statements cause a slight increase in the corporation's cost of goods. Therefore, it is vital to model the global production network so as to calculate the cost of manufacturing and logistics.

A global production network is a meaningful concept only if the same product (or the same subassemblies) is manufactured at several locations. Hence, the long-term importance of designing products with an eye to both cost and the special needs of target market segments in each nation. An artful standardization of subassemblies makes possible both production smoothing, and maneuvering liquid assets. Only if the product is somewhat standardized in design is it possible for actual sales data in one nation to be useful in revising sales forecasts in other nations. And only if a subassembly is so standardized that the total world demand is great enough to justify more than two plants, do corporate executives dare build a plant in the world's impoverished nations.

This summary has emphasized interconnections between decision modules. Whereas a manager is to do something, an executive is to care for the interfaces between managers, and adapt these interfaces as he or she foresees needs. From what one can now foresee for multinational corporations, they will need to nurture many multinational executives, viewing positions now as stepping stones to yet more demanding positions in the future.

Index

Adler, Michael, 68
Ad valorem import duty, 87
Advertising agencies, 298
Aguilar, Francis, 123, 141
Aharoni, Yair, 138, 141
Aiken, Michael, 29, 33
Alcan Aluminium Ltd., 56, 62
Alcoa, 296
Amariuta, Ion, 125, 141
Amdahl Corporation, 302
American Motors, in auto-pact, 108
Anti trust, 294
Arbitrage, 50
Argyris, Chris, 372
Arms length transfer pricing, 86, 188, 298
Ascendant Electric of England Ltd. case, 147-52
Auto pact, 108
Ayal, Igal, 275

Back-to-back loans, 55
Balachandran, V., 86, 103, 106
Ball, Robert, 166, 172
Bank of America, 3
Barcus, Al, 276
Barnard, Chester, 138, 141
Barriers, non-tariff, 318-23
Barthelmeh, Hans-Adolf (of Ford), 179
Bass, Bernard, 372
Beckering, Jack (of Black & Decker), 325, 326
Beedles, William, 58, 68
Begin, Robert of Paisley SA, 71-72, 75
Behrman, Jack, 30, 33, 132, 141

Belgium exchange rate, 50
    tax, 96
Bellamy, Christopher, 297, 314
Bergsten, Fred, 33
Bergstrom, Gary, 204
Black, Fischer, 68
Black and Decker, 31, 82, 315-31
Blake, David, 33
Blocked currency, 49
Bongers, C., 336, 343
Booth, Lawrence, 59
Boston Consulting Group, 12, 33, 82, 275, 314
Bowen, Murray, 362, 372
Bower, Joseph, 28, 33, 141
Brada, Joseph, 126, 141
Bradley, David, 137, 141, 235, 237
Brooke, Michael, 33
Brussels Tariff Nomenclature (BTN), 338
Bryant, D., 372
Burke, William (of Ford), 178
Burns, Jane, 106
Business board of a matrix, 26
Business International, 34, 46, 92-93
Butt, Ralph (of Black & Decker), 315
Buttles Corporation, 102

Calantone, Roger, 275
Canada, exchange rate, 50
Canadian Brewing, 264
Canadian General Electric, 31
Carley, William, 174
Carter, E. Eugene, 106
Cash flow portfolio, 61-64
Chaining invoices, 89-90

Chandler, Margaret, 27, 30, 34
Channels of distribution, 266, 267, 271
Channon, Derek, 33
Charnes, Abraham, 141, 268, 275, 364,
   373
Checklist
   to remind, 143
   to sort divisions, 128-31
Chemenceau, Marc (of Paisley S.A.), 71,
   74-75
Chemers, M. M., 373
Chemical Bank, 51
Chen, Andrew, 50, 68
Child, Graham, 314
Chorley, Lord, 166, 172
Chrysler Corp., 108, 294
Citibank, 58. *See also* First National
   City Bank
Cizaskas, Albert, 160, 172
Claycamp, Henry, 343
Clee, Gilbert, 21, 33
Cleland, David, 314
Clelland, Richard, 314
Colgate-Palmolive, 207
Comanor, William, 204, 298, 305
Comparability of markets, 255-65
Compensating balances, 83
Conjoint analysis, for market research,
   339-40
Containers, 148, 154
Cooper, William, 275, 268, 364
Costanzo, G. A. (of Citibank), 3, 4
Cost-benefit analysis, 131-38, 221-23,
   232, 235
Covariance between sales, 18, 183-84,
   259
Crowson, Wallace, 204
Crum, Roy, 98, 106
Cuffley, C. F. H., 172
Cultural bias, 18, 122-25, 361-63,
   370-72
Curham, Joan, 33, 34
Cyert, Richard, 138, 141, 275

Dalyrymple, D. J., 276
Daniels, John, 314, 373
Dantzig, George, 86, 106
Data General, 264
Davidson, William, 33
Davis, Stanley M., 2, 27, 33
Debt, locating, 61, 101, 132, 222, 228-29
De Groot, Morris, 275

Dellabita, Albert, 314
Dependency, 29
Deputization, 367-68
Devaluation, 44
Devanney, John, 156-67, 172
De Voe, James, 275
Digital Equipment, 264
Dillon, William, 275
Dirty float, 51
Dissonance theory, 48
Diversification, geographical, 18-22
Domestic International Sales Corporation
   (DISC), 90
Donahue, Kevin, 373
Dow Corning matrix organization, 25-27
Doz, Yves, 238
Dozier case study, 37-45, 47, 53-54
Dozier, Charles (of Dozier Inc.), 38
Drawback of import duty, 161
Drucker, Peter, 334-35, 343
Dufey, Gunter, 50, 68
Dumas, Bernard, 68
Dumping, 88
Dundas, Kenneth, 15-16, 33
Dunlop-Pirelli, 110, 115
Duty classification systems, 157-59
   maneuvering liquid assets, 86-90

Eaker, Mark, 38
Eastman Kodak, 260-61, 297
Economies of scale in plant size, 228
Edstrom, Anders, 373
Ehrenberg, A. S. C., 275
Eigenvector, 133-35
Eiteman, David, 106
Eli Lilly and Company, 88
Elton, Edwin, 68
Erikson, Erik, 370-72, 373
Erlenkotter, Donald, 228, 238
Errunza, Vihang, 50, 58, 68
Ethnocentric view explained, 12-18
   defined, 14
   exchange management, 56-59
   logistics, 153-62
   maneuvering liquid assets, 81
   multidivisional expansion, 125-31
   plant location, 228-31
   pricing, 303-305, 310-12
   product design, 333-34
   production smoothing, 182-84
   product launch, 255-59, 267-70
Etzioni, Amitai, 15, 33

Eurodollar, 37, 42, 105
Evans, Gareth, 350
Evolution of an organization, 11
Exchange Management ethnocentric
    guideline, 16, 37-69
  geocentric, 31
  polycentric guideline, 21
Expectancy theory, 48
Experience curve, 82, 294, 333
  defined, 12
Export incentives as a cheap loan, 160-
    61, 233
Exposure, illustrated in Dozier case,
    41-45
  U.S. definition of FASB-8, 57
  definitions of other nations, 59
  balance sheet v. cash flow, 61
Exxon, 20, 137

Fallon, Padraic, 44
Felixstowe, port of, 149
Financial Accounting Standards Board
    (FASB) of U.S.A., 56-67, 59
Firestone, 110, 115
First National City Bank case, 1-9
  currency forecasts, 58
Flexible factory, 191-93
Flory, Charles, 373
Foa, Uriel, 373
Folks, William R., 53, 68
Ford Motor Company hedging, 58
  in auto-pact 108
  Ford of Europe case, 174-81
Foreign Accrual Property Income, 97
Forward contract, defined, 47
Fouraker, Lawrence, 20, 33, 141
Fowler, D.J., 105, 106
Franko, Lawrence G., 207
Freedom of Information Act in U.S.A.,
    224
Fujitsu, 264
Futures, exchange rate, 41-43

Gaeteno, Lombardo, 238
Galbraith, Jay, 33, 373
Garstka, Stanley, 65, 68
General Electric, 320, 331
Generalized network, 82-86, 232
General Motors Corporation, 108, 294
  Opel subsidiary, 178
Generations of plant designs, 183

Generations of products, 101, 183
Geocentric view explained, 23-33
  exchange management, 60-66
  logistics, 164-69
  maneuvering liquid assets, 82-102
  multidivisional expansion, 131-41
  plant location, 231
  pricing, 302-3, 309-310
  product design, 334-41
  production smoothing, 187-202
  product launch, 263-67, 270-72
Geographical diversification, 18-22
Giddy, Ian, 50, 68
Giles, O. C., 166, 172
Gillen, Stanley (of Ford), 176
Glidewell, John, 373
Global product mandate, 31, 137
Glover, Frederick, 141, 364, 373
Gnome, a computer program, 103
Goeltz, Richard, 68
Goggin, William, 26, 33
Goodhardt, G. J., 275
Goodman, Stephen, 60, 68
Goodrich, B. F. Inc., 108, 110, 115
Goodwin, Richard, 137
Goodyear, 110, 115, 326
Goss, Richard, 172
Green, Paul, 258, 275, 339, 343
Grinold, Richard, 373
Gruber, Martin, 68
Gruber, William, 153, 172, 273
Gullotta, Thomas, 373
Gunn, John (of Southeastern National
    Bank), 38
Guthrie, Gordon (of Ford), 176-77

Hage, Gerald, 29, 33
Harari, Ehud, 373
Harrison, Roger, 373
Hauser, John, 276, 339, 343
Hausman, Warren, 204
Hayes, Walter (of Ford), 180
Hedging decision calculations, 53-55
Heeler, Roger, 275
Heenan, David, 34, 142, 238
Hill, C. J. S., 165, 172
Holt, Charles, 205, 275
Hopkins, Richard 373
Horen Jeffrey, 205
Horst, Thomas, 33
Hostage, plant perceived as, 220
Hustad, Thomas, 275

IBM, 5, 29, 171, 265, 302-3, 363
Ijiri, Yuji, 294, 314
Illiteracy, 191, 341
Imperial Tobacco Co. of Canada Ltd.,
    248
Incentives, paid by governments to lure
    factories, 222, 228-29
Industrial structure, 119-20, 131-37,
    294-97
Inflation, 49, 82, 297
Inflexibility as to production rate, 182
Insurance of balance sheet assets, 233
Integrators, 29
Interest arbitrage, 48-49
International executive development,
    349-77
  ethnocentric guideline, 17
  geocentric guideline, 32
  polycentric guideline, 22
International Monetary Fund, 5, 52, 53,
    67
Inventory for production smoothing, 185
Item produced at two or more plants,
    production smoothing, 188-202
ITT, 5

Jalland, Michael, 33
Joint ventures, 125-27
Jones, Roger, 165, 172

Kampe, William, 204
Kaufman, Herbert, 373
Keegan, Warren, 123, 141, 244, 275, 343
Kemp, Norman, 275
Kernan, Jerome, 276
Kets de Vries, Manfred, 16, 34, 373
Kienzle, Otto, 336, 343
King, William, 314
Klingman, Darwin, 141, 364, 373
Knickerbocker, Frederick, 34, 238, 293,
    314
Kodak, 260-61, 297
Kohlhagan, Steven, 58, 68
Kolde, Endel, 302, 304, 314, 343
Kotler, Philip, 314, 331, 334, 343
Kozmetsky, George, 142
Kramer, Robert, 23, 28, 34

Larson, John (of Ascendant), 148-52
Lawrence, Paul, 27, 29, 33, 34

Leach, Rodney, 155, 172
Leading and lagging of accounts re-
    ceivable, 92-93
Learner, David, 275
Leavitt, Harold, 14, 34
Lee, Fred, 373
Lefevres, Jean (of Paisley S. A.), 33-75
Leigh, Robert (of Southeastern National
    Bank), 38
Lent, George, 238
Levich, Richard, 50, 68
Levinson, Harry, 373
Levy, Haim, 68
Licensing technology and know-how, 85,
    90-92
Liechtenstein, 51, 95
Lietaer, Bernard, 62, 68
Lilienthal, David (of TVA), 138
Liner conferences
  explained, 155-57
  illustrated, 149
Livanos, V. M., 172
Lloyd, W. P., 68
Local content requirements, 29
Local loans, 98-99
Logistics, 174-205
  ethocentric guideline, 107
  geocentric guideline, 32
  polycentric guideline, 22
L'Oreal, 207
Lorsch, Jay, 29, 34
Lowest unit cost factory, 189-91

McConnell, J. Douglas, 276
MacCrimmon, Kenneth, 361
MacDonald Tobacco Co., 248
MacNeill, H. G. (of Goodyear), 119
Maintenance, delay or advance for
    production smoothing, 187
Malkiel, Burton, 49, 68
Manca, Plinio, 165, 172
Maneuvering liquid assets, 70-107
  ethnocentric guideline, 17
  geocentric guidelines, 31
  polycentric guidelines, 21
Manuge, Robert (of IEL), 111
March, James, 138, 141
Marer, Paul, 141
Market share, 82, 130, 182-84, 223-27,
    265, 294-96
Marshall, Kneale, 373
Martin, Warren, 276

Martyn, Howe, 15, 34
Mason, Richard, 124, 142, 293, 314
Massey, William, 343
Massey-Ferguson Ltd., 21, 62, 201
Mathewson, J. Frank, 89, 100, 106
Matrix organization
  in Citibank, 7-9
  defined, 23
  structural view, 25-27
  power view, 27-31
Mehta, Dileep, 153, 172, 273
Menzies, Hugh, 15, 34
Merton, Robert, 60, 69
Merville, L. J., 106
Mesak, Hani, 314
Metaxas, Bas, 172
Meyer, Herbert, 142
Michelin Tires case, 108-21
Miller, Joseph, 141
Miniature replica plant, 224
Mining, 61
Mobil, 5, 103
Modigliani, Franco, 205
Molitor, Graham, 142
Monroe, Kent, 314
Moore Corp. Ltd., 62
Moran, Theodore, 33
Morris, Anthony, 297, 314
Moyer, Reed, 276
Mueller, Gerhard, 69
Multidivisional expansion to new nation,
    108-42
  ethnocentric guideline, 17
  geocentric guideline, 32
  polycentric guideline, 22
Multinational plant location, 206-38
  ethnocentric guideline, 17
  geocentric guideline, 32
  polycentric guideline, 22
Muth, James, 205
Mutual fund, 50

Nationalization, 235
Neave, Edwin, 47, 69
Negotiating, 100-102, 131, 138, 197-
    200, 232
Nestle, 29, 332
New product launch, 243-76
  ethnocentric guideline, 17
  geocentric guideline, 32
  polycentric guideline, 22

New products
  cash flow effects, 82
  design, 335-38
  forecasting, 201, 261, 265, 323
  production problems, 182-84
Nicholson, Peter (of Nova Scotia), 109
Niehaus, Richard, 364, 372, 373
Nonmetric scaling, 123-24, 340-41
Norris, Richard, 238
Noyes, Geoffrey, 263

Officer, Lawrence, 156, 172
Ogram, Ernest, 314
Olsen, Bernhard, 14, 34
Oneida Silver Ltd., 263
Operant conditioning theory, 48
Options, 60
Overtime for production smoothing, 185
Overy, Colin (of Black & Decker), 317

Paisley S. A., case study, 70-80
Panama Canal, 147, 149
Parker, Worthing, 275
Pegged exchange rate, 52
Performance of subsidiary, 102-3, 104,
    190-95, 370
Perlmutter, Howard, 14, 34
Personnel transfer, 14, 368
Petty, J., 106
Philip Morris, 243-54
Philips, 31
Political forecasting, 162
Polycentric view
  exchange management, 49-56
  explained, 18-22
  logistics, 163-64
  maneuvering liquid assets, 102-3
  multidivisional expansion, 122-25
  plant location, 223-27
  pricing, 300-302, 306-9
  product design, 331-33
  production smoothing, 184-87
  product launch, 259-63
Prahalad, C. K., 238
Preempting a rival, 223-27, 265
Pricing, 277-314
  ethnocentric guideline, 17
  geocentric guideline, 32
  polycentric guideline, 22

Product design, 315-43
  ethnocentric guideline, 17
  geocentric guideline, 32
  polycentric guideline, 22
Production smoothing, 174-205
  ethnocentric guideline, 17
  geocentric guideline, 32
  polycentric guideline, 22
Product life cycle, 10, 298
Purchasing, 195-96

Quirin, David, 89, 100, 106
Quotas, 161, 224

Radebaugh, Lee, 314
Raiffa, Howard, 276
Rao, Ram, 226, 230, 238
RCA, 16
Reier, Sharon, 106
Replacement tables of managers, 364
Requirements, demanded by govern-
    ments, 222-23
Ricks, David, 50, 68
Risk spreading, 18-22
Robbins, Sidney, 81, 106
Roberts, Karlene, 373
Robertson, Thomas, 276
Robinson, Richard, 34, 303, 314
Robustness, of plant location, 232-35
Rodriguez, Rita, 106
Roll, Richard, 69
Rosow, Jerome, 20, 34, 131-32, 142
Rothschild, Richard (of Dozier), 38
Royalties and fees, 90-92
Rubber Association of Canada, 115-19
Rummel, R. J., 142, 238
Rutenberg, David, 34, 47, 53, 60, 65, 68,
    69, 106, 125, 141, 226, 230, 238,
    343

Saaty, Thomas, 133-35, 142
Sachtjen, Wilbur, 21, 33
Sadowski, Wieslaw, 343
Sapolsky, Harvey, 28, 34
Sarnat, Marshall, 68
Saudi Arabia, 15, 148
Sayles, Leonard, 27, 30, 34
Scanning the environment, 122-24
Scherer, Frederick, 224, 227, 238

Schlaifer, Robert, 276
Schwartzman, Harry, 294, 300, 314
Screening, 126-27
Seagram Co. Ltd., 257-58
Seasonal factory, 193-94
Section 482 of U. S. Internal Revenue
    Code, 88-89
Seghers, Paul, 107
Selznick, Philip, 138, 142
Senbek, Lemma, 50, 68
Senchak, Andrew, 58, 68, 69
Sethi, S. Prakash, 276
Shaftel, Timothy, 343
Shapiro, Alan, 53, 60, 69, 107
Shawky, Hany, 50, 68
Shulman, James, 107
Siegel, Sidney, 20, 33
Simon, Herbert, 138, 142, 205, 294, 314
Smith, Barnard, 204
Snake of European currencies, 52
Sobey, Frank (of IEL), 112
Sofer, Cyril, 373
Solnik, Bruno, 69
Sommers, Montrose, 276
Span of control, 359-60
Special drawing rights (SDR), 52
Spencer, William I. (President of Citi-
    bank), 7
Spot exchange rate, 41-44
Spread in banking, 5
Srinivasan, V. 229, 238
Staelin, Richard, 125, 141, 262, 276
Stakeholder, 131-38
Stansell, Stanley, 53, 68
Starks, Laura, 69
Starr, Martin, 343
Stewart, R. J., 172
Stobaugh, Robert, 81, 106
Stockpile
  factory where stockpiling inventory is
      cheap, 194
  purchasing, 196
Stonehill, Arthur, 106
Stopford, John, 34, 141
Strategic business units, 331
Subcontracting for production smooth-
    ing, 186
Subsidy, 58, 135-36, 194, 228, 368
Suri, Rajan, 33
Swap, 55

Tatonnement computational scheme of
    tentative bids and acceptances

product design 335-36
production smoothing, 198-200
Tax credit, 50-51, 222
Tennessee, Valley Authority, 138
Terpstra, Vern, 173, 257, 276
Texas Instruments, 294
Thain, Donald, 109
Theobald, Thomas C. (of Citibank), 8
Thompson, Gerald, 86, 103, 106, 229, 238
Thompson, James, 142
T-Mark, Japanese test board approval, 320-22
Topkis, Donald, 205
Transfer prices, 19, 76, 79, 81, 87-90, 102, 222
Transition matrix, of a job, 365-67
Translation in market research, 339-40
Truitt, J. Frederick, 138, 142
Tull, Donald, 258, 275, 339, 343
Turner, Ronald, 262, 276
Turner, W. V. (of RAC), 115-19
Two-boss managers (in matrix), 23
Tyler Abrasives Inc. case, 277-92
Tyndall, Gordon, 142

Unilever, 15, 207, 263
Uniroyal, 110, 115, 326
United Brewing of Copenhagen, 264
Urban, Glen, 276, 339, 343
U. S. Organization Chart Service Inc., 102

Value added tax, 89

Van Beusekom, Mark, 33
Vaughan, James, 372
Vaupel, James, 34
Verlag Hoppenstadt, 102
Vernon, Raymond, 10, 34, 101, 107, 153, 172, 273
Vroom Victor, 361, 373

Wagner, Harvey, 205
Walters, Robert, 33
Weighted distribution problem, 86, 232
Welam, Ulf Peter, 205
Wells, Louis, 34, 221, 238, 273, 276
Wentz, Roy, 107
Westinghouse Electric Corporation, 15
Williamson, Oliver, 19, 34, 173
Wilson, A. Thomas M., 373
Wilson, Godfrey and Monica, 373
Wilson, Thomas, 204, 298, 305
Wolfson, M. L., 343

Xenophobia, 15

Yoshino, M. Y., 276
Yuan, John, 205
Yugoslavia, 126

Zaleznick, Abraham, 16, 34, 373
Zeira, Yoram, 373